**Derek W**                    lor historians today,
having w                              alities and the period
in *In The Lion's Court*, *The Uncrowned Kings of England* and
the award winning *Brief History of the Circumnavigators*. He
is also the highly-acclaimed biographer of Hans Holbein and
Martin Luther. He runs the annual Cambridge History festival
and lives in Devon. His website is www.derekwilson.com.

Titles available in the Brief History series

A BRIEF HISTORY OF

# HENRY VIII

Reformer and Tyrant

# DEREK WILSON

ROBINSON

RUNNING PRESS
PHILADELPHIA · LONDON

Constable & Robinson Ltd
3 The Lanchesters
162 Fulham Palace Road
London W6 9ER
www.constablerobinson.com

First published in the UK by Robinson,
an imprint of Constable & Robinson, 2009

A copy of the British Library Cataloguing in Publication
Data is available from the British Library

UK ISBN 978-1-84529-903-3

3 5 7 9 10 8 6 4 2

First published in the United States in 2009
by Running Press Book Publishers

9 8 7 6 5 4 3 2
Digit on the right indicates the number of this printing

US Library of Congress Control Number: 2008931535
US ISBN 978-0-7624-3623-1

Running Press Book Publishers
2300 Chestnut Street
Philadelphia, PA 19103–4371

Visit us on the web!

www.runningpress.com

Printed and bound in the EU

# CONTENTS

# LIST OF ILLUSTRATIONS

# INTRODUCTION

'As the heavens are high and the earth is deep, so the hearts of
kings are unsearchable'

Book of Proverbs 25:3

Unfortunately, Hans Holbein Junior was a genius. Why unfortunately? Only because he has provided us with that image of
Henry VIII which, whether we like it or not, automatically
comes to mind whenever the name of the king is mentioned.
We see him standing belligerently, hands on hips, his barrel
chest adorned with jewel-encrusted vesture, his codpiece
thrusting forward. He glowers at us from the canvas, warning
us not even to think of contradicting him. The portrait is a
magnificent piece of propaganda which has proved its effectiveness from the time of its creation in 1537 right down to the
present day. However, (leaving aside issues of art appreciation)
that is all it is – propaganda. A starting point for a realistic
understanding must be the rejection of this forceful icon. This
is Henry as he wanted to be seen – strong, assertive, his own
man, not only powerful but worthy of power. This image of

'Henry the Magnificent' has always, in the popular imagination, seen off other less flattering evaluations. The Elizabethan poet, Ulpian Fulwell, declared the late king to have been a 'tender father' to his subjects. Lord Herbert of Cherbury called Henry 'one of the most glorious princes of his time'. James Froude exculpated the king's crimes by asserting that he 'sustained nobly the honour of the English name and carried the commonwealth securely through the hardest crisis of its history'.

Other commentators have thought differently. To Martin Luther, Henry VIII was a 'fool', a 'liar' and a 'damnable, rotten worm'. Sir Walter Ralegh said of him, 'if all the pictures and patterns of a merciless prince were lost in the world, they might all again be painted to the life out of the story of this king'. Jacob Burckhardt found him 'loutish and disgusting'. Charles Dickens was repelled by a man who was nothing more than 'a blot of blood and grease upon the history of England'. In our own day, Professor Diarmaid MacCulloch has not hesitated to compare the second Tudor to Joseph Stalin. The prevailing interpretation seems to be that of a monster but one who is nevertheless compelling – aggressive, macho and definitely sexy. Like him or loath him, there is absolutely no doubt that 'Bluff King Hal' remains everlastingly fascinating.

Why? There are several answers to that question. One is that he presided over – and was in some degree responsible for – the most sweeping cultural and social changes in English history. The England of 1547 was profoundly different from the England of 1509. It had been staunchly orthodox Catholic; it was now 'reformed' and under the papal ban. The Church had been a major landowner and a political partner in the life of the state at central and local levels; now the bulk of its wealth had changed hands, much of it going to augment an emerging propertied 'middle' class. In terms of international affairs, England had become a major European power, exercising an influence out of proportion to its economic standing. Then, of course, everyone knows that Henry VIII was the king who had six wives. This accomplishment has provided the material for a whole library of romantic novels and biographies, not to mention films and television series. To the aesthete Henry VIII will always be the vandal whose greed laid waste the monasteries and destroyed their garnered ancient treasures. For the aficionado of English history, this monarch uniquely compels attention. His personality was as massive as his frame and one cannot gainsay J.J. Scarisbrick's assessment that the thirty-seven-and-a-half years of his reign 'left a deeper mark on the mind, heart and face of England than did any event in English history between the coming of the Normans and the coming of the factory'.

All this suggests a powerful king who, for good or ill, deliberately set about transforming the realm he inherited from his father – and succeeded. A simplistic evaluation of the evidence neatly ties up the career of Henry VIII with Holbein's uncompromising image. The king assumes heroic proportions, whether as a tyrant or as a creator of a modern state. The picture I shall try to paint in the following chapters is very different. I shall argue that Henry VIII was a man whose blustering egotism covered a basic insecurity. He was both morally and intellectually limited and heavily dependent on others – ministers, courtiers, wives. He was too self-obsessed to have any vision of a greater or better England. The changes that came over the nation during his reign were in large measure the work of others and often emerged from the muddled interaction of external influences and internal factionalism. My argument in the following pages is based on two premises. First of all, many of the changes which overtook England would have occurred whoever had occupied the throne. The Renaissance and Reformation, disseminated through new information technology, profoundly refashioned the thought processes of those who lived through them. Church and state and the relations between them could not have remained unaltered during the four decades of Henry's reign. Of course, change has to be managed and it is no part of my thesis to assert that Henry had no ideas of his own and no impact on policy. However, what I do suggest, secondly, is that he was essentially reactive rather than proactive. He responded to events and was influenced by the powerful personalities of those around him (not to mention being a victim of his own passions). His greatest talent was an acute judgement of character. He chose some truly remarkable men and it was they who not only attended to the boring, day-to-day routine for which he had little taste, but shaped those policies whose effects were so profound.

What the Holbein portrait does reveal is Henry's keen interest in PR. This stemmed not from the belligerent self-confidence of a ruler determined to force his will on the nation, but from an awareness of the importance of public opinion. On a number of key occasions he gave way to it. Henry was a great showman, forever parading himself in court entertainments, tiltyard heroics and public spectacles. He needed the flattery of courtiers and the applause of the crowd. Over and above all else, he was constantly haunted by the ghost of his father. If he was driven by any principle it was the need to outdo the achievements of Henry VII, the parent from whom he had been estranged in life but who had notched up achievements which always lowered over him in later years. The first Tudor had won his crown by hazarding his person on the battlefield at Bosworth. His son espoused military glory and tried to win back the crown of France. The first Tudor had established a secure dynasty. His son's marital misadventures would be dominated by the need to provide a male heir. The first Tudor had cowed the nobility. His son was determined to bring the church to heel. The first Tudor had insinuated himself, by alliances and diplomacy, into the political life of Europe. His son entertained dreams of maintaining parity with his contemporary monarchs. The first Tudor had left a full treasury as the basis for strong, centralized government. His son would spend and spend without restraint in pursuit of unattainable objectives.

In pursuance of his ambitions Henry evolved from a spoiled adolescent into an unprincipled, unpredictable, paranoid and very dangerous eccentric. He demanded loyalty from those around him but it never occurred to him that they had the right to expect loyalty in return. It was not just his wives whom he treated abominably. He was profligate with the lives of his ablest servants. Remarkable men of the stamp of Thomas Wolsey, Thomas More and Thomas Cromwell were simply discarded on a whim or in pursuit of some passing advantage or to win popularity.

The 500th anniversary of Henry VIII's accession provides the occasion for fresh assessments and gives me the opportunity to offer the fruits of half a century of reflection and study. The historian David Starkey has suggested that an objective understanding of this king is inevitably shaped by changing fashions of historical discourse. I would like to believe there is more to it than that. Over the years, I have come to 'know' Henry obliquely through writing about contemporary personalities such as More, Wolsey, Cromwell, Thomas Cranmer, John Dudley, Thomas Howard, Holbein, Luther and Thomas Wriothesley: I hope that there is sufficient truth in the adage that you can tell a man by the company he keeps to make it worthwhile offering the insights I believe I have gathered. The result is not a work of political history; that would have made it too unwieldy. Nor, I think, is it a full-blown biography; that, too, would have weighted the project down with details more interesting than revelatory. I wanted to keep the focus as tightly as possible on the changing character of the king; to see how it responded to inner impulses and the often bewildering changes and chances of external events. What I have tried to present is a tragedy, in the Greek sense of the word. The life of Henry VIII, for me, fulfils most of the criteria identified by Euripides and Sophocles: a flawed hero, struggling in vain against fate and his own weaknesses who is eventually destroyed by them. It is a chronicle of cruelty, irony and passion, of unrealised dreams, unfulfilled loves and thwarted ambitions, so that, finally, we can say that, if there is any truth in Holbein's Henry, it lies in the king's defiant stance not against human adversaries, but against those demons which opposed and eventually destroyed him.

# Chapter 1

## ENGLAND'S HARRY

The king's grace is but a weak and sickly man, not likely to be a long-lived man. Not long since he was sick and lay at his manor at Wanstead. At that time a number of great personages discussed among themselves the shape of things that might come should his grace depart this life. Some of them spoke of my lord of Buckingham, saying that he was a noble man and would be a royal ruler. Others spoke of Edmund de la Pole. But none of them spoke of the Prince of Wales.[1]

Sometime in 1504 or 1505 a group of royal servants, in the relative safety of England's continental port of Calais, speculated on the future of their country. Such political gossip reflected two assumptions: the current regime of Henry VII was vastly unpopular and it would be succeeded by that of any rival to the house of Tudor who could command a large enough following among the leading magnates of the realm. The fact that the new dynasty warded off rebellions and coups and survived, for a further century, despite depending for that survival on a royal minor and two royal women, says much for the political tenacity and acumen of England's greatest reigning house. It also reflects the preoccupation of most of the crown's subjects with stability and continuity. Whatever scheming nobles might have thought in the twilight years of Henry VII's reign, the people at large had no taste for a return to the carnage and dislocation of the Wars of the Roses.

The boy who was to become Henry VIII would be the most absolute monarch England ever experienced and would preside over fundamental and far-reaching changes in the cultural, political and economic life of the nation. It is tempting to put all this down to his strength of character but the truth is more complex. It has to do with the impact of revolutionary ideas over which the king had no control and with a succession of gifted royal servants able not only to give Henry what he wanted but what they wanted him to want. It also reflects the passivity of a people unwilling to engage in major rebellion until pushed beyond endurance. Yet, at the beginning of the sixteenth century, those supposedly in the know could discount the possibility of young Harry succeeding to or maintaining his hold of the crown. To begin to understand the reign of Henry VIII we, too, must expunge from our minds what we know of Renaissance and Reformation England, the matrimonial convolutions of the king's life, the lavish royal rituals, the transfer of ecclesiastical wealth and power to the crown and the emergence of a new class of land-rich gentlemen and businessmen, who were partners in change but steadily developing an awareness of their own corporate interests. We must submit to the mental conditioning of Henry's contemporaries. They could only predict the future in terms of the past.

At the dawn of the sixteenth century there were very good reasons for discounting the accession to the throne of Henry VII's only surviving son, born in 1491. Twice during the previous 100 years the crown had passed to a minor and on both occasions the results had been disastrous. Henry V had been succeeded by Henry VI, a nine-month-old boy who became the pawn of aristocratic factions and was murdered, after a reign as chaotic as it was long, in 1471. Twelve years later the usurper, Edward IV, died and bequeathed his realm to the twelve-year-old Prince Edward. The new king and his brother were removed by their uncle, Richard of Gloucester, who was driven not only by his own ambition, but by the conviction that England could never be secure under the rule of a minor. As the movers and shakers of Gothic England waited for Henry VII to die, there seemed every reason to suppose that the future would lie in their own scheming hands and an effective military leader of their own choosing. The king disappointed their hopes. His last service to England was his eking out of his life until young Harry of Wales was within sight of his eighteenth birthday. The crown passed without challenge to the legitimate heir amidst demonstrations of wild rejoicing. The dynasty was secure – for the moment.

Our story, however, must start further back in time. A few months before Columbus gained his first sight of the Americas and the surviving Moors their last sight of Spain before being driven out by Ferdinand and Isabella, little Henry Tudor entered the world on 28 June 1491 in the palace of Greenwich, downriver from the fetid summer airs of the capital whither Elizabeth of York had resorted with her ladies for her lying-in. The birth process was always hazardous but the queen was robust and had already been safely delivered of one boy child (Arthur, 1486) and one girl child (Margaret, 1489). It was, nevertheless, a relief for the king to know that he had another healthy son, a 'spare' heir. The royal family continued to grow. Over the next few years Henry had three younger siblings, though only one, Mary (1496), survived infancy. By the standards of the day it was a good-sized brood, particularly valuable to King Henry because it enabled him to secure his position by negotiating a series of marriages with other royal houses. Childhood was short in those days. Long before puberty the young princes and princesses had become accustomed to the idea that they were destined for separation and dispersion to various European courts.

What little we can know about the upbringing of the royal children suggests that the dominant figure in their enclosed world was their grandmother. Lady Margaret Beaufort was a *femme formidable* in every sense. Scheming, ambitious and strong-willed, the king's mother had been one of the principle agents in Henry VII's acquisition of the throne. From a very early age she had been caught up in the sinister game of dynastic snakes and ladders. Because she was descended from Edward III, she was married off by Henry VI to his half-brother, Edmund Tudor, with the sole intention of producing more supporters of the Lancastrian cause. Edward lost no time in making his young bride pregnant by an act which must have been very close to rape. It left Margaret unable to have more children but she did have a son (the future Henry VII) and the two would always be very close. The bond was even stronger because Henry never knew his father, who died of plague before he was born. In 1471, when Henry was thirteen, the Yorkist Edward IV confirmed his grasp of the throne by murdering Henry VI. The young Tudor now became a theoretical rival and Margaret organized his hurried flight across the Channel. While Henry spent the next fourteen years in asylum in Brittany, his mother negotiated, plotted and schemed to gain the royal favour which would allow his return. However, the possibility of making a bid for the crown was never far from her thoughts and when Richard III's usurpation created a backlash among many of the nobility she grasped her opportunity to place her son at the head of a rebellion. Her scheming was as audacious as it was energetic. Her agents scurried secretly to and fro among disaffected Yorkist magnates, promising not a Lancastrian takeover but the union of the rival houses by the marriage of her son to Edward IV's daughter, Elizabeth. Meanwhile, other conspirators bargained with the rulers of France and Brittany for the provision of men and arms. The outcome of the rebellion was by no means a foregone conclusion and there were a number of false starts to the campaign before Henry Tudor landed safely at Milford Haven in August 1485. His eventual victory at

Bosworth had as much to do with defections from the royal ranks as with the accomplishments of Henry's mongrel army.

It was inevitable that Margaret Beaufort would exercise considerable influence in the new regime. Henry relied heavily on his mother's advice and she enjoyed greater prominence than Henry's new wife, Elizabeth of York. She assumed the royal coat of arms, signed documents 'Margaret R.' and appeared at court rituals beside the king. She maintained a large, magnificently appointed household not a whit less impressive than her that of her son. She wore sumptuous jewellery and beautifully tailored gowns, though almost always these were of simple cut and in chaste black. The portrait of her in Christ's College, one of two centres of learning she founded at Cambridge, reveals an austere woman in a nun-like habit, reading a devotional book.

There is no contradiction here. Margaret managed to combine worldly pomp and power with genuine religious devotion. Although she never entered a convent, she separated from her third husband in order to organize her daily life around a ritual of prayer and worship. She endowed ancient religious houses but was interested in modern developments in theology and religious art. And technology: she was the foremost patroness of the new, revolutionary printing industry. She ordered several devotional works from the presses of William Caxton and Wynkyn de Worde and bought copies as gifts for friends and protégés.

> The most devout King David. . .taught the people of Israel to praise God with their whole hearts and with voices full of melody to bless and praise him every day. If so great devotion was then used. . .what reverence and devotion ought now to be preserved by me and all Christian people during the ministration of the sacrament.[2]

These words from the early fifteenth-century devotional classic, *The Imitation of Christ* by Thomas à Kempis, were translated personally by Margaret for the first English edition and it is no surprise to learn that she took the writer's advice. Her chapel staff rivalled that of the king for numbers and musicality and was an important centre for the development of English polyphony. As a widow in her fifties who had experienced – and survived – many of the changes and chances of a troubled age, Margaret was an awe-inspiring old woman who wielded immense political and moral authority. According to the Spanish ambassador, she dominated her daughter-in-law and if Elizabeth was overwhelmed by the older woman the young princes and princesses must have been even more so. They were brought up in royal manors south of the Thames – Eltham, Greenwich and Richmond – and Margaret could easily visit them from her residence at Woking or her riverside town mansion of Coldharbour, near London Bridge. The grandmother they encountered in those early years was a strict disciplinarian with firm ideas about everything and everyone – especially education and religion.

The queen mother's confessor and closest adviser on things scholarly and spiritual was John Fisher, vice-chancellor of Cambridge University and one of the most advanced thinkers of the day. He belonged to that circle of international cognoscenti whom traditionalists dismissed contemptuously as trendy advocates of 'New Learning' because they had absorbed the Renaissance passion for classical scholarship and the original Greek and Hebrew texts of the Bible instead of being content with the time-honoured regurgitation of accepted patristic interpretations. Margaret naturally turned to Fisher when it came to selecting those men who should be employed as tutors for the royal children. Each of the siblings was appointed his or her own household staff and the academic avant-garde featured prominently among the appointees. The man installed as tutor to Prince Henry in about 1496 was the very remarkable poet and scholar, John Skelton. He had recently been appointed poet laureate at Cambridge and probably belonged to Fisher's circle. Skelton was in his mid-thirties and, if not exactly an 'angry young man', he was certainly a very intense one. His religious and moral earnestness displayed itself in his personal devotion (he took holy orders in 1498), in pedagogical books such as the *Boke how Men Shulde Fle Synne* and also in satirical verse. In 1499 he turned his pen to invective against the hypocrisy of the royal household in *The Bouge of Court*, in which he described an allegorical dream where certain characters representing established courtiers offered to guide him in the workings of the court:

> The first was Duplicity, full of flattery,
> With fables false, that well could feign a tale.
> The second was Suspicion which that daily
> Misjudged each man, with face deadly and pale,
> And Deceiver, that well could pick a quarrel,
> With other four of their affinity:
> Disdain, Riot, Dissimulation, Subtlety.

It seems that Skelton was determined to make his young charge aware of the unreality and false values of the enclosed little world in which he was growing up. The tutor certainly took his job very seriously. We know of several treatises written by him on subjects, such as grammar and the theory of government, which would have been useful for the education of a prince.

The queen, the queen mother and the king were all concerned to see the next generation of Tudors brought up not only by the best intellects of the day, but also by men who were at the cutting edge of intellectual enquiry. It was, perhaps, a concern inspired by their desire to establish the family as a dynamic dynasty, looking to the future, not the past. Henry VII had spent most of his formative years on the continent among cultivated men and women influenced by the Renaissance airs blowing across the Alps. He was well aware that England was regarded as culturally backward and he made a point of bringing into his realm the best artists and craftsmen who could be induced to come and work in the land of fogs and damp humours. Among the members of Prince Henry's entourage

was William Blount, Baron Mountjoy, a scholarly young man
who was a friend of Fisher and also of a London lawyer just
beginning to create a name for himself called Thomas More.
Blount made an intellectual pilgrimage to Paris in order to sit at
the feet of the doyen of the avant-garde movement, the great
Dutch scholar, Desiderius Erasmus, and the two became close
friends. When Erasmus arrived to visit his pupil in 1499,
Mountjoy arranged for the great scholar to be received by the
royal children. Thus it was that Erasmus and More made the
brief journey from Mountjoy's house to Eltham Palace.
Erasmus' account of the visit, written many years later, gives us
the only word picture we have of Henry VIII as a child. Arthur
was not present, for he had already left the nursery to begin his
serious training as future king. The eight-year-old Henry
assumed the role of host, greeting the visitors and engaging
them in self-assured conversation. He graciously received a
Latin tribute More had thoughtfully composed for the occasion
and asked whether the visiting international celebrity might
have a similar offering for him. This caught Erasmus on the
hop, for he had not thought to equip himself with a suitable
present. Only after returning to Mountjoy's home and burning
the midnight oil was he able to make good the omission.
According to Erasmus, Henry already had a good command of
Latin and French (the languages of scholarship and diplomacy)
and to these he later added some facility in Spanish and Italian.

However, Henry never fully embraced fashionable
humanism. Traditional influences were just as strong as challenging new ideas and the favourite part of his educational
syllabus was history – or what, then, passed for history. This
was a mix of courtly romance, moral tales and propaganda.
Europe was in the grip of a revolution in information technology. The invention of the printing press with its unlimited
potential for the instruction of children in well-to-do households raised the question of what texts should be set before
them. No one doubted what the author of *The Book of the
Knight of the Tower*, published by Caxton in 1484, pointed out:

that the past was a repository of improving stories from which the young could learn how to conduct themselves in the present. The immediate appeal of such tales in the classroom, however, was the *Boy's Own Paper*–style heroism lauded in accounts of knightly derring-do. Prince Henry, like many sons of royal and noble parentage, was brought up on the chivalric adventures recorded in Jean Froissart's *Chronicles*, Sir Thomas Malory's *Le Morte Darthur* (published in English by Caxton in 1485) and a wealth of other books and manuscripts of the same genre. They glorified personal combat and just war while extolling the pure code of honour which supposedly inspired all true knights. Such stories received vivid real-life illustration in the feats of arms performed in the 'lists', the enclosures where tournaments were held.

Here the young prince could thrill to the glorious spectacle of heraldically accoutred knights dashing their lances on one another's shields and enjoy the atmosphere created by cheering crowds, the clash of steel and the whinnying of horses. Henry longed for the day when he could take his place as a hero of the joust and the battlefield. As soon as he could handle small swords and bows he began to practise for that day.

Learning the martial arts intermeshed completely with the prince's religious and moral education. The business of bashing heads, besieging castles, burning villages and wasting farmland was to be considered highly commendable if the cause for which the knight was contending was just and holy, and as long as his own life was pure. In *Le Morte Darthur*, Lancelot rejects sexual temptation which would besmirch his knightly honour:

> To take my pleasure with paramours, that will I refuse: firstly for dread of God, for the knight who is an adventurer should not be an adulterer nor lecherous, for then he will be neither happy nor fortunate in the wars. Either he will be overcome by a simpler knight than he is himself or else he will by mischance and the curse upon him slay better men than himself. And so whoever resorts to paramours will be unhappy and everything about them will be unhappy.[3]

The disastrous consequences of Lancelot's subsequent liaison with Guinevere, of course, drive home the moral.

This code of honour was subscribed to by all young noblemen and gentlemen but for the son of the king of England it carried greater weight, for was he not directly descended from the hero-king who presided over the Round Table? When Henry VII ensured that his firstborn was brought into the world at Winchester, the ancient capital of England, and christened with the unusual name of 'Arthur' these were propaganda acts and parts of an overall plan to use every means possible to give his regime credibility. He was deliberately linking his dynasty with ancient legend and with the genealogy proposed by Geoffrey of Monmouth, the twelfth-century chronicler in his *Historia Regum Britanniae*. Geoffrey claimed to have discovered ancient sources which linked the rulers of England not only with King Arthur, but also with fugitives from the fall of Troy. Fifteenth- and sixteenth-century readers had no accurate sense of chronology. 'History' was for them a radiant tapestry in which kings, saints, knights, magicians and heroes all had their interconnected panels.

Henry VII was determined to weave his family into this imposing fabric. He commissioned the Italian scholar, Polydore Vergil, to write an updated history of England which would be very much a narrative with a Tudor spin. Prince Henry was brought up to see himself as the inheritor of this melange of romantic, militaristic, idealized, politicized mumbo-jumbo. If he had a favourite personal hero it was Henry V, the warrior-king whose spectacular military exploits were still celebrated in legend and ballad. His cross-Channel campaigns had added Normandy and much of northern France to England's continental possession of Gascony in the south-west. By his death in 1422, approximately one-third of what we now call 'France' owed allegiance to the English crown and he had been named as heir to the French throne. That was before England's warrior-class split into factions and began to turn their swords against each other. By 1453 everything had been lost except Calais. Since then the political map of nearer-Europe had changed considerably. Louis XI (1423–83) united most of the independent duchies west of the Rhine by a combination of war and diplomacy and made of France a centralized monarchy. The union of Aragon and Castile and the expulsion of the Moors turned Spain into a formidable state. It was the relationship between these two nations which would determine the shape of European politics throughout the ensuing century and introduce the concept of the 'balance of power'. England had ceased to be a major player. For Prince Henry, however, Anglo-French rivalry was a matter of unfinished business and the relegation of England to the status of second-rate nation, a mere spectator in the Habsburg-Valois struggle, was not to be borne. From an early age he dreamed of emulating the exploits of his illustrious ancestors.

As well as the time he spent at his lessons, Henry's days were passed in the company of two groups of people, his female relatives and his *socii studiorum*. The latter were the sons of noble parents who shared the prince's classroom and leisure hours. They were selected as suitable companions and as a means of tying their families more securely to the Tudor regime. It was with this peer group that Henry took exercise – in the tennis court, in the butts, in the hunting field and in the tiltyard. These recreational activities developed and expressed his macho self-image and his intensely competitive nature, which were also reinforced by the fact that he spent much of his time in a household of women in which he was the leading male figure. He was much in the company of his admiring mother and his sisters and always in the background was the dominatrix, Lady Margaret. Young Henry never really had a male role model. He saw little of his father and his elder brother. Arthur would always remain a shadowy figure. Francis Bacon, writing in the early seventeenth century, asserted that Henry VII's heir was 'strong and able'. The fact that, by his early teens, he had received various important offices and that plans for his marriage were pursued with

vigour may suggest that there was no long-standing concern
about his health. On the other hand, portraits of the prince
show him with the rather pinched features of his father and
other Lancastrians. His tutors reported that he was a studious
boy and an apt learner. (We might be tempted to respond,
'They would, wouldn't they?') There are no references to his
appearing in the tiltyard or participating in athletic exercises
apart from archery. This evidence – such as it is – may support
the generally accepted opinion that Arthur was a sickly child.
In any case, his contact with the brother who was five years his
junior was limited. Arthur had his own household and, as the
heir, received a distinctive upbringing.

It is interesting, and not entirely fanciful, to speculate about
what would have happened to Henry if Arthur had lived. The
two brothers were very different. One might almost see them
as representing the Lancastrian and Yorkist elements of their
ancestry. Henry grew up tall, athletic and passionate, like his
grandfather, Edward IV. If we are at all correct in portraying
Arthur as studious, reserved and pious, like his father or even
the unfortunate Henry VI, there could hardly have been more
difference between the siblings. Would the younger have
settled happily as a loyal subject and supporter of the elder?
The immediate family of Edward IV had destroyed itself by
fraternal rivalry. George, Duke of Clarence, was impelled by
ambition and hubris to those acts which obliged his brother to
order his execution. Richard of Gloucester had come to grief
as the result of grasping the crown rightfully belonging to
Edward's son. Might Henry have decided, like his great-
uncles, that he was a more worthy candidate for kingship than
his bookish brother? The forceful, impatient Henry known to
history could only have found a subservient role irksome and,
perhaps, intolerable.

Nor should we neglect the impact of Arthurian legend. The
heir to the throne bore the magical name of the 'once and
future king'. Henry VII had sought to merge the mystical past
with the promise of a radiant future, safe in the hands of a

dynasty which would restore internal unity and make England once again great. Around 1500 there existed a very real sense of new beginnings. Many English men and women felt that somehow they were on the cusp of a golden age. They looked to the Tudors with expectancy. However, if the heroic mantle of 'Arthur' sat only loosely around the slender shoulders of a weak king might not his brother have felt that it was imperative for him to make good the deficiency? And even if Henry had given loyal support to the anointed king, what would have happened if that king had died young, bequeathing the crown to a minor? For the third time in a century England would have been faced with the disastrous reign of a child. It is difficult to imagine Henry standing passively by while noble factions once again threatened chaos. These possibilities are not just make-believe scenarios of no real interest to the historian. They certainly occurred to Henry VII and members of the political nation. As we saw at the beginning of this chapter, 'what ifs' were certainly questions for debate and speculation among the nation's leaders. They were no less so for members of the royal family whose very survival was bound up with the smooth transfer of the crown to men of stature able to wear it with dignity and conviction. As for little Henry, he emerged from the chrysalis of infancy not knowing what his future might be. There was even a suggestion that he might be pushed into the church, presumably to prevent him appearing as a rival for the crown.

If Henry saw little of his father during his childhood years it was only partly because he was lodged in his own residences. The king was preoccupied in establishing his throne. From 1491, the year of his second son's birth, to 1500 Henry VII was seldom able to feel secure. He was repeatedly involved in dealing with rebellions and rumours of rebellions. Yorkist plots, centred round the pretender Perkin Warbeck, obliged him to despatch or lead armies to Ireland, Scotland and France as well as make frequent sorties into various parts of his realm. These military activities were expensive and the tax burden

imposed by the government was the heaviest England had had
to bear for more than a century. In the spring of 1497 the men
of Cornwall had had enough. They raised the standard of
revolt and marched eastwards. The five-year-old Prince Henry
was staying at his grandmother's house at Coldharbour when
news arrived that the Cornishmen had reached Farnham.
Margaret hastily packed her daughter-in-law and her children
into barges and had them rowed down to the Tower. There, in
the safety of the ancient royal apartments, they waited
anxiously for news while the king gathered his forces together
to confront his disobedient subjects on Blackheath Common.
Defeating the ill-disciplined revolt was not difficult but simul-
taneous risings in other places made this the most hazardous
summer of the reign. Henry sent troops northwards while he
led his main army into the heartland of the revolution. In
Devon the last vestiges of rebellion were dispelled and
Warbeck was taken prisoner. However, the troubles were not
over. Eighteen months later, another pretender, Ralph Wilford,
put himself forward and no sooner were his pretensions
brought to an end than the leading Yorkist contender, Edmund
de la Pole, Earl of Suffolk, fled abroad to make a nuisance of
himself in foreign courts. It is hardly surprising that the king
and his younger son were able to spend little 'quality time'
together. By the time that all immediate military threats were
past it was 1502 and in that year Prince Henry's life changed
dramatically.

From about 1496, King Henry was involved in frenetic
diplomatic activity aimed at securing his own and the nation's
position by means of a network of marriage alliances. His elder
daughter, Margaret, was to be espoused to James IV of
Scotland. Other matches were sought for the infants Henry
and Mary, while Arthur was to be wed to Catherine of Aragon,
the daughter of Ferdinand and Isabella. The various negotiations dragged on over several years, chiefly because, in the
beginning, Henry VII was punching above his weight. In
foreign eyes he was a usurping adventurer whose dynasty was

unlikely to last long. However, as the English king stamped his authority within his realm other monarchs took him more seriously, realizing that his neutrality or military cooperation could be a significant factor in their rivalries. The marriage of Margaret and James (1503) bestowed much needed peace upon England's northern border. Before the end of his reign Henry had agreed a match between Mary and the Archduke Charles (the future Emperor Charles V). Had this materialized, the course of European affairs over ensuing decades would have been very different but the proposal died with Henry. His major coup was the marriage of Arthur and Catherine, the most prestigious English dynastic alliance since Henry V's marriage to Catherine of France in 1420. The treaty was drawn up in 1496 and the couple were betrothed the following year. It was not uncommon for such initial agreements to be set aside in the light of subsequent political or diplomatic complications and King Henry could not rest easily until the ring was on the princess's finger. He obtained a papal dispensation to allow the union to take place before the couple reached marriageable age and Arthur and Catherine were wed by proxy in May 1499 when they were twelve and thirteen respectively. Still, there could have occurred a slip twixt cup and lip and it was November 1501 before the king could allow himself a sigh of relief. That was when Catherine arrived in her new homeland. Henry VII has often been represented unfairly as a parsimonious, cheese-paring monarch. The truth is that when he wanted to impress English and foreign spectators, no one put on a better show. To celebrate his diplomatic triumph he threw back the lid of the royal coffers.

No expense was spared in welcoming the Spanish princess and her suite with what was 'perhaps, the supreme masterpiece of English civic pageantry'.[4] Londoners love a parade and they turned out in their tens of thousands to catch a glimpse of their future queen. The Tudor propaganda machine did not disappoint either them or the foreign contingent. As they rode through the heart of the capital the guests were greeted by a spectacular series of allegorical scenes, the like of which the citizens had never seen. Catherine and her attendants could scarcely have understood much of the convoluted astrological and mythical allusions that confronted them but the general drift will have been clear. At each stage elaborate constructions covered in painted and gilded canvas provided platforms from which elaborately-robed figures recited adulatory verses extolling the virtues of the princess's husband and father-in-law. Confident prophecies assured the young bride of future happiness and even an enthroned 'God' was enrolled to pronounce a benediction:

> Blessed be the fruit of your belly
> Your substance and fruits I shall increase and multiply.[5]

From the utter failure of this pseudo-divine promise sprang all the ills of the next half century.

However, this was only the beginning of splendours. The wedding was celebrated two days later (14 November) in St Paul's Cathedral, magnificently draped in silken bunting for the occasion, and was followed by a week of court celebrations. These took the form of sumptuous banquets in Richmond Palace, recently enlarged and refurbished at immense cost, and tournament combats staged in an arena set up in front of Westminster Hall. Here, Henry and his guests beheld from specially-erected galleries a spectacle which was not just a feat of arms. Tournaments had taken on a highly theatrical character. Combatants and their attendants were applauded as much for their skill at 'disguisings' as for their athletic prowess. So, for example, one knight entered the lists on a simulated ship 'floating' on painted water; another appeared in a gilded carriage drawn by fabulous beasts; a third was borne along in a mobile castle, set with 'turrets and pinnacles of curious work'.[6]

For Prince Henry, now ten years old, this must have been the most exciting week of his life so far. For months the court had been in a fever of eager anticipation and the boy, who loved theatricality and dressing up, had particularly looked forward to the role allotted to him in the ceremonial. His most important part in the lavish rituals occurred at the marriage service. It was he who met the beautiful Spanish bride in her dazzling wedding gown at the west door of the cathedral and escorted her the entire length of the building to the high altar. Afterwards, he walked behind the newlyweds as they emerged from the church while bells rang, fountains gushed wine and crowds cheered. For anyone who, like Henry, loved an audience it was a thrilling experience – even if he was not the centre of attraction. Observers noted how much the little prince enjoyed himself, dancing with such vigour that he had to put off his outer garments. Yet, might there not have been a reverse side to the coin? It would be understandable if he had experienced at least a twinge of envy. Arthur was being feted with an expensive exuberance which would never be a younger brother's lot. Whatever foreign princess was found for Henry, it was unlikely that such an extravaganza would be laid on for him. He would always be obliged to play second fiddle. And when Arthur and his lovely queen were crowned, Henry would be their subject.

However, if the little green demon had taken up lodging in the prince's mind a tragic sequence of events soon drove it hence. The events of the wedding day ended, as tradition demanded, with the ceremonial 'bedding', a mix of good-natured Hymen worship and bawdy buffoonery during which the groom was conveyed to the bridal chamber and seen safely ensconced between the sheets with his new wife. History would love to know what happened next, not out prurient curiosity, but because the nature of the relationship between Arthur and Catherine would become a matter of the highest importance years later. The following morning the boasting prince claimed that he had spent much of the night in 'the midst of Spain'. Catherine insisted, in the 1520s, that the marriage had never been consummated. Who should we believe – the bragging adolescent defending his macho image

or the middle-aged woman clinging desperately to her reputation and her position?

Before the year's end the newlyweds had left the capital in
order to set up home for themselves. For the next stage of
Arthur's training in kingcraft it had been decided that he
should assume control of his principality of Wales. Actual
administration was in the hands of a council of trusted Tudor
agents but Henry VII wanted to establish a dynastic presence
in this distant part of the realm which had its own identity and
traditions. Although Welsh support had been vital in his own
progress to the throne, the loyalty of the whole country could
not be relied upon and the king aimed to secure his grasp of the
land beyond Offa's Dyke and provide the people with a
personal focus for their allegiance. It was important that, in any
disturbance which might mark the beginning of Arthur's reign
the new king should have a strong power base in the west. The
location chosen for the princely court was Ludlow Castle. This
formidable Marcher fortress, set on high ground above the
Teme and Corve, was an excellent stronghold but it had long
been the centre of English administration and, as medieval
castles went, it was comfortably appointed. With apparently
no qualms, the king bade farewell to his elder son and settled
down to the next priority of his diplomatic programme, the
marriage of Margaret to the Scottish king. He was quite unpre-
pared for the news with which he was awakened on a Tuesday
morning four months later.

Ludlow Castle, for all its sixteenth-century mod cons, was
not an ideal residence for anyone with a weak constitution. By
the end of March 1502, winter had yet to relax its grip on the
border country. Viruses flourished in the dank airs wafting up
from the valley. Icy winds moaned round the battlements.
Draughts defied the shutters and drapes covering doors and
windows. Several of the castle's inhabitants succumbed to
chills and agues. The prince and princess were among them.
Anxious royal physicians hovered round the curtained beds
where the feverish young couple lay. They were relieved when

Catherine's temperature came down and there was hope, perhaps even expectation, that her husband would also make a complete recovery. But Arthur failed to respond to their primitive medical practices. On 2 April, the young Prince of Wales died – 'suddenly' according to the contemporary record. The dolorous news was rushed to London and it was Henry's confessor who was delegated to break it to the king. A contemporary chronicler provides a touching picture of Henry's grief and how the queen tried to comfort him:

> She with full great and constant comfortable words besought his grace that he would first after God remember the weal of his own noble person, the comfort of his realm and of her. She then said that my lady his mother had never no more children but him only and that God by his grace had ever preserved him, and brought him where he was. Over that how that God had left him yet a fair prince, two fair princesses. . .and that we are both young enough[7]

This underlines the fact that what most concerned Henry VII was the succession. Elizabeth's suggestion that there was still time to have more children (she was 38) was immediately acted on. Ten months later she was delivered of another daughter. Mother and baby survived the birth by only a few days.

Not surprisingly, the atmosphere in the royal court changed drastically from this time. Much of the gaiety went out of it after Elizabeth's demise, to be replaced by a new anxiety. The king was only forty-six but he had witnessed the death of his younger wife and most of their children. He had worked with patient intensity to secure the dynasty and now, just when the Yorkist cause had been thoroughly weakened, rebellions crushed, the nobility brought to heel and the arrangement of an impressive edifice of foreign alliances taking shape brick by painstaking brick, fate had whittled the Tudor succession down to one eleven-year-old boy. If the accession of his son was to be peacefully achieved, the king would have to devote more energy to the task, be more vigilant in spying out possible

trouble-makers and devise new policies to shore up the
dynasty. According to contemporary chroniclers, in the last
years of his reign Henry Tudor underwent a profound change
of character. He became a secretive, obsessive, money-
grubbing tyrant. The king who had ventured the royal person
on campaign against his enemies and delighted in lavish public
spectacles now secluded himself in his chamber, crouched over
account books, personally supervising every penny of royal
expenditure and working out ways of afflicting 'over-mighty'
subjects in their purses rather than their bodies. Nor was it
only wealthy landed magnates who, according to historian,
Edward Hall, were marked for plunder:

> It came into his head that Englishmen did little pass the obser-
> vation and keeping of penal laws and financial statutes, made
> and enacted for the preservation of the common utility and
> wealth and, therefore, if inquisition were had of such penal
> statutes, there should be few noblemen, merchants, farmers,
> husbandmen, graziers, nor occupiers but they should be found
> transgressors and violators of the same statutes.[8]

Whether or not Henry underwent quite such a dramatic,
sudden and sinister transmogrification is debatable. The
machinery created to explore the statute books in search of
laws which might be profitably exploited and to send officials
into every shire snooping into private muniments (the Council
Learned in the Law) had been in existence some six or seven
years before 1503. However, there is no doubt that he now
focused fresh endeavours on a series of legal and financial
measures which would bind substantial subjects to him with
golden cords and provide the crown with a well-filled treasury
capable of financing any counter-measures it might be
necessary to take against military threats. Those on the
receiving end accused the king of miserliness and oppression.
Henry labelled his policies 'prudence'.

If the rule of the first Tudor had degenerated into tyranny the
impact of his autocratic rule was most keenly felt in his own

household, and especially by his son. The king's behaviour became erratic in the extreme. He suffered long bouts of illness and was given to sudden rages, of which his son often felt the full brunt. The effect of Arthur's death on the status of his brother was, of course, momentous – but not immediate. If he expected to be promoted to the titles and honours of the late Prince of Wales, Henry had to possess his soul in patience and remain content for the time being with the numerous honours he already held. As one aspect of the king's policy of cutting England's powerful nobles down to size, he had loaded numerous important offices on his infant sons rather than on ambitious barons. As well as the royal dukedom of York, young Henry had already been appointed Earl Marshal, Lord Warden of the Scottish Marches, Lord Lieutenant of Ireland, Lord Warden of the Cinque Ports and Constable of Dover Castle. The duties attendant on these offices were, of course, carried out by deputies but the titles – and the revenues – remained firmly in royal hands. For good measure little Henry was also a knight of the Garter and of the Bath before he reached the age of four. On Arthur's death Henry exchanged the dukedom of York for that of Cornwall. However, it was not until 18 February 1503 that he was invested as Prince of Wales. The delay was occasioned by the possibility that Catherine might be pregnant. There was lively speculation on this subject. Even Catherine's Spanish attendants were divided on the issue. Her duenna was adamant that her charge was still *virgo intacta* but this did not prevent everyone else around the princess waiting and watching intently for signs that the young widow might be carrying the heir to the throne of England.

Young Henry felt the loss of his mother more keenly than that of his brother but it was the combined effects of these deaths which inevitably made an impact on his character. On the cusp of adolescence, he was deprived of the two people who, more than any other, had provided his life with its shape. At about the same time he also lost his much-loved tutor. John Skelton was paid off by the king and left the court to become a country parson. Despite his cynicism about life in the royal household, Skelton did not enjoy his new role and was eager to return. The fact that Henry VIII brought him back to court soon after his accession suggests that he, too, regretted the break in their relationship. Now that he was heir to the throne, Henry's education entered a new phase. He was setting out on the path to an unexpected future and doing so without the support and affection of those upon whom he had relied most closely. It was unlikely that in the future he would find it easy to form and sustain close relationships.

He was subjected to a rigid regimen within a claustrophobic court. After the fate which had befallen his brother there was no question of sending Henry to the Welsh border to take charge of his principality. The heir was now confined to his father's court where he could be protected from disease, accident and conspiracy. And, perhaps, from himself. The athletic teenager who enjoyed boisterous and potentially dangerous sports had to be kept on a tight reign. Tiltyard exercise was strictly rationed. Now there was little dancing or music in the king's house and the prince's leisure hours were closely monitored. He was only allowed out in the company of his bodyguard. Even within the palace his movements were restricted. We know, for example, that he was forbidden to have communication with Catherine of Aragon even when they were living under the same roof. His father was, to Henry, a grim and distant figure. The Spanish ambassador described him as 'so subjected that he does not speak a word except in response to what the king asks him'.[9] And always behind Henry's father was the figure of his grandmother, the formidably pious Lady Margaret.

What explanation is there for the unwholesome regimen of Henry's teenage years? For the king it was a matter of the utmost importance to protect his son but that does not explain the lack of love or understanding he displayed. Was it just an example of the personality clash of the old lion and the young lion? English history is replete with instances of conflicts between the monarch and the heir to the throne, e.g. Henry IV and Prince Hal, George III and 'Prinny', Victoria and 'Bertie', George V and Edward. There is an almost inevitable clash of interests between the sovereign and the sovereign-in-waiting. In the fifteenth century, tensions within royal families were particularly disruptive. The Yorkists had destroyed themselves through fratricidal strife. Henry VII was almost paranoiacally insecure in his later years. Just as Henry IV had believed rumours that the popular Prince Hal was plotting against him, so Henry VII may have feared that if his son was allowed too much freedom discontented elements (of which, as he knew, there were many) might make him a figurehead for rebellion.

Possibly, the root of the problem is more simple – Prince Henry was not Arthur. By 1503 the king's younger son was a spoiled, ebullient, fun-loving extrovert, quite unlike his serious and bookish brother. Henry VII had been able to mould his intended heir in his own image. If Arthur had lived, the old king could have died happy in the knowledge that his policies would be continued, but the boy on whom all Tudor hopes now rested was a frivolous prince preoccupied with his own pleasures and with a head full of romantic, chivalric ideas. The young boy showed signs of growing up to be the image of his maternal grandfather – a charmer with a penchant for glitzy display and jovial camaraderie, far too easygoing to continue the ruthless work of strengthening the position of the monarchy.

We do not need to rely on pure conjecture to understand something of the relationship between father and son. Over thirty years later, Henry VIII proclaimed to the world just how he saw himself in relation to the previous king. In 1537, he commissioned an impressive mural for the privy chamber at Whitehall Palace. In it he had himself displayed, with his mother, father and third wife, grouped round a plinth whose long Latin inscription deliberately compared and contrasted the achievements of the first two Tudors:

Between them there was great competition and rivalry and [posterity] may well debate whether father or son should take the palm. Both were victorious. The father triumphed over his foes, quenched the fires of civil war and brought his people lasting peace. The son was born to a greater destiny. He it was who banished from the altars undeserving men and replaced them with men of worth. Presumptuous popes were forced to yield before him and when Henry VIII bore the sceptre true religion was established and, in his reign, God's teachings received their rightful reverence. [10]

Three decades after the death of his father Henry still felt the need to exorcise the old man's ghost. Despite his parents' lack of faith in him, he insisted, he had proved himself a better king, even outdoing Henry VII in Christian piety.

In Freudian psychoanalytical theory the Oedipus Complex is identified as one cause of neurosis. It results from the subject's unresolved, unconscious rivalry with a same-sex parent. The young Henry's essential self (what Freud labelled the 'id') was certainly repressed and confined not only by the physical restraints placed upon him, but also by the unfavourable comparisons frequently drawn between himself and his dead brother. This was underlined in the closing years of his father's reign by the policy fluctuations concerning his marriage. The situation after Arthur's death was that his young widow remained a 'guest' in England, lodged for the most part at Durham House, one of the palatial town residences on the Strand with grounds running down to the river. Her fate remained undecided while her father and father-in-law discussed what should be done about her and her dowry. Both kings were eager to maintain the alliance and Henry VII was certainly not prepared to forego any of the money he had received from Ferdinand and Isabella. Catherine was still eligible for an English royal spouse because a papal dispensation had been obtained for her to marry a close relative of her late husband. According to the wording of this document the parties had to be dispensed from the demands of canon law, not only because they were in the first degree of affinity, but because, it was conceded, Catherine's marriage to Arthur had been consummated. At the time, this was of purely academic interest. No one could possibly have foreseen how world-changing it would prove to be. Henry's first proposed solution was that he, himself, should marry his seventeen-year-old daughter-in-law. This was indignantly rejected by Catherine's relatives, not out of moral repugnance at the age gap, but because the marriage would put the princess in a humiliating situation. Instead of being Queen of England after Henry VIII's accession, she would have been merely the king's step-mother, a political nonentity.

Thus it was that, in the summer of 1503, a contract of marriage was agreed between Catherine and Henry, Prince of Wales. However, within a couple of years, the two kings had fallen out and the marriage was off. The fourteen-year-old Prince Henry was forced to take responsibility for the change of policy and to make a humiliating climb down. He was brought before a committee of the council and obliged to make a solemn affirmation that the match had been without his permission when he was a minor and that he now renounced it. Meanwhile, as a result of the changing cloudscape of international politics, the king selected a new bride for his son. He was to be betrothed to Princess Eleanor of Austria. It can scarcely be wondered at that in later years Henry VIII was adamant about choosing his own wives on his own terms.

As long as his father lived Henry was permitted no share in government, attended no council meetings and was not consulted on the framing of policy. It was as though the old king had given up all hope of training his heir. His thoughts were increasingly turned towards the next world and calling to mind the many sins he needed to confess. If King Henry was waiting for his death, it may be imagined that his son was looking forward to it no less impatiently.

Henry's character traits germinated in the soil of his childhood and adolescence. Therein lies his tragedy. Aristotle described tragedy as a character's descent into catastrophe as a result of *hamartia*, a Greek term borrowed from archery and meaning, literally, 'falling short of the target'. An Aeschylus or a Sophocles, dramatizing the life of Harry of England, would have pointed out those defects of character which rendered him unequal to the tasks he was set and which were later punished by the gods. The king who came to the throne at his father's death on 21 April 1509 was a young man forced into aggressive self-assertion by years of being suppressed; an eager competitive player with something to prove; an impetuous and impatient ruler determined to assert himself and determinedly smothering self-doubt. For the time being, the gods smiled on him. Ultimately, they would vent their indignation.

# Chapter 2

## CAMELOT

Merlin went forth unto King Lodegreance of Camelard and
told him of the desire of the king that he would have unto his
wife Guinevere his daughter. 'That is to me,' said King
Lodegreance, 'the best tidings that ever I heard, that so worthy
a king of prowess and noblesse will wed my daughter. And as
for my lands, I would give it him if I wist it might please him;
but he hath lands enough, he needeth none. But I shall send him
a gift shall please him much more, for I shall give him the Table
Round, which Uther his father gave me. And when it is fully
complete, there is a hundred knights and fifty; and as for a
hundred good knights, I have myself; but I want [i.e. lack] fifty,
for so many have been slain in my days.' And so King
Lodegreance delivered his daughter Guinevere unto Merlin and
the Table Round with the hundred knights; and so they rode
freshly with great royalty, what by water and by land, till that
they came nigh unto London.[11]

Arthurian legend played mightily on the imagination of
England's new eighteen-year-old monarch. His dead brother
might have borne the name of the once and future king but

Henry VIII would show himself to be the real spiritual heir of the great hero – and also of his own namesake, Henry V, the victor of Agincourt. If any leader could claim to 'feel the hand of history upon him' that leader was Henry VIII. He could not possibly have come to power under circumstances that lent themselves more potently to the acting out of his fantasies. There were no rivals for the crown. The royal treasury was full to bursting. Best of all, his grandmother, the formidable Lady Margaret Beaufort, had survived her son by only sixty-four days and with her passing the last restraints upon her grandson were removed. There was now nothing to stop him being the complete playboy-king. Not that this is a description he would have acknowledged. He saw himself as the focus of all national and dynastic pride, the man appointed by God to take up the unfinished international business which had been interrupted by the Wars of the Roses: the conquest of France. He also regarded himself as the complete Christian prince, presiding over a glittering court, more cultured and refined and, in its way, more devout than any other in Christendom. However, for the moment, the realization of such golden dreams had to wait upon the leaden workings of politics. England had to be prepared for the change of regime and important issues had to be resolved.

Henry VII died around 11 p.m. on Saturday, 21 April 1509, at his favourite palace of Richmond. His son was immediately informed and played his part in the acting out of a macabre charade. For more than thirty-six hours courtiers came and went in the privy apartments at Richmond, as if nothing had happened. The wheeling and dealing took place secretly in other rooms. Councillors and royal attendants jostled for power as though their very lives depended on it. And, indeed, they did. No one was in any doubt about young Henry's feelings towards his father. The new king would select his own advisers and close servants to be the main pillars of his regime and he would want to distance himself from his predecessor's more unpopular policies. The best public advertisement that the times were changing would be to sacrifice officials who had been associated with Henry VII's morally and legally dubious practices. There could, of course, be no acknowledgement of the late king's own guilt; the official verdict fell back on the old chestnut excuse that the sovereign had been misled by evil advisers.

As soon as Henry VII's death was announced it was accompanied by a London-wide demonstration as soldiers scoured the city seeking out men suspected of being royal agents and informers and placing them in the stocks. The purge went on for several weeks. As Thomas More exulted, informers now went in fear of being informed against. By giving disgruntled citizens the opportunity for revenge, the new government diffused much of their stored resentment. Four prominent leaders of the old regime were singled out for severer punishment, 'by malice of them that with their authority in the late king's days were offended, or else to shift the [blame for] the straight execution of penal statutes in the late king's days'.[12] One of the four suspects wriggled out by quickly resigning the office of Surveyor of the King's Prerogative, which he had only held for a few months. The others were arrested and clapped into the Tower. William Smith, a notorious accumulator of lands confiscated by royal order, was eventually released. That left Richard Empson and Edmund Dudley, who had to sit in their cells while they waited to see what crimes they were to be charged with. There is no doubt that the two unfortunates were victims of factional intrigue but the new king was certainly involved in their persecution. He was determined to put clear water between himself and his father's reputation. In effect, within hours of his father's death, he demonstrated that he, too, was prepared to stretch justice and equity in his own interests.

However, there was something that interested him far more in those early, exciting, promise-filled days of his new freedom: marriage. There was still an 'understanding' with Margaret of Savoy for a union with her daughter, Eleanor, but now that young Henry was king he could have the pick of several eligible European princesses. Meanwhile, Catherine of Aragon remained in limbo, an unwilling guest of her late husband's family. Her father was still demanding her return and, perhaps more importantly, the return of the portion of the large dowry that he had already paid. Prudence might well have suggested a period of sitting back and weighing the options, but Henry did not wait. He immediately announced himself in favour of the Spanish girl he had, four years previously, rejected. The reason he offered to Eleanor's mother was that he was honouring his father's dying wish and that he felt obliged to stand by existing Anglo-Hispanic treaty obligations. And this is the only documented motive we have for the most momentous royal marriage in English history!

Should we take it at face value? There can be little doubt that the late king's ministers urged Henry to go through with the Spanish wedding for sound political reasons but can we really believe that, in a matter touching him so closely, the headstrong and determined young king meekly did as he was told? Was the young man who was so determined to step out of his father's shadow submitting to the old man's will in this most intimate area of his life? No, Henry married Catherine because he wanted to. Various reasons present themselves. Political considerations may have played a part in his decision. From the outset Henry was determined on a military showdown with France that would restore to the English crown those territories lost by the incompetence of his recent ancestors. A firm alliance with Spain was a necessary precondition of an effective anti-French policy. However, a simpler and, in my view, more compelling explanation is that Henry knew his chosen bride and liked her. Perhaps he even believed himself to be in love with her.

Throughout his chequered matrimonial career Henry only once married a woman he had not previously met and got to know – usually intimately. He was simply not disposed to tie himself to some stranger, be she never so comely or diplomatically desirable. Catherine had been in England for eight-and-a-half years most of which had been spent at the royal court. She was pretty, intelligent and well-tutored in fashionable accomplishments. She combined youthful high spirits and feisty Spanish pride with a serene reserve and a strength of character she had certainly needed as a widow in an alien land whose ill-tempered king refused to allow her to go home. She would make an eminently suitable consort in the kind of court Henry was determined to establish; someone to preside at the lists where he showed off his athletic prowess with his knightly comrades, to sit beside him at banquets arrayed in the finest silks and jewels money could buy, to match his tireless energy for dancing into the small hours. In short, she would be the ideal Guinevere to his Arthur. And that suggests another motive for the king's decision. He was replacing his dead brother and was determined to prove himself the better man. Arthur had wedded and bedded Catherine – to no effect. Four-and-a-half months of cohabitation had produced no children. Henry would stuff his wife with a procession of princes and princesses.

However, there was an even stronger bond between the two young people. Both had suffered at the hands of the irascible Henry VII. The old king, increasingly suspicious and tenaciously hanging on to personal control of government despite bouts of illness, frequently lashed out at those around him. There were times when the very sight of his son was sufficient to send him into paroxysms. As for Catherine, she had suffered the humiliation of having her Spanish household reduced and her own allowance so slashed that in over four years in England she had only been able to afford two new dresses. The experience had strengthened her. Instead of meekly and patiently awaiting the outcome of the ill-natured diplomatic exchanges between her father and father-in-law, she had taken a personal role in Anglo-Spanish negotiations – and learned the hard way all about tough bargaining, deviousness and duplicity. She was determined to bring about her marriage to the new Prince of Wales and, as she knew through Princess Mary and other intermediaries, he supported this ambition. This, of course, only angered Henry VII further. As we have seen, he ordered that the couple were to be kept apart – even when they were both living in the palace. Such behaviour could only have one result; the cords of mutual sympathy binding Henry and Catherine were made stronger. Tension at court had become even tighter in the last weeks of the old king's reign. In early March 1509, Catherine had reached the extremity of desperation. She had written to her father begging to be allowed home and actually threatening him: 'I might do something which neither the King of England nor your Highness. . . will be able to prevent'.[13] Nothing exposes more clearly the emotional background to the ill-fated marriage of Henry Tudor and Catherine of Aragon.

As soon as the old king was dead, the negotiations which had limped along so uncomfortably for six years, and with such bad grace, galloped wildly to the finishing post. Spanish diplomats were taken aback at the speed with which obstacles were swept aside. Within six weeks, the 'i's and 't's were dotted and crossed and on 11 June Henry met his first bride at the altar. The wedding was no grand affair, such as had marked Catherine's union with Arthur. It took place in the 'closet' at Greenwich, the little room in the royal privy apartments set aside for the private devotions of the king and queen. Doubtless the reason for this was that preparations were in hand for the coronation and nothing could be allowed to overshadow the spectacle of the great public holiday which was to mark the inauguration of the reign.

The coronation was scheduled for 24 June. Three days before the king and queen travelled overland, by way of the south bank of the Thames and London Bridge to the Tower. They availed themselves of the good summer weather to show themselves to their subjects, rather than travelling by river as was the custom. Henry was a young man revelling in fame. Wilful he certainly was, and he became notoriously more so with the passing of the years, but public acclaim and the goodwill of the people mattered to him. Celebrity is not celebrity without an audience. Having arrived at their destination, the couple lodged

in the antiquated palace quarters to the south of the White
Tower. Henry did not like the old building. It did not provide
the degree of comfort and luxury he desired and he ordered
considerable modernization before he consented to stay there
again. Thus, he seldom set foot in the sinister fortress which
was to become so closely connected with his name. Over the
next thirty-seven years far more crown prisoners would be
incarcerated there than in any other reign. Empson and Dudley
were the first of that sorry assemblage of victims. From their
cells, only yards away, they must have heard the fanfares that
greeted the royal pair and the clatter of their escort as they
crossed the moat and passed the Byward and Bell Towers.

On Saturday 23 June, Henry and Catherine received the
adulation of the capital. People love a spectacle and the king's
event managers did not disappoint:

> If I should declare what pain, labour and diligence the tailors
> embroiderers and goldsmiths took both to make and devise
> garments for lords, ladies, knights and esquires and also for
> decking, trapping and adorning of coursers, jennets and
> palfreys it were too long to rehearse; but for a surety, more rich,
> more strange nor more curious works hath not been seen than
> were prepared against this coronation.[14]

So the chronicler, Edward Hall, enthused about this first lavish
parade of the reign. The City fathers, of course, matched the
exuberant display of the court. The serpentine processional
route, from Tower Hill, via Tower Street, Gracechurch Street,
Cornhill and Cheap to Newgate was decked with bunting and
tapestries (some of which were torn down immediately afterwards and cut into strips by souvenir hunters). Fountains
gushed wine. At stages along the route loyal addresses and
elaborate tableaux were presented. Everywhere crowds craned
forward to gain a sight of their sovereign. He, of course,
presented the most stunning of all the images which passed
before the dazzled eyes of the populace. Clad in scarlet and
gold spangled with myriad gems, he rode a magnificent horse

and acknowledged the deafening cheers. Hall's sycophantic description may, in this instance, be taken at face value: 'His goodly personage, his amiable visage, princely countenance, with the noble qualities of his royal estate, to every man known, needeth no rehearsal, considering that for lack of cunning I cannot express the gifts of nature that God hath endowed him withal.'[15] Henry did look every inch the model Christian monarch – over six feet tall, ruddy of complexion, muscular, a fine horseman, a veritable sun king. The cavalcade made its way to Westminster where the royal couple spent the next hours quietly and, presumably, in prayer and solemn reflection, preparing themselves for the responsibilities they were to take on the next day.

What image of kingship did this young demigod embrace? Its elements were worldly magnificence, religious responsibility and Arthurian destiny. Monarchs had to demonstrate materially their superiority over all their wealthy subjects. Extravagant display was essential to the assertion of royal power and Henry did not invent 'conspicuous consumption'. What he did do was transform it into an art form. He built and refurbished more royal residences than any English ruler before or since. He was less concerned than his predecessors to leave permanent architectural memorials of his piety by funding new churches or monastic buildings. Apart from completing the great chapels at Westminster and King's College, Cambridge, Henry spent no money on religious foundations. Egocentricity governed his extravagant expenditure.

A contretemps which developed within months of his accession indicates his sense of priorities. Lady Margaret Beaufort had designated a part of her estate for the creation of St John's College, Cambridge, but this bequest was not clearly set out in her will. Henry was determined to benefit as hugely as possible from his grandmother's demise and set his lawyers to divert her endowment into his own coffers. He would undoubtedly have got his own way had he not found himself up against an adversary as tenacious as himself. Bishop John

Fisher, chaplain to the late queen dowager and her executor, led a vigorous campaign which, though not totally successful, did retain most of Lady Margaret's benefaction. The new foundation rapidly established an impressive reputation for scholarship and was the foremost college in Cambridge until, at the very end of his reign, Henry (at the urging of his last wife) endowed Trinity College, right next door, which was more grandiose than that of his grandmother. The king was no aesthete. His palaces were rambling affairs which 'grew' according to need rather than in fulfilment of any overall design. The wealth of gold and silver plate, enamelled jewellery, tapestries and paintings with which he adorned his homes had more to do with prestige and self-aggrandisement than artistic patronage. Not until the 1520s, when he was employing some of the leading European painters and sculptors, did Henry demonstrate any concern to be seen as an avant-garde, Renaissance prince in cultural competition with the courts of France, Burgundy and Italy.

Static, permanent artefacts – buildings, paintings, sculptures, *objets d'art* – were only the backdrops and props which existed to enhance the drama of monarchy. Henry was, above all else, a performer. His cultural passion was invested in the performing arts. He delighted in ever more ingenious and elaborate tournaments and court masques. His basic insecurity revealed itself in a compulsion to show off and a need for the reassurance of applause. Other monarchs were content to lay on elaborate shows for their guests and to hire performers to entertain them. Not so Henry. He had to be the centre of attention. At a Shrove Tuesday banquet for foreign ambassadors the king took a lead role in the cabaret. Having seen everyone else seated, he did not assume the presidency. He installed Catherine in the chair of state. Then,

> suddenly the king was gone. And shortly after, his grace with the Earl of Essex, came in apparelled after Turkey fashion in long robes of baudekin [gold-embroidered cloth], powdered

with gold, hats on their heads of crimson velvet, with great rolls of gold, girded with two swords called scimitars, hanging by great baldrics of gold. Next came the Lord Henry, Earl of Wiltshire, and the Lord Fitzwalter in two long gowns of yellow satin, traversed with white satin. . .after the fashion of Russia.[16]

The show was not over. When the tables had been cleared for dancing, once again Henry,

withdrew himself suddenly out of the place, with certain other persons appointed for that purpose. And within a little while thereafter there came in a drummer and a fifer apparelled in white damask and green bonnets and hose of the same suit. Then certain gentlemen followed with torches apparelled in blue damask. . .and on their heads hoods with long tippets to the same [with] blue damask masks. Then after them came a certain number of gentlemen, whereof the king was one, apparelled all in one suit of short garments, little beneath the points of blue velvet and crimson with long sleeves all cut and lined with cloth of gold.[16]

The one artistic talent Henry certainly possessed was music. He had a good voice, an excellent command of notation and could perform on several instruments. He wrote love songs, religious anthems and motets and those that survive indicate an ability that, in other circumstances, would have placed him in the ranks of professional musicians. His enthusiastic interest in contemporary trends and his curiosity about the developing techniques of instrument-making brought to court some of the most talented musicians of the age. Under Henry's patronage the English court led its rivals in the development of church and secular music. Italy and the Netherlands were unsurpassed as homes of the plastic arts but no nation outshone England for choral and instrumental music.

One of Henry's first acts on becoming king demonstrated his instinctive recognition of genius. He elevated Robert Fairfax to be First Gentleman of the Chapel Royal with a huge lifetime annuity of 9l. 2s. 6p. Fairfax had been for a few years a junior member of the king's choral staff and a particular favourite of Lady Margaret Beaufort but it was Henry who appreciated his true worth. He placed the musician, who held doctorates from both universities, in charge of the choristers who travelled with the court and performed daily in chapel services. For his royal master Fairfax produced numerous mass settings, anthems, canticles and part songs (mostly now lost) which demonstrated innovation and subtle ornamentation combined with a masterly marriage of words and music. Fairfax was one of the founders of the distinctively English choral tradition, the main link between the age of John Dunstable and that of Thomas Tallis, John Taverner and William Byrd. For more than a century his music formed part of the staple of performance in churches and cultured salons. He was a particular favourite of Henry's and annually he exchanged New Year gifts with the king. It is thanks to the secure employment and encouragement Henry provided that this great musician's talent was able to develop and flourish. The royal chapel, of course, depended on a steady input of unbroken boys' voices and Henry did not hesitate to 'steal' choristers from cathedrals and noble households. He did not rely on native exponents alone. He had his agents scouring foreign courts for masters he might poach. As the reign wore on, Henry's reputation as patron grew and England became a magnet which attracted several fine European musicians.

An attribute of Fairfax which must have appealed to Henry was the way he used music not as an adornment to the text, and certainly not as something to be admired in its own right, but as a moving way of expressing and expounding the text. This brings us to Henry's religious convictions. They are difficult to fathom but the effort must be made because none of the more important developments of the reign can be understood without some knowledge of how Henry saw himself in relation to the beliefs and personnel of the church. No less than that of any other thinking man, Henry's belief system was a compound of convention and personal preference. He had a genuine interest in theology and enjoyed debating it with his bishops and confessors. He dissented from no article of the Catholic faith – at least in his early years. He was regular in his attendance at mass and relished the musical adornment of worship in his chapel. However, there were aspects of traditional devotion to which he was indifferent and, in some instances, potentially hostile. These included religious imagery, pilgrimage and monasticism.

Henry was also aware, and acutely aware, that the English church constituted a political problem. At the climactic moment of the coronation he had holy oil or chrism applied to his head and breast. It must have been an emotional moment for him. Perhaps he even experienced a mystic thrill. What we can say about that ceremony is that ever after Henry thought himself to be in a special relationship with God. The theory of divine right of kings was not formulated for another century, largely in opposition to the proposition that sovereignty came from below rather than above. No such potentially anarchic idea troubled Henry VIII or any of the political elite. The king stood at the top of a hierarchal pyramid held together by duties and responsibilities. Everyone owed supreme and unquestioning allegiance to the king as the deputy of God. Well, not quite everyone. The clergy were a special case. They were primarily the pope's subjects and enjoyed privileges denied to the laity. The English church was also immensely rich, its monasteries and dioceses sitting, as they did, on the accumulated endowments of centuries. They constituted, in effect, a semi-independent estate of the realm with vast resources and a territorial base more formidable than that of any potential baronial alliance. In his coronation oath Henry swore to 'preserve to God and Holy Church and to the people and clergy entire peace and concord before God'. This was nothing more nor less than a commitment to maintain the status quo but it was open to a more interventionist interpretation, should the king ever decide that the state of the church demanded his personal attention. There is evidence that from very early in the reign he was contemplating such decisions concerning the relationship between church and state. It would never have occurred to him that reform of externals could not be achieved without calling in question the very beliefs on which Catholic orthodoxy rested.

There was nothing new about the conflict of spiritual and temporal authority. Traditionally, it centred on two issues: control of the worldly aspects of church life (property and senior clerical appointments) and authority for reforming the spiritual aspects of church life. The pious Henry VII had not flinched from exerting royal authority over the church in his domains. A Venetian ambassador reported that the English king would have loved to be able to rule in the style of his French counterpart, Louis XI, but that he was inhibited by the freedoms enshrined in Magna Carta. Louis it was who broke the power of France's mighty vassals, annexed Brittany and Burgundy, established centralized administration and made the crown autonomous. In his relations with the pope he adopted the principles later dubbed 'Gallicanism', which combined conciliarism (the belief that a general council of senior ecclesiastics had more authority than the pope) with the reduction of papal influence in France. Under Louis XII (1498–1515), the establishment of a French national church went even further. The king failed in his attempt to set up an ecumenical council but within his own dominions he established royal control over the church with the right to carry out much needed reform. In Spain subjection of the ecclesiastical to royal authority had gone much further. Ferdinand and Isabella (Catherine of Aragon's parents) had, by 1494, established the Inquisition as an organ of state control, annexed the property of the old military orders and established the right to appoint bishops and to carry out reform by decree.

With such role models readily available it was inevitable that the first two Tudors would aim to minimize the interference of Rome and set their own ecclesiastical house in order. Henry VII made it clear to bishops that they were first and foremost his servants. Abbacies and bishoprics were held by men he could trust rather than with those approved by Rome or elected by their own people. Since he was more interested in having the English church run by efficient administrators who would guard crown rights rather than improving educational or pastoral standards, he appointed canon lawyers to episcopal office in preference to theologians. As in the secular sphere, the king used the law to circumvent the law. Thus, when it came to the exaction of fines and bonds, lords of the church fared little better than their temporal counterparts. By decree and by Act of parliament, Henry VII nibbled away at clerical privileges. He blocked appeals to Rome. He exerted royal authority over ecclesiastical authority whenever he could. For example, church courts could no longer depend on the secular arm to inflict punishment on excommunicated offenders. The king's agents insisted on reviewing such cases. Other methods of making money from the church, such as appropriation of benefices and dissolving minor religious houses, were not original to Henry VII but were certainly employed by him to the full. Edmund Dudley, while awaiting his trial, wrote a treatise on government called *The Tree of Commonwealth* in which he intimated that Henry VII had gone too far in his subordination of church to crown. He exhorted his successor:

> to be that Catholic king that shall not only support and maintain his church and the true faith thereof in all rights as far as in him lieth, but also to see that such as he shall promote and set in Christ's church. . .be both cunning [i.e. educated] and virtuous.

Dudley warned the king against simony, appointing his cronies, keeping bishops at court rather than allowing them to properly oversee their dioceses and loading senior churchmen down with secular offices. Finally, Dudley suggested:

> it were a gracious and noble act that the Church of England were restored to her free election after the old manner and not to be letted thereof. . .Also for the honour of God let your grace

refrain yourself from the appropriation of benefices or to unite
any house of religion to another for if this do continue it shall
by all likelihood destroy the honour of the Church of
England.[17]

Good Catholics, like Thomas More, also expected or hoped
that the new king would revert to earlier practice and be
content to help the bishops administer discipline.

Henry, however, from the very beginning of his reign, had a
different perspective. He knew well, from Catherine and from
the reports of diplomats, that in Spain King Ferdinand kept the
church on a very tight leash. Not only did he exercise political
and economic control by appointing his own yes-men to episcopal office and siphoning off a substantial amount of their
income, he also set his agents to purge the church of notorious
abuses. By 1510, Henry's father-in-law had established in his
territories a state church well on the way to being reformed.
Furthermore, he had obliged the pope to treat him with
respect. Alexander VI had bestowed upon the Spanish king the
title of 'the Catholic'. This provided Henry with a very
attractive model, combining the extension of royal power and
wealth with pious zeal. He, too, would seek to exercise
ultimate control over the church in his dominions while jeal-
ously guarding his reputation as a thoroughly orthodox
member of the body Catholic.

The third element in Henry's understanding of his kingship
may be summed up in the word 'imperium'. One of the high
points of Malory's *Le Morte Darthur* was the king's visit to
Rome:

All the senators that were alive and the cunningest cardinals
that dwelled in the court. . .besought him as sovereign, most
governor under God, for to give them licence. . .in the city of
Syon that is called Rome to crown him there kindly with
chrismed hands, with sceptre for sooth as an emperor should. 'I
assent me,' said the King, 'as ye have devised, and comely by
Christmas to be crowned; hereafter to reign in my estate and to

keep my Round Table, with the rents of Rome to rule as me likes; and then as I am advised, to get me over the salt sea with good men of arms, to deem for his death that for us all on the Rood died'. . .at the day assigned, as the romance tells us, he was crowned emperor by the Pope's hands, with all the royalty in the world to wield for ever. There they sojourned that season till after the time and established all the lands from Rome unto France, and gave lands and rents unto knights that had them well deserved.[18]

Henry believed this mishmash of history and fable which conflated the exploits of Arthur with those of Charlemagne. He played out the old chivalric romances in the tournaments which were soon regular court entertainments and these feats of arms became increasingly adorned with theatrical embellishments featuring the heroes of Arthurian legend. This was not just a sugary coating on court life. Henry's mind was soaked in mythology and he made no separation between patriotic display and practical politics. At Winchester there was – and still is – a massive wooden circle made up of several planks. It was confidently identified as the original Round Table, bearing the names of many of King Arthur's knights. In 1522, when he wanted to impress a visitor, the young Charles V, Henry ordered it to be repainted with alternating panels of green and white (the royal colours), a Tudor rose at the centre and himself in the position of Arthur. He took great pleasure in pointing out to his guest the remarkable similarity between himself and the former king. The glories of his Arthurian inheritance pointed to a destiny in which anything was possible. In 1519, Henry actually attempted to have himself elected Holy Roman Emperor.

Henry believed that the Tudors had come to inaugurate a new era and put behind them the humiliations England had experienced in recent decades. The new dynasty would reclaim the extensive tracts of continental territory which had been lost since the 1440s. Essential to this ambition was the concept of imperium, which for sixteenth-century theorists meant absolute rule not derived from the country so ruled. Sovereignty was God-given and reposed in the sovereign. This meant, in international terms, that the king of England was on a par with his brother monarchs irrespective of their comparative wealth or the extent of their kingdoms. On the same day in 1489 that the marriage treaty of Arthur and Catherine was ratified, Henry VII commissioned the striking of a new gold coin. He called it the 'sovereign' and it bore his effigy wearing a closed, 'imperial' crown instead of the more conventional open crown of England. It was a statement of his equality with Ferdinand. Henry was no petty prince, ruler of a small offshore island: he was asserting his right to a seat at the 'top table' of European monarchs. The use of the crown imperial henceforth featured prominently in all Tudor propaganda:

> In chapels, halls and churches...commissions for windows and painted screens reveal a further dimension of the new emphasis on the iconography of the crown imperial, Henry VII's desire to link himself and his kingship visually to those considered to be his most worthy progenitors, Edward the Confessor, Henry V, Henry VI, as well as the legendary Arthur and the first of the Christian Roman Emperors, Constantine.[19]

History, or what passed for history, was plundered by Henry VII and his son for any material that would bolster the image of the upstart Tudor dynasty. Public display of the imperial image kept official political doctrine before people's eyes just as church decoration impressed them with religious doctrine. The imperial ideal had important internal significance. If Henry's imperium was a reality, it followed that no other monarch had any rights within his realm. That exclusion might be extended to include the pope but exactly what aspects of Rome's 'interference' were challenged by imperial theory? Did imperium imply no more than royal superiority over the secular aspects of church life – property ownership and the operation of church courts – as Henry VII asserted, or did it have a spiritual dimension? Such questions went unasked, for the time being, but if ever a crisis should occur which demanded that imperium should be more minutely defined Henry VIII would set his scholars to pore over old documents in search of the evidence he wanted them to discover. He would show himself to be more like his father than was immediately apparent.

Certainly, no one around the court during the first years of the reign would have observed any similarity. 'Our time is spent in continual festival,' Catherine reported to her father.[20] Her showman of a husband filled his days with court entertainments and public displays. The energetic agenda for Henry's first summer progress in 1510 was that of a young man determined to live life to the full. It included:

> Shooting [archery], singing, dancing, wrestling, casting of the bar [a sport similar to tossing the caber], playing at the recorders, flute, virginals, and in setting of songs, making of ballads [The king] did set two goodly masses, every of them five parts, which were sung oftentimes in his chapel and afterwards in divers other places. And when he came to Woking, there were kept both jousts and tourneys. The rest of this progress was spent in hunting, hawking and shooting.[21]

These events were semi-public affairs. Local people would turn out to get a glimpse of the king and the fine ladies and gentlemen who shared in his outdoor pursuits. Crowd control could be a problem. The tournay of 1511 ended in mayhem when fans of the champions broke through the barriers, grabbed souvenirs from the decorations and rich horse trappings and even plucked gold ornaments from the king's own costume.

This particular highly theatrical and elaborate contest of arms was the most sumptuous of the reign. The preparations and publicity build-up were extensive, and for a very good reason. The king and the nation had a splendid event to celebrate – the birth of a prince. The dynasty was secure. For two February days in a specially constructed arena at Westminster

Henry and the cream of England's young aristocracy vied with each other at chivalric rituals. The weather may have been cold but long before the scheduled start there was no seat or standing room to be had. At last trumpets sounded and a frisson of excitement went through the audience. Then, at one end of the arena a strange apparition appeared: a troop of wild men or woodwoses, 'their bodies heads, faces, hands and legs covered with green flushed silk'. These savage creatures were leading two shimmering 'great beasts', horses decked out to resemble a silver antelope and a gold lion. Mounted on each fabulous animal was a 'richly apparelled' lady (equivalent, I suppose, to the scantily clad models without whom it seems no modern motor car can be launched on to the market). The beasts of burden were hauling, by golden chains, a large pageant cart decorated to resemble a gilded castle set amidst a forest. 'All the herbs, trees and flowers of the same forest were made of green velvet, green damask and silk of divers colours, satin and sarcenet.' In front of the castle the audience was delighted to observe a gentleman making a garland of roses for the new prince.

This complex apparition came to a halt before the queen's gallery, whereupon 'foresters' appeared who blew upon their horns. This was the signal for the cart to open up and out rode 'four knights, armed at all pieces, every of them a spear in his hand on horseback with great plumes on their heads, their [coverings] of cloth of gold'.[22] It would be hard to imagine any modern carnival float rivalling such a spectacle. Alas, the baby in whose honour all this extravagant flimflam was staged died within a few days. This was a severe blow for the king who had so publicly advertised his proud parenthood and it doubtless explains why no celebration on such a lavish scale was ever seen again throughout his entire reign. It was the first serious check he had received since coming to the throne; the first ambition which had been thwarted; the first object of desire he had been denied. We should not underestimate the impact of such setbacks.

The young man within the gaudy, ebullient carapace of brilliantly stage-managed display was insecure. The extravagant clothes, the endless round of entertainments, the boasting of athletic and sexual prowess, the identification with Arthurian mythology – all these were like conjurer's slight of hand through which the audience's attention is diverted away from what the performer is really doing. The reality was that Henry was, as a king, inexperienced and untrained and, as a man, emotionally immature. 'Psychohistory' is rightly viewed with suspicion but we do not need to enter the speculative realms of Sigmund Freud and Alfred Adler to recognize the overcompensation and constant need for adulation experienced by those who have been deprived of love and encouragement in their early years. Hans Holbein has done us all a disservice by his famous and brilliant representation of the magisterial, assertive king which has become the standard image for Henry VIII. His portrait was a royal icon, painted to order. Even if it were a perceptive image of the king in his forties (which it is not), we should not allow it to colour our understanding of England's Harry as he was at the beginning of the reign. In these early years he had two preoccupations: he was finding his way politically while, at the same time, presenting himself to the world as completely in command of the situation.

He had two corps of supporters: the body of advisers bequeathed to him by his father and his own 'gang'. The latter were the king's chosen companions, mostly the young men with whom he hunted and jousted, gambled and roistered. However, there were also scholars, drawn from among the ranks of fashionable humanism, men with whom he loved to talk when he had a mind to more serious matters than ordering another suit of tilt armour or composing a love song. Lord Mountjoy, a cultured member of the inner circle, reported to his friend Erasmus how the king, in a rare moment of self-analysis, had deprecated his own lack of scholarly accomplishment. Mountjoy dutifully replied that it was for his majesty to rule and to command the attendance of the realm's wisest men to advise him. Most of Henry's daily companions, the 'inner core' of his vast household, constituted the staff of the privy chamber. They were those he admired for their athleticism and love of fun. Most of these young heroes of the tiltyard, such as Edward Howard, Charles Brandon, Nicholas Carew, Francis Bryan, William Compton, Thomas Knyvet and Henry Guildford (a creative impresario of court entertainments), were a few years older than the king and some had seen military service.

Henry looked up to them as men of the world, men of the rising generation whose gung-ho attitude he admired. They became his mentors. He spent almost every day in their company, from the moment that he rose (about 8 a.m.) and was dressed by his squires of the body. He was accompanied to the closet by his most intimate companion (soon to be designated groom of the stool), before he mounted his hunter with the aid of his master of the horse to spend a day in the field, or else he went to practise in the tiltyard or the butts, or enjoyed a few games of tennis. The inner circle accompanied him right through to his evening entertainment at the card table or in the great hall for dancing or 'disguising'. These favourites set the tone of the court, the fashions of dress and music, the mix of formality and boisterousness. The more sober royal advisers and attendants looked on disapprovingly, anxious at the power the king's friends had over him. They were both a barrier, keeping at bay people the king did not wish to see, and a conduit, offering their own clients access to the royal person to present petitions or to seek favours. In other words, the privy chamber staff enjoyed considerable influence. They were among the first to be appointed to military posts when Henry went to war and to represent the king in foreign diplomacy. Consequently, they developed a political significance not always in accord with their political ability. This band of 'goodly knights' set the ethos of the court – a decidedly Arthurian ethos.

Arthurianism was the freemasonry of the day – the *raison d'être* of a highly-ritualized, pseudo-religious brotherhood. It

provided the behavioural code for the Henrician establishment, which was adopted by all members of that establishment as well as those who aspired to be members of it. It
almost goes without saying that it was exclusively male;
women were assigned a respected but essentially passive role
within the Arthurian scheme of things. In Malory's tale, the
fellowship of the Round Table is destroyed when Sir Lancelot
abducts Queen Guinevere and kills several of his brother
knights in the process. Arthur's reaction to the news is
revealing: 'much more am I sorrier for my good knights' loss
than for the loss of my fair queen; for queens I might have
enough, but such a fellowship of good knights shall never be
together in no company'.[23] Henry and his friends identified
themselves with this lofty image of loyal brotherhood.
'Honour' was their watchword, the dominant motif of tiltyard
ritual and court masques.

However, we must not allow ourselves to be dazzled by the
spectacle of the joust and the hyperbole of the knightly code.
What was happening in the inner circles of Henry Tudor's
entourage was the strutting of a self-important gang leader
who looked to his friends to bolster his image, just as they
looked to him for the tangible rewards he was able to
distribute. Henry was certainly an enthusiastic sportsman but
he was not foolhardy. The reign was nine months old before he
appeared publicly in the lists and when he did so his 'good
knights' who competed with him were left in no doubt that
their principal responsibility was to make the king look good.
An accomplished horseman could convincingly 'throw' a
course so that his opponent appeared to have genuinely bested
him and this happened almost every time that one of Henry's
friends was drawn against him in the lists. For example, in the
February 1511 tournament Charles Brandon, a talented
performer, excelled in all his bouts, until he came up against the
king. At the half-way point the scores were close but in the last
three courses Brandon was careful to miss his target and to
allow Henry to break his lance against him and, thus, to

emerge as the victor in a 'hard fought' contest. None of the
accounts of early tournaments speak of Henry being unhorsed
or sustaining injury. On the contrary, contemporary chronicles
relate the king's accomplishments and invite the reader's awe at
his all-round athleticism:

> His grace with two other with him challenged all comers to
> fight with them at the barriers with target and casting the spear
> of viii foot long and that done his grace with the said two aids to
> fight every of them xii strokes with two-handed swords, with
> and against all comers...where the king behaved [i.e. acquitted]
> himself so well and delivered himself so valiantly by his hardy
> prowess and great strength that the praise and laud was given to
> his grace and his aids, notwithstanding that divers valiant and
> strong persons had assailed him and his aids.[24]

Henry always had to win, whatever he was doing.
Unfortunately, a group of Italian bankers visiting the court in
1511 were not party to this unwritten rule. They played at dice
with the king and several courtiers and the king lost heavily.
Petulantly, Henry complained of cheating and threw the
foreigners out.

Henry was no reincarnation of the valiant King Arthur and
the vision of a new Camelot was no more than a gaudy
baldachin erected over the self-indulgent court of an immature
monarch. Nor does the chivalrous code as it applied to sexual
mores stand much scrutiny. Theoretically, knights wielded
lance and sword in honour of their ladies but this principle was
only tangentially associated with conventional morality. The
rules of courtly love loosely cloaked sexual licence. In this
macho world women might be the idealized objects of desire
but they certainly did not always remain unattainable. It was
not long before Henry found himself at odds with his wife and
some of her more prudish companions over what they
considered the moral laxity of the court. He had become
attracted to Anne Herbert, Lady Hastings, sister of the
Edward Stafford, Duke of Buckingham, and used William

Compton, his Groom of the Stool, as an intermediary with her. Anne's sister, Lady Fitzwalter, was head of the 'queen's side'. When she got wind of what was going on she told their brother. This led to a furious row between Buckingham and Compton. Henry supported his closest friend against Catherine's circle. Not only did he confront Buckingham, who left court in a huff, he also dismissed Lady Fitzwalter. Catherine was not prepared to submit meekly to having her household disrupted, especially when she believed that her companion had been in the right. The result was a very public tiff between royal husband and wife. Clearly, there were differences between the mores of the twin establishments of the court – the king's and the queen's.

Henry did not consider himself confined by his marriage vows but he still had a conscience. The love songs he wrote and performed were dedicated to his wife and he protested in one of them:

I hurt no man, I do no wrong;
I love true where I did marry. . .
Thus saith the king, the eighth Harry[25]

This probably explains why, having been 'found out', he was stung into angry defensive reaction. The Hastings affair was nipped in the bud and does not seem to have permanently damaged royal marital relations. The couple slept together frequently but Catherine's pregnancies put a natural limit on sexual activity and it may well have been at such times that Henry found release elsewhere. However, we simply do not know the details of any of his liaisons or one-night-stands, or, indeed, whether there is much to know. He boasted that he 'never spared a man in his anger or a woman in his lust' but that may have been the testosterone speaking. Certainly, nothing came of his infatuation with Anne Herbert. We only know of two royal mistresses and Henry only ever acknowledged one illegitimate child. In 1513, a beautiful teenage girl, Elizabeth

Blount, joined the queen's entourage and almost immediately Henry fell under her spell.

Things were not going well in the royal bed. Within months of her marriage Catherine had miscarried a daughter and this was followed by a false pregnancy which the king found particularly humiliating. He had proudly announced the queen's condition, only to become aware of sniggering ridicule around the court when it became clear that the royal physicians had blundered in their diagnosis. This was followed by the sad fiasco of the birth and early death of the couple's first son in 1511. Henry persevered in his efforts to sire an heir but, progressively, his endeavours were just that – efforts. What passion there had been steadily seeped out of the marriage, which was soured by the repeated disappointments of further miscarriages in the years 1514 and 1515 and the birth of a princess in 1516. And yet, not until 1518 did Henry's mistress become pregnant. She might, of course, have suffered miscarriages before then, which no one considered it sufficiently important to record, but the bare facts we do have certainly do not support the image of Henry VIII as a rampant stud. It is, perhaps, significant that he had to get Compton to carry out his seduction of Anne Hastings. It was one thing to engage in bawdy talk with his chamber cronies but quite another to open himself to the vulnerability implicit in a deep relationship. Henry wanted, as do all sane men, to love and be loved but his ego was ever at hand to elbow aside any woman who got too close.

While the king was enjoying himself with his close companions in his palaces around the capital and on regular tours during these early years, the country, of course, had to be ruled. The centralized government established by Henry VII demanded the efforts of a dedicated executive backed by a large staff of clerks, scribes and messengers. This caucus was the council, an amorphous body comprising officers of state together with leading nobles and ecclesiastics. In practice, day-to-day policy-making was in the hands of a smaller working body of advisers chosen by the king. Henry inherited the council left by his father. Its principal members were William Warham, lord chancellor and Archbishop of Canterbury, Richard Fox, Bishop of Winchester and lord privy seal, Thomas Ruthall, Bishop of Durham and secretary, Thomas Howard, Earl of Surrey and lord treasurer, and Charles Somerset, Baron Herbert and chamberlain of the household. However, listing the names of prominent councillors does not imply stability. Ambitious men were just as eager to gain places on the council as they were to be admitted to the charmed circle of the privy chamber. Before the new reign was many months old, the jockeying for power had begun. In August 1509 Bishop Fox received a letter from Thomas, Lord Darcy, one of the wardens of the Scottish Marches:

> The common saying with every market man that comes from London is that the Lord Privy Seal, seeing of his own craft and policy he cannot bring himself to rule the king's grace and put out of favour the Earl of Surrey, the Earl of Shrewsbury, the Bishop of Durham, Mr. Marney, Mr. Brandon and the Lord Darcy, now he will prove another way; which is to bring in and bolster himself to rule all with the Duke of Buckingham and the Earl of Northumberland. And doubtless fast they curse and speak evil of my Lord Privy Seal beyond measure.[26]

Reports reaching the north were somewhat garbled but significant facts can be gleaned from the prevailing gossip which came Darcy's way, including the suspicion that the old king's principal servants were trying to 'rule' the new king – a suspicion not without foundation. Those who had been in government for some years had their own ideas about how England should be run. Broadly speaking, they were for keeping the ship on a steady course while throwing overboard some of the officers, such as Empson and Dudley, to give the impression that the tiller was now in safer hands. Yet how could one deal carefully but firmly with a headstrong young monarch who might present them with a different chart? Some were for taking the king's education in hand while others thought it better to encourage Henry's preoccupation with establishing a lustrous Renaissance court and counselling him to leave the tedious minutiae of government to the 'experts'. Theirs was a tricky situation. They could not be sure of keeping control of the levers of power until they had taken the measure of their new master.

Their master was the victim of rival instincts. The traditional assessment of Henry VIII is that he was too lazy to bother himself with business, which enabled policy to be determined by his ministers. Recent revisionism has swung to an opposite opinion and credited the king with working towards a series of clear objectives. The truth lies in neither extreme, nor in the middle, but in both extremes. Henry was determined to be his own man but in the early years of the reign he totally lacked the dedication and application to detail that would enable him to become a successful 'hands-on' monarch. The prospect of spending hours every day solemnly debating with greybeard counsellors or personally checking pages of accounts smacked too much of his father. Henry's inclination was to be primarily concerned with governmental style and he was dependent on others to take care of the substance. Furthermore, he was impressionable and tended to be influenced by the last person who had spoken to him. Ambitious men knew that it was vital to gain a prominent position at court where they would be noticed by the king. Then, once admitted to the charmed circle, it was essential to remain there. A courtier's worst nightmare was to be sent away from court, for whatever reason. Out of sight was out of mind and he would be unable to counteract the machinations of his rivals. While Henry refused to attend council meetings or become bogged down in the complex business of government, he was intelligent enough to realize that he had to keep executive control. He knew that he must not allow his council to assume that he would rubber stamp whatever they decided. His normal method of dealing with councillors was to approve their decisions and agree to their proposals but periodically to issue a veto, usually forcefully. Within weeks of his accession he lambasted the council for presuming to send a polite message to Louis XII assuring the French of the King of England's continuing friendship. He told Fox and his colleagues that the king alone determined foreign policy.

Henry did have his own agenda and relations with other monarchs headed the list of issues on which he felt passionately. At his accession he had two major concerns: war and the relationship of crown and nobility. These priorities were completely intertwined. Henry was determined to disassociate himself from his father's negative attitude towards the peers of the realm. He wanted the great men of the nation and their impressive entourages to be adornments of his court. Particularly, he needed their involvement when it came to the war with France which he was determined to relaunch. For their part, the great families of the land were eager to reassume that part in the running of the country which they considered to be theirs as of right. The nobility, and especially the younger nobility whom Henry welcomed to court, were his obvious allies in his contest with the council and his bid to establish his own, more adventurous, style of leadership. Henry was, of course, always on the receiving end of petitions from his own intimates to advance them or their relatives. When he rewarded their importunity he was motivated by policy as much as by friendship.

Thus it was that Henry embarked on a strategy of creating new peers and cancelling restrictions imposed by the previous regime. Among those singled out for favour in the early years were several men who became players in the political game. The Staffords were the most noteworthy beneficiaries of the change of policy. Edward Stafford, Duke of Buckingham, was England's only surviving non-royal duke. He could trace his ancestry to Edward III, was immensely rich and connected with several of the leading noble families. For all these reasons Henry VII had treated the Duke of Buckingham with a degree of reserve. Immediately after the old king's death, the council had moved against his younger brother, Lord Henry Stafford, and imprisoned him on suspicion of involvement in Empson and Dudley's 'rebellion'. The new king ordered Lord Henry's immediate release and appointed him to the privy chamber staff, while Buckingham was created Lord High Constable. The following January, Lord Henry was made Earl of Wiltshire.

Henry also promoted some of his friends and close companions in the early years of the reign. Charles Brandon became Viscount Lisle and, subsequently, Duke of Suffolk. Sir Henry Marney of the privy chamber was awarded a barony. George Talbot, Earl of Shrewsbury was made Lord Steward of the Household. More significantly, all these 'new men' were appointed to the council at the start of the reign. When Darcy wrote to Fox, he was aware of all the shuffling for power and prestige that was going on, which is why he was fishing for information about how the bishop was responding to the new dynamic of court and council. He need not have worried. For the time being government was more or less 'business as usual'. The old hands on the council remained in control. A few of Henry VII's notorious bonds were cancelled for show but the screws on the nobility were not noticeably lessened. If the government got away with domestic policy change which was more promised than delivered, it was partly because potential malcontents were dazzled by the splendours of the new court. Creations and promotions served more of a propaganda function than any shift in political power:

> Every grant served one basic purpose: to project the image of a munificent prince, glorified in the distribution of honours. The investiture focussed attention upon the king as the source of nobility. The ceremonies for the award of the higher titles were great occasions carefully stage-managed by the heralds and attended by as many noblemen as could be gathered together.[27]

'Policy' in the first few years was something that emerged from the interaction of the privy chamber, the council and the dominant personalities of the establishment. It would be a mistake to look for consistency. This is well illustrated by the final chapters in the Empson and Dudley story. Henry VII's henchmen were tried publicly but separately. In his defence Sir Richard Empson pulled no punches. He confronted his judges with a defiance that would prove prophetic:

> Whoever yet saw any man condemned for doing justice, especially when by the king, the chief dispenser of the laws, the whole frame of the proceeding hath been warranted and confirmed?. . .And will you alone hope to escape this heavy judgement? If contrary to all equity and example, you not only make precedents for injustice and impunity, but, together with defaming, would inflict a cruel death on those who would maintain them, what can we then expect but a fatal period to us all?. . .Only if I must die, let me desire that my indictment be entered on no record, nor divulged to foreign nations lest, from my fate, it be concluded that in England all law and government are dissolved.[28]

The two lawyers were found guilty and sentenced to death. They were returned to their cells in the Tower and there they stayed. Despite their unpopularity, the House of Lords declined to endorse an Act of attainder passed by the lower house. A whole year went by and the prisoners had no idea whether they had been forgotten, or whether they might receive pardons such as several offenders had already received at the hands of a magnanimous prince. Their fate lay in Henry's hands and he, it seems, did not know what to do with them. He had a straight choice between clemency and the rigorous enforcement of the law. The only question he seems to have considered was which would be the more popular course. According to Edward Hall, he did not make up his mind until the summer of 1510, when he heard fresh murmurings against Empson and Dudley while he was on progress in the Midlands. Only then did Henry issue the execution warrant. The prisoners met their end on 17 August, but not by the means set down by the law for traitors. Their sentences were commuted to simple beheading and afterwards their bodies were not unceremoniously interred in the chapel of the Tower; their families were allowed to remove them for private burial. Their estates were not confiscated and their children did not suffer from their fathers' disgrace. All this seems like the behaviour of a government acting out of expediency rather than conviction.

There is an even more remarkable coda to this dismal tale. The Dudleys did not dwindle into obscurity. Fifteen months after Edmund's execution a new husband was found for his widow. This was none other than the king's only unmarried uncle, Arthur Plantagenet, bastard son of Edward IV. The family thus remained within the ambit of the court and Edmund's heir achieved a place in the privy chamber as soon as he came of age. Henry VIII could not admit to being troubled in conscience over the punishment of his father's devoted servants but his actions do suggest that he felt the need to make restitution to their families. He was a man who acted on impulse and was susceptible to public opinion. If, in this case, he regretted taking a decision he could not reverse it would certainly not be the last time he found himself in such a situation.

As members of the political elite took stock of their new king they discovered an immature young man who rarely bothered to exert his not insignificant intelligence on important matters of state. He was jovial and easy-going but became petulant when thwarted. He tended to lose his temper with those who pressed him for decisions and was easily influenced by those around him. On 30 September 1511, the king's almoner (responsible for distributing alms on behalf of the household) reported from Windsor to Bishop Fox, who had been kept away from court by illness:

> My lord, for divers urgent causes it is thought very expedient that you should repair to the King, for all his great matters be deferred unto your coming, which is daily looked for and desired of all those that would the King's causes should proceed in good train. . .My Lord Treasurer at his last coming to the King, which was this day sevenight, had such manner and countenance showed unto him that on the morrow he departed home

again and, as yet, is not returned to the court. With little help now he might be utterly, as touching lodging in the same, excluded, whereof in my poor judgement no little good should ensue. . .Mr Howard [Sir Edward Howard] marvellously inciteth the King against the Scots, by whose wanton means his grace spendeth much money and is more disposed to war than peace. Your presence shall be necessary to repress this appetite.[29]

The shrewd observer who wrote this letter was a certain Thomas Wolsey and his brief observations give us a good picture of the impatient young man who occupied the throne. Wolsey, as the king's almoner and confessor, had easy access and segued imperceptibly into the role of secretary and liaison between king and council. Fox found him very useful, especially as the only time Henry seemed to be amenable to signing papers or giving thought to important matters was during daily mass, when he was obliged to sit still for a while or at the end of the day, when he had returned, tired and hungry, from a day's hunting. The issue which Wolsey reported as currently inflaming the royal ardour and temper was that of war and peace. Lord Howard, Henry's cautious Treasurer, advocated a continuance of Henry VII's non-belligerence but his younger son, Sir Edward Howard, was a hot-headed young man who had won his spurs on an earlier Scottish campaign and was eager for military action. Henry, egged on by Sir Edward and his other close companions, was determined to wage war on France at the earliest opportunity and, inevitably, that would involve action against France's old ally, Scotland. This issue was driving a wedge between privy chamber and council and would render it impossible for the two to work together.

Sometime in the early years of the reign, Henry's former tutor John Skelton wrote a verse play entitled *Magnificence*. Its central character is a ruler depicted as choosing his principal adviser. The candidates include Felicity, who urges him to subordinate his desires to sober reason, and Liberty, who, contrariwise, insists that a constrained king is no king at all:

. . .how can you prove that there is felicity,
And you have not your own free liberty,
To sport at your pleasure, to run and to ride?
Where liberty is absent, set wealth aside!

The third member of the triumvirate is Measure (i.e.
Moderation) who points the hero to a middle way:

Where Measure is master, Plenty doth none offence;
Where Measure lacketh, all thing disordered is;
Where Measure is absent Riot keepeth residence;
Where Measure is ruler, there is nothing amiss.
Measure is treasure; how say ye, is it not this?[30]

The inexperienced king wisely agrees to be guided by Measure
but another allegorical character, Fancy, appears and, in
alliance with Liberty, seduces him into a life of shallow
amusement and vice. Magnificence slips down the greasy slope
to ruin and is only saved at the eleventh hour from remorseful
self-destruction by the Seventh Cavalry in the shape of Good
Hope. It is impossible not to see this play as having direct
reference to the political situation of Henry VIII's 'Camelot'
years. Perhaps the poet still saw himself as having some tutorial
role in the king's household. If so, it must have saddened him
that the moral, of necessity wrapped in fable, went unheeded.
In his conflict with the council Henry set aside Felicity.
Nothing would deter him from the pursuit of glory, not even
two sadly empty seats at the Round Table. By the spring of
1513, Henry had lost two of his closest and bravest friends, the
first casualties in his attempt to live out the Arthurian dream.

# Chapter 3

## 'FOR HARRY, ENGLAND AND SAINT GEORGE!'

It is interesting, and not utterly fanciful, to compare Henry VIII and Pope Julius II – a king who made himself a little pope and a pope who was more at home acting the king. Both were ambitious and restless men who found war glamorous and coveted the rewards it might bring. Both ruled small states on the political periphery of Europe. Both were determined to regain territories which had fallen from the grasp of their antecedents over the previous century. Both sought to ring advantage by playing the two major powers of Spain and France off against each other. There was even a degree of physical similarity, for it was written of Julius that, 'in body and soul he has the nature of a giant. Everything about him is on a magnified scale, both his undertakings and his passions'.[31] Julius was the more successful of the two because he was the better politician. He knew precisely what he wanted, could calculate the most likely way of achieving his ends – when to wage war and when to offer peace – and allowed no inconvenient emotions such as loyalty or sincerity to hamper him in the gaining of his objectives. When Henry rushed enthusiastically into war in 1512 and 1513, it was without any of these advantages. He was outclassed both by his enemies and his allies.

We can only make sense of these early conflicts by placing them in a European context. For eighteen years Italy had been the focus of attention because, in their efforts to make territorial gains at the expense of their neighbours, the northern city states had summoned the might of Spain and France to their aid. They would have done better to stick with the devils they knew rather than sell their souls to such powerful, alien demons. The two superpowers had their own reasons for intervention: they aimed to achieve a permanent foothold in the central Mediterranean. Thus, once engaged in the peninsula, they had no intention of quitting and fought fiercely for control, particularly of the duchy of Milan and the kingdom of Naples. In vain did Niccolò Machiavelli seek a 'Prince' who would be the saviour of an independent Italy. That unhappy land was doomed to years of intermittent warfare and to be a tool in the hands of Spain, France, the Holy Roman Empire, the Swiss cantons – and England. What added further complication was the fact that Italy was also the seat of the papacy, that institution which, theoretically, guaranteed the unity of Latin Christendom and could call on the loyalty of all Christian rulers. However, those 'sons' of the Church, as well as squabbling among themselves, had their own ideas about their 'father' and his administration of household affairs. By 1512, scholars, diplomats and politicians were united in being appalled at the corruption coursing from the heart of Rome through all the arteries of the ecclesiastical establishment. The office of pope still commanded respect but the holders of that office were not seen as men equipped to provide Catholic monarchs with the leadership they had a right to expect. Few of them now doubted the crying need for reform. Thus, spiritual and moral issues were inextricably bound up with the very unspiritual and amoral ambitions of contending parties.

At the end of 1508, Julius II (1503–13) masterminded the League of Cambrai which pledged most European nations (not including England) to join with a group of Italian states in assisting his holiness to oust Venice from mainland territories it had acquired over the years. The warrior-pope boasted that he would reduce proud Venice to the status of a fishing village for its presumption in encroaching on papal territory and its assertion of a measure of spiritual independence from the Holy See. France played the major role in the ensuing war, which saw Venice swiftly and comprehensively defeated and stripped of most of its territory. Now Julius had a bigger problem on his hands than a recalcitrant Italian republic; the French had come and were in no hurry to depart. Moreover, Louis XII had further provoked papal wrath by summoning an ecumenical council to consider church reform and to dethrone the corrupt pope, widely known to be a self-indulgent, irascible pederast. With his political and spiritual authority both being threatened, Julius had to take serious action. He denounced the 'barbarians' and formed a new alliance – including the recently humiliated 'fishing village' – to drive them back over the Alps. The Spaniards and the Swiss were the most active components of the pope's 'Holy League' but, at the end of 1511, it was also joined by Henry VIII.

From the beginning of the reign his representatives had been active in Rome. Good Catholic that he was, Henry determined to have effective influence in the headquarters of the church. As early as September 1509 he despatched Christopher Bainbridge, Archbishop of York, to the Vatican as his resident ambassador. Bainbridge was the last and the most successful ecclesiastic of the old order. His position as chaplain to Henry VII had been the launch pad for his meteoric rise through the episcopal ranks and he held several lucrative appointments. He easily ingratiated himself with Julius, who made him a cardinal within eighteen months of his arrival (he was the only English churchman to become a resident member of the Curia, the governing body of the Catholic church) and favoured him with his confidence. Bainbridge was an excellent choice from Henry's point of view because he was a skilled politique, able to obtain impressive proof of the pope's support for his young master and also to further the intrigues of the anti-French party. Bainbridge, unlike several of his conciliar colleagues back in Westminster, was a zealous francophobe. His success was very gratifying to the king. Bainbridge obtained from Julius a special indulgence for all who participated in military action against France. The pope, as well as sending to England generous gifts of wine, cheese and the much-coveted Golden Rose, promised to bestow upon Henry the title 'Most Christian King', which had just been stripped from Louis XII. Moreover, he declared that he would travel to Paris and personally place the French crown on Henry's head – after Henry had defeated Louis in battle. The quid pro quo demanded of the English king was that he would mount a campaign which would deflect Louis from his military activities in Italy. Plans for military action were already well in hand with Ferdinand of Spain who had his own reasons for courting Henry's aid and was bringing pressure to bear via his daughter as well as through the usual diplomatic channels.

Everything seemed to be falling into place to support Henry's own belligerent inclination: he was being flatteringly courted by the head of the church and by one of Europe's most powerful princes: he had the prospect of gloriously inaugurating his reign by reuniting the crowns of England and France; and he could claim to be marching his armies on to foreign soil in the interests of Christendom. In international relations, Ferdinand, no less than Louis XII, used the need for widespread church reform as a plank of his diplomacy. Italy had become a major cockpit in the long-running conflict between France and Spain and both monarchs found it necessary, at times, to woo the pope. However, when it suited either of them to pursue peace the message went out for all the leaders of Christendom to join in a league for the purpose of summoning a council which would carry out those sweeping moral and doctrinal reforms that the scandalously worldly Alexander VI (Rodrigo Borgia) and the warrior-pope Julius II were neither willing nor able to undertake. On this issue Henry found himself in something of a dilemma. He was, and wished to be recognized as, a loyal son of the Holy Father but he was also determined not to be left out of any summit conference. He let it be known that he was in favour of an ecumenical council but only if it was convened and headed by the pope.[32] Henry's Arthurian destiny could scarcely be beckoning more clearly. While his captains made their military preparations, his diplomats distanced themselves from their French counterparts. He declined an invitation by Louis to send delegates to his council in Pisa and, when Julius trumped Louis' ace by calling his own council (the Fifth Lateran) to meet in Rome, Henry sent as his representative, Silvestro de' Gigli, Bishop of Worcester (a name destined to reappear in one of the more unsavoury diplomatic intrigues – see below, p.78).[33] All the parties to these labyrinthine negotiations were so blinkered by pursuing their own ends that they could not see the signs of the coming crisis which would overwhelm them. Thus, for example, the Lateran Council, having, apparently, achieved its object of bolstering papal authority, was wound up in March 1517. Seven-and-a-half months later Martin Luther issued his *Ninety-Five Theses*, and changed forever Europe, the church and the world.

Such eventualities were well beyond the horizon as Henry prepared for war. Between, on the one hand, the glorious spectacle of multicoloured heraldry, nodding helms, prancing steeds, glinting armour and ranks of soldiers marching to the sound of pipe and drum and, on the other, the realities of victorious combat there is, of course, a great gulf fixed. Troops have to be mustered, transported, equipped, fed and paid. Strategies have to be developed. Tactics have to be planned and constantly adapted to give effect to those strategies. The king had no talent for, or interest in, the fundamentals of military logistics. Nor, it seems, was he capable of planning and preparing for the long haul. Government propaganda projected the grandiose vision of Henry regaining the ancient territories of the crown – Anjou, Maine, Gascony, Guyenne and Normandy – but there is no evidence that the king understood just how difficult it would be to realize such an objective, nor that he calculated whether he had at his disposal the resources necessary for it. Henry and his hawkish coterie psyched themselves up with gung-ho rhetoric. They were neither the first nor the last to believe that waging war for 'king and country' was a self-justifying occupation which would be divinely blessed with success.

Careful observation of and reflection on what was happening on foreign battlefields would have led to a more effective preparation for Henry's campaigns. Warfare was developing rapidly in this period. Handguns were challenging bows and arrows. Field artillery was coming into its own. The balance of cavalry and infantry was changing. The emergence of professional mercenary armies (notably those of Switzerland) armed with the long pike was beginning to dominate battlefield tactics. However, it was not until later in the reign that English armies began to take on a new shape. The forces that crossed the Channel between 1511 and 1513 still relied on the longbow and the cavalry charge. An important development that was inaugurated early in the reign was the tentative beginning of a permanent navy, but even this was more a matter of royal prestige than of being at the cutting edge of technology.

When Henry learned that James IV of Scotland had taken delivery from a French dockyard of the *Michael*, the biggest warship afloat, he immediately ordered a vessel that would outclass it, the *Henry Imperial* or *Henry Grace à Dieu,* launched in 1513. Soon afterwards, being impressed by the effectiveness of oared vessels, he commissioned the 800-ton *Great Galley*, an impressive three-masted warship which had a gun deck above the rowing deck. He was inordinately proud of this ship but its effectiveness is doubtful. There is something stirring about the sight of a great man-of-war and there is no reason to doubt that, even in the days before steam power, people's hearts were moved by the spectacle of a stately great ship under full sail. The showman in Henry certainly responded to these magnificent fighting machines. At the launching of the *Great Galley* in 1515, he strutted the deck dressed as a sailor – but in cloth of gold! Immediately on coming to the throne he began to augment the royal navy and, by the time of the French campaign of 1513, he had, by building, purchase and capture, more than doubled the fleet inherited from his father. This, of course, was a necessary concomitant of his intention of invading France. To convey troops across the Channel and to keep it clear of enemy shipping he had to have naval supremacy, but his programme was only a beginning. It contributed nothing to the development of naval warfare or to place England in a position to challenge the supremacy of Spain and Portugal in transoceanic endeavour.

This reincarnated Henry V, then, demanded war. Through his diplomats he prepared for war. He equipped himself with the materiel of war. In the tiltyard with his friends he played at war. However, someone else had to shoulder the massive burden of actually organizing war. Into that office the king's almoner slipped adroitly.

According to his biographer, George Cavendish, Thomas Wolsey made it his business to 'satisfy the king's mind, knowing right well that it was the right course to bring him to high promotion'.[34] This was scarcely an original or profound conclusion to reach; all royal favourites attain and maintain their position by pandering to the whims of their masters. What made Wolsey different was his omnicompetence. He was the executive officer par excellence. His mind was a well-filled and finely-organized filing cabinet. He was compulsively industrious and few details escaped his attention. He had the mental facility to evaluate arguments and the intuition to weigh up people. This did not mean that he was a funless bureaucrat, far from it. Even those who disliked Wolsey acknowledged his eloquence and wit. If, as his power grew, he could threaten frighteningly, he could also charm disarmingly. Few men of his time, and perhaps no Englishmen, were more cultured. He was a lavish and discerning patron, a generous host and bon viveur. The wealth he acquired from his ever-growing portfolio of offices and sinecures was expended on display – houses, clothes, jewels, music for chapel and hall, tapestries, carpets and table plate.

Like his royal master, Wolsey was a theatrical extrovert, but he was never an uncontrolled one. Perhaps this explains the hold he came to exercise over the young Henry. Wolsey was always careful never to appear in competition with the king. His splendour was a complementary splendour, designed to enhance Henry's reputation. The royal almoner appealed to Henry because his personality straddled court and council. He was a fun-loving bon viveur but also a serious man of affairs, capable of giving sound advice. Like the king, he intended England to be a major player in the affairs of Christendom and that meant presenting an impressive front to the world. He provided the young monarch with a magnificent object lesson in how a splendid Renaissance prince should live. God was robed in splendour and it behoved his representatives in church and state to reflect something of his effulgence. Henry paid frequent visits to Wolsey's palaces at York Place and Hampton Court, and Wolsey was always ready with lavish entertainment – even, apparently, when the royal party was unannounced. His biographer tells the story of one such occasion. The churchman and his guests were in the middle of a banquet when a group of 'foreign shepherds' arrived. These rustics had never spent a night on the hillside looking after flocks and they were all dressed in vivid silks. When they had been invited to join in the eating, drinking, dancing and gambling and when the fun was at its height, the host suggested that perhaps there was among the strange guests one who outranked him and who should take the seat of honour. Indeed there was, came the reply, but could Wolsey penetrate the great man's cunning disguise? This was, of course the signal for Wolsey to humbly unmask the king, which he proceeded to do. Unfortunately, he got it wrong and pointed to Sir Edward Neville, who was much like Henry. Laughter all round!

Wolsey thus entered enthusiastically into setting a tone of conspicuous consumption, a tone eagerly taken up by courtiers, nobles and gentlemen who could afford to do so (or who borrowed heavily to maintain their place among the social elite). The example set by Henry and Wolsey encouraged a spate of competitive domestic construction and created a demand for land and convertible buildings that (without knowing it) was hungrily waiting for the dissolution of the monasteries in the 1530s. Every commodious country mansion and every town house enhanced by the artistry of foreign craftsmen demonstrated to England's continental neighbours that the Tudor elite were not boorish back-woodsmen but shared with Frenchmen, Burgundians and Italians an appreciation of all the latest fashions. Wolsey's exuberant lifestyle matched that of Henry and was based on the same philosophy. For this reason and because Henry enjoyed Wolsey's company and respected the intellect of this man who took uncongenial burdens from his shoulders, Henry trusted Wolsey more and more. Wolsey became, by degrees, the king's right-hand man, his chief adviser, the inter-mediary between the itinerant court and the council at Westminster. He took on himself the arrangements for equipping and victualling the royal forces employed in the 1512 campaign but the strategy was that of the king.

The results of its implementation were humiliatingly disas-trous. The plan was for an Anglo-Spanish invasion of Guyenne, in south-west France. Ferdinand would supply his son-in-law with cavalry, cannon and wagons and help him to claw back part of the territory of Aquitaine, which had once been annexed to the English crown. The Spanish king, however, had different priorities. He intended to use the English attack as a diversion while he overran Navarre, immediately to the south. This ancient kingdom, bordering Aragon, Castile and France, controlled the principal Pyrenean pass used by pilgrims, merchants and armies and its independence was, therefore, an irritant which Ferdinand was determined to remove. Ignorant of his ally's duplicity, Henry embarked on the great enterprise with typical bravura. High offices were distributed to his close companions. Thomas Grey, Marquis of Dorset, was appointed commander of the land operation and Edward Howard was made admiral of the fleet, charged with keeping the Channel approaches clear of French warships. Other privy chamber members, including, Charles Brandon, Henry Guildford and Thomas Knyvet, clamoured for positions of honour and were rewarded with commissions. The assembly of the force in Southampton was an impressively theatrical event:

> To see the lords and gentlemen so well armed and so richly apparelled in cloths of gold and silver and velvets of sundry colours, pounced and embroidered, and all petty captains in satin and damask of white and green and yeoman in cloth of the same colour, the banners, pennons, standards. . .fresh and newly painted with sundry beasts and devices, it was a pleasure to behold.[35]

When news arrived in June of the successful landing of Dorset and his 10,000 men at San Sebastian, near Biarritz, Henry ordered a celebratory joust at Greenwich. This was followed by a naval review at Portsmouth for Henry to inspect his fleet and send forth the chivalric brotherhood on further triumphant enterprises: 'The king made a great banquet to all the captains and everyone swore to another ever to defend, aid and comfort one another without failing, and this they promised before the king, who committed them to God, and so with great noise of minstrelsy they took their ships.'[36]

Howard led his fleet on a seek-and-destroy mission to locate and eradicate the French marine. At the beginning of August 1512 he tracked the enemy down to the well-fortified port of

Brest and, on the 10th, his opposite number, Hervé, Sieur de Portzmoguer, came out to offer battle. Warships at this time were not gun platforms designed to pound the enemy to pieces but troop carriers whose captains tried to grapple and board the opposition vessels. It was while Henry's capital ship, the *Regent*, was thus shackled to the French carrack, *Marie La Cordelière*, that a horrific incident occurred which shocked both combatants and put a swift end to the action. Either by accident or design, the *Cordelière's* powder store was ignited. Within moments both the ships, locked in a deadly embrace, were blazing. Officers and men were doomed to burn to death or drown since the heat was too intense for other ships to rescue them. Seven hundred English sailors perished and among them was Thomas Knyvet.

Reporting these 'lamentable and sorrowful tidings' to his mentor Bishop Fox, Wolsey urged him to keep the news secret, commenting that 'only the king and I' were party to the full details. He went on, 'To see how the king taketh the matter and behaveth himself, ye would marvel, and much allow his wise and constant manner. I have not on my faith seen the like.'[37] We would expect Wolsey to praise the king's stoical self-control and it is frustrating to have no other indication of Henry's true feelings at the loss of his friend. Did he privately nurse a deep grief or were other emotions uppermost as he received bulletins on the progress of the war? They were far from reassuring. Dorset and his men were effectively trapped in the environs of St Jean de Luz. Immobilized by lack of supplies and by divided counsels. Ferdinand failed to send the men and equipment he had promised. He also tried to persuade Dorset to march his army south over the Pyrenees. The English commander refused to abandon his instructions, which were to move north and invest Bayonne. The result was that he did nothing. His demoralized troops fell prey to idleness and dysentery; some 1,800 died. Eventually, they mutinied, demanding to be taken home. Dorset, now ill himself, yielded to them. Henry was incandescent. He wrote to Ferdinand asking him to prevent the English troops abandoning their enterprise but his instructions arrived too late. Howard, meanwhile, was raiding along the French coast, burning, looting and capturing enemy ships in an orgy of revenge. In a message to Wolsey, he vowed never to return to court until he had made the French pay heavily for Knyvet's death.

It is scarcely surprising that Howard was in no hurry to face the king. The expedition which had started out so bravely had all gone horribly wrong and Henry, as he well knew, did not like losing. Dorset, on his return, went to his country estates, claiming to be too ill to present himself at court. Whether his affliction was physical or diplomatic, he was well advised to maintain a low profile. Back at Greenwich his subordinate officers were being put through the mincer of royal wrath. Ferdinand had sent envoys roundly blaming English incompetence for the Guyenne debacle and Henry, not wishing to offend his ally, accepted the Spanish analysis – officially, at least. Several of the English captains were subjected to a humiliating 'trial' in front of Ferdinand's representatives. Henry cowed them with threats of stringing them up from the highest gallows but no punishments were subsequently handed out. They may well have considered themselves hard done by. They had supported Dorset in refusing to depart from the strategy outlined by the king. Their inability to carry out that strategy had been entirely due to Ferdinand's failure to stick to his side of the bargain.

What does emerge from this sorry sequence of events is Henry's tendency, even at this young age, to use anger – often theatrical – to cow those who provoked his displeasure. It was an effective weapon, even when turned on those who knew him well. It silenced offenders, precluded further debate and absolved the king from calmly weighing up the pros and cons of complex problems. It was to become a feature of all Henry's relationships over the years. He was not yet given to the towering rages which would mark his later years. Rather, he displayed his disapproval in petulance and the sulking withdrawal of favour.

His ministers, diplomats and captains were increasingly motivated less by a desire to please him than by the desperate need
not to displease him. While this undoubtedly drove royal
servants to achieve results which would not have been possible
under the rule of a more even-tempered monarch, it could also
be counter-productive. Ambassadors in far-off capitals or
generals on distant battlefields who were in the best position to
decide how to respond to changing situations effectively had
their hands tied by fear of exceeding the instructions they had
received from the king. Thus, individual initiative and creativity
was stifled.

In the spring of 1513 Edward Howard, embroiled in the
frustration of another inconclusive naval campaign and
knowing how impatiently Henry would be waiting for good
news, had the temerity to invite the king to come and take
charge of the action for himself. Of course, he wrapped up the
challenge in suitably flattering words: Henry's presence would
ensure victory, he suggested. He was really saying: 'Instead of
grumbling, come and see for yourself what it is like out here.'
His invitation, needless to say, received a curt reply.

Within weeks Howard became another member of the
'Round Table' to lay down his life for the king. Somewhat like
a losing gambler who goes on throwing the dice in the
conviction that his luck will change, Henry pledged himself to
a continuation of the war. This time he upped the stakes. He
would personally lead an army to invade northern France. If a
force of 30,000 was to be safely conveyed to Calais it was
essential, first of all, to clear the Channel of French ships. This
was the task assigned to Howard in the spring of 1513.

Once more he located the enemy fleet at Brest. This time the
French declined an open battle, preferring to sit it out in their
safe haven until their opponents were forced, by weather or
shortage of victuals, to withdraw. They would not come out of
port and Howard could not get in. When he tried, one of his
capital ships came to grief on the rocks. The stalemate
continued for two weeks; a battle of nerves. It was Howard

who broke first. Knowing how the king would interpret his continued inactivity, he resolved on a typically rash, death-or-glory escapade. He launched an attack by rowing boats across the shallow waters of the anchorage. He and his men reached and boarded the French admiral's ship. Fierce hand-to-hand fighting ensued but the attackers were greatly outnumbered. Howard was among those forced over the side where he drowned in the water, weighed down by his armour. His dispirited captains upped anchor and sailed for home, while the French sallied forth to raid at will along the Sussex coast.

It is not recorded that Henry stoically contained his grief. He was, in fact, far more concerned at the threatened disruption of his master plan. His immediate reaction was to appoint Edward Howard's brother, Thomas, to take his place, put some fight back into his men and execute the pre-ordained strategy without any more bungling. Thomas was an altogether more cautious man than his sibling. Whatever else he did, he made sure to watch his back. As day followed frustrating day in Plymouth, where he was supposed to be mustering his force, the admiral bombarded Wolsey and the king with letter after letter excusing the delay and blaming everyone except himself. The ships needed repair. The sailors were too cowardly. Supplies were sub-standard or non-existent. He even rode to London himself to explain the situation in person. To his chagrin, neither the king nor his almoner would see him. It was the end of June 1513 before Howard was able to bring his ships round to the Thames estuary to escort Henry and the main part of the invasion fleet.

Henry would always claim the 1513 campaign in France and Scotland as a great personal triumph. It was nothing of the sort. The vanguard of the army, led by Charles Brandon, and the rearguard under the command of Charles Somerset, Baron Herbert (the long-serving councillor Henry had inherited from his father), had already crossed the Channel by the time Henry began his stately progress through Kent, attended by his liveried guard of 600 spearmen and a mile-long retinue of splendidly accoutred nobles with their own levies that wound its way along dusty lanes and through villages of jingoistic countrymen who had turned out to cheer their champions setting out to bash the 'frogs'. Before embarking, Henry had a nasty surprise for the Howard clan. Thomas and Edward's father, the Earl of Surrey (also called Thomas) was Earl Marshal and assumed that an honoured place would be found for him in this prestigious enterprise, but he had opposed Henry's expansionist ambitions. He had been at odds with his younger son, Edward, who had valiantly laid down his life in the service of his king. As for the older boy, Thomas, he had scarcely given an impression of competence in handling the maritime arrangements. Henry now took delight in informing Howard senior that he was not to join him in France. Instead, he was to make his way to England's bleak and distant northern border. It was known that James IV of Scotland would support his old ally, the French king, by making trouble in the Marches. Surrey was now detailed to contain the expected incursion. Later, Thomas and his remaining brother, Edmund, were detached from the army in France to go to their father's aid. It was an important commission but it was not the high profile one Surrey had hoped for and it lacked any semblance of glory. Whatever his private feelings about Henry, Surrey publicly vented his ire on the Scottish king. 'Sorry may I see him,' he told his companions, 'or die that is the cause of my abiding behind, and if ever he and I meet, I shall do all that in me lieth to make him as sorry if I can.'[38] Reluctantly, the earl took his leave of his glory-seeking sovereign. Neither could anticipate the irony that would unfold over the ensuing weeks.

The English army besieged and captured with relative ease Thérouanne in Artois and Tournai, a city in Flanders which Louis had taken from the Emperor. The only battle in the field occurred when a French relieving force was put to rout, an engagement contemptuously referred to by the victors as the Battle of the Spurs because of the speedy withdrawal of the enemy. It was old-fashioned warfare fought largely in accord with chivalric convention. Can it have been entirely coincidental that insignificant Thérouanne was a mere 20 miles (30km) from Agincourt or that the king made a nocturnal tour of the English camp putting heart into his men, as Henry V had done before his famous battle? The only immediate advantage to the English was the capture of several prominent and eminently ransomable French notables. Henry's 'great battle' could scarcely have been more different from the one his father had won at Bosworth, hazarding himself in the clash of arms to snatch a crown, but it was a victory and one he was determined to trumpet loudly. Meanwhile, he had left Queen Catherine as his regent during his absence and she it was who energetically prosecuted the war against the Scots.

On 22 August 1513, James IV crossed the border with a force of about 30,000 men, including a small contingent provided by his French ally. (In his reports Surrey inflated this figure to more than 80,000.) Surrey had been energetically recruiting and had around 20,000 troops to face the invasion, but this was only part of the national response. Catherine and the council had reacted industriously and intelligently to the threat. Sir Thomas Lovell, a seasoned Tudor servant who held various offices including Constable of the Tower and Steward of the Household, was ordered to gather men in the Midland counties as a second line of defence. For her part, the queen became a veritable Boudicca, riding from Richmond to the muster-point at Buckingham at the head of a third army behind bravely fluttering banners, some of which she and her ladies had sewn themselves.

In the event, her mettle was not tried in battle because the Scots were halted some 2.5 miles (4km) south of the Tweed on the heights above Flodden Field. The English victory at the Battle of Flodden (or Brankston Moor) on 9 September was the result of a rare flash of tactical brilliance on the part of the Howard leadership, combined with the rash incompetence of the Scottish king. It may also indicate the gulf between chivalry and the bloody reality of war. According to legend,

James refused to allow his artillery to blast the enemy to pieces as they struggled across the marshy terrain on the grounds that it would be 'dishonourable'. He allowed himself to be lured from his commanding position in the hope of winning the day in a downhill cavalry charge. Howard had been counting on such a headstrong response in order to achieve the pitched battle his disciplined men were equipped to fight. Even so, the conflict was long and bloody and went on until evening. By the time the Scottish standards were captured, the king, several of his nobles (the 'flowers of the forest' long-remembered in minstrelsy) and some 10,000 soldiers lay dead on Flodden Field.

It was one of the major turning points in Anglo-Scottish relations. For the rest of Henry's reign the demoralized Scots were in no position to intervene effectively in affairs south of the border. James was succeeded by an infant son whose regency was vested in Queen Margaret, Henry's sister. The result of Flodden was, therefore, much better than the king could have hoped for. It removed one irritating chess piece from the complex board of foreign policy. However, it was also a personal embarrassment. It was obvious to anyone who calmly assessed the recent military activities that the Howards' achievements had put Henry's in the shade. No one, of course, said as much openly. Quite the contrary. When Catherine forwarded to her husband a fragment of James' bloodstained surcoat (tunic), she was careful to affirm that the triumph was Henry's, carried out in his name and for his glory.

After taking possession of Tournai on 24 September, the victor spent three weeks in lavish displays of celebration. The Howards were not invited to come and join in the festivities and when, subsequently, Thomas Howard, Earl of Surrey, was awarded the dukedom of Norfolk (a title which had been stripped from the Howards by Henry VII), he had to share the investiture with the captains of the French campaign, Charles Brandon, who became Duke of Suffolk, and Lord Herbert, who was elevated to the earldom of Worcester. However, no one shared more handsomely in the fruits of victory than Thomas Wolsey. He was appointed Bishop of Lincoln and Bishop of Tournai (a position he later relinquished in return for a pension of 12,000 livres). Negotiations began in Rome for his elevation to the cardinalate. And before 1514 was out, he had become Archbishop of York.

More cold water was poured on Henry's achievements by the behaviour of his allies. It had been agreed between the rulers of Spain, England and the Holy Roman Empire that their league against France would continue and that it would be cemented by a marriage between Henry's sister, Mary, and Charles, ruler of the Netherlands, who was the grandson of both Maximilian and Ferdinand (and, therefore, Queen Catherine's nephew). It was an impressive diplomatic coup, signifying clearly that Harry of England had 'arrived'. By the spring of 1514, though, it was all off. Ferdinand and Maximilian had made a truce with Louis. This time Henry was not prepared to ride the diplomatic punches; he hit back. After the events of recent months he had more standing in the councils of Europe – and he also had at his elbow an arch-intriguer, well able to play the game of deception and counter-deception. Wolsey knew that England could not afford an open-ended commitment to war. The country needed an honourable peace. Possibly, the achievement of this had been his goal all along; having given the king his moment of glory he may well have entertained hopes of steering him into more irenic and positive policies. He was already using his influence in Rome where the death of Julius II in February 1513 and his replacement by the Medici, Leo X, had inaugurated a very different regime.

Exhausted by the turmoil engendered by the belligerence of the old pope, Rome wanted peace at almost any price. Cardinal Bainbridge was still using his influence to maintain an anti-French party and that did not suit Wolsey at all. He now set about undermining the English ambassador. Silvestro de' Gigli, officially in Rome for the Lateran Council, was his

chosen instrument for this task. Bitter rivalry broke out
between the two ecclesiastics and Bainbridge's influence
rapidly waned. Then, in July 1514, he died suddenly, poisoned
by a member of his own household. Under torture, the
murderer claimed to have been in the pay of Gigli and subsequently committed suicide. The bishop managed to shake
off the accusation but not the opprobrium attached to it and
his career never recovered. Was a contract against the great
Cardinal Bainbridge taken out by Gigli or his patron back in
England? The crime remains an unsolved mystery. What is
undisputed is that the man who replaced the unfortunate
ambassador as Archbishop of York was none other than
Thomas Wolsey and, thanks to the energetic advocacy of Gigli
in the Medici camp, the king's right-hand man received the
coveted cardinal's hat a year later.

Wolsey was undoubtedly behind the foreign policy U-turn
of 1514 but Henry was wholly in favour of it, if for different
reasons. He was furious at having been betrayed by his allies
and was determined to outmanoeuvre them in the diplomatic
arena. If they could go behind his back and do a deal with the
French, he could and would top their bid. He proposed a
treaty with Louis XII, to be cemented by marriage between the
ill and aging monarch and Princess Mary. It was a brilliantly-
conceived coup against Ferdinand and Maximilian. It pointed
out that Henry did not need an alliance with a young
Habsburg prince when he could have an alliance with a Valois
king. And the possibilities of the marriage between the fifty-
two-year-old Louis and the twenty-eight-year-old Mary were
exciting indeed. Louis had no male heir. If Mary could make
good this deficiency she would become regent of France if
Louis died during the infancy of their son, as seemed likely.
With his sisters ruling both Scotland and France, Henry would
emerge as the arbiter of Europe. He would have control of the
seaway between the Mediterranean world and the northern
markets of the Netherlands, Germany and Scandinavia. He
had gained new mainland territory and a handsome French

pension to boot. He had taken his fellow monarchs by surprise and won a place at the top table. His international reputation had reached a peak it would never attain again. And he owed most of this to Wolsey.

It is Henry's sense of indebtedness to the cardinal that explains Wolsey's rapid, even meteoric, rise to wealth and power. His friend had stood by him throughout the struggle to implement his war policy, had shouldered the burden of organizing the military and diplomatic effort and masterminded the new direction of policy. He deserved his reward. Of course, showering ecclesiastical preferment on Wolsey cost Henry little but he was not slow in raising his friend to leading positions in the state. The aging Archbishop Warham and Bishop Fox were hangovers from a previous reign that was now essentially out of sympathy with the new regime. In the winter of 1515–16 they resigned as lord chancellor and lord privy seal respectively. To what extent they were eased out by Henry is a matter for conjecture. Wolsey was immediately appointed the new Chancellor and the Privy Seal was entrusted to Thomas Ruthall, Bishop of Durham, who was, according to the Venetian ambassador, so close to the cardinal as to be thought of as 'singing treble to Wolsey's bass'. With control of the two seals which authenticated all royal orders Wolsey was now, *de facto*, in control of the government and his extraordinary 'reign' was to last for more than a decade. Within the space of a few months, death and resignation had removed some of the major personalities from the court and the privy chamber, and created a new dynamic at the heart of national affairs.

There was another purely fortuitous event that enabled Wolsey to occupy his centre-stage position without any rivals. In 1512 something happened which made it impossible for Henry to continue to live in the place that had been the centre of royal government since the reign of Edward the Confessor. A disastrous fire ravaged the domestic buildings of the palace of Westminster. The great hall, the Star Chamber (where the council frequently met) and adjacent offices were spared, which meant that routine judicial and executive business could continue, but it was no longer possible for Henry to hold court there. He became a king without a grand residence within his own capital. Wolsey, by contrast, now had nearby York Place as his archiepiscopal town mansion, a mansion he soon set about enlarging and beautifying. Here the cardinal ensconced himself while the king moved around his perimeter palaces of Greenwich, Richmond and Eltham. The phenomenon of a king *in absentia* and a resplendent churchman daily progressing, in great pomp, to the council chamber or the courts of justice was one whose extraordinary nature was not lost on Englishmen or foreign diplomats with business to transact with the crown. The Venetian ambassador was just one representative who felt obliged to point out the reality of the situation to his superiors: 'I have informed the Signory at least a thousand times that. . .were it a question of neglecting his majesty or his right reverend lordship the least injurious course would be to pass over the former.'[39]

It is highly significant that Henry took no steps to rebuild the ancient residence. From time immemorial Westminster Palace and the Tower of London had physically represented royal authority and power. Henry neglected the royal apartments in the latter and now completely deserted Westminster. In effect, he let out the traditional home of the monarchy to Wolsey. It might help us to gauge something of the impact of this if we consider what the public response might be to the current queen vacating Buckingham Palace in order to accommodate the prime minister and his staff. Even though the executive and judicial elements of constitutional monarchy have long been separated from the ceremonial, there would, undoubtedly, be an outcry. Wolsey's apparent usurping of royal dignity provoked just such resentment, especially among the nobility. To see an Ipswich butcher's son exalted above them in both church and state and to have to go cap in hand to this creature were almost unbearable. As that eccentric poet, John Skelton, pointed out, England now had two courts and the cardinal's was the most prestigious. Verses which he circulated among courtiers, who eagerly read and discussed them, claimed that Wolsey scorned his betters. Wolsey was, according to the poet, overbearing:

In the Chancery where he sits
But such as he admits
None so hardy to speak!
He saith, 'Thou hoddypeak [simpleton],
Thy learning is too lewd,
Thy tongue is not well-thewed [well-mannered]
To seek before our grace!'. . .
And in the Chequer he them checks
And in the Star Chamber he nods and he becks,
And beareth him there so stout
That no man dare rowt (contradict)!
Duke, earl, baron nor lord,
But to his sentence must accord;
Whether he be knight or squire,
All men must follow his desire.[40]

It was one of the ground rules for royal servants that one should gain and keep a position as close to the king as possible, not only to see and be seen, but also to be able to counter the influence of rivals and enemies. Wolsey knew the jealousies and resentments his power occasioned and, as we shall see, he took pains to be well informed about daily events at court and the comings and goings of those who had access to the king. However, he was sufficiently confident of Henry's backing to maintain a separate, semi-independent existence.

What is more important is that Henry also was aware of the cardinal's growing unpopularity but refused to be influenced by it. We have already seen how Wolsey gained and earned his master's support but we need to explore further this relationship which was foundational in setting the tone for the reign. It has often been suggested that Henry let his deputy 'run the country' because he was lazy; that he had limited

capacity for mental application. He certainly had no inclination for his father's style of close personal supervision of
administrative minutiae. Nor did he intend to spend hours
every day listening to the reports and supplications of the
scores of men and women who thronged his audience chamber.
It was, therefore, valuable to him to have in the cardinal's
sumptuous establishment a court of first resort where ambassadors, regional officials and humble suitors could be dealt
with. However, this by no means meant that he resigned decisions to his minister. Wolsey was very careful to keep his
master fully informed. He had a stable of horses at his disposal
and it was very rarely that a day passed when he did not
despatch a succession of messengers to the king. Once a week,
unless Henry was on progress, it was his routine to process
with his usual pomp from York Place via the City to the
waterside where his barge waited to convey him up or down
river to wherever his master was keeping court.

Henry, like most egotists, recognized people he could use.
That is why, throughout his reign, he was attended by an
extraordinary array of talented men. Wolsey, More, Cromwell
and Cranmer were only the ones who rose to the top positions
in church and state. Others, variously gifted, served in lesser
capacities. In Wolsey, he had found someone very special. The
king's minister was a workaholic:

> Henry leads his usual life, leaving all the cares of state to
> Wolsey, who is so very ill that he is in danger of losing an eye,
> and the rest of his body seems almost equally affected. There
> seems little hope of his immediate recovery, especially as he will
> not abandon the affairs of the kingdom to others and must see
> many people daily.[41]

So the imperial ambassador reported in March 1522 and many
other observers testified to Wolsey's tireless industry. Nor were
his labours merely those of an administrative hack, lacking the
ability to delegate. The Venetian ambassador reckoned that the
cardinal paid personal attention to the range of business matters

that, in his own country, occupied the attention of several state departments. Wolsey was a creative, energetic reformer. As lord chancellor he not only streamlined the working of the courts; he also took a personal interest in many of the cases that appeared there. Unlike the king, he had a genuine interest in and concern for the wellbeing of the English people and used his position for the increase of justice and equity. In May 1516 he made a 'manifesto' statement to the king and council. He pointed out that justice was all too often being perverted by great men who considered themselves above the law. This state of affairs, he warned, must cease. To that end, he intended to give the law stronger teeth – teeth which would bite all offenders, regardless of rank. To drive the point home, that very same day he found the Earl of Northumberland guilty of raping a royal ward and sent him under guard to the Fleet prison. Henry let it be known that he fully supported this policy and was determined to ensure 'the indifferent ministration of justice to all persons, as well high as low'.[42]

This inevitably brought Wolsey into conflict with the powerful men of the realm who believed that the courts existed to uphold their authority and for whom overawing judges and juries was second nature. It was Wolsey's determination to stand up to the nobility which gave the king another reason for supporting him. Henry realized the importance of the work his father had done in bringing to heel potentially over-mighty subjects and was not going to let the reins of centralized power slip from his grasp to be taken up by some noble caucus. On the other hand, he needed the support of his magnates in the administration of the shires, in attendance at court and, especially, in times of war. Having as his principal agent a man who had no family connections with the country's leaders and who was also no respecter of persons enabled him to exercise discipline at one remove. Wolsey had already shown his hand as early as 1515 when he had the cash-strapped Earl of Derby fined a swingeing £1,000 for affray. It must have seemed to many that the financial exactions of Henry VII had not been

consigned to the scrapheap. And, just as the first Tudor sheltered behind Empson, Dudley and the Council Learned in the
Law, so his son now used Wolsey as a shield to deflect the
enmity of disaffected nobles.

Where the king was less enthusiastic about the cardinal's
activity was his domination of the council. Only gradually did
he realize just how completely Wolsey had come to change the
workings of government. It was not just that, by sheer force of
personality, he overawed the council; he actually changed its
function. Originally, it had been a body with a dual purpose.
Its members, drawn almost exclusively from the spiritual and
temporal nobility, advised the king on all matters and assisted
in the operation of royal justice. Wolsey increased its burden of
judicial business to such an extent that it had little time or
energy left to debate affairs of state. These were now
considered by Wolsey, who discussed them with the king
(personally or by messengers) and then brought them to the
council, for 'information'. Henry grew restless about this
development. Basically, it suited him well to be freed from the
tedium of government but he felt that his status was to some
extent diminished by not having with him a 'council attendant'
of wise men with whom he could at any time discuss important
matters. This unease was something Wolsey had to take into
account in the years ahead.

Of course, Henry still had his other attendants, his
companions of the privy chamber. Since the death of Knyvet
and Edward Howard, the man who had assumed the leading
place in Henry's affections was Charles Brandon, now Duke of
Suffolk. Like others to whom the young Henry was drawn, he
was a few years older. By 1514 he was in his early thirties. That
was the year that the astute Countess of Salisbury granted him
an annuity of £100 to look after her interests at court. She only
considered Wolsey to be worth an investment of £66 at that
time. Brandon was the complete courtier – athletic, fun-loving,
fashion-conscious, arrogant and unprincipled. Despite the
generous gifts lavished on him by the king, keeping up his

position at court meant that he was constantly broke. Like a modern celebrity playboy, he was possessed of an animal magnetism women found irresistible. His matrimonial life was a tangle of dishonourable commitments and desertions beside which Henry's pale into insignificance. The king was so attracted by this macho, ebullient man that he was prepared to overlook his failings – a state of affairs that encouraged Brandon to push his luck to the limit. By 1512, he had been married twice. He had wriggled out of his first union with Anne Browne in order to take on a more lucrative prospect, Margaret Mortimer. Subsequently, he threw over Margaret and went back to Anne. She died in 1512 and Brandon took the opportunity to contract a marriage with his infant ward, Elizabeth Grey, in order to administer her fortune. This temporarily eased his financial problems while he looked out for something more profitable.

The following year saw Henry and his friend on campaign in France and Flanders. They were frequent guests of Margaret of Austria, daughter of the Emperor Maximilian and Regent of the Netherlands. Margaret kept a court which, in order to provide some kind of moral framework for the relationships between her male and female attendants, was governed by the rules of chivalric love. The English visitors enthusiastically fell in with the amorous rituals of courtship and Brandon extravagantly protested his love for Margaret. It is doubtful that he had any serious pretensions to marry so far above his station but his sighing vows of devotion were vigorously seconded by the king. What began as a game soon became a diplomatic embarrassment. The story spread that a serious proposal of marriage had been made. Maximilian was affronted. He protested to Henry, and the king, in order to extricate himself from any involvement in the debacle, made a great show of seeking out those responsible for spreading the scandalous rumour. Margaret and her father suggested that the least Henry could do was order Brandon to marry Lady Lisle, to whom he was betrothed, and thus put an end to speculation. This Henry declined to do. When friendship was weighed in the balance against diplomatic relations it proved to be heavier. Yet this extraordinary episode was only the curtain raiser to the adventure the Duke of Suffolk plunged into the following year.

Princess Mary was married by proxy to Louis XII on 13 August 1514. The French king was looking forward impatiently to his union with a younger – and very attractive – woman. One of Wolsey's correspondents reported from the French court, 'I assure you, the king thinketh every hour a day until he seeth her; he is never well but when he hears her spoken of. I make no doubt she will lead a good life with him, by the grace of God.'[43] Mary, by contrast, had mixed feelings. The prospect of being pawed by a prematurely aged, gout-ridden spouse was far from appealing. On the other hand, to be Queen of France and mistress of the glittering Louvre court was a prize worth making some sacrifice for and she could always comfort herself with the thought that her marriage was not likely to be of long duration. On 9 October, the couple came together in Paris for the festivities surrounding the consummation of their union. Louis greeted his bride attired in the fashionable garments of a young buck, showered her with magnificent jewels and, on the 'morning after', boasted of his lusty performance in the marital bed. The political implications of the marriage were, of course, paramount and the man sent over to conduct discussions with the French about an offensive alliance against Spain was Charles Brandon. It was an important mission, Suffolk's first foray into top-level diplomacy, and the fact that it was entrusted to the king's closest friend was meant to demonstrate the importance Henry attached to it. Brandon arrived to find the queen in a state of some distress. She was feeling homesick and, moreover, had reasonable cause to complain about her husband's conduct, as she had recently explained in letters to her brother and to Wolsey:

> On the morning next after the marriage my chamberlain with all other men servants were discharged and likewise my mother

Guildford [Sir Richard Guildford's widow, who had been Mary's closest attendant for many years], with other my women and maidens. . .as my mother Guildford can more plainly show your grace than I can write, to whom I beseech you give credence. And if it may be by any means possible, I humbly require you to cause my said mother Guildford to repair hither once again. . .I am well assured that when you know the truth of everything as my mother Guildford can show you, you would full little have thought I should have been thus intreated.[44]

Had matters had time to settle down, and particularly if Mary had soon had babies to think about, doubtless she would have established and settled into an acceptable routine. That was not to be her lot. Twelve weeks to after her wedding her husband died. She now set about making her own life and her brother's more complicated.

To understand the background to what happened next we need to go back at least a couple of years. Then Mary had been happily ensconced in the Tudor court with the prospect of being married sometime to her cousin Charles, who was four years her junior. She was a lively teenager who enjoyed being part of all the entertainments at her brother's court with their attendant chivalric ballyhoo. She thrilled to the spectacle of dashing young men locked in tiltyard combat. And who more dashing than Charles Brandon? He paid court to her as deftly as only he could and she fell in love with him. There was no possibility of anything developing between them because princesses were not free to follow the dictates of their heart, but Mary had a full measure of Tudor wilfulness. She later claimed that she had struck a deal with Henry: she would marry first at his dictation if she was allowed the freedom to choose her own second husband. She and Brandon had some sort of 'understanding'. The duke, as we have seen, was adept at wooing royal women and his courtship of Mary may have been no more serious than the attentions he paid to Margaret of Austria. At most, the possibility of marriage to Mary was just another card in his hand. By the time she was free to accompany him to the altar, he would probably have found some rich widow eager to be a duchess. Matters did change when it was decided to marry Mary off to old Louis but any real prospect of marrying his king's sister still seemed remote. Apparently, he did not even mention the matter to Henry until after Louis' unexpectedly sudden death and even then, we may assume, he did so with caution.

At the beginning of 1515 the political situation which had seemed so settled was thrown into confusion by the threatened breakdown of the Anglo-French alliance. Louis' death played into the hands of council members who persisted in regarding France as England's inevitable enemy (as did much of the country at large) and who resented Wolsey's control of foreign policy. The first reaction of Henry and his minister was to save the situation by marrying the young widow to Louis' cousin and heir, Francis I. Everything, however, conspired to wreck this strategy. France's new twenty-year-old king was, like Henry, a vigorous, martially-inclined young monarch bent on glory and, specifically, on reversing his country's recent humiliation. He intended to renew the conflict in Italy with Spain and its allies and his only interest in England was to prevent it interfering with his plans. Initially, he welcomed the idea of marriage to the dowager queen. Should that prove impossible, his fallback position was to extract diplomatic advantage from her by placing her on the international marriage market. Henry's plans were identical: pledge Mary to Francis and, failing that, use her in his own dynastic negotiations, preferably by renewing the offer to Prince Charles of Burgundy. The poor girl's plight was desperate. She shrank from Francis' advances, which she regarded as lewd attempts at seduction, and was confused by his bland assurances that, as matters stood with her brother, her only choice was between himself and Prince Charles. She countered with the only weapon she had; she told the French king that she was not free to marry any great monarch because she was foresworn – she had consented to marry the Duke of Suffolk.

For Francis this was marvellous news. The dowager queen had inadvertently handed him the diplomatic equivalent of a loaded gun. By forwarding the Suffolk match he could trump Henry's ace. An English marriage alliance with a potentially alien power would be impossible. It was at this point that Brandon turned up in France. Once again he had been sent as his king's representative, this time to try to negotiate the immediate return of his sister. On his arrival he found himself completely fazed by the wiles of Francis and the hysterical importuning of Mary. The one crucial piece that is missing from our understanding of this complex jigsaw is any impartial evidence about what may have passed between Henry and his ambassador before the latter left England. If Suffolk did raise the issue of a possible marriage to the king's sister, Henry's response is likely to have been, 'We'll talk about it after you've brought Mary home', for his immediate concern was to get her out of Francis' clutches. Brandon's first meeting with Mary indicated that achieving this would be a problem. He may well have exaggerated his report of it to Henry but he was obviously faced by a woman who was in an emotional state yet not so distraught that she could not calculate how to extricate herself from her dire situation. Tearfully, she implored Suffolk to marry her without delay because she knew her brother could not be trusted to honour whatever verbal pledges he may have made to herself or her intended husband:

> She said that the best in France had [said] unto her that and she went into England, she should go into Flanders [i.e. be married off to Prince Charles]. To which she said that she had rather to be torn in pieces than ever she should come there and with that she wept. Sir, I never saw woman so weep.[45]

Undoubtedly, she was right in her assessment of Henry's intentions and brave in seeking to thwart them. Perhaps she was emboldened by the headstrong behaviour of her elder sister in Scotland, who had just astonished everyone by taking a dashing young chevalier for her second husband. When Suffolk assured

Mary that Henry had no intention of marrying her against her will, she responded with a straightforward challenge:

> If the king my brother is content and the French king both. . . that I should have you, I will [choose] the time after my desire, or else I may well think. . .that you are come to take me home [so that] I may be married into Flanders, which I will never [do, even though] I die for it.[45]

When in perplexity Brandon turned to the French king, Francis assured him that he would write personally to Henry to ease the situation. A more clear-headed and resolute envoy would not have allowed himself to be manoeuvred into a perilous marriage but Suffolk was not the sort of man who could carefully weigh up the implications of a course of action or think his way through any set of circumstances that were at all complex. He allowed himself to believe that Henry's affection for his friend and his sister would overcome the anger he would initially feel. He rushed into marriage and, to put the matter beyond any possibility of being disentangled by clever lawyers, he and Mary immediately consummated their union.

It was not just Henry's freedom of movement in international affairs that was compromised by this headstrong act of personal rebellion; the marriage had its implications for the delicate balance of political forces at home. Wolsey and Brandon were the king's closest confidants and were, therefore, the targets of jealous intrigue by rivals, led by the Howards, in court and council. Buoyed up by Suffolk's presumption, these rivals now had high hopes of seeing him at the very least banished from the realm, the pro-French policy reversed and Wolsey brought low for having engineered it. They even spread rumours that the king's evil advisers were in league with the devil and that their influence over him had been brought about by necromancy. In later years such tactics would very probably have proved successful. Henry's forcefulness covered an underlying insecurity. Despite appearances to the contrary, he was sensitive to popular opinion and this would on more than one occasion cause him to sacrifice a faithful servant who had become the victim of court factions. In 1515 he was well aware that his relations with France were intensely unpopular and it would have been easy for him to put the blame for current policy on Wolsey and Brandon and leave them to the mercy of their enemies. However, at this time Henry could not be without Wolsey and did not choose to be without Suffolk. As long as the French alliance remained intact and Henry could extricate himself from the marriage debacle without too much loss of face, he was prepared to forgive the lovers and receive them back at court. Unfortunately, he was about to learn another hard lesson about the cynical world of diplomacy.

Francis I was a canny and ruthless young statesman. He had Henry over a barrel and was determined to take full advantage of the fact. The instructions Brandon received from London were that his master's bruised ego would be salved if Mary brought home with her both her dowry and the trousseau of glittering gems that her doting French husband had lavished upon her. However, when Francis was approached, he refused point blank to part with the jewels and countered with a demand to which Henry could not possibly agree – the relin-quishing of his great prize of Tournai. Months of haggling now ensued and it was mid-April before a compromise was reached which permitted the English couple to return home. When they reached Calais they discovered just how unpopular they had become. They were barricaded in their lodgings by a furious, stone-throwing mob. If that made them uneasy, they were, naturally, much more concerned about the reception they would receive from Henry. They need not have feared. The king, having decided to back his sister and his friend, did so in style, leaving their enemies in no doubt where his favour lay. Henry came as far as Barking with his court to greet the couple and he ordered a fresh wedding ceremony to be held at Greenwich in May, when he personally gave his sister away.

Whatever the front Henry put up, there was no disguising the fact that he was singularly irritated by the turn the international situation was taking. Francis was not satisfied with the renewed Anglo-French treaty. He was about to march for Italy to renew the combat with Spain for control of the peninsula and he was determined to bolt and bar his back door. He secured the neutrality of Prince Charles with a new treaty and then turned his attention to Scotland. The politics of that country were rent by pro-French and pro-English factions. In the previous summer, Margaret had tried to strengthen her position by marrying the young Earl of Angus. In fact, this only united opposition to her rule. She was challenged for the regency by John Stewart, Duke of Albany, who was the heir presumptive, currently in exile in France. While the Tudor court was celebrating the nuptials of Henry's younger sister in May 1515, news arrived that Francis had sent Albany to Scotland to make trouble and deflect the king of England from any continental ambitions he might be harbouring. The council in Edinburgh stripped Margaret of the regency and awarded it to Albany. In September, Margaret fled across the border. Hard on the heels of this news came information about Francis I: the young king had confronted Swiss and Milanese troops at Marignano and won a famous victory.

For Henry, the military and diplomatic triumphs of the French king were as bitter as gall. Once again he had been bested by someone posing as his ally. This time it was not a seasoned monarch who had got the better of him. It was the 'new kid on the block', a fresh force in European politics, a younger man and one who, like Henry himself, set much store by chivalric display. Henry felt personally affronted. He had been scarcely seven years on the throne, yet the world seemed to have changed drastically in those years. Perhaps Henry had now grown up and been forced to realize that public affairs, at home and abroad, were more complex than the stories in Mallory's *Le Morte Darthur*.

# Chapter 4

## WAGING PEACE

The years 1516–21 were ones of frustration and mounting anxiety for Henry. His two major interests were, as ever, securing the dynasty and securing his own place as a lead player in Europe. Dark shadows fell across both and refused to be dispelled. The international scene changed with the deaths of Ferdinand of Spain (1516) and the Emperor Maximilian (1519). Continental affairs came to be dominated by the clash of Francis I and the Emperor Charles V (elected in 1519), both charismatic leaders younger than Henry and both more intent on their own rivalry than on accommodating the wishes and ambitions of the King of England. By the end of this period, Queen Catherine was virtually past child-bearing, had not done her duty of providing her husband with a prince and had ceased to be physically attractive to him. As he entered his thirties – that phase of life when many men look to see some fruit from the tree of their hopes and plans – Henry felt himself hemmed in by fate. Good Catholic that he was, he tried to prise blessings from the hands of an inexplicably reluctant God by entering the theological fray against a heretic monk who was proving pestilential to the church. Here, too, he ran into problems. Not only did Martin Luther refuse to be cowed, his opinions began to make headway among some of Henry's brightest subjects.

The king, angry at being outwitted by Francis, was eager to continue the war. In theory, further military action would have been popular; most Englishmen were still francophobes. In fact, the council and the taxpaying public were not enthusiastic for more expensive adventures. This left Wolsey in the position of having to gratify Henry's militancy while avoiding the cost of another full-blown campaign. Some historians have suggested that king and minister were at odds over foreign policy during this difficult period. They certainly saw things from different perspectives. Henry's concern remained what it always had been – establishing himself as a major arbiter in the affairs of Europe. Wolsey was now, by virtue of his cardinalate, not just a royal servant but a senior figure in the western church and therefore obliged to take a wider view. His new building at Hampton Court provided ample evidence of his identification with other princes of the church universal. The country palace created for him beside the Thames by Italian craftsmen brought in for the purpose was a little bit of Italy in England. With its symmetrical layout, internal cloister and its terracotta images of classical heroes, it was modelled closely on the kind of lavish Renaissance palazzos built by his colleagues in Rome and Florence. When critics protested at Wolsey's pomp, it was this alien magnificence they had in mind. Not only did it speak of worldly power and wealth which were at odds with his holy calling; it also seemed to set him above temporal rulers:

> By the mass we had high authority,
> In heaven and earth taking our pleasure.
> Kings and princes for all their dignity,
> To displease us feared out of measure.[46]

Henry, as we have seen, did not (for the time being) share this common conception of ecclesiastical exhibitionism. He regarded his minister's extravagant display as an extension of his own. Wolsey was his cardinal. Indeed, he persuaded the pope to appoint the cardinal as a *legate a latere* in 1518. Theoretically, this empowered Wolsey to speak with the authority of Rome but what Henry intended was the opposite; he wanted Wolsey's ecclesiastical eminence to give papal sanction to his policies. There was certainly a tension inherent in Wolsey's position but it did not amount to a clash of loyalties. His own preference in 1516 was for peace but he would pursue war – until such time as he could convince his master of the value of ending hostilities. Somehow, he had to find a way of keeping Henry in a central position on the diplomatic stage without the military presence which would give his role some substance. If Wolsey could pull that off it would be a very neat trick.

In his international negotiations Wolsey was playing from a poor hand against very canny opponents. The situation called for reliable intelligence, careful analysis of a rapidly changing situation and the ability to adjust tactics accordingly. The policy he embarked on in 1516 was to get other people to fight the French. He financed military activity in north Italy by Maximilian and his Swiss allies and promised that Henry would once again invade France from the north. However, the emperor was a very slippery customer who was eager to pocket English gold but less enthusiastic about meeting his obligations. In fact, while supposedly prosecuting the war, he was carrying on clandestine negotiations with the enemy, but Henry and Wolsey had been here before and they were not to be fooled again. They informed their agent in Switzerland, Richard Pace, that there would be no English contingent sent across the Channel. Interestingly, though, Pace was ordered to persuade the mercenary leaders (for a fee) to write to Henry saying that it was they who wished to abort the enterprise. No one, especially Francis, should be encouraged to suspect that the English king had chickened out of the war.

The situation on the continent called for great flexibility. It would be a mistake to look for any foreign policy plan on the part of king and minister. Their objectives remained clear but their actions, viewed in historical retrospect, appear inconsistent. Take, for example, Henry's pursuit of the imperial crown. The title of Holy Roman Emperor was conveyed by the electoral college of German princes upon a prominent royal of their choice. As early as 1513, Maximilian had offered to adopt Henry as his successor. If Henry was flattered by the suggestion he certainly did not show it. His councillors probably pointed out that the emperor did not have the final say in the matter and was merely trying to extract money from England in return for his good offices. Certainly, at the time the offer was made, Henry was a young man full of self confidence who had no need of extra titles to enhance his standing. He regarded himself as an emperor in his own dominion and was about to add France to his possessions. For all that, Maximilian thought it worthwhile to keep the possibility alive. He repeated the offer in 1516, 1517 and 1518. Perhaps his spies told him that Henry's rejection was not absolute; that, like Julius Caesar, he was thrice offered a crown and put it by, 'but for all that. . .he would fain have had it'. Such an assumption is offered credence by Henry's behaviour after Maximilian's death. Then, when the electoral college was already assembling in Frankfurt, he despatched Pace on a hectic round of German capitals canvassing votes. Either Henry had seriously decided to throw his hat in the ring or he was trying to draw support away from the two front-runners, Charles and Francis, in order to prevent either of them being elected. Either way, the campaign was badly handled and Charles of Spain became the new emperor, thereby creating an awesomely mighty empire comprising Spain, Burgundy, the Netherlands and the possessions of the Austrian Habsburgs, as well as extensive colonial territories in the New World.

A similar story can be told of Henry's interest in a crusade against the Turks. In 1517, Pope Leo X floated the idea of a grand, united Christian enterprise for the recovery of Constantinople. In part he was motivated by a desire to divert the Valois and Habsburg rulers from their clashing ambitions in Italy. Neither Maximilian nor Francis was interested. Nor was Henry. Constantinople was too far away to be of any concern to him; the fish he had to fry were to be found in home waters. Then, in the immediate aftermath of the imperial election, he dictated to the pope a long letter expressing his avid enthusiasm for the holy cause. He promised a royal army of 35,000, plus private contingents provided by the pious nobility of England. He even hinted that he might lead the expedition himself. The king was taking this bold initiative, he declared, in the hope that his brother monarchs would follow. Nothing came of this valiant offer and, perhaps, Henry never really thought that it would. However, even if that is the case, should we dismiss his uncharacteristically detailed and zealous epistle as a piece of cynical flimflam?

It was just one manoeuvre in a long-running campaign which was, in itself, but one aspect of Henry's marathon contest to achieve equality with his continental counterparts. He was not interested in spilling English blood and gold for the pope, hence his cool reception to earlier appeals for a crusade, but he was interested in the prestige it was in Leo's power to impart. Titles were immensely important in political and diplomatic circles and the pope alone had the authority to bestow hereditary titles which resounded throughout Christendom. Maximilian was, of course, 'Holy Roman Emperor', Ferdinand had been accorded the soubriquet 'Catholic King' and Louis XII was permitted to call himself 'Most Christian King'. It was a matter of the utmost importance to Henry to join this 'holy club'. In 1512, when the French king fell out with Julius II, English agents at Rome had petitioned for his title to be removed and conveyed to Henry. Thereafter, it became their constant objective to obtain an equivalent honour for their master. 'Orthodox' and 'King Apostolic' were just two of the titles which were suggested – and which failed to find favour. The problem was essentially

the same as that which the English king had to face in all his
foreign policy: he was not important enough. For all his show-
manship and military posturing, he was a lower-league player
trying to gain promotion to the top flight. Rome was not in the
business of dishing out empty titles. Accolades had to be
earned. Habsburg and Valois monarchs had the power to
perform real services for the church – usually military or
financial – but what could Henry do? It was a question the
Curia had every reason to ask – and did ask. For the moment,
there was no very convincing answer.

A kind of schizophrenia governed the relationships of all the
princes of Christian Europe with the holy see, and Henry was
not the exception to this rule. On the one hand they were the
servants of God's representative on earth. On the other, they
were, themselves, divine appointees charged with the spiritual
oversight of their subjects. National and dynastic interests
could clash with their allegiance to Rome. Thus, for example,
both Louis and Ferdinand had achieved virtual control over
senior ecclesiastical appointments within their dominions.
However, the potential for conflict ran at a deeper level.
Church reform was in the air, canvassed by a wide spectrum of
activists including radical bishops, scholars of the New
Learning and out-and-out heretics. Protestors railed against
corruption in the Vatican centre of the church, the worldliness
of prelates such as Wolsey and the venality governing ecclesiastical appointments. The lecherous monk and the money-
grubbing parish priest were stock figures of fun and had been
for as long as anyone could remember. It would probably be an
exaggeration to speak of a groundswell of anticlericalism but
every time a scandal involving the clergy hit the 'headlines' it
encouraged a 'them-and-us' prejudice among the laity. One
such scandal had hit London in 1514 and its reverberations
long continued. A prominent merchant, Richard Hunne, had
fallen foul of his parish priest and threatened to bring him to
court. Before he had a chance to do so the Bishop of London
arrested Hunne on suspicion of heresy. When the merchant

was found hanged in his cell the City was up in arms. A coroner's jury accused the bishop's chancellor of murder. There were demonstrations in the streets, questions in Parliament and Henry personally presided over a council meeting at which the matter was discussed. The bishop appealed to Wolsey and ecclesiastical ranks closed. There was a cover-up which, of course, ensured that the case would not be forgotten. At a higher level, as we have seen, there were demands for a general council of the church. Reform was in the air. It was part of the tenor of the times. It could not be permanently ignored.

Where did Henry stand in all this? To find a strong clue we need to fast-forward twenty years. As we have seen, in 1536, the king commissioned his court painter, Hans Holbein, to create a mural for the privy chamber of his new palace of Whitehall, which depicted Henry, his current wife, Jane Seymour, and his parents, Henry VII and Elizabeth of York. The figures were arranged around a plinth bearing a Latin inscription eulogizing the achievements of the first two Tudors and inviting the beholder to compare the merits of father and son. Henry VII was lauded for reducing the barons to order and creating internal peace. However, the son was declared to be the greater of the two, because he, 'banished from the altars undeserving men and replaced them with men of worth. Presumptuous popes were forced to yield before him and when Henry VIII bore the sceptre true religion was established and, in his reign, God's teachings received their rightful reverence.'[47] This was the nearest Henry ever came to writing his own obituary and it is revealing to see what he wanted to be most remembered for. Not his military exploits. Not his diplomatic achievements. Henry staked his claim to a place in history as a religious reformer.

Henry was religious. He did not simply use Christian theology and sentiment to wrap his selfish policies in shiny but bogus sincerity. Whenever he embarked upon a course of action he believed that it was right (or he persuaded himself that it was right, which amounts to the same thing.). Exactly what he believed in terms of religious dogma changed with the passage of time and was individualistic but we can detect three strands in his religious thought. The liturgical routines established in childhood stuck with him. Probably the earliest example of his signature in existence is on a prayer roll which he gave to a certain William Thomas and which bears the written inscription, 'I pray you pray for me your loving master Prince Henry'. The illuminated scrolls of which this is an example served as both practical aids to devotion and relics. They carried religious images and written prayers and were designed to fit into a purse. William Thomas would have been able to use this gift to recite the orisons but its very presence on his person acted as a charm, protecting him from evil and assuring him of heavenly reward. The coming together of word and image was something comparatively new in lay devotion, a trend reinforced by the advent of printing. While orthodox piety was stimulated by it, so also was the habit of reading about the faith and this could be a threat to traditional belief because it opened people's minds to divergent possibilities. Henry regarded himself as a conventional Christian insofar as he subscribed to the basic tenets of Catholic doctrine and maintained a strict, though variable, regimen of orthodox devotion. No day passed in which he did not hear mass, sometimes three or more times. Yet, although not an ardent reader, he also spent time with books and liked to think of himself as something of a theologian.

The second strand was a genuine, if desultory, interest in the New Learning. The beginning of the reign had coincided with an intellectual revolution. In fact, we can say that the combination of the arrival of a new, young king and the publication of a remarkable book in 1509 together created a buzz of excitement throughout the academic world. The book was *The Praise of Folly* and its author was Desiderius Erasmus. The arrival in England of the man who had become the doyen of the scholarly world was, in itself, something of a coup for the radical intellectual minority. When he went to Cambridge in 1511 his lecture hall was crammed, but it was *The Praise of Folly* which started an unquenchable fire. This instant bestseller which satirized all sorts and conditions of men soon had its readers chuckling – but also nodding sagely about the author's analysis of what was wrong with society and the urgent need for reform. Erasmus' devotees, the circle commonly known as Christian humanists, included Thomas More (soon to enter royal service), John Colet, Dean of St Paul's, the diplomat Richard Pace, Cuthbert Tunstall (later Bishop of Durham and a royal councillor) and several young academics and lawyers en route for careers in the service of the crown. They saw themselves as men with a mission:

> More and Erasmus and many of their friends were full of the excitement of new discovery – the discovery, they believed, of a method of understanding the message of Christianity and the life and teaching of their Lord Jesus far superior to the method current in their own day. Into a world gone stale and sour they hoped they could bring a sense of the good and true, which would freshen and sweeten it.[48]

Their reforming programme entailed ridding the body ecclesiastic of various diseases: obscurantism in the universities, ineffectiveness of the clergy, corruption in high places and erroneous doctrine. Central to this programme was the Bible; not the traditional Vulgate, set forth by St Jerome 1,100 years before, but a purified version based on fresh insights into the original Hebrew and Greek texts. In 1516 Erasmus provided the preachers of a revivified religion with an essential basic tool, *Novum Instrumentum*, a new version of the Greek New Testament. Not even Erasmus appreciated that the Bible is a subversive book. It sets forth an interiorized religion and challenges every human institution. Some of the first Christian humanists, More among them, were horrified to see the cat they had let out of the bag. The authority of the church was brought into question when traditional doctrines and practices were exposed as incompatible with Scripture, and the humanists could not stop the movement they had helped to start. From the universities and the inns of court the new ideas rippled outwards, picking up as they went the flotsam of anticlericalism and earlier native heresy.

The king could not remain insulated from the current of criticism and affective religion flowing through the English church. His court steadily filled with bright young men who had been brought up on the educational principles now in fashion. He followed the career of Erasmus, albeit at a distance, and accepted the scholar's principle that reform would only be achieved if it was sponsored by the leaders of secular society.

However, his attitude towards the need for royal action in church affairs does bring us to the third, and basic, element in Henry's religious makeup: his conviction that he had authority over the English church. What exactly that meant was not clear. The king was bound by his coronation oath (and, indeed, by Magna Carta) to maintain 'the laws, customs and liberties granted to the clergy and people'. 'Clergy and people' were two separate estates whose ultimate allegiance was a matter of debate. While the laity was answerable for its actions in the royal courts, men in any of the seven grades of holy orders had their cases heard at ecclesiastical tribunals (an arrangement known as benefit of clergy). The laity was bound by both common law and (in matters such as matrimony and inheritance) canon law. Bishops as well as civil authorities had the power to detain suspects in prison. When verdicts reached in church courts required action against the persons or goods of offenders (for example, in heresy cases) secular authorities were expected to carry out the prescribed sentences without further enquiry. Any appellant with the necessary determination and money to take his case to the highest authority might find himself, according to the alleged offence, having to plead before judges appointed by the king or the pope. These overlapping systems resulted in frequent clashes but, in the early years of the reign, it was in no one's interest to press the issue of church-state relations to the ultimate.

Just how pragmatism and compromise held sway is well illustrated by the outcome of the Richard Hunne case. The House of Commons was up in arms at the way the religious establishment was protecting its own. They claimed that the trial of the bishop's chancellor in the episcopal court was an abuse of benefit of clergy. The issue reached a wider audience when the Abbot of Winchcombe denounced the MP's protest in a blistering sermon at St Paul's Cross. Henry was sufficiently alarmed by this clash of secular and religious lawmakers to order a public debate to clear the air and appointed one of his spiritual advisers, Henry Standish, to argue the case for the trial of suspected heretics in royal courts. Tempers flared and Standish was actually threatened with investigation for heresy before Convocation, the church assembly. Henry defended his champion. He told Standish's accusers that 'the kings of England in times past have never had any superior but God alone.' However, he judiciously avoided a contest which would have put this claim to the test. He ordered Hunne to be tried in King's Bench – and acquitted. In return Convocation dropped its action against Standish. In such ways was a fundamental constitutional and religious issue fudged – for the time being.

The wider problem of church reform continued to fester like a wound that refused to heal. Every informed observer knew that something had to be done. More and more people were agitating for it. The church itself could not or would not do it. So who would? Many people throughout Europe were asking each other that question. Then, in October 1517, a professor of theology in a new university in an obscure north German city raised doubts about the validity of indulgences – relief for souls in purgatory issued in return for acts of devotion or, much more commonly, cash payments to the church. Martin Luther's superiors refused the debate he had called for. Instead, they accused him of heretical presumption in daring to question an established practice which was currently being enthusiastically

promoted by Pope Leo X (who urgently needed money, ostensibly for the rebuilding of St Peter's basilica in Rome). The
renegade monk was ordered to recant. He refused. Since
Luther based his arguments on the Bible, the indulgences
question rapidly turned into an issue of authority: God's
earthly representative versus God's written word. This was the
spark, the catalyst, the starting pistol which incipient
reformism had been waiting for.

Within two years a little local difficulty had become a
Europe-wide *cause célèbre*. Luther staunchly defended his
original *Ninety-Five Theses* against indulgences and, within
months, his challenge was being read in academic centres everywhere. We know that Thomas More had a copy by March 1518.
He was appalled by what he read and repented of his earlier
advocacy of radical theology. Others were excited, even intoxi-
cated by Luther's bold assertion of a different kind of Christian
faith. What he offered them in the works which now poured
from his pen was a well-argued intellectual schema for building
personal faith as opposed to institutionalized religion. Now
critics of clerical abuse realized that they had scriptural support
for challenging oppressive or corrupt ecclesiastical regimes.
Small wonder that the demand for Lutheran books had become
so great by the early 1520s that German merchants were
importing them by the shipload, even when they ran the risk of
having their cargoes confiscated on the orders of the bishops.

Henry VIII, who was always interested in theological
debate, personally entered the fray in 1521 (see below) but for
the time being he had other things on his mind – or, rather, he
was still governed by his main preoccupations of the
succession and his standing in Europe. In January 1516, Queen
Catherine had, for the first time, given birth to a baby which
actually survived the critical early months. That was the good
news. The bad news was that the child was a girl. The royal
couple were relieved that the long succession of miscarriages
and infant deaths seemed to have come to an end and their
hope that they might yet be blessed with a son was quickened.

However, it was another two-and-a-half years before Catherine knew that she was pregnant again. In November 1518 she gave birth to another girl who died after a few days. A few months later Henry did have a son. Christened Henry Fitzroy, the boy was brought into the world by Henry's established mistress, Elizabeth Blount. This birth, of which Henry was inordinately proud, reassured him that he was able to sire male children. Deficiencies in this area were generally assumed to be the fault of wives and the appearance of little Fitzroy seemed to confirm Henry's conviction that the fault lay not with him, but with Catherine.

However, the truth was not that simple. The possibility of Henry suffering from some congenital sexual malfunction has often been mooted. Whether or not he experienced physical difficulties from the beginning, it is obvious that, as time passed, mounting anxiety over the absence of a male heir inevitably created psychological pressure and this may, in turn, have had physiological manifestations. He got his first wife with child seven or eight times in nine years but, in the five years that Elizabeth Blount was his mistress, she only bore him the one son. The only other adulterous attachment he is known to have formed – to Mary Carey (née Boleyn) – resulted in no bastards. After 1519, when he was only twenty-seven, he sired only two more children and, in the 1530s, the hushed rumour circulated in court circles that the king was 'no good in bed'. About the same time, Henry took to sporting enormously exaggerated cod pieces, which must be seen as a defiant assertion of his virility. Every time he searched for a new wife he insisted that she should excite his passion. This was unusual in an age when kings tended to regard sex with their wives as duty and with their mistresses as pleasure. So, what can we say with any certainty about the king's love-life? Sifting out the truth from circumstantial evidence is difficult. If Henry was a poor sexual performer it would be the last thing he would admit to and the only people able to comment – his wives – would have done so at their peril.

Unfortunately, it is very important that we should try to understand this aspect of his life. It is not mere prurience. When Henry made his long and tortuous marital pilgrimage he took the country with him and the consequences were profound. By the time he was middle-aged, Henry was suffering from an impotence that was, at least, sporadic. I believe that he had always lacked a strong sex drive. He covered up this weakness with male braggadocio. Unable to accept that he was responsible for his marital problems, he blamed his wives. It was this denial of his own inadequacy which drove him, with growing desperation, to find marriage partners who sufficiently stimulated him. And we should not ignore the spiritual and moral struggle that he went through. He was conventionally devout, which means that he believed in the sanctity of marriage. His dalliances were for the most part chivalric rather than carnal, flirtations rather than full-blown affairs. He was very far from being the horny stud portrayed in later fiction. It was precisely because he took marriage seriously that he agonized in prayer over the non-appearance of a male heir. Convinced that he was not to blame, he automatically held Catherine responsible but, as time passed, he began to ask himself whether the real culprits were those who had arranged his union with his brother's widow – his father, his father-in-law and the pope. Could this be what God was trying to tell him? After Catherine's disastrous last confinement in 1518 the couple rapidly grew further apart. She was no longer the fiery Spanish beauty Henry had married. She was shapeless and, according to one diplomat, 'rather ugly than otherwise'. No amount of wishful thinking could now cast her in the role of Guinevere to Henry's Arthur. With the souring of royal relations something of the spontaneity and joy went out of court life.

Yet there were still things to celebrate with appropriate panache and spectacle. In August 1518, Wolsey pulled off his greatest diplomatic coup. If he could not present his master to the world as a champion resplendent with military trophies, he would cast him as a beatific mediator garlanded with the laurels of peace. In achieving this he was doing no more than making a virtue of necessity but, nevertheless, it required diplomatic endeavours of Trojan intensity. Early in 1517 Henry's allies, Charles and Maximilian, entered into peace negotiations with Francis which left the English king high and dry. Wolsey's agents on the spot assured him that nothing could be done to break the resultant Treaty of Noyon but the cardinal persevered doggedly. He was playing for high stakes. If he failed, not only would England be relegated to the ranks of a second-rate power but his own position would be in jeopardy, for his enemies in court and council would be sure to take advantage of the fact. On the other hand, if he succeeded the prize would be universal peace (a desirable thing in itself) and the placing of England and its king at the heart of Europe.

With the concentration and forward planning of a chess master, Wolsey gathered his intelligence and calculated his moves. On examination, the situation could be seen to offer some possibilities for profitable English intervention. The seventeen-year-old Charles of Burgundy had been obliged to accept somewhat humiliating terms from Francis because he was unable to continue hostilities. It was imperative that he travel to Spain to take possession of his inheritance and that would mean leaving his Netherlands territories vulnerable to French attack. The young man might be open to offers of assistance from his Uncle Henry. Then there was the fact that the king did now have a bargaining counter in the person of little Princess Mary. In terms of the succession she was a disappointment but her person could be bartered on the marriage market. Thirdly, there was the pope. If Leo X wanted his crusade it would have to be preceded by an outbreak of universal peace in Europe. To achieve that he would need the services of an honest broker and Wolsey could think of no one better suited for that role than himself. Finally, there was Tournai. Francis wanted it back and it was of no earthly use to Henry. The time had come to turn it into cash.

Throughout much of 1517 and 1518, despite suffering recurring bouts of serious illness, Wolsey organized a series of diplomatic meetings. He and Henry both pulled out all the stops to impress the diplomats who came to London. The king showed off his skills in the tiltyard and gave a demonstration of horsemanship which left the audience gasping. The Venetian ambassador, Sebastian Giustinian, reported that Henry seemed to make his horse 'fly rather than leap'. The English promised to aid Charles in his difficult task of stamping his authority on his disparate territorial inheritance and to sell Tournai back to France for 600,000 crowns. Amity between the two nations was sealed by the betrothal of Princess Mary to the infant dauphin. These were only the main planks of what came to be known as the Treaty of London, for the wider negotiations embraced all the principal nations of Europe (the papacy, England, France, Spain, the Empire, Portugal, Denmark, Scotland, Hungary, the Swiss republics and the German Hanse towns) in a non-aggression pact, a uniquely impressive diplomatic feat, and all based on the ending of the old animosity between France and England.

This impressive festival of Christian brotherhood culminated in five days of lavish celebrations in October 1518. On Sunday the 3rd, Henry, his court and all the ambassadors with their trains assembled at Durham Place, halfway along the Strand, and processed in gaudy splendour along the Strand and Fleet Street via Ludgate to St Paul's for a solemn mass. It was celebrated outdoors on a raised platform, 'that the king and the ambassadors might be seen'.[49] Richard Pace delivered a speech on the blessings of peace, after which Wolsey presided at the mass and the treaty was signed at the high altar. As the day faded the procession made its way to Westminster where the cardinal hosted a banquet which, according to the Venetian ambassador, outdid any party which might, in ancient time, have been thrown by Cleopatra or Caligula. After the feasting, bowls filled with ducats and dice were brought out 'for such as liked to gamble'. Then, there was dancing until midnight.

Tuesday witnessed another set of solemnities and festivities at Greenwich. The proxy marriage of the French and English infants was celebrated. There followed entertainments of such variety and magnificence as to draw more breathless prose from Giustinian. They were, he reported, 'of such a sort as are rarely seen in England'. Allegorical scenes were presented involving elaborate 'conceits' created from wood, canvas and paint. To the applauding throng a triumphal car was revealed on which stood a castle set upon a rock in which was a cave. From it there emanated the sound of music. Dimly glimpsed within were nine 'goddesses' bearing candles. Set about the rock were five trees representing the pope, the emperor and the kings of England, France and Spain. This placed Henry firmly on a par with his brother monarchs. The audience was allowed time to work out the meaning of the elaborate symbolism of these and other elements of the pageant before a rider on a winged horse rode forward to explain that the beautiful and firm rock represented peace, whereon the greatest rulers of the world rejoiced to take up their abode. At this point actors dressed as Turks came out to challenge the pacific intentions of the Christian princes. This led to a tourney in which, we may presume, the Muslim infidels were vanquished. Then came the presentation by Henry of costly gifts to members of the French delegation, before the assembly gave itself up to dancing into the small hours. There followed two days of thrills and spills in the tiltyard before the guests all made their way home, having, presumably, been dazzled by spectacle and stirred by high-sounding rhetoric. Wolsey received plaudits from all: 'I. . .told him that he could do nothing more glorious in the world. . .than in the midst of great strife amongst princes to prove himself that corner stone which joined the two detached walls of the temple [France and England].'[50] Cardinal Wolsey was careful to reflect the glory on to his master and Henry, the showman, revelled in being the centre of universal attention.

However, despite the glitzy celebrations of peace, the two issues which threatened it – international rivalry and Lutheranism

– had not gone away. As we have already seen, none of the signatories of the Treaty of London was interested in a crusade, which had been the ostensible reason for it, and they soon had other things to think about. Within three months, Maximilian died, sparking off rivalry for the imperial title. The success of Charles radically changed the balance of power. His territories now encircled those of Francis I. Countering this was the Anglo-French alliance which potentially closed the Dover-Calais straits to commerce between Spain and the Netherlands. For the next couple of years Henry and Wolsey maintained their pose as peace brokers and conducted important summit meetings with Francis and Charles. Yet, they ended up by invading France again in 1522. Before we try to unravel the tangled diplomatic cords which produced the resumption of hostilities, we need to consider the more important events which were taking place in the religious life of Europe.

Leo X and his minions were quick to discover that Professor Martin Luther of Wittenberg University was no ordinary heretic. He was dogged in his opinions, determined in his refusal to abandon them and unflinching in holding to the further revelations that came to him from Scripture. The more he studied, the more discrepancies he discovered between the beliefs and customs of the first-century church and those emanating from contemporary Rome. In October 1520 he published his most outspoken diatribe to date, *A First Trumpet Blast Against the Babylonian Captivity of the Church*. It attacked the sacramental system on which the power of the priesthood was based by reducing the number of sacraments from seven to three. Out went non-biblical ordinances – extreme unction, marriage, confirmation and ordination – and the doctrinal basis of the mass was savaged. Luther rejected the 'magical' claims of the priesthood to 'make God' on the altar and the philosophical theory of transubstantiation which purported to explain this miracle. Six months later he was summoned to appear before the emperor and the imperial Diet at Worms. He had already been condemned by the leading

church authorities. It remained only for him to be outlawed by
the secular power as a prelude to his arrest and inevitable immo-
lation by fire. The story of the confrontation at Worms between
this one man and the assembled might of church and state was
soon spreading throughout Europe. Sympathizers repeated
Luther's defiance, 'Unless I am convicted by Scripture and plain
reason. . .I cannot and will not recant anything.' Soon they
added the embellishment which has rung down the centuries:
'Here I stand; I can do no other. God help me. Amen!' Whether
villain or hero, Luther became, in 1521, the most famous man in
Europe.

Henry VIII was as outraged as any other orthodox Catholic
by the German's blasphemous effrontery but the *Babylonian
Captivity* offered him an opportunity to pursue his political
objectives. In the Treaty of London he had paraded himself as
the champion of Christian unity. He had assured the pope of
his ardent desire to play a lead role in a crusade. Subsequently,
he had gone cold on that idea. Now, without going to great
expense, he could grasp the initiative once more. He would,
himself, enter the lists of the theological tiltyard and vanquish
this upstart monk. This would earn him the applause of all
orthodox Europe and, if Wolsey handled the PR efficiently, it
would induce the pope to convey on him the title he had so
long coveted. It was Wolsey who induced the king to embark
on this holy project. He presented Henry with a copy of
Luther's book, perhaps carefully annotated, early in 1521. He
knew that Henry had earlier toyed with the idea of publishing
something against the *Ninety-Five Theses* but his enthusiasm
had run into the sand after a few pages, as was usually the case
with anything that demanded from his young master any
degree of mental application. This time, however, Henry's
imagination was captured by the new project. Doubtless
Wolsey suggested that the king could be 'assisted' by some of
the leading theological brains in the country and the resulting
work was definitely a team effort, though we cannot know
how much of it came out of the king's own head. By April 1521

he had started work on what would emerge as *Assertio Septem Sacramentorum* (*Defence of the Seven Sacraments*). The English controversialists were much encouraged at the end of the month when news reached them from Germany. Charles, in the first test of his leadership in this part of his empire, had not made an impressive showing. While all the pope's agents bayed for blood and expected the emperor to clap the heretic in prison, he had sent Luther back to Saxony under a safe conduct, where he was protected by his sovereign, the Elector Frederick. Charles had shown himself to be more concerned about offending some of the influential German princes than in defending the unity of Christendom. From that moment, Germany began to divide along confessional lines.

It was the ideal opportunity for Henry to show that England was one kingdom where heterodoxy would not be tolerated. On 12 May, Wolsey went in procession to St Paul's, accompanied by a retinue of clergy and courtiers, as well as most of the diplomatic corps. In the churchyard, where they were joined by a large crowd of citizens, the aged Bishop Fisher of Rochester preached for two hours against Luther's opinions. Then a bonfire was made of Luther's books and Wolsey announced that the king would be personally venturing into print against the heretic. The promised book was published in July with a dedication to Leo X, who was presented with a copy bound in gold. A string of letters to Rome had kept the Curia informed of every move made in England to stamp out the insidious ideas infiltrating from Germany and, in October, Henry received his reward: a papal bull bestowing the title, *Defensor Fidei*. Meanwhile copies of the *Assertio* had been sent to several foreign capitals so that all Christian rulers would be 'bound to this good and virtuous prince for the vehement zeal he beareth unto the church'.[51]

In a letter to the pope Henry wrote, 'Nothing is more the duty of a Christian prince than to preserve the Christian religion against its enemies.'[52] He probably believed it with one level of his mind but he was more concerned with the practicalities of international power politics. The apparent ardour of their official anti-heresy response should not deceive us into thinking that Henry or Wolsey really grasped the fact that the Lutheran threat was more important than the clash of dynastic ambitions. The holy unity to which they appealed was no more than a burnished coating on a vessel that was rusting away beneath the surface. Habsburg-Valois rivalry was too corrosive to be expunged by appeals to Christian brotherhood. The princes of Europe were no more prepared to sink their differences to present a united front against internal heresy than they were to join together in a crusade against the infidel. For Francis and Charles, the Treaty of London was no more than a truce; a respite allowing them to gather their forces for the next round of warfare. Over the next two years both wooed Henry in the hope of enlisting his support against the other. It is to Henry's credit that he honestly tried to keep the peace with both of his powerful neighbours.

During the treaty negotiations of 1518 the English, French and Spanish representatives had decided that their achievement would be crowned by personal meetings of their respective monarchs. Preoccupation with the imperial election in 1519 delayed the arrangements for this summitry and it was not until the following year that elaborate preparations were set in hand for what would become known to history as the Field of Cloth of Gold, which, according to contemporary opinion, was either the eighth wonder of the world or a wasteful Renaissance folly of mammoth proportions.

However, before we probe the intricacies of this diplomatic spectacular, we should direct our gaze to the domestic scene and the significant events taking place at the Tudor court in the immediate years leading up to it. Wolsey's power rested on a 'three-legged stool'. One leg was his efficiency in carrying out the work of government. The second was his skill in persuading the king that his own policies and the royal will were as one. The third was manipulating the personnel of the court so that no one could undermine the king's confidence in his minister.

Perhaps a better metaphor would be that of likening the
cardinal to a juggler keeping three balls in the air, for maintaining his position called for skilful coordination. The
dramatic events of 1517 showed both how vulnerable Wolsey
was and how adroit he was in handling rapidly changing events.
In June, a devastating disease made its first appearance of the
reign. The sweating sickness, or 'English sweat', was, in its way,
more terrifying than the plague. It struck suddenly, seemingly
indiscriminately, reached its usually fatal climax within hours
and appeared to favour the wealthier members of society. The
symptoms, which bear some similarities to influenza, were,
according to one contemporary, 'a great sweating and stinking,
with redness of the face and body and a continued thirst, with a
great heat and headache because of the fumes and venoms'.[53]
The 1517 outbreak carried off between a third and a half of the
population in the worst hit towns (including Oxford and
Cambridge). More important politically, it decimated the royal
court, where it was observed that a healthy, energetic lady or
gentleman dancing at nine o'clock could be dead by eleven.
Wolsey himself was one of the sweat's first victims. He survived
a bout in June but had to endure two further attacks before the
epidemic finally subsided in December. Henry's reaction to the
disease was one of very reasonable panic. He fled to Windsor
and when members of his entourage continued to drop like flies
he moved to another royal residence – and kept on moving.

This was inevitably disruptive of the business of
government. It was essential to the pattern established by
Wolsey that there should be regular meetings between king and
minister and that no one should be allowed to interpose
himself between the two men who ran the country. This was no
longer possible. The most influential men at court were now
those who attended him daily and they gave Wolsey serious
cause for concern. Since the campaigns of 1512–13, death and
promotion had changed the personnel of the privy chamber.
Some of the king's earlier companions had been replaced by
younger men. They still performed the same functions in the

chamber, the hunting field, the banqueting hall and the tiltyard but they were different – brash, arrogant, callow youths, scarcely out of their teens. By encouraging and sharing in the exploits of this swaggering gang who called themselves the king's 'minions', Henry clung to his athletic youth. Their company was more immediately congenial than that of his older councillors and even his middle-aged wife. They, much encouraged by their older relatives among the nobility, intruded more and more into political affairs and began to usurp the role of councillors.

Wolsey's first response was to place his own trusted agents at court. They had to be men of intellectual ability and personal charm able to outface the minions. Richard Pace, churchman and seasoned diplomat, and Thomas More, accomplished lawyer and author, were admirably suited to the roles Wolsey now designed for them. Pace had enjoyed the position of royal secretary for some months but had been abroad. On his return he was lodged at court with instructions to take care of all Henry's correspondence. More, though officially appointed to deal with poor men's pleas discussed in council and referred to the king for endorsement, was, in effect, joint secretary and the cardinal's eyes and ears. What they reported back confirmed Wolsey's suspicions about the minions. They were monopolizing Henry's time and attention, distracting him from the serious concerns of government and creating an atmosphere of unseemly frivolity. Pace grumbled that the king was so obsessed with hunting as to convert what ought to be a pleasurable pastime into a 'martyrdom'. Inevitably, there were tensions at court between the boisterous young men of the privy chamber and those more concerned with royal gravitas. The minions did not always win clashes between the factions. Early in 1518, Sir Nicholas Carew, a great favourite of Henry's, was banished from court. His return in March drew the sour comment from Pace, 'too soon, after mine opinion'.

Negotiations for the peace treaty brought the French and English courts close together for the first time in living memory. In the autumn of 1518, as part of the 'twinning' exercise, the minions were invited to Paris where Francis I went to great lengths to impress them with both the sophistication and the freedom of his court. It was all part of a Valois strategy to influence Henry through his close companions. Among the entertainments laid on for his guests were drunken carousings through the city streets, pelting passers-by with eggs and stones, led by the king himself. It was all a great adolescent lark and the immature young men were completely won over by their French holiday. They returned as ardent Francophiles, flaunting their fashionable clothes and manners and singing the latest Parisian songs. The fact that their elders were almost to a man contemptuous of the 'frogs' added spice to their little rebellion. As an outraged chronicler recorded, 'they were all French, in eating, drinking and apparel, yea and in French vices and brags. So that all the estates of England were by them laughed at. The ladies and gentlemen were dispraised, so that nothing by them was praised but if it were after the French turn.'[54]

It might be thought that this would suit Wolsey's policy of rapprochement but nothing could be further from the truth. He saw through Francis's attempt at backdoor diplomacy. He intended to maintain freedom of manoeuvre in his relations with France and the Empire and was not going allow his policy to be circumvented by the French king. He had the whole council and much of the court (including Queen Catherine) behind him in protesting about the antics of the minions. As a result they were despatched for a few months to Calais, where they soon had the silliness knocked out of them by residents who had a better understanding of their French neighbours and their motives. By the time the minions returned in the summer of 1519, the staff of the privy chamber had been augmented by four older men, who were also members of the council. This sequence of events provides yet another example of the importance of personal relationships to any understanding of Henry VIII and his policies. Great events could and sometimes did depend on an idea spoken or a joke shared in the intimate confines of the privy chamber.

For us the affair of the minions has a significance which is out of proportion to its immediate importance. It acts as a probing light on to the development of Henry's character and also on to the atmosphere in the court. It shows us that Henry was no longer simply the fun-loving extrovert who lived for pleasure and was obsessed with the glamour of kingship. Nor was he yet the tyrant whose will no one dared question, whose desire no one dared thwart. Such a king would not have allowed his young favourites to be sent away from court. His was a personality in transition. As he approached the age of thirty the vagaries of fate were chipping away at his confidence and optimism. His first ten years as king had not yielded the glorious conquests he had expected. He had not been able to fulfil that most basic of royal responsibilities – securing the dynasty. In international affairs he found himself in competition with two other young, ambitious monarchs who possessed greater resources. And his own treasury was emptying rapidly, as his ministers pointed out to him. Beyond the comfortable confines of the court all was not well nationally, as even Henry was aware. There was little sign now of the euphoria which had greeted his accession. Price inflation, that mysterious economic disease which baffled sixteenth-century financiers, had begun to infiltrate the mercantile and agricultural arteries of the kingdom. Grain prices doubled between 1509 and 1519. Harvests were disastrously bad in 1519, 1520 and 1521. Householders struggling to make ends meet did not respond enthusiastically to demands for taxes to pay for Henry's foreign wars. At the same time, ominous cracks were appearing in the two main pillars of the monarchy. The great aristocratic families were resentful of Wolsey's power and the church was under unprecedented attack from heretics.

It is hardly surprising that Henry found it difficult to understand and, therefore to cope with, the complexities of domestic and foreign policy. Strains and tensions, changes and challenges were multiplying. It took a man of industry and intellect like Wolsey to keep abreast of all aspects of government, and even Wolsey made mistakes. For years Henry had been content to leave the political and diplomatic minutiae in the cardinal's capable hands but now he began to feel that he ought to take a more personal interest in what was going on. There was a new seriousness in his demeanour which showed itself in several ways. We have already noted his flirting with the idea of going on crusade and the hitherto uncharacteristic application he brought to his written attack on Luther. He now enjoyed the company of scholars. Thomas More's biographer has left a vivid picture of the relationship between the king and his secretary. In his *Life of Sir Thomas More,* William Roper describes many occasions on which the king kept More up until late at night discussing subjects as varied as astronomy, theology and diplomacy. Together they would stand on the palace roof gazing at the stars or wander the corridors and gardens, with Henry's arm round his servant's shoulder, deep in conversation.

More had been in two minds about responding to the summons to court. One of the 'big questions' raised in *Utopia* was whether a philosopher should become involved in politics, which inevitably had a corrupting influence. He evidently decided that as an adviser to the king he might be able to contribute wise and restraining counsels. In these years Henry showed himself not only willing but eager to listen to sage advice. No longer was he complicit in the system Wolsey had installed which separated him from his council and left him dependent on the cardinal and the intermediaries who reported directly to the cardinal. He decided that he wanted his own itinerant council which would be on hand and instantly available to discuss whatever agenda he wished to set. It was partly to satisfy this requirement that Wolsey attached the four senior members (known as 'knights of the body in the privy chamber') to the royal household. However, such organizational changes, which might have resulted in a system of hands-on, chamber

government, were always vulnerable to being undermined by
the two men who were responsible for them. The problem with
Henry was that the spirit was willing but the flesh weak. He was
simply incapable of settling down to a routine of government
that involved daily – or, at least, regular – meetings with
household officers and councillors. Wolsey also was lukewarm
about the king's greater involvement. He was quite happy with
the existing arrangement which located him securely at the
centre of the political web. That was why, while providing
Henry with his own conciliar staff, the cardinal ensured that
they were answerable to him. What finally emerged from the
administrative changes of 1518–19 was no-change or, rather, it
was the old system but with new, built-in uncertainties.

The affair of the minions helps us to see the extent to which
rivalry and suspicion had come to stalk the chambers and
antechambers of the royal household. It astounded people that
Wolsey's rule extended to the very heart of Henry's entourage.
The minister's unpopularity with the aristocracy was growing
year on year and some of it was rubbing off on the king.
Members of the political class frequently discussed the relationship between monarch and minister. Skelton suggested
that Wolsey's usurping of royal prerogative must be due to
some kind of necromancy:

> It is a wondrous case
> That the king's grace
> Is towards him so minded
> And so far blinded
> That he cannot perceive
> How he doth him deceive.
> I doubt, lest by sorcery
> Or such other rascality
> As witchcraft or charming.[55]

However, the only spells involved were concocted in Henry's
unconscious. They convinced him that he was in control
because he wished to be so convinced. Wolsey simply went

along with the king's self-deception. Yet the cardinal did have
to watch his back at all times. He relied on his appointees to
spy on members of the court and he even came to question the
loyalty of his own protégés. By 1521, for example, he had come
to believe that Richard Pace was trying to undermine him and
he had the secretary sent on embassy to Rome. Henry, too, had
to be watchful lest the jealousy and ambition of frustrated
nobles should turn into treason. In 1520 he sent a secret,
personally handwritten note to Wolsey:

> To this that followeth I thought not best to make [the
> messenger] privy, nor none other but you and I, which is that I
> would you should make good watch on the Duke of Suffolk, on
> the Duke of Buckingham, on my Lord of Northumberland, on
> my Lord of Derby, on my Lord of Wiltshire and on others
> which you think suspect.[56]

Paranoia is seldom absent from the corridors of power and
it certainly had secure lodging in the court of Henry VIII.
Whatever the reason for Henry's anxiety on this occasion, it
was not mollified until blood had been spilled. The choleric
Edward Stafford, Duke of Buckingham, would have been
hard put to it to say which he hated more – France, the old
enemy, or Cardinal Wolsey, the new upstart – so the prospect
of peace with Francis I engineered by the cardinal was more
than enough to push him beyond the very narrow limit of his
patience. The two men clashed often at court, and at least
once in the king's presence. At a banquet Henry was handed a
bowl to wash his greasy fingers. Immediately afterwards
Wolsey took the vessel to clean his own hands. This
presumption was too much for Buckingham to endure. He
grabbed the bowl and threw it at Wolsey. This proud peer,
descended from Edward III and linked with most of
England's noble houses, spoke for many when he grumbled
about the king's minister, but he allowed his unbridled tongue
to run away with him in angry criticism of the king himself.
According to evidence gathered by Wolsey, he denounced

Henry as unfit to rule, declared himself willing to assassinate him and boasted that any rebellion would have the support of most of his brother peers. On 13 May 1521, Buckingham was tried for treason. On the 17 May, he was beheaded on Tower Hill. Such events indicate the atmosphere which pervaded the English court as preparations were made for the stupendous meeting between Henry VIII and Francis I in a field between Guines and Ardres.

By the time the postponed Anglo-French summit meeting finally came about in the summer of 1520 both the emperor and the French king were already making their plans for resumed hostilities and both were anxious to gain either the English king's support or his neutrality. This provided Henry and Wolsey with two alternative strategies: they could maintain their stance as the peacemakers of Europe or they could play the rival nations off against each other to secure maximum advantage for England. As they made their preparations throughout the early months of the year they had not decided which course to adopt; they were keeping their options open. Historians have debated whether the grandiose celebration of friendship at the Field of Cloth of Gold was a genuine endeavour to sustain the peace and concord established by the Treaty of London or an elaborate cynical camouflage to disguise hostile intent. It seems to me that, as far as Henry was concerned, it was both. He was committed to the ideal of peace throughout Christendom but he was also still encumbered by the Arthurian baggage of the warrior-king. He had to decide which would most enhance his image – peacemaking or warmongering. Only this dilemma can explain why he made a hugely expensive and showy demonstration of amity towards Francis at the same time that he was inclining towards an anti-French agreement with Charles.

When the emperor heard that Europe's impresario, Thomas Wolsey, was actively engaged in preparations for an Anglo-French summit in May 1520 he was determined to get in first and made arrangements to visit England. A serious rebellion in

Spain was threatening the unity of his empire and was also encouraging Francis to reopen hostilities. He needed England's support and was ready to promise almost anything to gain it. Queen Catherine was eager to meet her nephew and also to scupper her husband's accord with Francis. She begged Henry to invite Charles. He agreed and negotiated a further slight delay in his departure for France but he insisted on informing Francis and assuring him that the proposed meeting was a family affair and that only commercial matters would be discussed. He was keeping everything open and above board – just about. Charles duly arrived but it was a close run thing. Henry had set 26 May as the last day he could reasonably wait. The emperor's embarkation was delayed by contrary winds and Henry was already at Sandwich, preparing to cross the Channel, when a messenger hurried into his presence announcing his nephew's arrival. Had the emperor been delayed any longer the diplomatic results might have been very different. The two monarchs rode to Canterbury for three days of feasting and dancing while Wolsey fretted over the impact of the delay on his complex logistics.

For the Anglo-French spectacular over the Channel, 5,000 English men and women and almost 3,000 horses had to be transported, fed, housed and decked in suitably resplendent costume for the diplomatic encounter. The flower of English aristocracy was in attendance, as were most of the senior clergy and each county provided representative gentry to swell the English ranks. For everyone participating, it was a horren-dously expensive exercise. Estates were mortgaged, manors sold and loans negotiated so that the leaders of English society could acquire clothes, tournament armour and equipment. Most of them did so willingly, eager to be seen as men of substance loyal to the crown. One valuable side effect of this whole enterprise was the reinforcement of the ties which bound the rulers of the shires to central government. The gaily-accoutred company met up with their French counterparts on a dusty, wind-swept plain within the pale of Calais where carpenters, bricklayers, glaziers, painters, tent-makers and engineers had spent months creating a fairyland setting of pavilions and prefabricated palaces. The effect was somewhat spoiled by the weather, which was wet and windy by turns, but this did not seriously disrupt the programme which centred on intense competition in everything from martial feats in the tiltyard to culinary extravaganzas on the banqueting tables, elaborate 'disguisings', exchangings of costly gifts and intricate musical mass settings. There was little in the way of serious discussion because there was little to discuss. This gathering was in essence only the fancy wrapping to the Treaty of London. The two kings congratulated themselves on having made peace and pledged eternal friendship. After two-and-a-half weeks the royal parties went their separate ways and the work of dismantling the camp site began.

Henry rode to Gravelines for further talks with Charles and then returned with him to Calais in order to conclude their conference. Again, there was nothing underhand about these sessions. Henry had told Francis that he had arranged to report to the emperor on the outcome of the Anglo-French meeting. Once again, Charles tried unsuccessfully to detach his uncle from the French alliance. Henry reminded the emperor that by the terms of the Treaty of London he was obliged to come to the aid of whichever major power was attacked by the other. However, beneath the surface niceties of diplomacy the tectonic plates of French and imperial interests were already grinding against each other. The very tents and pavilions which Francis' workmen were dismantling outside Ardres were being shipped south for use on his next projected campaign. Charles was fully aware that the French king was awaiting his moment to strike. At the same time Pope Leo had abandoned his irenic stance and was urging Charles to join him in a drive against French interests in north Italy, but the emperor was preoccupied for most of the next year with the troubled situations in Spain and Germany. He needed time to pacify his own domains before he could gather his forces to face an external threat. This was why he desperately needed an alliance with England. In Henry's court the prevailing mood was still one of incipient franco-phobia, encouraged by the queen, the imperial ambassador and several members of the nobility and supported by the mercantile community who were dependent on the textile trade with Flanders. However, the king and his minister were still feeling the bruises inflicted during their previous military involvements in Habsburg-Valois rivalry. They were not about to rush into another war.

Then, in the spring of 1521, Francis attacked Navarre and a pro-French sortie was launched by the Duke of Bouillon, a military freelance, against imperial Luxemburg. Neither invasion was successful but that did not matter; France's intentions had become clear. There followed weeks of frantic diplomatic exchanges. Charles prepared to strike back. Wolsey was despatched by Henry on a final attempt to keep the dogs of war on the leash. He went to Calais and there summoned French and imperial diplomats to discuss a peaceful resolution to their differences. However, a fall-back position had already been decided on. Should it prove impossible to secure a truce there was to be no question of the English delegation slinking home having failed totally in their mission. Henry would, under these circumstances, throw in his lot with Charles. Wolsey travelled on to Bruges and there, on 25 August, a secret Anglo-imperial treaty was signed. It was agreed that England would declare war on France the following May and that a joint invasion would be launched in May 1523. Amity between the two nations would be sealed by a marriage contract between the emperor and Princess Mary. For his part, Charles undertook to divide the territorial spoils of victory with Henry and to put his weight behind Wolsey's candidature at the next papal election. These were future undertakings and anything might happen before the parties were called upon to honour them. Henry was delighted with what Wolsey had achieved. In a congratulatory letter he conceded that he could not have done better himself.

John Skelton summarized the diplomatic toings and froings of these years with his usual acerbity:

There hath been much excess
With banqueting brainless,
With rioting reckless,
With display thriftless,
With spend and waste witless,
Treating of truce restless,
Prating for peace peaceless,
The arguing at Calais
Hit us in our purses.[57]

Many of the poet's fellow countrymen shared his frustration but, then, they knew little about the tortuous reality of diplomacy. What Henry and his minister had done, against all the odds, was keep England at the centre of European affairs. When pitted against its powerful neighbours, Henry's kingdom could never win a war but it had just won the peace. Unfortunately, it was now heading for war again.

# Chapter 5

## 'ALL PEOPLE CURSED...'

The 1520s was the decade in which everything changed. As England's Harry journeyed through his thirties he saw his dreams fade and his ambitions unravel. Even his basic assumptions came to be questioned. All this happened at a time when Harry's England was confronted by ideas which challenged age-hallowed traditions and the beliefs that undergirded them. However, this intellectual and spiritual shift was not, strictly speaking, brought about by the advent of Protestantism.

There was no such thing as Protestantism in Henry VIII's England. The word 'Protestant' originally applied to a group of German princes who, in 1529, protested against the pope's reaffirmation of the ban pronounced against Luther's adherents at the Diet of Worms. It only entered common English parlance in the 1550s to describe people who rejected the pope's doctrinal authority.

This is not just a piece of quibbling over semantics. Something was happening in the 1520s – something immensely powerful – and we shall not understand it if we get our terms of reference wrong. We have become accustomed to think of the English Reformation as the process by which England changed from a Catholic to a Protestant country. This basic assumption has led historians to try to evaluate the various contributions to that change – humanism, Lutheranism, Lollardism (see below), religious radicalism, anticlericalism, etc – but those 'isms' are simply labels we put on various manifestations of religious experience to help us understand spiritual realities which were much more profound and complex. The real conflicts which became increasingly fierce throughout the 1520s and 1530s were between Religious Commitment, Religious Conformity and Scepticism (I use capitals to help us identify the contenders clearly.) Under the heading of Religious Commitment I include people who found a deep personal faith either in the traditional teachings of the church or in the new ideas which were in circulation. Religious Conformity embraces all those (the majority) who went along with the status quo as well as those leaders in church and state who were determined to maintain the status quo. Scepticism includes people who were critical of the prevailing religious establishment and/or the doctrines undergirding that establishment. Inevitably, these categories overlapped to some extent. Thus, for example, Erasmus could pillory the professionally religious whose morals contradicted the faith they professed, while being appalled at the extremism of enthusiasts who threatened to overturn the established order of things. It would probably be true to say that most English men and women were content for the clergy to 'do' their religion for them while, at the same time, grumbling about paying tithes and expressing outrage at events such as the Hunne case, which showed the clergy to be above the law. In the 1520s, something happened which focused aspirations, discontents and personal rivalries in a new way.

Evangelion (that we call the gospel) is a Greek word; and signifieth good, merry, glad and joyful tidings, that maketh a man's heart glad, and maketh him sing, dance and leap for joy. . .Now can the wretched man (that [is] in sin and danger to death and hell) hear no more joyous a thing, than such glad and comfortable tidings of Christ; so that he cannot but be glad, and laugh from the low bottom of his heart, if he believe that the tidings are true.[58]

The words quoted above from the introduction to William Tyndale's translation of the New Testament (1525) identify for us the explosive ingredient which was dropped into English society in this crucial decade. I use the word 'crucial' advisedly. We think rightly of the 1530s as the era which produced the English Reformation but the legislative and religious innovations which came later were the results of changed lives, emancipated lives, and lives which, to use C.S. Lewis's phrase, had become 'surprised by joy' in the 1520s. They were developments which did not wait for the permission of Martin Luther to happen. Since, for ease of discussion, we need a label for this movement, it is more accurate to call it 'evangelicalism' and it emerged from what we must still call Catholicism.

As Tyndale explained, the *evangel* is the Christian gospel, as set out in the church's foundation document, the Bible. Many of those who had, over the centuries, discovered it, had found the encounter life-changing, just as Tyndale described. It was a fourteenth-century archbishop, later a candidate for canonization, who wrote:

I used to think that I had penetrated to the depths of Your Truth with the citizens of Your Heaven; until You, the Solid Truth, shone upon me in your Scriptures, scattering the cloud of my error, and showing me how I was croaking in the marshes with the toads and frogs.[59]

Over the centuries many mystics and independent-minded students had come to the same conclusion. Thomas à Kempis, whose *The Imitation of Christ* by this time had already gone through more than fifty imprints since its publication in 1486, had urged the genuine seeker after holiness to study the plain word of scripture and to read each part 'with the same spirit wherewith it was written'.[60] However, for the vast majority of theology students simple truth had become encrusted with centuries of dogma and the intricacies of university teaching methods (scholasticism). As a result, theology had been stood on its head. Instead of being used as a tool to help people understand the Bible, the Bible had come to be regarded as a bundle of proof texts to support 'orthodox' doctrine. It was this that Erasmus and the Christian humanists rebelled against. They took their stand – as, indeed, did Luther – on 'scripture and plain reason' and believed – as, indeed, did Luther – that once the Bible was freed from the shackles of obscure allegorical interpretation it would transform society. They were absolutely right.

What neither they, nor Luther, bargained for was the power of the exuberant, emotional reaction of people who responded to the *evangel*. Tyndale said that the experience of 'conversion' might well make a man 'sing, dance and leap for joy' and there is no reason to doubt that he was writing from personal experience. What the gospel 'tidings' offered the eager, anxious, devout or troubled soul was assurance and certainty, something that the church's penitential system could never provide. The parish priest or confessor could direct his spiritual charges along the pathway of contrition but he could not promise them entrance to heaven or intimate how long might be their passage through purgatory. The plain word of scripture, on the other hand, taught seekers that they could trust completely in the finished work of Christ. This was heady stuff.

It may be difficult for a secular age to comprehend how intoxicating this revelation was to our sixteenth-century ancestors. They had been taught that this world was but the testing ground for eternity. Most of them took seriously their obligation to live well and to die well – and to aid with their prayers and worldly goods their loved ones who had preceded them into the greater reality. Now, at a stroke, the burden of indulgences, pilgrimages, penances and the whole paraphernalia of ritual religion was lifted. Such, at least, was the logical conclusion of the evangelical way of salvation. Certainly, in the 1520s, there were few who reached, or were ready to acknowledge, that logical conclusion. The gospel way of faith was open only to those who could read the Bible (or who had it read to them by ardent 'gospellers'), whether in Erasmus' Latin or in a smuggled vernacular text. Of that minority there was only a small percentage again who desired or were courageous enough to stand up and be counted, to challenge openly that orthodoxy to which their neighbours subscribed. However, it takes only one match to start a forest fire and the zeal of some early converts was enough to create a real problem for church authorities. Within a decade, that faith which dared not speak its name was being embraced by some of the highest in the land and the parliament of England had begun to cut the country adrift from western Christendom. It is this incipient spiritual and intellectual revolution which provides the background to the next ten years of the reign of Henry VIII. The king never understood it but he was quite prepared to try to harness it for his own purposes.

The career of William Tyndale during this period provides some kind of a template for what was happening in the world of thinking men. In 1520 he was about twenty-seven, a bright intellectual just concluding his studies at Cambridge. He had earlier taken his master's degree at Magdalen Hall, Oxford, which, as well as being the institution where Thomas Wolsey had spent his formative years, was also the most 'advanced' college in the university, committed to the principles of the New Learning. Tyndale became a disciple of the modern approach to religion and went on to Cambridge, which was even more radical. He would have been too late to hear Erasmus lecture but the great humanist's wit and erudition had left a radiant afterglow. Students and lecturers still repeated the barbs he had launched against banal religious externals and his Latin version of the New Testament was required reading. Its impact on Tyndale was profound and, like Erasmus, he too longed for the time when the sacred text might be available in English, so that, 'the farmer might sing snatches of Scripture at his plough, that the weaver might hum phrases of Scripture to the tune of his shuttle, that the traveller might lighten with stories from Scripture the weariness of his journey'.

Having left the university and taken holy orders, Tyndale went in search of a patron in his native Gloucestershire. This brought him to the household of Sir John Walsh of Old Sodbury, where he earned a modest living as a tutor to Walsh's sons and as a chantry priest who prayed for the souls of Walsh's deceased parents. He also picked up the odd fee for preaching in the neighbourhood. In other words, he slipped into the traditional role of an educated chaplain, who augmented the ranks of the local clergy and, presumably, waited hopefully to be offered a benefice. He gained something of a reputation as a proclaimer of novel, unorthodox opinions but there is no evidence that he was regarded by local church leaders as anything other than a precocious young man come fresh from the university with his head full of the latest fashionable notions. When he fell foul of the bishop's chancellor he received no more than a severe dressing down. To his backbiting critics he said he would be perfectly happy if 'they should bring him into any country in all England, giving him ten pounds a year to live with, and binding him to no more but to teach children and to preach'. Here was no firebrand revolutionary.

However, Tyndale was growing steadily more frustrated with both the ignorance of the ordinary people and the stubborn sophistries of the ecclesiastical establishment, as he later recorded:

I perceived how that it was impossible to establish the laypeople in any truth, except the Scripture were plainly laid before their eyes in their mother tongue, that they might see the process, order and meaning of the text. For else, whatsoever truth is taught them, these enemies of all truth quench it again, partly. . .with apparent reasons of sophistry and traditions of their own making, founded without ground of Scripture; and partly in juggling with the text, expounding it in such sense as is impossible to gather of the text.[61]

Tyndale decided to undertake, himself, the translation of Erasmus' *Novum Instrumentum*. He knew, of course, that reactionary elements would oppose him but he believed that the ecclesiastical top brass would support so obviously bene- ficial an undertaking or, at least, that they would not mount a determined campaign against it. He knew that he would need the help of someone more influential than his Gloucestershire patron for, according to existing law, no Bible translation was permissible without episcopal warrant. So, in the summer of 1523, he set out for London armed with a letter of introduction to Sir Henry Guildford, Henry's master of the horse. The courtier passed him on to Cuthbert Tunstall, Bishop of London. Tunstall was a noted humanist scholar and Tyndale had high hopes of a sympathetic hearing for his enterprise, but the bishop turned him away on the, probably sincere, grounds that he had no vacancies in his entourage. The scholar now found himself in the capital among evangelicals of a very different stamp. Members of the merchant community were in contact with their German counterparts; men familiar not only with Luther's writings, but with the white-hot controversy raging over them on the continent. They brought the clash of ideas to London, where others who had come into direct contact with the New Testament through Erasmus' translation or fragments circulating in underground Lollard cells were excited by what they read. Controversy was soon raging within elite circles. Lawyers, university and inns of court students, radical priests and friars, courtiers chasing intel- lectual fashion and people who liked to consider themselves avant-garde argued in the taverns, read the diatribes published by both sides and listened to sermons pro or anti the new ideas. The capital and parts of the Home Counties were, by 1525, in the grip of what later centuries would recognize as evangelical revivalism. For the individual, 'the sense of undergoing a profound change, of experiencing a "conversion", and of being able to rationalise and, to some extent, systematise that expe- rience, was a profoundly important aspect of a new religious and social existence'.[62] Those who did not or did not wish to share that experience found ardent evangelical preaching aggravating. Those responsible for the peaceful ordering of church and state saw it as a potential threat.

There were two interconnected reasons why the establishment felt threatened by the Bible and the people of the Bible. For the leaders of the church it was inconceivable that the truth revealed to saints and doctors over fifteen centuries could be at variance with the truth as revealed in the sacred foundation document. Conservative theologians were angry with Erasmus for producing a fresh Latin version which differed from the Vulgate text of St Jerome. Archbishop Lee of York took Erasmus to task and airily pointed out that wherever his text varied from Jerome's it was he and not the fourth-to-fifth-century saint who was in error. As for allowing ordinary laymen access to the Bible, such an idea was anathema. Holy writ was complex and only theologians who had devoted years of patient study to it could begin to understand it. Part of the priesthood's role was mediating God's word to the people in forms shaped by ecclesiastical tradition. The church operated a two-tier spirituality; it was for the clergy to understand the faith and for the laity simply to believe what they were told. It was when the people stepped out of their role as passive pupils that alarm bells rang. Several years earlier, Thomas More had mused that society could only go seriously awry:

When an hatter will go smatter
In philosophy,
Or a peddler wax a meddler
In theology.[63]

In 1519, when Erasmus was being attacked by Archbishop Lee, More had sprung to his friend's defence but before seven summers had passed he had become an ecclesiastical bloodhound, energetically sniffing out caches of forbidden books and bringing their owners into court.

More parted company with some of his radical humanist friends because he saw with a greater clarity the second reason why laypeople should be kept well away from the Bible. If folk were free to read and interpret the word of God for themselves this had the potential to undermine the entire fabric of society. Christendom was a divinely ordered, hierarchic cosmos, in which every person had his or her place. It was a pale reflection of the kingdom of heaven. Thus, for example, just as an English petitioner might approach a courtier to lay his case before the king, so he might call upon one of the saints who gathered in God's audience chamber to be his 'especial good lord'. Anything that challenged the theoretical basis of this society attacked the pillars which supported the elegant fan tracery and the polychromed oriels of the Gothic world. It was certainly heresy and, quite possibly, treason. Once the uneducated man was encouraged to play the scholar and the layman to play the priest, it could not be long before subjects would usurp the roles of kings and popes.

It is a remarkable fact that England was alone among major European states in outlawing vernacular scriptures. In France, Germany, Italy, Spain and the Netherlands printed versions of the whole or parts of the Bible were in circulation and had been since the previous century. Church authorities were not everywhere happy to encourage laypeople to read the holy text for themselves but they mounted no concerted campaign to prevent them. This may have been because most translations were from the Vulgate and contained no obnoxious glosses. It may also represent a certain pragmatism on the part of the bishops, who might well have reasoned that any attempt to forbid Bible reading would only drive the activity underground. The tradition of lay devotion, based on the contemplation of Scripture, had its roots back in the centuries before printing when Bibles, psalters and gospels were expensive and could only be owned by the wealthier (and, therefore, more responsible) members of society. What had been encouraged in earlier generations was tolerated now that the holy text was more widely available. So why were English ecclesiastics so twitchy about vernacular scriptures? Largely because they had, long since, come to be connected with a 'pernicious' religious cult.

In the late fourteenth century, those who followed the teaching of the condemned heretic, John Wycliffe, had made and circulated their own biblical translations. These 'Lollards' (the derogatory word is of uncertain origin) had never been more than a minority but they had stubbornly refused to be exterminated. They tended to marry within the faith, set up households where fellow believers could gather for instruction, were expert at concealing their banned books and operated colportage networks throughout much of south-east England. Since the Inquisition did not exist on the western side of the English Channel, control of heresy was in the hands of the bishops, who often had better things to do than initiate and maintain persecution. Clampdowns on heresy were sporadic, sometimes half-hearted and could result in popular demonstrations against episcopal officers. Therefore, English authorities were particularly sensitive to Bible translation and heresy which, in their minds, were inextricably woven together.

In London Tyndale came to the attention of Humphrey Monmouth, a well-to-do draper who gave the newcomer board and lodging and introduced him to his own underground network of radical thinkers. Monmouth was not a Lutheran nor, he would later insist, any kind of heretic but he did have contact with local Lollards and foreign, unorthodox believers. He was, probably, no more than what we might call a freethinker. He supported his parish church and he had even made a pilgrimage to Rome. Others among the 'evangelical brethren', a very loose association of religious radicals, were less reticent. Scripture taught that it was not enough for the believer to enjoy his faith in secret; he was obliged to 'go into all the world and proclaim the Gospel'. By bold preaching and personal proselytizing the brethren sought to spread their convictions. To aid them in this process they needed a good supply of English

Bibles. Monmouth and some of his colleagues agreed to finance Tyndale and, through their international contacts, to enable him to do the translation in a safe European haven and see it through the printing process. In 1525 he set off for Cologne but, within months, had to move on when the print shop was raided. It was, therefore, the city of Worms which, for the second time, gained an important place in the evangelical story. Here Tyndale produced that masterpiece of English literature which was to be formative in all English Bible translations, the 1526 New Testament. The evangelical brethren did their work well and soon thousands of copies, smuggled in cloth bales and wine casks, were in circulation.

The only word to describe the reaction of the religious authorities is 'panic'. The Archbishop of Canterbury called upon all his colleagues to contribute to a fund for buying up and destroying every New Testament translation that could be found. Tunstall organized a bonfire of several hundred books containing 'that pestiferous and most pernicious poison'. With all the militant zeal of modern drug-squad officers, officials raided homes and put people on trial for dealing or possession. With the hysterical frenzy of McCarthyite witch-hunters, they denounced with ringing pulpit rhetoric the 'seditious' and 'unpatriotic' activities of those who made ideological war on Christendom. They pointed to Germany, where, in 1524–5, the savage Peasants' War was raging, as proof that rejection of church teaching led to anarchy. Secret agents were sent to the continent to track down Tyndale and other religious refugees. The slanderous word was put about that the translator had gone to Wittenberg to become Luther's disciple. The urbane Thomas More turned savage persecutor, embarking on a series of polemical books against Luther and Tyndale, raiding the London premises of the German merchant community and personally arranging the arrest and interrogation of suspected heretics. By the end of the decade, England was well on its way to the most severe, nationwide campaign of religious persecution in its history to date.

At this stage few men and women paid the ultimate price for their beliefs but there were burnings and the authorities made sure that they were given maximum publicity. Many more suspects were arrested, grilled, forced to recant or locked up so that they could not infect others with their heresy. The vast majority abjured under pressure and went in public procession, 'bearing their faggot', as a sign of the worse fate – death by fire – they had narrowly escaped. By no means all of the king's subjects who were so troubled were Lutherans and many had never had sight of Tyndale's masterpiece. What was happening was that the growing awareness of new ideas and the mounting criticism of the papal church were subtly changing the prevailing mood. Scepticism and intellectual rebellion, long harboured in secret, were coming into the open. For example, John Simonds was examined by the Bishop of Lincoln for saying that he did not believe in purgatory and that, in his opinion, priests should be free to marry (a heresy to which he had converted several clergy of his acquaintance!).[64] John Ryburn, caught up in the same persecution, was accused of being infected with Lutheranism for declaring that 'what the priest doth hold above his head [at mass] is but bread and if you cast it to the mouse it will eat it'.[65] However, Luther never rejected the miracle of the altar. Canny countrymen did not need the permission of a foreign reformer to assert what to them seemed to be plain common sense. Disaffection was most pronounced in London and the southern and eastern counties. Elsewhere, the majority of people continued with their age-old religious practices. However, it was the capital and its environs that really mattered, for this was the hub of the nation's social, commercial and political life. And at its centre lay the royal court.

In November 1528, a certain Richard Foster was among those who 'bore his faggot'. He seems to have been lucky to have got away with his religious rebellion, for this was not the first time he had been in trouble. The previous year he had been accused of expressing opinions 'more extreme than the Lutherans'. Foster stood in danger of the full rigour of the law.

Might it have been his important connections that saved him? This religious radical was a yeoman usher at court and in frequent attendance on the king, but there were others still closer to Henry whose religious orthodoxy was in doubt. Tyndale, still in hiding in the Low Countries, continued to publish and, in 1528, he sent to the press *The Obedience of a Christian Man*. This little treatise for the first time linked the authority of Scripture and the authority of kings over church and state. Someone at court thought that Henry would find the arguments of Tyndale's book helpful in resolving his own current problems. That 'someone' was Anne Boleyn.

No woman has made a greater impact on the history of England than Anne Boleyn. There are elements of her tragic story which have always carried a touch of mystery. Those elements cluster round her rejection and death but it may be that we can penetrate that enigma rather better if we understand more about the beginnings of her relationship with the king. She arrived on the scene when Henry was at a particularly low ebb. He was approaching the halfway point of his three score years and ten and had very little to show for it. He had seen his hopes dashed in foreign policy. He had been humiliated by his own people. He had no male heir and no prospect of siring one. He was trapped in a loveless marriage. He was beginning to put on weight and his body was telling him that he was no longer young. Henry, the extrovert who was always driven to compete – against tiltyard rivals, against other monarchs, against the accomplishments of his father – found himself in the lists against fate. And losing. He was not prepared to admit it – least of all to himself.

First of all, let us pick up the story of his foreign adventures. In August 1521 Henry had decisively thrown in his lot with his nephew, Charles V. The following summer the emperor paid another visit to England to ratify the anti-French agreement reached by the ambassadors. Like all summitry, this was an exercise of rivalry cloaked in effusive expressions of friendship. London welcomed the two monarchs with lavish pageants, lovingly described by the chronicler, Edward Hall. All along the processional route a clear message was delivered over and over again:

> The citizens well apparelled stood within rails set on the left side of the streets and the clergy on the right side in rich copes, which censed the princes as they passed and all the streets were richly hanged with cloths of gold, silver, velvet and arras. . .and in every street were these two verses written. . .

> Long prosperity to Charles and Henry,
> Princes most puissant.
> The one of faith, the other of the Church
> Chosen defendant.[66]

(It is ironical that the two rulers who prided themselves on being the champions of the Catholic church within a few years turned savagely upon it.) Henry pulled out all the stops to impress his guest with the extravagance of his hospitality. Charles capped this by putting on display some of the spectacular Aztec treasures recently sent home by the conquistador, Hernán Cortés.

Yet, as with the Field of Cloth of Gold, the dazzling, gilded amity was the beautiful wrapping of an empty box. There was personal goodwill between the principals, industriously fostered by Queen Catherine, but their ambitions could not coexist. Each monarch wanted to extract maximum profit from the downfall of France and wanted to use the other to achieve that end; each was prepared to make extravagant promises to involve the other in a war of aggression, grandiosely referred to as the 'Great Enterprise'; and each was conscious of the exorbitant cost such a war would entail. In the haggling that went on at Windsor in mid-June 1522 Henry managed to obtain a postponement of the English invasion until 1524 but he was obliged to make his departing guest a loan of £30,000. In his turn, the king had to look to his people for the money. Their reaction was cool and might have warned a less thick-skinned monarch that he should not regard his country as a milch cow to which he could take his pail whenever he wished.

> The king about this very time sent to the city of London to borrow £20,000, which sore chafed the citizens, but the sum was promised and for the payment the mayor sent for none but for men of substance. Howbeit, the crafts sold much of their plate. This sum was paid and the king sent his letter promising [re]payment of the same and so did the cardinal. The poor men were contented with this payment and said, 'Let the rich churls pay, for they may well.' Like loan was practised throughout all the realm and privy seals delivered for the repayment of the same.[67]

The cold truth was that England simply could not afford the grandiose plans Henry was making on its behalf. He was not entirely oblivious to the problem and Wolsey was certainly very sensitive about the difficulties of raising war finance. Furthermore, both men were cautious about Charles' intentions. They had had their fingers burned more than once in Habsburg alliances. So, while Charles fretted over the non-appearance of English troops which should have been diverting Francis of France from the southern theatres of war, his allies watched the situation closely, determined not to move until they could see clear advantage in doing so. Then, in the summer of 1523, something happened that brought out the old bellicose, eternally-optimistic Henry. The duc de Bourbon, France's premier nobleman and Constable of France, rose in revolt against his liege lord. He looked to Francis' enemies for support and he was not disappointed. All Henry's glory dreams were revived. Once more he saw himself entering Paris to reclaim his heritage. This was not quite the way Charles regarded the situation. He had no intention of replacing one troublesome northern neighbour with another. The deal he hammered out with Bourbon said nothing about crowning Henry as King of France. However, the emperor gave his uncle sufficient encouragement to ensure his military intervention and, by the end of August, the Duke of Suffolk was in Calais at the head of a fresh, 10,000-strong army. Daily, the king waited eagerly for the latest news from the front. It was not encouraging.

Everything started so well. Wolsey had talked Henry into abandoning the original scheme, which was for a long and, inevitably, costly siege of Boulogne. Instead, Charles Brandon was ordered to strike straight for Paris. After two months he was within 50 miles (80km) of the capital. Then everything went pear-shaped. The strategy of invasion at the end of the campaign season depended on England's allies doing their stuff. The armies of Charles and Bourbon were to move up from the south and Suffolk's army was to be reinforced from the Netherlands. None of this happened. Charles was more concerned about securing his Pyrenean frontier and bothered about the war in northern Italy. Having regained Fuenterrabia, he halted his march. Bourbon's revolt crumbled. The aid promised by Margaret of Burgundy simply did not materialize. Once again, an English army on the continent was left high and dry to face the vagaries of nature. The weather turned depressingly cold, then even more depressingly wet. Floundering in mud, Suffolk's men could neither advance, nor dig in comfortably for the winter. Despite royal urgings from the comfort of the court, the English force dribbled back to Calais.

For several months Henry was in denial. Messengers passed back and forth between the allies with plans for the resumption of the campaign in the next season. Wolsey did his best to damp down the war frenzy, preferring to follow the lead of the new pope, Clement VII, who was trying to broker a peace between the main combatants. That said, Henry's passion for pouring more men and gold into the restoration of his French empire was also waning. The king craved glory – as long as he could have it on the cheap. Wolsey told Richard Pace that he would only go again to war if there was a real prospect that he might 'facilely, without any great resistance' regain his inheritance. Disillusionment with his allies was bringing Henry into line with his cost-conscious cardinal and Wolsey went on to outline a host of reasons for not resuming military action in 1524:

> Treasure would thereby be wasted and the French gain encouragement. Besides Picardy is barren of victuals and forage and there is great scarcity in Flanders. . .A shoulder of mutton is sold in Valenciennes for 12d. Fl. The Lady Margaret has informed the king that she cannot assist his army and therefore all provisions must necessarily come from England, which alone is sufficient impediment to prevent the expedition. Even if a mean army of 10,000 men were sent over it would be useless, as the French king would be sure to carry away all the provisions in the country through which it would pass. . .It is better to save treasure for [an invasion in 1525] and merely to [sustain] Bourbon for this year.[68]

Everything came down to money in the end and there was, according to Hall, considerable resentment at the government bankrolling Bourbon. If there had to be war, people grumbled, 'it were much better that the king should maintain his wars with his own subjects and spend his treasure on them than to trust the Duke of Bourbon, being a stranger, to spend his money'.[69] Wolsey's policy was to keep his options open. While official policy discussed with the imperial ambassador maintained the promise of military and financial aid *mañana,* a secret embassy was received from Paris to explore the possibility of a reversal of English policy. It did not remain secret for long. Charles spies reported to him that the French were handing out lavish 'sweeteners' to Henry's councillors and courtiers. This infuriated the emperor and confirmed his suspicion that his 'dear uncle' was playing a double game.

1525 was the year that changed everything. The diplomatic and military advances and retreats might, like some pavan, have continued interminably. Wolsey, in the king's name, might have continued trying to extract from troubled continental affairs the maximum advantage at the minimum cost, while keeping tight control of government at home, but in this year several fundamental problems were poured simultaneously into the alembic and their combined results were explosive. The lives of Harry and Harry's England would never be the same again. The complex international situation, the mounting unpopularity of Wolsey, Henry's marital problems, the preservation of the dynasty, religious conflict, the emergence of court factions – all these lurched the nation in a new and unpredictable direction.

Anglo-imperial hostility was emphasized at the beginning of February 1525 by what can only be seen as a deliberately provocative act on Wolsey's part. He intercepted a letter sent by Charles' ambassador, complained of its contents, harangued the ambassador before the council and demanded his recall. The timing could scarcely have been worse for, within days, imperial forces won a spectacular and unexpected victory at Pavia. Not only were the French soundly beaten, but their king was among the scores of leaders taken prisoner. Henry was ecstatic. This seemed to solve all his problems. The allies were in a position to impose on France whatever terms they wished. Without having had to go to the expense of a new military expedition, the prize of the French crown or, at least, considerable French territory would fall into his lap. Waving aside the recent contretemps, he warmly congratulated Charles and also presented a shopping list of his requirements. Unsurprisingly, Charles did not see things the same way. He was thoroughly frustrated with the behaviour of his supposed ally. Not only did he ignore English interests in his peace negotiations with Francis, he also broke off his engagement to Princess Mary and sought the hand of Isabella of Portugal. This humiliation stung Henry but there was worse to come.

The diplomatic response of king and cardinal was sharp and decisive. Having made sure that there was an Anglo-French string to their fiddle, they vigorously applied their bow to it. By the end of May, a new treaty had been signed at The More, one of Wolsey's country houses. The French were in no position to haggle over terms and the agreement included a sizeably war indemnity. This addition to the king's coffers was particularly welcome in view of another reverse the government had recently received. When the prospect of a further French campaign had been on the cards, the council had made a desperate and extraordinary attempt to raise revenue. It was only a couple of years since commissioners had been sent out to collect taxation approved by parliament. Now they were despatched again to collect a 'gift' from Henry's loving subjects. It was given the grandiose name of the Amicable Grant. In fact, there was nothing remotely amicable about the common response and many subjects simply refused to grant anything: 'All people cursed the cardinal and his coad-herents as subversor[s] of the laws and liberties of England. For they said, if men should give their goods by a commission, then were it worse than the taxes of France, and so England should be bond and not free.'[70]

Householders in several parts of the country were prepared to resist the king's officers because they could not afford to pay and because they considered the demand unconstitutional. Civic leaders protested that the levy had not been approved by parliament and the clergy objected that their representatives in convocation had not agreed it. Lavenham, in Suffolk, was one of the country's more prosperous towns and, therefore, one of the worst affected by the proposed tax. When Charles Brandon turned up there to supervise collection, he was faced by a 4,000-strong army of protestors. Their spokesman explained the knock-on effect of crippling taxation:

> You ask who is our captain. Forsooth his name is Poverty; for he and his cousin Necessity have brought us to this doing. . .the cloth makers have put all these people and a far greater number from their work. . .husbandmen have put away their servants. . .They say the King asketh us so much that they be not able to do as they have done before this time.[71]

The king was, despite all his bluff and bluster, acutely conscious of popular opinion. The recent near-rebellion had genuinely worried him, as well it might bearing in mind the current upheaval caused by the Peasants' War in Germany. It may be that the events of 1497 arose from the mists of memory – the hurried flight to the Tower with the royal women while his father rode out to face the Cornish rebels at Blackheath. His solution was to deny all knowledge of the Amicable Grant. He 'graciously' pardoned all who had resisted and assured them that it was his advisers who had attempted this unconstitutional imposition. Wolsey commented to the council that he was ready to shoulder the blame 'but the eternal God know'th all'.[72] Hardly surprising, but certainly not courageous or honest, was this decision to pass the buck. 'Now here is an end of this commission but not an end of inward grudge and hatred that the commons bare to the Cardinal and to all gentlemen that vehemently set forth that commission and demand.'[73]

It may be that this issue brought to Henry's attention for the first time just how unpopular Wolsey was (and how useful that unpopularity could be to him). In their correspondence with the king, the Duke of Norfolk (Thomas Howard the younger, elevated to the dukedom on his father's death in 1524) and Charles Brandon, Duke of Suffolk, had pointed out that most people blamed the cardinal for their tax burden. In response Wolsey had shrugged off his adverse PR. 'It is the custom of the people when anything miscontents them,' he pointed out, 'to blame those that be now about the king and when they dare not use their tongues against their sovereign their malice will not fail to give evil language against them.'[74] It seems clear that Wolsey had no conception of the contempt and, in some cases, downright hatred in which he was widely held. Something of it was expressed in a long verse satire written in the safety of Strasbourg by two ex-Franciscan friars, Jerome Barlowe and William Roye. Both were reformist propagandists. The latter enjoyed the patronage of Humphrey Monmouth and helped Tyndale with his translation work. They were members of that

trickle of exiles already beginning to flee the prospect of persecution in England. Their book, *Rede Me and be Nott Wrothe*
(which would reach England in 1528), indicated Wolsey as the
personification of a corrupt and over-powerful church:

> ...though he threaten thee be not dismayed
> To publish his abominable estate
> For though his power he doth elevate
> The season is verily come
> Ut inveniatur iniquitas eius ad odium [For his iniquity to be
> smelled out]...
>
> Thou knowest very well what his life is
> Unto all people greatly detestable,
> He causeth many one to do amiss
> Thorough his example abominable
> Wherefore it is nothing reprobable
> To declare his mischief and whoredom
> Ut inveniatur iniquitas eius ad odium.[75]

Ironically, one of Wolsey's unpopular recent activities was
one of which the reformist authors would have approved: he
had obtained papal permission for a complete review of
English monasticism. He was aware of the gap that had opened
up between the spiritual significance of the religious orders in
national life and the immense landed wealth they had accumulated. Some of this wealth could beneficially be put to other
causes, notably educational, as Lady Margaret Beaufort and
others had demonstrated. Whatever genuinely reformist
agenda Wolsey might have conceived was, inevitably, skewed
by his desire for personal and lasting celebrity. One objective
(perhaps the primary objective) of his investigation was to
suppress a number of establishments in order to apply the
proceeds to a college he was founding at Oxford (Cardinal's
College, later Christchurch). Twenty-nine monasteries and
nunneries were sacrificed for this noble enterprise and another
foundation in Wolsey's native Ipswich; this inevitably led to a

certain amount of upheaval and ill-feeling in their several local-
ities. At Bayham in Sussex, 'a riotous company, disguised and
unknown, with painted faces and vestures, came to the same
monastery and brought with them the canons and put them in
their place again and promised that whensoever they rang the
bell that they would come with a great power and defend
them.'[76]

The writers of *Rede Me and be Nott Wrothe* lamented that
the only person who seemed to be blind to Wolsey's manifest
vices was the king, something that must, they insisted, have
been attributable to the influence of Satan. However, the relationship between king and minister was changing. At court,
the end of the distressing year 1525 ended with what came to
be called the 'Still Christmas'. Because of lingering plague in
London, Henry kept the festival at his comparatively small
residence at Eltham. The celebrations of the reduced royal
retinue were uncharacteristically muted. Meanwhile, Wolsey
'lay at the manor of Richmond and there kept open household
to lords, ladies and all other that would come, with plays and
disguisings in most royal manner; which sore grieved the
people and in especiall the king's servants to see him keep an
open court and the king a secret court'.[77] There could scarcely
have been a more dramatic demonstration of the fact that
Henry was being overshadowed by his servant and there was
no lack of aristocratic Iagos to pour jealous thoughts into his
ear. Norfolk and Suffolk, as we have seen, had been delighted
to point out Wolsey's unpopularity over the Amicable Grant
and there must have been many other occasions when
disgruntled courtiers took the opportunity to draw the king's
attention to examples of the cardinal's hubris and the failure
of his policies.

Wolsey was well aware that the insidious drip-drip-drip of
criticism must affect his standing with the king. As soon as
Twelfth Night was passed he hastened to Eltham and spent two
weeks there. During this time he set in hand a major reshuffle of
government and household personnel (the Eltham Ordinance).

Ostensibly, this was a necessary reform of court expenditure aimed at reducing the number of hangers-on claiming free board and lodging. It was also a response to Henry's complaint that he was not properly served by an itinerant council. In reality, Wolsey's fundamental objective was to reinforce his own position. He ordained that henceforth the king was to be attended at all times by twenty leading councillors. That appeared to deal with Henry's grievance and it would have seriously interfered with Wolsey's government of England if the proposed itinerant council had ever met. However, the cardinal sabotaged his own 'reform' by ensuring that all the major office holders were needed in London and that the only councillors available to Henry were a sub-committee of four. From this time on there developed a divergence between Henry's public and private attitudes towards Wolsey. Writing to Luther in 1526 (a letter intended for publication) he sprang to the cardinal's defence. Luther had written an apology for his earlier diatribe and suggested that the king had fallen under the evil influence of his minister, 'that baneful plague and desiccation'. In his reply Henry riposted that he had complete confidence in Wolsey and yet this was also the year that the king began to take political initiatives without consulting the cardinal and, indeed, sometimes specifically kept them secret from Wolsey. It has become conventional to believe that king and minister fell out over the latter's mishandling of Henry's divorce proceedings. In fact, their relationship was already coming under pressure before the divorce issue forced Henry to turn to other advisers, supporters and comforters.

Henry's falling out with Charles V had placed new strains upon his marriage to his Spanish wife, though 'marriage' is scarcely the appropriate word to describe the relationship between Henry and Catherine by the mid-1520s. They were no longer sleeping together and the queen rarely presided over court entertainments. Her principal comforts now were her religion and her daughter. There was no longer any prospect that she would bear him a son and the severing of the marriage plans between Mary and Charles meant that no male heir to the English throne would emerge through that union. The problem of the succession now began to loom large in Henry's mind and its urgency was signalled dramatically by an accident which befell him in the spring of 1525. He had a brush with death. While out hawking he attempted to ford a flooded dyke with the aid of a pole. The pole snapped and he was thrown head-first into the muddy water. His head stuck in the bottom of the ditch and had it not been for the quick thinking of Edmund Body, one of the royal footmen, Henry would have drowned.[78] Such mishaps certainly concentrate the mind and Henry must have been badly shaken by it. It reminded him that, as powerful as he was, he was not immortal. His father's shadow was forever at his shoulder, demanding to know what he had done with his inheritance. Henry VII had ventured his person in battle to deliver England from decades of dynastic strife and had established the house of Tudor, placing it on a par with the other royal houses of Europe. If his son were to die now what would his legacy be? There would be little to show for a dozen years of intermittent warfare and strenuous diplomacy and England would be left in the hands of a woman for the first time since the unhappy and contested governance of the Empress Matilda in the twelfth century. It was a depressing prospect and Henry began to take serious thought for the future.

His first solution to the succession problem (and it has all the appearance of a knee-jerk reaction) was to bring his bastard son out of the shadows and commence the process of grooming him as a prince of the blood. Little Henry Fitzroy was the king's only offspring by his mistress, Elizabeth Blount, and had been discreetly kept in the background but, in June 1525, he was paraded before the court. With all the pomp of ancient cere-monial, he was invested with the Garter and the royal dukedoms of Richmond and Somerset, appointed Lord Admiral and Warden of the Northern Marches and provided with his own household. This unexpected development was another cause of friction between Henry and his wife. Not only was Catherine affronted by the attention bestowed on the king's illegitimate son, she also feared that her own daughter was being shouldered aside. All the queen's hopes and dreams were concentrated in Princess Mary. Now that she was estranged from her husband, all her love was directed to her only child, of whose interests she became ferociously protective. Catherine intended that Mary should inherit the crown. Such an eventuality might be anathema to the English but the Habsburg tree had produced many women who ruled either in their own right or as regents. She made her feelings very clear. There was a row and Henry dismissed some of his wife's Spanish attendants, but eventually he caved in. At the end of July, Mary's household was increased and she was sent to Ludlow to take up her position as Princess of Wales. Meanwhile, there was talk of a French marriage for her.

This might have solved the immediate problem but it was no answer to the long-term difficulties facing the dynasty. Indeed, the equal honours bestowed on the royal children bore the seeds of future conflict. It was not difficult to envisage a situation in which the Duke of Richmond and the Princess of Wales became armed rivals for the throne. It was vital to make unambiguous provision for the succession. For Henry, the amateur theologian and Defender of the Faith, his anxieties inevitably took on a religious hue. Why, he asked himself, had God declined to bless him with a male heir? Might the answer lie in his relationship with Catherine? There had always been an unsatisfactory element about his marriage and the papal dispensation that had made it possible. Could it be that in his youthful haste to take to bed his brother's widow he had offended the Almighty? At some point in his thinking, Henry came across a verse in the third book of the Bible which seemed to be a direct answer to his question: 'If a man marries his brother's wife, it is an act of impurity; he has dishonoured his brother. They will be childless.' (Leviticus, 20.21) On the face of it, this prohibition seemed to fit Henry's case. It did involve wrenching the words out of context but, then, subtle medieval exegetes were adapt at doing just that and using the Bible as a bunch of proof texts to be applied to the issues of the day. In fact, the words from Leviticus bore no relation to Henry's situation because they referred to bigamy involving the marriage of a woman to two brothers simultaneously (something Luther was at pains to point out later when he was appealed to for a decision on the royal divorce). Furthermore, a Deuteronomic text advocated that a brother *should* marry his brother's relict in the interests of family and tribal unity.

However, to a genuinely religious man, desperate to understand and deal with his tragic situation, Leviticus 20.21 was more than a straw to be clutched at; it was a plank and one whose buoyancy was confirmed when the king discussed it with his confessor, Bishop Longland of Lincoln. Julius II had absolved Henry from the provisions of canon law relating to marriage within the prohibited degrees but God's written word carried much more force than church regulations and no pope had the authority to dispense with it. That being the case, Henry and Catherine had never been lawfully married and the solution of the king's problem was blissfully simple. The current pope must be persuaded to undo what his predecessor had erroneously done. Henry would then be free to contract a new 'first' marriage and sire legitimate heirs.

Fortunately, there was a woman to hand who would admirably fill the bill. When Henry revealed his misgivings to Wolsey, the cardinal assumed that his master would be looking abroad to negotiate a marriage which would have important diplomatic consequences. He was less than pleased to learn that Henry was determined to marry for love. Anne Boleyn was the daughter of Thomas Boleyn, an ambitious, grasping, upwardly mobile courtier, and Elizabeth Howard, daughter of the Duke of Norfolk and sister to Edward and Thomas Howard. She arrived in 1522 to take up a place in the queen's entourage at the age of 21 and had spent some years at the highly sophisticated French and Burgundian courts acquiring all the accomplishments of a well-educated lady of fashion. She was not, by all accounts, stunningly beautiful but she possessed the vivacity and animal allure that attracted men as moths to a candle. Several courtiers fell prey to her charms and her father was set on making the most of her magnetism to secure a favourable marriage for her. When it came to wooing the most desirable young woman at court, Henry was not to be left out. Having already had an affair with Anne's elder sister, Mary, he now transferred his attentions to Anne. In all probability the 'affair' began as a conventional chivalrous courtship but developed rapidly on Henry's part into passionate love.

It is at this point that chronology is crucial but maddeningly difficult to determine. By the early spring of 1526 Henry was pursuing Anne, and other suitors were being warned off. Over the course of the next year his feelings deepened, as evidenced by a series of love letters written by him. The humiliations and anxieties of 1525 had left Henry feeling 'ragged' and in need of someone to whom he could turn for emotional support. He had also reached the susceptible age when some men feel the need to prove their virility by attracting younger women. But how does all that correspond with the emergence of the king's serious doubts about his marriage? In other words, which came first, his desire for Anne or his political need to secure the dynasty? Traditionally, Anne has been identified as the one who determined the pace at which the relationship developed. It is claimed that her ambition or modesty induced her to cool the ardour of her royal stallion by refusing to sleep with him as his mistress and demanding nothing less than marriage. That is something readily recognizable from the conventional 'love triangle' in which the 'other woman' is blamed for the subsequent divorce and all that flows from it. This interpretation has been the stock in trade of Catholic historiography since 1536. However, what we are dealing with here is not a conventional situation.

The concept of any woman playing a reluctant king like a hooked salmon for six years is not an easy one to come to terms with. And Henry was no lovesick swain. If he felt an overmastering passion for Mistress Boleyn, he certainly experienced a no less emotional need for a legitimate male heir. That need received a strong boost in May 1527 when Charles V sent couriers speeding round Europe bearing the happy tidings that he had just become the father of healthy son. If God thus blessed other monarchs, why did he not bless the king of England? Professor Bernard has recently made out a good case for Henry as the party who was determined on marriage. As he points out, sex with Anne, resulting in another royal birth, would not have helped the succession issue at all and, once annulment proceedings had begun, would only have provided ammunition for Catherine's partisans who could claim that Henry was being driven by nothing more nor less than lust.[79] I believe we are wrong if we think of Henry as being driven either by lust or by desire for a male heir. The two are inextricably intertwined. Henry needed a son and he needed him urgently. He was now in his mid-thirties. If he was lucky he might reckon he had some twenty or so years ahead of him – just about enough time to see his successor grow to maturity. He was therefore in immediate need of a new wife. She had to be someone he found sexually stimulating for I believe that his virility was flagging and that he knew it (See below, pp.258ff). With Anne he could experience – and express – real passion. Therefore, he had to have her – no matter what or who tried to get in the way.

As for Anne, it may well have taken some time for her to be convinced that Henry was in earnest. Kings did not marry ladies of non-royal blood. They used them for their pleasure (as Mary Boleyn had discovered). Anne's dedicated suitor might promise wedlock but he would certainly not be the first or last man to do exactly that in order to get the object of his desire into bed. Anne wanted to be a wife and mother and there had been earlier possibilities of arranged marriages that would have suited her very well. Could it be, she must often have asked herself, that what her father told her was really true –

'Play your cards right and you will soon be Queen of England'? It seems to me to be unnecessarily cynical to attribute Anne's reticence to anything more than maiden modesty and the desire not to have her matrimonial chances ruined by being labelled as another of Henry's cast-offs.

Some clue to the timing of events is offered by the dates when those events became public knowledge. As far as extant records are concerned, no one seems to have been very interested in the latest royal affair. Either the couple were being very discreet or Henry's involvement was not considered worthy of note. It was in the spring of 1527 that Henry unburdened his conscience to Wolsey and informed him that he desired an annulment. The cardinal was delighted. Anything that further estranged Henry and Charles suited well his pro-French policy. There was no mention at this time that the king was bent on marrying one of the women of his own court. Even more astonishingly, no hawkeyed foreign ambassador had detected any whiff of sensational marriage speculation around the court. It was not until September 1527 that any documentary evidence appeared suggesting that Henry and Anne had agreed to wed. On 17 May, the cardinal convened a tribunal under his authority as papal legate to decide whether the king's marriage was or was not valid. The hearing was adjourned at the end of the month, perhaps because the issue was theologically not as clear cut as had at first appeared, but certainly because startling news arrived from across the Channel which would involve Wolsey in another trip to France. The unexpected and shocking turn taken by the war in Italy pushed Henry's matrimonial dislocation well into the shade. In fact, the timing of his suit could not possibly have been worse.

In 1526, realizing that Charles and Francis (now released) might soon be at each other's throats again, the cardinal had put in place an insurance policy in the form of the League of Cognac. This was an alliance, brokered by England, of the Papal States, Florence, Milan, Venice and France aimed at deterring or resisting further imperial incursions into northern

Italy. Wolsey was back to his old routine of projecting Henry as the arbiter of universal peace – and cheap peace at that. He would not join England to the league or promise military aid. He hoped to obtain his ends for no more than a modest cash subvention, as he reported to Henry:

> Your grace shall have high and notable thanks of the pope's holiness, the French king, the Venetians and all the league; you shall not be driven to expose any treasure more than this exile sum; your grace shall conserve your amity with the emperor, acquiring with God's grace, great thanks of him for concluding the peace; and finally the glory and honour thereof.[80]

This was a complete misreading of the character of Charles. Stung by Francis' repudiation of their recent treaty, following his release from captivity, and angry at the new alliance ranged against him, the emperor was determined to continue the war in Italy. What particularly enraged him was that the French king had made common ground with the Ottoman Sultan, Suleiman the Magnificent, whose troops delivered a massive blow to imperial forces at the battle of Mohács. Charles now sent an army against the league under the leadership of the duc de Bourbon, scarcely the most reliable of commanders. On 6 May 1527, this motley mercenary invasion force, underpaid and bent on plunder, fell upon Rome and subjected the eternal city to eight days of unimaginable rape and pillage. Bourbon could not be blamed, since he had been killed in the first assault, but it is very doubtful that he would have been able to control his men. The pope escaped via a secret tunnel to the Castel Sant'Angelo, where he remained under personal siege, but the bulk of the populace was not so fortunate during what was the worst experience the capital of popes and caesars had suffered since the invasion of Genseric's Vandal horde more than a millennium before.

> What Goths, Vandals, what Turks were ever like this army of the emperor in the sacrilege they have committed? Volumes would be required to describe but one of their misdeeds. They

strewed on the ground the sacred body of Christ, took away
the cup and trod underfoot the relics of the saints to spoil their
ornaments. No church nor monastery was spared. They
violated nuns amid the cries of their mothers, burnt the most
magnificent buildings, turned churches into stables, made use
of crucifixes and other images as marks for their arquebuses. It
is no longer Rome but Rome's grave. They dressed the old
wooden crucifix, revered by all nations, which stood on one of
the seven altars of St. Peter's in the uniform of a lanzknecht.[81]

So read just one report received by Wolsey of the atrocities
visited on the eternal city. The sack of Rome was one of those
rare events that jolt the thinking of a generation. It tore up the
rule book by which Christendom politics had been conducted.
The army that ravaged Rome was made up of both Catholic
and Lutheran elements which vied with each other in the
performance of atrocities. Roye and Barlowe were not alone
among religious radicals in seeing this tragedy as God's wrath
against the popish Antichrist. Erasmus did not shrink from
placing some of the blame on Clement VII's shoulders. 'How
long is it to be suffered,' he complained, 'that the pope should
ally himself first with one prince and then with another, until
peace becomes hopeless?'[82] However, most people, of course,
held the emperor responsible. The Venetians urged Henry to
come to Italy with main force to prevent Charles making
himself 'monarch of the world'. His only response was fine
words. He was, he affirmed, burning with grief and indignation. He vowed, 'as a champion of the faith' that he would
leave nothing undone to free the pope from their 'degrading
bondage' and sent Cardinal Wolsey to discuss with the French
king the best means for achieving that end.[83]

However, other concerns were uppermost in the king's mind.
It seems insensitive to the point of obscenity that, with Rome in
ruins, the government of the church in tatters, Clement holed
up (until December) in his castle and the Turks advancing on
Vienna, Henry should have been pestering the pope with his
matrimonial problems, but that is precisely what he did do.

Maintaining a sense of proportion was never prominent among Henry Tudor's character traits. The marriage/succession issue now dominated his thoughts and actions and widened the fissure that was opening up between him and Wolsey. While the cardinal attempted to deal with the complex European agenda resulting from the recent crisis, to use it to England's diplomatic advantage and to win support at Rome for his master's 'secret matter', Henry went behind Wolsey's back, took his own initiatives and, in doing so, damaged his own case, probably irreparably. The rift developed because the two men saw the problem from different perspectives. Wolsey knew that the argument for annulment was not straightforward; it would require considerable casuistical pleading and winning important people in Rome to the king's side, something which had been made much more difficult by recent events. Henry, by contrast, saw the issue in clear black and white. His case was sound and he expected the pope to do what, under normal circumstances, he would readily have done – oblige an important client for a suitably impressive fee.

It is all too easy to isolate Henry VIII's matrimonial ills as though they were unique. He will always be, in the popular perception, 'the king who had six wives' but, as Henry looked about him in 1527, he saw several notable contemporaries whose private lives were anything but 'regular' and who, nevertheless, were able to steer their own courses, often with the blessing of the church. His sister, Mary, had married for love and her spouse, Charles Brandon, had a notoriously chequered marital career. The Duke of Norfolk was living openly with one of his own servant girls, Bess Holland, despite the shrieking protests of his harridan of a wife. In this very year, his only other sibling, Margaret of Scotland, obtained from an obliging Pope Clement a divorce from her second husband. Wolsey had lived with a mistress for several years and had children by her. And as for the pope, all the world knew that he only occupied his position because his cousin, Leo X, had declared that Clement had been born in lawful wedlock, although the truth was that he was a bastard. It seemed to Henry that what he was seeking, for the best possible motives, was perfectly reasonable and not at all out of the ordinary.

Wolsey was aware that things were not that simple and the king convinced himself that his minister's caution indicated a certain lukewarmness. Wolsey was driven to write, 'at the reverence of God and most humbly prostrate at your feet', to assure him that this was not the case, but Henry was in a hurry and any procrastination on the cardinal's part only worsened the niggling pain of doubt. This meant that, as the cardinal once more departed for foreign parts, he was vulnerable. His enemies had espied the chink in his armour and the imperial ambassador was reporting as early as mid-May 1527 that Norfolk and Tunstall were heading up an opposition faction.

There was, however, one other reason why the paths of king and minister diverged. Henry had not been altogether honest with Wolsey. He had not told him of his plans to marry Anne. When the cardinal left for France in early July he still believed that the king's secret matter revolved entirely round the validity of his marriage. Such evidence as is available suggests that it was only at this point that the lovers actually agreed to wed. It was while Wolsey was preparing to depart that Anne's father Thomas (now Viscount Rochford) arrived at court. He had just been summoned back urgently from a diplomatic mission in France and thereafter was numbered among the king's intimates. Rochford would certainly have had to be a party to any wedding plans involving his daughter, though such plans would have to remain secret for the time being. If Henry was economical with the truth in his dealings with Wolsey it must have been because he knew that his desire to marry his mistress would show up the annulment affair in a more lurid light. However, since this was sure to become known at some point, Henry was, in effect, sending his champion into the ring with one hand tied behind his back.

The news, and the mode employed to relay it to the cardinal, came as a very unpleasant surprise. William Knight, the king's secretary and, supposedly, Wolsey's ears and eyes at court, arrived at Compiègne, France, en route for Rome on a secret mission for Henry which he was under strict orders not to divulge to the minister. This was to obtain a papal bull permitting the king to marry a woman to whom he was already related. What was all this about? Back in England someone had realized that there was another impediment to the union of Henry and Anne. According to canon law, Henry's affair with Mary Boleyn, although adulterous, constituted consanguinity. Wolsey had his own spies at court and discovered the nature of Knight's mission. He was devastated for four reasons: the plans for the new marriage would hugely complicate negotiations with the pope; his enemies were undermining his authority; the king was keeping secrets from him; and Knight's mission involved a hair-brained scheme proposed by a king and royal advisers who were plainly incompetent in such matters and which would blow the gaffe on Henry's real intentions. Wolsey tried to stop Knight going on to Rome and, in an exchange of urgent correspondence, Henry agreed to be entirely guided by his cardinal. At the same time, he instructed Wolsey to allow Knight to continue his journey to Rome because he had 'other' matters for the secretary to attend to there. Needless to say, once Knight reached his destination he proceeded with the original plan. The result was a bull which was totally worthless. Henry had papal permission to marry Anne as long as his existing marriage was declared invalid.

Wolsey was chafing with frustration. He was attempting the impossible, namely to keep England – and, primarily, himself – at the centre of affairs. Those affairs were immensely complex. In the midst of this, he had to try to satisfy the demands of a king who no longer trusted him and to keep one eye on the machinations of his enemies in England. His impatience occasionally surfaced in his letters home. In the midst of a long report to Henry, he suggested, somewhat tartly, 'If your Grace will take a little patience. . .your intent shall honourably and lawfully take the desired effect'.[84] During his sojourn in France that summer he gambled all on a diplomatic outside bet; he tried to turn himself into a surrogate pope. He summoned his fellow cardinals to join him in Avignon and jointly exercise the authority which Clement was currently unable to exercise. Had he been successful in this endeavour he would have been able to decide the king's case himself and all would have been well, but Clement issued orders forbidding anyone to aid the Englishman in this attempt to subvert his position and the imitation papal court never came into being. Wolsey returned home at the end of September 1527 with nothing to show for his earnest labours.

It took him no time at all to assess the changed atmosphere at court. At his first audience with the king he found Anne at Henry's side and, when it became clear that she was not going to be asked to withdraw, he had to make his report in her presence (something he never had to do in front of Queen Catherine). However, all was not lost. Consummate politician that he was, he knew how to worm his way back into the king's good graces. Clearly, he now had a formidable rival for influence with Henry. Whenever he had been faced with opposition from courtiers and nobles he had dealt with them firmly and had them removed from proximity to the king. Even now, it took him little time to have the Duke of Norfolk despatched back to his East Anglian estates to supervise 'pressing affairs' there. This woman was different. Nothing Wolsey could say would prise the lovers apart. Very well, he would use other tactics. He made himself as pleasant as possible to the king's mistress, plying her with precious gifts and laying on sumptuous entertainments for her and Henry. He also applied himself to the problem of disentangling the king from his wife. A letter sent, in December 1527, to Sir Gregory Casale, the English agent at the Curia, shows that Wolsey understood full well exactly what was at stake in the annulment issue. He listed the arguments the representative was to use in making his appeal to the pope:

1. The friendship I have inspired in the king towards his holiness – a friendship which will be permanent unless some

occasion should be offered for alienating the king's mind in which event it will never be in my power to serve his holiness.

2. ...this affair concerns the king's conscience, the prosperity of his kingdom and the security of his succession.

3. This concession will be honourable to his holiness and agreeable to God.

At this point the writer abandoned enumeration, continuing more discursively:

There are secret reasons which cannot be entrusted to writing, certain diseases in the queen defying all remedy, for which and other causes the king will never live with her as his wife...the king's friendship is of the utmost moment to the pope, as his enmity is fraught with the most terrible consequences. If the pope is not compliant my life will be shortened and I dread to anticipate the consequences...the king is absolutely resolved to satisfy his conscience; and if this cannot be done he will of two evils choose the least and the disregard for the papacy must grow daily, especially in these dangerous times...If [the pope] refuses I can do nothing hereafter in his behalf.[85]

Doubtless Wolsey was exaggerating for effect – even to the point of inventing some unspecified illness from which Catherine was supposedly suffering – but his basic assessment of the situation was starkly accurate: nothing would deter Henry from the course he had embarked upon and if he was forced into a trial of strength with the head of the church the results could be dire – for the church.

This letter is important because it shows that Wolsey understood well, a full decade before the Reformation flood burst upon England, that the cords binding church and state were stretched to breaking point and that a political crisis would be sufficient to snap them. It was only months later that a new, scurrilous book was circulating among the avant-garde, written by someone with whom Wolsey had already had a distasteful brush. Back in 1525, Simon Fish had lampooned the cardinal in a play presented at the inns of court and deemed it wise, afterwards, to make himself scarce. Now, from the safety of the Low Countries, he issued a tract entitled *A Supplication for the Beggars.* It took the form of an appeal to the king of England to remedy abuses in the church. Fish spared not to enumerate all the ills of which reformist elements had been complaining and then pointed out that the ecclesiastical establishment, 'these greedy sort of sturdy, idle, holy thieves', had been milking the country for years. The poor people had paid their tithes and other dues under threat of eternal punishment at the same time that the king had only with difficulty been able to extract lawful taxes for the defence of the realm:

> Is it any marvel that the taxes, fifteenths and subsidies that your Grace most tenderly of great compassion hath taken among your people to defend them from the threatened ruin of their commonwealth have been so slothfully, yea painfully, levied, seeing that almost the utmost penny that might have been levied hath been gathered before yearly by this ravenous, cruel and insatiable generation?. . .And what do all these greedy sort of sturdy, idle holy thieves with these yearly exactions. . .Truly nothing but exempt themselves from the obedience of your Grace. Nothing but translate all rule, power, lordship, authority, obedience and dignity from your Grace unto them. . . For the which matter your most noble realm wrongfully (alas for shame!) hath stood tributary, not unto any kind, temporal prince but unto a cruel, devilish bloodsupper, drunken in the blood of the saints and martyrs of Christ.[86]

It was an argument well calculated to appeal to Henry in his present difficulties and it was not long before it came to his attention. The *Supplication* was brought to Anne Boleyn's notice and she showed it to the king, who was so impressed by it that Thomas More thought it necessary to pen a riposte (*A Dialogue Concerning Heresies,* June 1529). That did not stop Henry inviting Fish to return to England under royal protection. Did this mean that the Defender of the Faith was

*(left)* The formidable Lady Margaret Beaufort, Henry's domineering grandmother.

*(right)* Henry VII by Pietro Torrigiano – the father with whom Henry never bonded.

*(left)* An early suit of tournament armour made for the young Henry.

*(right)* Henry in the tiltyard

*(above)* A miniature by Hans Holbein representing Henry as Solomon receiving the adulation of the Queen of Sheba (perhaps representing the Church).

Several artists made portraits of Henry. They form useful correctives to the official propaganda pieces commissioned from Holbein.

A portrait of Henry by Cornelius Matsis, 1544.

*(above)* Henry's reformation of the English Church consisted largely in persecuting those he disagreed with. He 'trampled' the Pope and burned evangelicals.

*(above)* Henry VIII authorized the first English Bible in 1539.

Hampton Court Palace
Henry collected houses to ease his annual progresses and express his grandeur. He confiscated Hampton Court from Wolsley and commissioned the elaborate Nonsuch.

Nonsuch Palace

The vast wealth Henry gained from the church and taxes was largely lavished on war. He built up a large Royal Navy and ringed England with defensive fortifications like Deal Castle *(below)*.

contemplating abandoning Roman orthodoxy? Clearly not. While Wolsey and his minions were feverishly working on Clement to secure the annulment, Henry could not offend Rome by appearing to succour heretics. Thus, the same king who was reading Fish's diatribe simultaneously issued a proclamation deploring the effusion of Christian blood during the Peasants' War, and warning his subjects not to be seduced by 'certain heretical and blasphemous books lately made and privately sent into this realm'. He ordained that, 'no man within the king's realm or other his dominions, subjects to his highness [shall] hereafter presume to preach, teach, or inform anything openly or privily, or compile or write any book, or hold exercise or keep any assemblies or schools in any manner or wise contrary to the Catholic faith or diminution of holy church'.[87]

In the pursuance of what he conceived to be his own interests Henry was steadily parting company with moral and intellectual consistency. He would grasp any idea that appeared to suit his purpose, just as he would use any person he thought could most effectively carry out his bidding. Simplistic explanations of the king's character have represented his moral decline as being the result of his infatuation with Anne Boleyn but, while the annulment issue demonstrated his deterioration, it was not the sole cause of it. Indeed, it might be that historians and biographers have overstated Henry's amorous passion. In the summer of 1528, when the couple were supposedly aching to consummate their love, Anne, along with thousands of others, succumbed to the sweating sickness. Suddenly, Henry could not quit her side fast enough. Leaving her only with his chief physician, Dr William Butts, he toured several royal manors, accompanied by a bevy of doctors and advising his beloved not to be too hasty in rejoining him. Henry was something of a hypochondriac, probably as the result of being cosseted as child, and it was, of course, only sensible for reigning monarchs to be careful about their health, but Henry's interest in potions and treatments bordered on the obsessive. Now his own welfare certainly took precedence over his concern for that of his beloved. At the same time, he enjoined Wolsey to remain as close to the royal tour party as possible so that he could be kept abreast of latest developments and so that the cardinal would have recourse to the king's medical team in the event of his being overtaken by the sweat.

For a better understanding of the king's character we have to look to the pressures which had built up over twenty years in the life of an essentially weak and egocentric man. He was facing failure on every front. His military exploits had brought no solid gains. His diplomacy was in tatters. His people were divided and discontented. Trade was suffering badly as a result of his falling out with the emperor. His marriage was empty – in every sense of the word. And Wolsey, who until now had been his 'Mr Fix It', was making heavy weather of his wife-swap. In response, Henry had grown secretive and deceitful and, like many dishonest people, he was often most successful in deceiving himself. This lover of 'disguisings' had reached the point where reality and role-play sometimes became confused. He certainly entertained no doubt that in seeking to end his marriage to Catherine he had the highest possible religious motives. In November 1528, he summoned a crowd of notables to Bridewell Palace and there delivered himself of a carefully prepared speech in defence of the annulment proceedings:

> Think you these doings do not daily and hourly trouble my conscience and vex my spirits? Yes, we doubt not but if it were your own cause every man would seek remedy when the peril of your soul, the loss of your inheritance is openly laid to you. For this only cause I protest before God in the word of a prince I have asked counsel of the greatest clerks in Christendom. . . And, as touching the queen, if it be adjudged by the law of God that she is my lawful wife, there was never thing more pleasant nor more acceptable to me in my life both for the discharge and clearing of my conscience and also for the good qualities and conditions the which I know to be in her.[88]

Hall recorded that many who heard this speech went away 'much sorrowed' because they were sympathetic to Catherine, while others 'sighed and said nothing'. Doubtless, their disquiet sprang as much from disillusionment with a king who lied to them as from their affection for his put-upon wife. Perhaps all this would not have mattered so much if it had not come at a time of particular hardship for Henry's subjects. The goings-on of royalty and the nobility were remote from the lives of ordinary people but the cost of a loaf of bread was not. A bad harvest in 1527 had pushed grain prices up by 65 per cent. The government had to issue orders forbidding farmers from hoarding their stocks to maintain high prices. Trade disruption had led to unemployment in the cloth industry. As these misfortunes began to bite they spurred many people to talk of, and plan, sedition. There were demonstrations throughout southern England in the spring of 1528 which called for prompt action by the magistrates and a situation developed in Kent which could have turned very ugly. Over an area extending from Penshurst to Sevenoaks, villagers congregated and planned to take the local gentry prisoners, raid their armouries for weapons and march on London. There, they would demand redress of sundry grievances and get rid of Wolsey for good and all. They even worked out in detail the means of the cardinal's execution. Since killing the pope's representative in England would result in the country being place under the papal ban, they proposed to tow him out sea in a leaky boat and there scupper him!

By the time he was driven to make his public defence, Henry knew that the legal proceedings were going badly. Pope Clement had finally been freed in December 1527 and had removed to his villa at Orvieto to escape the plague in his devastated capital. However, fighting continued between imperial and league forces (Wolsey had finally been persuaded to declare war on the emperor in January 1528) and, until he saw which way the wind was blowing, Clement was careful not to commit himself irrevocably to either Charles or Henry.

Both monarchs were spreading propaganda abroad and were taking the high moral ground. Henry painted Charles as the devastator of Rome and Charles insisted that Henry was in the pocket of his cardinal who was prosecuting war for his own ends and had induced the king to renounce his wife. Now it became clear just what a diplomatic blunder Henry's mishandling of his 'great matter' had been. The emperor had no great affection for his aunt but she was his best agent at the English court and, for that reason, he was anxious not to see her set aside. However, her plight did provide her nephew with an effective propaganda weapon. It helped to distract European opinion from the outrages perpetrated by his own army. During the course of 1528 the military situation, which had for months been finely balanced, turned unexpectedly in the imperialists' favour. Charles could now set his agents to conclude advantageous peace terms, plan a personal visit to Italy to be solemnly crowned by the pope, secure his control of the peninsula and concentrate on problems elsewhere in his vast domains. Viewed from a wider perspective, Henry's 'great matter' was only a European sideshow but its progress was inevitably affected by major events.

Throughout these months, numerous missions were despatched from London urging the pope to send some impartial representative to adjudicate on the king's case. Understandably, Clement used every delaying tactic. It was not until August 1528 that Cardinal Lorenzo Campeggio set out from Italy equipped with a papal commission to try the case in company with Wolsey. Even then, he managed to make the trans-European journey last nine weeks. The poor man was plagued by gout and had to travel much of the way in a slow horse-litter but, painful though his affliction may well have been, he made the most of it as an excuse for restricting his progress still further. Henry had planned to celebrate Campeggio's arrival and mark it with a pageant-strewn progress through London. The optimistic king may well have glimpsed the writing on the wall when his important guest declined all the 'fuss' and asked to be conveyed directly and quietly to his lodging.

The proceedings of the legatine court pursued an equally leisurely course. Campeggio and Wolsey interviewed witnesses who could testify to the relationships between Catherine and her two husbands, and particularly sought to determine whether her marriage to Arthur had been consummated. The queen, of course, insisted that it had not been and therefore she had never, in canon law, been the wife of Henry's brother. After nineteen years the truth of the matter could not be established one way or the other. What was more important was that Catherine refused to appear before the legatine court and appealed her case to Rome. And it was in Rome that the annulment proceedings hit the buffers. In June 1529 Charles' army gained a definitive victory over the French and their allies at Landriano. Within days peace terms were agreed between pope and emperor, to be sealed by a marriage between Clement's nephew and Charles' illegitimate daughter. The pope could no longer prevaricate or maintain the fiction of impartiality. He informed Sir Gregory Casale that he had decided to hear the annulment case in Rome. Back in London, before the arrival of this papal bombshell, Campeggio attached his own less powerful explosive charge to the king's plans. He declared that the court was in recess for the duration of the Roman law vacation – mid-July to 1 October! Henry and his council, who had come expecting the legates to present their verdict, were stunned. Charles Brandon shouted out a protest. This led to a slanging match between him and Wolsey. Henry stalked out.

At that point the cardinal must have known that the prophecies he had made in his letters to the Curia were on the brink of being realized, but it was the news that the king's case was to be heard in Rome which was, for Henry, the final straw. The prospect of appearing (personally or by proxy) before the papal throne as a humble appellant was not to be borne. The only course now open to the king was to try to bully Catherine and Clement into abandoning the appeal. There seemed to be no other way open to Henry and his advocates. What had become clear from the lumbering legal proceedings of the last two years was the potential conflict that existed between the king's law and the pope's law and from hereon in the annulment issue would widen into proceedings aimed at resolving this conflict. In a sense, there was nothing new in this. One of the grievances which fed anticlericalism arose from civil lawyers' frequent clashes with their ecclesiastical counterparts. Hitherto such rivalry had not touched the king. Now circumstances forced him to look deeper into the boundaries of juridical authority.

He was, according to some contemporary writers, assisted in this by William Tyndale. The exile's latest book was *The Obedience of a Christian Man* (1528), in which he expounded the biblical teaching on all kinds of authority. A copy came into Anne Boleyn's hands and this caused a storm in a court teacup. Dr Richard Sampson, dean of the royal chapel, confiscated the book from one of her attendants. Anne went straight to Henry and he ordered it to be returned. When she had recovered it, she suggested that the king might like to cast his eyes over it. He did so and declared himself delighted with it. According to the story, he commented, 'This book is for me and all kings to read.'[89] Well might he say so after perusing such passages as this:

Whosoever voweth an unlawful vow, promiseth an unlawful promise, sweareth an unlawful oath, sinneth against God and ought therefore to break it. He needeth not sue to Rome for a licence; for he hath God's word and not a licence only, but also a commandment to break it. They therefore that are sworn to be true to cardinals and bishops, that is to say false unto God, the king and the realm, may break their oaths lawfully, without grudge of conscience, by the authority of God's word. . .Let kings. . .rule their realms themselves, with the help of laymen that are sage, wise, learned and expert. Is it not a shame above all shames and a monstrous thing that no man should be found able to govern a worldly kingdom save bishops and prelates, that have forsaken the world.[90]

The words touched Henry's situation precisely, and were doubtless intended so to do. They were encouraging him to reflect on the question 'Who rules England?'

At that moment none of Henry's subjects had any doubts about the answer to that question. It was Wolsey. He was the government and since it is every Englishman's birthright to be against the government every Englishman – or so it seemed – was against Wolsey. He was blamed for all the ills that had befallen the realm. Catherine's supporters accused him of beginning the annulment issue. Henry's friends believed that he was trying to thwart the annulment. Radicals condemned him for persecuting suspected heretics. Reactionary churchmen resented his 'softly, softly' approach to heterodoxy. Taxpayers held the cardinal responsible for England's involvement in costly wars against France and merchants grumbled about the effects on trade of his anti-imperial policies. Wolsey represented the overweening pride and power of the church, yet, by his closure of monasteries, he was seen to be milking the church for his own ends. The aristocracy were jealous of the power he had usurped from them. Everyone abhorred the semi-regal pomp by which he flaunted his vast personal wealth. For almost two decades Henry had winked at his minister's enormities because the alternative was to take more responsibility on his own shoulders. If Wolsey had got too big for his boots it was because the king had allowed him to do so, but in the current crisis the king's attitude was seen to cool. He did not dismiss Wolsey or subject him to a private or public dressing-down. That would have involved too much mental effort. He simply distanced himself from the cardinal. That was a strong enough hint.

Others were emboldened to take their own initiatives:

When the nobles and prelates perceived that the king's favour was from the cardinal sore minished, every man of the king's council began to lay to him such offences as they knew by him and all their accusations were written in a book and all their

hands set to it, to the number of thirty and four, which book
they presented to the king.[91]

The list was as comprehensive as its compilers could make it
and, though bizarre in some of its details, does indicate the sort
of behaviour the leading men of the realm particularly
resented. It included the issuing of official documents in the
name of 'the king and I'; having himself appointed papal legate
which gave him authority over all English church dignitaries
without the king's permission; paying huge sums to Rome to
obtain his privileged status; and breathing on the king when he
had the French pox. Hall, who could not, of course, find fault
with the king, represented him as being completely taken
aback by these revelations: 'he marvelled not a little' when he
'perceived the high pride and covetousness of the cardinal'. In
fact, Henry was far from being so obtuse. For example, it was
scarcely a year since he had taken the cardinal to task over his
dealings with the monasteries, precisely because he knew the
discontent Wolsey's dissolutions were causing. His letter of
reproof was almost apologetic in tone. He was, he wrote:

> . . .right glad that, according to mine intent, my monitions and
> warnings had been benignly and lovingly accepted on your
> behalf, promising you that the very affection I bear you caused
> me thus to do. As touching the help of religious houses to the
> building of your college, I would it were more, so it be lawfully
> [done], for my intent is none but that it should appear [so] to all
> the world and the occasion of their mumbling might be
> secluded and put away, for surely there is great murmuring of it
> throughout all the realm.[92]

Henry, then, was well aware of public opinion. He knew
how unpopular Wolsey was; he saw at court a caucus gathering
around the Boleyns; but he fully appreciated how much he
owed to the cardinal. These were the balls he was juggling as he
set off on his usual summer progress in 1529. This was the time
of year when Wolsey's influence was always at its weakest

because he saw the king less often and his enemies had access to him on a more regular basis. The minister spent much of his time working hard at the two political priorities on the agenda – the annulment and the French peace treaty. The French ambassador, Jean du Bellay, reported a conversation with Wolsey in which the latter had declared that once he had secured a permanent peace with France, seen Henry and Anne married and rejoicing in the birth of a son, he would consider his work done and would retire from politics to spend his declining years in holy contemplation. The ambassador, though, did add a rider: the cardinal, he thought, was making a virtue out of necessity because, 'if this marriage is accomplished he will have much to do to maintain his influence'.[93] Du Bellay put his finger on the crucial political change that had taken place at court. Henry always needed others to lean on for advice and emotional support. For years Wolsey had been his main prop and stay. He had become a habit, not always wholesome but difficult to break. Now another had interposed herself between king and councillor. Henry did not rely on her for political advice but she could work on his prejudices and provide a bridgehead for her father, her brother, her uncle, the Duke of Norfolk and their allies who realized that they now had their best opportunity in years for removing the hated cardinal.

It was, therefore, with great interest that the whole court (or as many as could fit into the royal hunting lodge at Grafton) jostled to observe the arrival of Wolsey on 19 September 1529. A showdown was widely expected. The onlookers were disappointed. The event was an anticlimax. King and minister held long conversations and, though Anne was able to lure Henry away for an outing and so prevent further discussions, the two men parted, it seems, on reasonably friendly terms. It was apparently 'business as usual'. However, behind the scenes there was a distinct change of mood. Courtiers and senior officials sensed the growing influence of the Boleyn clique and hastened to adjust their own allegiances. Henry, meanwhile, was once more going behind his minister's back over the annulment issue. In seeking support for his theological position his agents had gathered opinions from various scholars and divines at home and abroad and the king now decided to summon parliament. Exactly what role he hoped it would play in the resolution of his 'great matter' is not clear and it may not have been clear to him either. It was, however, another body which could be manipulated so as to enhance his own authority. Henry had always favoured having the marriage issue resolved in England. Since the pope was dragging his feet and since, realistically, Henry's chances of obtaining a favourable verdict if he did have to submit to a hearing in Rome were slim, he needed a fallback position.

During the late summer Henry made plans with his lawyers and councillors in great secrecy to establish parliament's authority. Some canny legal expert had suggested that a notoriously vague statute of 1393 might be stretched to cover the existing case. This was the Statute of Praemunire which was intended to defend 'the king's regality' from incursions by foreign courts. Predominantly, it existed to cover eventualities when royal and papal jurisdiction came into conflict. As soon as the new legal term was opened in October 1529, Wolsey was indicted in King's Bench under this statute, his offence to obtain and publish papal bulls appointing him as legate and using that authority, in certain specified cases, in ways prejudicial to the crown. Wolsey knew better than to contest the case. He pleaded guilty. The sentence was imprisonment and forfeiture of goods. Henry remitted the former but eagerly took possession of the cardinal's great houses, stuffed with treasures. Days later, Norfolk and Suffolk were sent to demand the return of the Great Seal and to dismiss Wolsey from his office of lord chancellor. The most hated man in England had fallen – and great was the fall thereof. News spread around the capital and when the cardinal made his way, as ordered, into rural retirement the citizenry turned out to witness the spectacle. This time no impressive retinue accompanied the pseudo-king. He tried to slip away quietly, using the Westminster privy stairs. No chance! The river was a scene of unofficial carnival: 'at the taking of the barge there was no less than a thousand boats full of men and women of the city of London [sailing] up and down in Thames. . .supposing that he should have gone directly to the Tower; whereat they rejoiced'.[94]

The cardinal's enemies were cock-a-hoop but their triumph was far from complete. When Wolsey's party reached the Surrey bank and began their overland ride to Esher, they were suddenly met by Sir Henry Norris, the groom of the stool and the king's close friend, who had ridden post haste from the court with an urgent message:

> Although the king hath dealt with you unkindly as ye suppose, he saith that it is for no displeasure that he beareth you, but only to satisfy more the minds of some (which he knoweth be not your friends) than for any indignation. And also ye know right well that he is able to recompense you with twice as much as your goods amounteth unto. And all this he bade me that I should show you. Therefore, Sir, take patience. And for my part I trust to see you in better estate than ever ye were.[95]

The image of Henry conjured up by this sequence of events is not an attractive one. He had acted to please Anne and her friends even though he knew his treatment of Wolsey was shoddy. He was not man enough to confront the cardinal face-to-face but sent others to do his unsavoury bidding. Having made his decision he could not stand by it. He wanted to enjoy the popularity that accrued to him for having encompassed Wolsey's fall without, necessarily, depriving himself of the ex-minister's services.

Harry of England had only just passed the halfway point of his reign but his character was already beginning to unravel.

# Chapter 6

## 'RESTORING THE FAITH AND RELIGION OF CHRIST'

A famous *Punch* cartoon of 1890 was captioned 'Dropping the Pilot'. It related to the sacking of the German chancellor, Otto von Bismarck, by the young Kaiser Wilhelm II and showed the former, the architect of the German Empire, descending a ship's gangway while his royal master looked on, having taken personal command of the bridge. The implied question was whether the inexperienced emperor would be able to steer the ship of state through the turbulent waters ahead. Subsequent history would return a disastrously negative answer to that question. A parallel with Henry's dismissal of Wolsey is apt. The cardinal had many faults but, as quasi-monarch, he had kept England in the forefront of international affairs as well as making some attempt at tackling social problems and ensuring the more equitable running of the law courts. Above all, he had prevented the political disease which is endemic to the government of virtually all weak rulers – factionalism. In the remaining sixteen years of the reign, after Wolsey's restraining hand had been removed, the royal court and council became the battle ground not only of nobles and courtiers whose ambitions and animosities had, at long last, escaped the leash, but also of bitterly opposed ideologies.

In the summer of 1529, Norfolk, Suffolk and the Boleyns had tried to persuade the king that Wolsey was not merely dragging his feet over the annulment; he was actually opposed to it; he was a man of divided loyalties who, in the last analysis, would always obey pope rather than king. Did Henry believe them? Probably not. In his biography of his master, Thomas Wolsey, George Cavendish recorded a conversation between Anne and the king in which she catalogued the cardinal's many failings. 'If my lord of Norfolk, my lord of Suffolk, my lord my father or any other noble person within your realm had done much less than he,' she insisted, 'they should have lost their heads before this.' Henry was, apparently, less than convinced. 'There is no blame in him,' he is reported to have responded, 'for I know that matter better than you or any other'.[96] He spoke the sober truth. Henry, of all men, knew just how much he owed to the organizing genius who had managed the nation's affairs for him for more than half his lifetime. If, over the ensuing weeks, he allowed himself to be steered into drastic action his principal concern was to send a message to the pope: the king of England was, under God, supreme in his empire and would not tolerate interference in his affairs by any foreign prince. As for Wolsey, Henry was soon relaxing his punishment. Within weeks he lifted some of the Praemunire penalties and in February 1530 he issued a complete pardon. Moreover, Wolsey was allowed to take up residence at Sheen, an easy barge ride from Westminster or Greenwich. Every indication was that the king was preparing the ground for his ex-minister's rehabilitation. Perhaps he hoped that, once he had made his point in Rome, room might once more be found for a chastened Wolsey beside the throne.

All this was extremely worrying to the Boleyn faction. They had committed themselves totally to the cardinal's destruction.

Throughout the winter of 1529– 30 they must have frequently wondered whether their objective could really have been so easily attained. Had they, in fact, seen the last of the man who had dominated the realm and been their hated master for so long? One thing was certain: if Wolsey managed a comeback heads would roll. Nor did they have confidence in the king to stand by his decision to end permanently Wolsey's political career. In the autumn of 1529 the project to remove the cardinal had seemed to be all done and dusted. A reshuffle of jobs and titles placed Anne's circle of family and friends in an apparently unassailable position. Thomas Boleyn rocketed his way into the peerage when Henry gave him the earldoms of Ormonde and Wiltshire and also appointed him lord privy seal, the third most important office of state. Anne's brother, George, now became Viscount Rochford and a gentleman of the privy chamber. Other members of the Boleyn clique were elevated to become Earls of Sussex and Huntingdon. Suffolk was made president of the council (a new post) but, as he demonstrated little enthusiasm for committee work, it was, in fact, Norfolk who assumed the lead political role.

Thomas More became the new lord chancellor, a sign that the senior law office would, henceforth, be in lay hands. More had adroitly deserted his former patron and cemented his new allegiance with a sickeningly sycophantic attack on Wolsey when he opened the new parliament:

> Amongst a great flock of sheep some be rotten and faulty, which the good shepherd sendeth from the good sheep. So the great wether [ram] which is of late fallen as you know, so craftily, so scabbily [as of sheep afflicted with scab], yea and so untruly juggled with the king, that all men must needs guess and think that he thought in himself that [the king] had no wit in himself to perceive his crafty doing. . .but he was deceived, for his grace's sight was so quick and penetrable that he saw him, yea, and saw through him, both within and without, so that all things to him was open, and according to his desserts he hath had a gentle correction.[97]

The wording of the speech, obviously approved beforehand by the king, was an indication to both sides in the power struggle of just how far he was prepared to go against the cardinal – Wolsey would receive a 'gentle correction'.

Small wonder the atmosphere at court throughout the winter months was jittery. One can almost feel sorry for Henry at this time. He was caught between two termagant women, his queen (still officially presiding over the distaff side of the court) and his mistress, whose assertiveness was becoming daily more pronounced. The rivalry of the women and their support camps created a poisonous atmosphere reminiscent of the worst kind of television soap opera. No sooner had Henry walked away from one altercation with Catherine than he was pounced on by Anne. She scolded:

> Did I not tell you that whenever you disputed with the queen she was sure to have the upper hand? I see that some fine morning you will succumb to her reasoning and that you will cast me off. I have been waiting long and might in the meanwhile have contracted some advantageous marriage, out of which I might have had issue, which is the greatest consolation in this world. But, alas! Farewell to my time and youth spent to no purpose at all.[98]

Anne drove home her sulking displeasure by refusing to join the king for Christmas. A few months later, news that Clement had had the temerity to order Henry to separate from his concubine brought on another demonstration of Anne's fury. She upbraided Henry for his weakness and threatened to leave him. This time the king was reduced to tears. The image of Henry VIII cowed by a woman is not a familiar one but it is one we have to accommodate if we are to get the true measure of this man. He was always vulnerable to stronger personalities and with the passing of the years his emotional dependence on those close to him grew. He shunned direct confrontation and increasingly depended on the exercise of naked power to exert his will – usually at third hand.

Anne was no less frustrated with her allies. They had failed to achieve the destruction of Wolsey and they were totally incompetent in finding any way of disentangling the king from his marriage. The Boleyn 'faction' was, in reality, no such thing. It was a bunch of opportunist courtiers, each of whom had his own agenda. Norfolk, who knew full well that the king held no real affection for him, was a loose bundle of hatred and hubris held together by only the weakest fronds of political competence and creative ideas. He was essentially a negative character – anti-Wolsey, anti-France, anti-annulment (though, of course, he kept that to himself) and anti-reform. Suffolk was, as Eric Ives has succinctly described him, 'work-shy'. Boleyn *père* was only interested in personal advancement. Boleyn *fils* was something of an evangelical firebrand, concerned for root-and-branch church reform. More saw his prime responsibility as leading a major crusade against heresy.

Thomas Howard, Duke of Norfolk's contribution to the anti-Wolsey campaign was to try to put as much distance as possible between the king and his ex-minister. He persuaded Henry to despatch the Archbishop of York to his diocese, ostensibly to tend the flock he had never visited since his inauguration fifteen years earlier but actually to make sure that he was out of sight and out of mind. Wolsey, of course, knew precisely what his adversary was up to and stubbornly refused to budge. The contest went on until April 1530 when Norfolk, in a typical rage and with a typical degree of Howard rhetoric, sent a messenger to tell the cardinal that, 'if he go not away shortly, I will, rather [than that] he should tarry still, tear him with my teeth!'[99] Eventually, Wolsey began his leisurely progress northwards, his journey sweetened by a financial gift and messages of encouragement from the king. His behaviour was certainly not that of a defeated and deflated has-been. Without seeking royal approval, he began arranging his impressive enthronement in the great minster at York. He kept himself informed via his agents (chief among whom was his right-hand man, Thomas Cromwell) of events at court and maintained his foreign contacts. If he remained sanguine about his future, he had good cause. With his enemies in disarray, the annulment no nearer achievement, support for Catherine and Mary growing among ordinary people, the emperor as much in command of Rome as ever and the king showing no signs of abandoning his old minister completely, he had no reason to believe that fortune's wheel had ceased turning. With Clement now threatening Henry with excommunication, the crisis was deepening and no one had better curial contacts than Wolsey. It could only be a matter of time before Henry came to his senses and discarded the self-seeking rabble of advisers who had presumed to try to take his place. In the summer of 1530 the smart money would have been on the cardinal's return.

The Duke of Norfolk belatedly realized that sending his adversary to the north might not, after all, have been the wisest course of action. In this distant and 'backward' region where conservative sentiment was strong among the leaders of society as well as the rank-and-file, the ex-minister might be able to build up a personal following on behalf of the queen. It was difficult for the duke to keep close watch on the cardinal's household and all who came and went there. Desperate to ensure that his enemy's downfall was permanent, he posted his own spies in Wolsey's establishment and prided himself on 'turning' some of the cardinal's men, but it was not till the autumn of 1530 that he managed to gather what he thought would be damning evidence against the cardinal. He inter-cepted letters sent by Dr Agostino Agostini, Wolsey's Venetian physician and his main intermediary with members of the diplomatic corps. They were addressed to a French emissary, Jean Passano, Sieur de Vaux, and we have no means of knowing their content. All that is clear is that Norfolk was able to persuade the king that they referred to plans for drawing Henry into war with Charles V, which would be so unpopular as to create a grave domestic crisis and thus force the king into reinstating his old major domo. What followed casts grave doubts as to whether Wolsey had been so careless as to put such inflammatory material in writing. The king had no alternative but to send officers to arrest Wolsey and bring him back to London to face charges of high treason. Agostini was also apprehended but, instead of being racked and accommodated in the Tower's least comfortable apartments, he was, according to Eustace Chapuys, the imperial ambassador, 'treated as a prince in the house of the Duke of Norfolk, which clearly shows that he has been singing to the right tune'.[100] Thomas Howard was preparing the ground for a state trial from which not even royal favour could save the victim.

In the event, Wolsey was saved this final humiliation and the possible ordeal of a traitor's death. During his leisurely journey southwards he succumbed to dysentery at Leicester and died on 29 November 1530. Anne and her allies received the news with unrestrained rejoicing. George Boleyn commissioned a masque for performance at court which dramatically signalled the end of the old order and the coming of the new: it was entitled *Of the Cardinal's Going into Hell*. As Norfolk and his cronies laughed at the antics of a fat, red-robed figure struggling with horned demons, they may have permitted themselves a brief interlude of gloating but the fact must have penetrated even Howard's slow brain that, though the cardinal might be dead, England's problems were still very much alive. The king remained locked in a barren marriage. Religious strife was growing. The treasury was empty. The duke had no answers to offer. What he urgently needed were new men, men whose fresh and unconventional ways of thinking might be able to sever these Gordian knots tying down the realm. Enter the two T.C.s – Thomas Cranmer and Thomas Cromwell.

Who was the chief draughtsman of the English Reformation? Who decided, not only that the English church should be sundered from Latin Christendom, but that it should be provided with a vernacular Bible and liturgy and a radical, evangelical theology? That question leads unavoidably to another: what do we mean by 'Reformation'?

Several reform movements were buzzing around Europe in the middle years of the sixteenth century. There were changes to university syllabuses and the whole educational ethos. There were demonstrations against clerical corruption and privileges. There were political innovations designed to give national governments more control of ecclesiastical property and personnel. There were translations of the Bible aimed at making every reader his own theologian. There was a rising tide of religious controversy which manifested itself in pamphlet warfare, heresy prosecutions and popular revolts. These movements gained impetus because the religious establishment was unwilling and unable to set its own house in order and also because the issues involved engaged the minds of many leaders of opinion, nationally and internationally: 'What made the Reformation successful was not the support (if any) it received from the deviants and the marginalised, but the support it received from the established elites in Church and state'.[101] This being so, it is not surprising to discover that an almost disproportionate number of radically inclined men and women were to be found in that place where ambition and talent carried many of England's finest – the royal court.

By 1531, the most influential religious radicals in and around the Tudor household were Anne Boleyn, her father and brother, Thomas Cromwell and Thomas Cranmer. They provoked a conservative backlash and a group emerged, headed by the Duke of Norfolk, Thomas More and Bishops Fisher and Tunstall, which, for the first time, had a religious identity. Each of these people (and their supporters in the country at large) played a part in the evolution of the English church but each worked to a different agenda. As the pace hotted up, various elements in English life collided with each other, divided and coalesced like globules of quicksilver in an alchemist's dish. Therefore, what began to emerge in the 1530s – the most formative decade in English history – was not something conceived in a single creative mind, nor an end product manufactured by a combination of interactive forces, but rather a muddled, incomplete politico-religious compromise which disturbed many and satisfied none.

Let us begin our investigation by considering the activities and motivations of the person who, at the turn of the decade, was daily uppermost in King Harry's mind. Who was this woman he was so determined to marry that all other affairs of state were shuffled further down the agenda? As Professor Eric Ives has well established, 'Anne Boleyn was not a catalyst in the English Reformation; she was a key element in the equation'.[102] To this point, Anne had spent almost all her life in the heady, sophisticated and superficial atmosphere of royal courts. It was an ambience in which she flourished, like a fine orchid in a hothouse. She was born into an upwardly mobile Norfolk family which had contrived, in recent generations, to become well-connected and moderately wealthy. Her mother was a daughter of the previous Duke of Norfolk and her father, Thomas Boleyn, was descended in the maternal line from the Earls of Ormonde and Salisbury. Thomas entered royal service early in the reign, became a favoured courtier and, from 1519, a leading diplomat. His accomplishments fitted him well for the role of foreign representative: he was cultured, intelligent, well-educated and fluent in French and Latin. He was a believer in the Renaissance principle that women should receive an education and he sent both of his daughters, Mary and Anne, to be 'finished' in foreign courts. Undoubtedly, his motives were mixed. Not only did he want his girls turned into 'proper ladies' who could attract wealthy, titled husbands, he also intended that they should acquire those accomplishments which would equip them, eventually, to gain places in the English queen's household, there to promote even further the Boleyn interest. Thus it was that, from the ages of approximately thirteen to twenty-one, Anne belonged to the entourages of, first, Margaret of Austria, who ruled the Netherlands as regent for Charles Duke of Burgundy (the future Emperor Charles V), and, secondly, Claude, Queen of France.

The households of these two royal ladies represented the pinnacle of Renaissance culture where places were eagerly sought by the great families of several nations. Here patronage was bestowed on the most accomplished painters, musicians, sculptors and scholars of Europe. Anne became acquainted with the works (and, perhaps, the persons) of such masters as Jan van Eyck, Hieronymous Bosch, Josquin des Prés, the celebrated tapestry-makers of Bruges and the great Flemish masters of illuminated manuscripts. In the Archduchess Margaret's court the code of chivalric romance had been brought to its apogee and transformed into a veritable art form. The plighting of troths, the giving of tokens, the choosing of champions, the expressing of devotion in sighing verse and sweet, lute-accompanied song, the intricate body language of stately dance – all these were brought to perfection in the sheltered world of Margaret's young ladies. Other courts, including the English, aped the manners of these model courts and beside them must have seemed boorish. We have already seen how Charles Brandon and Henry got into hot water through the former's inept failure to appreciate the subtleties of courtship as defined by Margaret. Anne learned well. She was one of the most refined and accomplished products of the system. Not only could she sing, dance and converse in French and Latin, she also possessed the poise, learning and intelligence that enabled her to shine in any company. Add to this a natural vivacity and a ready wit and it is not difficult to see why she turned so many heads.

Anne brought into Henry's life that combination of youthful charm and mature sophistication that Catherine possessed no longer. She was adept at the game of courtly love and her relationship with Henry began as just another chivalric flirtation. Indeed, Anne's behaviour in the early days of their relationship can be explained as the anxiety of one who perceived that the game was getting out of hand, that her knight errant was becoming too serious. Like Catherine, Anne was strong-minded but knew when to be submissive. Henry liked to have people around him who were clear-thinking and intelligent – provided that they were tactful enough not to show him up. He enjoyed debate, particularly religious debate. At least three of his wives were women of sincere devotion and strong religious opinions. This brings us to the aspect of Anne's upbringing and character of which we would dearly love to know more. Writing half a century later, during the reign of Anne's daughter, the martyrologist John Foxe wrote this obituary of Queen Elizabeth's mother: 'for the rare and singular gifts of her mind, so well instructed, and given towards God, with such a fervent desire unto the truth and setting forth of sincere religion, joined with like gentleness, modesty and pity toward all men, there have not many such queens before her borne the crown of England.'[103]

Writing for Anne's daughter, in a Protestant ethos and aspiring to steer England still further along the path that led away from Rome, Foxe was scarcely an impartial chronicler. Fortunately, there is an abundance of evidence that attaches Anne to the beginnings of the English Reformation. She was the patroness of men like Tyndale and Fish, who were outlawed for heresy. She had her own copy of Tyndale's New Testament and kept an open English Bible in her chambers for anyone so disposed to read. She was in contact with Erasmus and, more particularly, with French reformers. She gave succour to persecuted radicals, one of whom, the poet, Nicolas Bourbon, poured out his gratitude in gushing evangelical sentiment: 'How can I express my thanks, still less, Oh Queen, repay you? I confess I have not the resources. But the Spirit of Jesus which enflames you wholly with his fire, He has the wherewithal to give you your due.'[104] Only someone who enjoyed the unquestioning love and protection of the king could have associated with a coterie of friends and protégés such as Anne's without facing examination for heresy.

Circumstantial evidence and intelligent guesswork point to her teenage years at the court of Queen Claude as the time when Anne began to deviate from Catholic orthodoxy. In French royal circles she came into contact with the friends of Margaret of Angoulême, the sister of Francis I and later Queen of Navarre. Margaret was the leading patroness of advanced thinkers in France and there were among her protégés those who suffered exile, imprisonment or death for espousing religious opinions that were non-PC. As a mere attendant on Queen Claude, Anne could not have been on intimate terms with this redoubtable free-thinking lady but she certainly admired her and later, when her own station in life had been remarkably enhanced, she was able to address Margaret on more equal terms. There was nothing she so much desired, she insisted in 1534, 'as the Queen of Navarre's company, with whom to have conference, for more causes than were meet to be expressed'.[105] It is tempting to think that religion had its place among those topics of conversation about which it was necessary to be discreet.

No less than in England, intellectual circles in France were abuzz with the new ideas of Erasmus and the Christian humanists and the more dangerous challenges presented by Luther. The leading scholar of Margaret's 'salon' was Jacques Lefèvre d'Etaples. Though of an older generation (he was born in 1455), his career had similarities to that of William Tyndale. His passion was to make the Bible widely available. He translated various parts of it, such as the epistles and gospels, for liturgical use and brought his endeavours to a conclusion with his vernacular Bible of 1525, the same year in which he was forced to flee to Strasbourg. Anne possessed a number of Lefèvre's works but her favourite reading was his Bible. Her own copy (now in the British Library) bore embossed texts on its covers asserting basic evangelical teachings on the all-sufficiency of Christ and salvation by faith, rather than works of the law: 'As in Adam all die, so in Christ shall all be made alive' (I Corinthians, 15.22); 'The law was given by Moses but grace and truth came by Jesus Christ' (John, 1.17). If these citations were meaningful for Anne, as we must assume they were, it is reasonable to imagine that she became an adolescent convert to evangelical faith while in France.

However, it may be that we should look nearer to home for the main evangelical influence in her life. Anne was very close to her only brother, George, Viscount Rochford, who was her junior by three or four years. He was one of the bright young things of the court, sophisticated, well-educated (possibly at Oxford), a fluent linguist and no mean poet. He was, needless to say, a member of the intellectual avant-garde, familiar with the religious issues of the day; a man who attended radical sermons, read banned books and enjoyed vigorous debate. He wore his evangelical faith on his sleeve. Chapuys dreaded invitations to dine with George Boleyn, who he knew would spend the entire meal trying to engage him in religious argument. George had beautiful presentation copies of Lefèvre's works made for his sister and may well have used his position to smuggle into the court even more radical English tracts. He certainly encouraged Anne to show the king Fish's *Supplication for the Beggars.* To the end of his days George remained a convinced evangelical. In his scaffold speech he acknowledged, 'I was a great reader and a mighty debater of the word of God and one who favoured the gospel of Jesus Christ.' Standing on the brink of eternity, which was no place for deceit or dissimulation, he repented, not his faith, but his failure to live up to it and he urged his hearers 'for the love of our Lord God hold by the truth and speak it and embrace it'.[106] Brother and sister, at the centre of the court's 'in' group, shared a fresh, personal faith rendered all the more exciting by being outrageously anti-establishment. Their sheltering behind royal favour to encourage 'heresy' was a cause of anger and jealousy to many outside the charmed circle and this would eventually contribute to their downfall. Particularly infuriated was Jane, George's wife. Theirs was a loveless marriage and Lady Rochford bitterly resented her exclusion from the privileged clique of her husband and his friends. In the claustrophobic royal household, where all emotions tended to become exaggerated, it did not pay to make enemies like Jane Boleyn but, at the dawn of the 1530s, Anne had little regard for her spiteful sister-in-law.

How far Anne went in discussing theological core beliefs with the Defender of the Catholic Faith we cannot know but she certainly urged him, with increasing boldness, towards those aspects of reform which related to the relative powers of king and pope.

As the king's exasperation and frustration rose, so the possibility of taking some kind of draconian action against the papal regime assumed a concrete form. Henry realized that wielding a royal stick among the ecclesiastical hierarchy would go down well in certain quarters and he now had at his side one who, from personal conviction, was dedicated to reform. To Anne, Wolsey represented everything that was bad about the hierarchy of the international church but, in the early days of their relationship she had to be nice to him. The cardinal's influence at Rome represented the only available means of achieving what she wanted – marriage to Henry. Once she had made the emotional leap of commitment to her royal lover and embraced the responsibility of her future as England's queen, she must, in her prayers and meditations, have begun to prepare herself for that role. Her evangelical conscience would have urged her to think more in terms of responsibility than of power, wealth and the enjoyment of luxury. We know from a notorious sermon preached by John Skip, one of her chaplains, in 1536 (see below) that Anne was familiar with the biblical book of Esther, and it is not at all fanciful to see her finding a role model in the ancient heroine of that story. Esther belonged to an Israelite family living in exile in the Persian empire during the reign of Xerxes. The emperor put aside his wife, looked for a replacement and his choice fell upon Esther. When a persecution arose against the Israelites, Esther's guardian appealed to her. 'Who knows but that you have come to royal position for such a time as this?' he urged (Esther, 4.14). As a result of her clever tactics in handling her tyrannical husband, Esther was able to avert the catastrophe.

Anne must have asked herself (and would certainly have been encouraged in this by her evangelical mentors) for what purpose she was being raised from obscurity to a throne. The answer was readily available: to succour the latterday people of God. Her mission was to encourage Henry to reform the English church, a process which would include improving the educational standards of the clergy, placing the Bible centrally in the life of the people, stripping the pope of his power in England and purifying doctrine. That being the case, she was inevitably set on an ultimate collision course with Wolsey. For the time being, however, she had to support the trust Henry still reposed in his minister. It was as month followed tedious month and letter followed optimistic letter from Wolsey's office, and still the annulment proceedings remained stalled, that Anne's patience wore thin. She was fast approaching her thirties. If the way was to be cleared for her to marry Henry and bear him sons time was not on her side. By 1529 she had joined with her father and the leaders of the anti-Wolsey clique at court in active campaigning against the cardinal. What precise part she played in the downfall of the great minister in the autumn we can never know. The stories of her boldly exposing Wolsey's failings to the king and intriguing to keep the two men apart are apocryphal.[107] Her rejoicing at his death was genuine but she still had to endure the agony of knowing that, as far as her own situation was concerned, it had changed nothing.

The two years following the cardinal's initial downfall were years of phoney war. Henry and Clement had taken up a confrontational stance but neither made the first move to open up direct hostilities. It steadily dawned upon interested and concerned parties that the issues at stake were so enormous that one or other of the contenders would have to back down. They waited to see who it would be. However, the pope was in no position to yield and anyone who expected the competitive Henry to throw in the towel did not know his man. He had been accustomed since childhood to getting his own way. His tiltyard contests had to be rigged to ensure his triumph. In war and diplomacy he always expected his representatives to do his bidding, no matter what difficulties they faced. And, when changes of policy were forced upon him, as with the Amicable Grant, he blamed underlings for failure and disassociated himself from their actions. At the same time, he was, as we have seen, not insensitive to public opinion. Indeed, he now looked to the possibility of harnessing it. One way of demonstrating that, in the current ideological impasse, he was in the right was to accumulate an impressive body of support. When Henry summoned parliament in the autumn of 1529 it was (as well as for the purpose of raising much-needed revenue) with vague ideas in mind of demonstrating national solidarity. Events proved that this was a miscalculation. If parliament was to become a major element in the king's campaign, it would have to be very carefully 'managed'.

Parliament was far from being a united body. There was a considerable anticlerical element in the lower house, particularly among lawyers and country gentlemen who were most affected by the incursion of clerical power in their affairs. This did not, however, imply automatic support for the annulment. Sympathy for Catherine and Mary was widespread, even among the more radical members of the Commons. There seems to have been some idea of using the assembly to organize a mammoth petition signed by as many as possible of the nation's leaders imploring the pope to accede to their king's wishes but the project was set aside and only reappeared eight months later in a much diluted form. Sometime between November 1529 and the summer of 1531, a draft bill was produced to enable the king's matrimonial matter to be decided by the English archbishops instead of the pope. This, too, was dropped. It had quickly become clear that parliament was not the key that would automatically unlock the door for Henry into a resumed bachelor state.

In reality, all the king had done was give licence to members of the national talking-shop to air their grievances and to state their opinions on the disturbing new ideas that were spreading outwards from the capital like ripples on a pond. It soon became evident that the Parliamentarians' concerns were not the same as those of the king. From the Commons house came a chorus of complaints against the clergy. They ranged from bias against the laity in ecclesiastical courts and clerical non-residence to excessive fees charged for conducting funerals and proving wills. When some of these measures were passed to the upper house, the ordure hit the fan. The bishops, as Hall recorded, 'frowned and grunted, for that touched their profit' and the veteran John Fisher lambasted the Commons, comparing its members to the Hussite heretics of Bohemia:

> My Lords, you see daily what bills come hither from the Commons house and all is to the destruction of the church. For God's sake, see what a realm the kingdom of Bohemia was and when the church fell down then fell the glory of the kingdom. Now with the Commons is nothing but 'Down with the church!' and all this me seemeth is for lack of faith only.[108]

Once the bishop had got into his stride he painted a picture of total anarchy and even suggested that limiting the privileges of the clergy would lead to the collapse of Christianity and usher in 'the tyrannical government of the Turk'. The squires and burgesses were not disposed to take this attack lying down. They appealed to the king and he summoned Fisher and some of his colleagues to explain themselves. It was all, from his point of view, very unsatisfactory. This squabbling was not what the parliament had been summoned for. No mention had been made of Henry's quarrel with Rome and soundings from courtiers who were members of parliament must have made it abundantly clear that no universal support for the annulment could be expected from a body which was divided in itself. On 17 December 1529, parliament was prorogued until after Easter. When April came it was postponed to June, then to October and did not finally reconvene until January 1531. Henry and his advisers simply did not know what to do with it.

As for the grand petition, what that eventually came down to was a letter cobbled together by Henry's secretariat and signed by eighty-two people hand-picked from those who supported the annulment. Even this document was not achieved without difficulty. There were significant gaps in the list of signatories. Lord Chancellor More was not invited, nor were seventeen of England's twenty-three bishops. Even some of the nobles, courtiers and senior churchmen who were prepared to support the exercise demurred at the first draft and the missive had to be toned down. However, it still extended a veiled threat. After urging his holiness to make a speedy res-olution of the king's great matter it stated that his failure to comply would oblige Henry 'to seek remedy elsewhere'. There had been a time when that assertion would have been a bluff and it may still have been regarded as such in Rome but Henry's inner convictions, shored up by the Boleyn group, sycophantic courtiers and religious enthusiasts, would not be denied. And yet, and yet, and yet, by the autumn of 1530 no one had discovered a way out of the king's dilemma.

It was not for want of trying. Anne's family was feverishly active in following every avenue which might lead to the desired destination. The prize of unassailable influence and all that meant in terms of wealth, prestige and power was tantalizingly close but might yet elude their outstretched fingers. They used their patronage network of scholars and printers to produce pro-annulment propaganda and in the process discovered an unlikely champion. In August 1529 two of the king's advisers had a chance meeting over supper with Dr Thomas Cranmer of Jesus College, Cambridge. Their discussion of the burning topic of the day was couched in terms of academic debate and Cranmer pointed out that the substantive issue was one of Christian ethics and not canon law. It would, therefore, be appropriate to canvas the opinions of Europe's leading theological faculties. This was not a startlingly original idea; some foreign scholars had already been approached for their views on the question of the validity of the king's marriage, but the concept of a continent-wide campaign was very much flavour of the month – or the decade. At a time of theological ferment the universities were not infre-quently called upon to adjudicate on the rival claims of Rome,

Wittenberg, Geneva and Zurich. As soon as the conversation was reported to Henry, he embraced the idea wholeheartedly, ordered Cranmer back from Cambridge, installed him in George Boleyn's townhouse and set him to work to draft a proposition to be set before the great brains of Europe. This set off a quite extraordinary Christendom-wide debate. If the great matter had not been an international *cause célèbre* before, it certainly became one now. One hundred and sixty scholars and twenty-three universities were canvassed by pro and anti partisans. As Diarmaid MacCulloch has pointed out, 'it must have been the single most lucrative source of consultancy fees for academics during the whole sixteenth century'.[109]

In the spring and summer of 1530, Cranmer, Thomas Boleyn and his son headed the mission that toured foreign universities gleaning support for the king. It goes without saying that the verdicts given by the university faculties were not purely the result of unfettered academic debate. Money played an important part, as did political considerations. For example, the Sorbonne was unable to come to a decision as long as Francis I's two sons were held hostage in Spain. As soon as they were released the Parisian professors suddenly discovered that Henry's case was crystal clear. Anti-papal sentiment was another influential factor. There was general acceptance, certainly in humanist circles, that Rome was too powerful and too corrupt. The conciliar movement was growing in strength and a decision in Henry's favour was sometimes given as much to clip the pope's wings as to please the king. As soon as Thomas Boleyn, Cranmer and their party returned in the high summer of 1530, Henry interrupted his summer progress to convene a special meeting of leading coun-cillors at Hampton Court. This gathering was a crucial moment in the campaign. The emissaries reported in detail on opinions in Europe about the king's conflict with the pope and England's leaders considered the tactics now to be adopted. However, some-thing more important happened in those few days at Wolsey's old palace. The concept of royal supremacy was defined, accepted by the king and made the cornerstone of future policy.

The Boleyns' hired scholars had been busy ferreting out anti-papal ammunition. At the Hampton Court meeting Cranmer was able to offer the king a taste of what they had come up with. Henry was so excited that he demanded to see written proof as soon as possible. This must explain why, a few weeks later, the king was presented with, not a finely-bound volume setting out the royal case, but a bundle of manuscript pages known to history as the *Collectanea satis copiosa* ('The Sufficiently Abundant Collections'). As the title suggests, this was a collection of proofs texts drawn from old chronicles, the church fathers and holy scripture which purported to demonstrate that the Bishop of Rome had no rightful claim to exercise spiritual supremacy over the universal church and that, certainly in England, the king enjoyed a plenitude of jurisdiction in all matters. Henry loved it. He spattered his own copy with personal annotations. This bundle of documents supported everything he believed about himself and his heritage. Specifically, it took him back to the congenial historico-mythology on which he had been raised, for the *Collectanea* drew extensively on Geoffrey of Monmouth's, *Historia Regum Britanniae*, which was the principal source for Thomas Malory's *Le Morte Darthur*. Geoffrey was the literary originator of the stories about Arthur, the Round Table and the chivalric code which, for Henry, were of the very essence of English kingship. The manuscript provided him with a potted history of his kingdom stretching back to Roman times and argued that, so far from his seeking to challenge papal authority, it was popes who had subtly, over the centuries, usurped the power rightfully belonging to his predecessors.

There can be little doubt that the arguments contained in the *Collectanea* provided the content of the conference held in August 1530. The one principle that leaped out of the pages of scholarly quotation and interpretation was this: 'the custom of England [is] that no-one should be compelled to go to law out of the kingdom'.[110] This assertion was pregnant with consequences for the future but for the present it answered Henry's case superbly and he immediately despatched messengers to

Rome to inform Clement that he had discovered ancient and inviolable proof that his holiness had no right of involvement in the issue of the king of England's marital arrangements. This was new. It was a dramatic shifting of ground and it placed in the king's hands the scalpel which would soon sever the muscles, nerves, veins and arteries connecting the English church to continental Christendom. The name of that surgical instrument was 'royal supremacy'.

This raises vital questions which have provoked debate among generations of historians. Was Henry or anyone else at that fateful meeting aware of the implications of what they were proposing? Did the idea of the king's supremacy over the church in England emerge from the Boleyns' carefully garnered scholarly opinions? Or did the *Collectanea* merely provide chapter and verse for a conviction Henry had long held? Professor Bernard argues cogently that, from very early in his conflict with Rome, Henry was minded, if necessary, to act unilaterally over the annulment issue. From the time of Wolsey's fall he was more energetic in pursuing his political objectives.[111] For one thing, he was back at Westminster. Ever since the fire of 1512 Henry had been a king *in absentia*. He had occasionally decided that he wanted to be an effective executive head and had protested about not having his own council around him as he toured from palace to hunting lodge to royal manor but, as we have seen, the cardinal had always managed to keep the reins in his own hands and, most of the time, the king had been content for him to do so. However, one of Henry's first acts after the minister's condemnation for Praemunire had been to confiscate York Place, Wolsey's power base. The cardinal had protested that the palace was the London residence of the Archbishops of York and not his personal possession but Henry was not to be put off by such a mere technicality.

The building programme he now set in train proclaimed his intention to locate himself at the centre of government. On land bought from Westminster Abbey and Eton College he erected new buildings and enclosed a hunting park (now St James's Park). By 1536, Henry had 'most sumptuously and curiously builded and edified many and distinct beautiful, costly and pleasant lodgings, buildings and mansions for his grace's singular pleasure, comfort and commodity, [with] a park walled and environed with brick and stone'.[112] The new headquarters sprawling along the Thames from Charing Cross to Westminster Hall were renamed the Palace of Whitehall.

Right at the very centre of this royal complex he installed what he intended to be a permanent statement of his own magnificent achievement. It was a self-apotheosis, almost an early obituary. It declared to those admitted to this inner sanctum how Henry VIII wished to be regarded by contemporaries and remembered by posterity. As discussed earlier, in 1537 the king's painter, Hans Holbein, created a fresco for the new privy chamber, the innermost of all the public rooms, accessible only to the king's intimates and those guests who were especially favoured with an invitation to the richly furnished hub of the Tudor state. If there was a room which gave physical expression to Henry's personality this was it. The life-size painting celebrated the achievements of the two Tudor monarchs. Henry VII, Henry VIII and their wives were positioned round a stone plinth bearing, in Latin, the following inscription:

If it pleases you to behold the glorious likeness of heroes, look at these, for no inscription ever represented finer men. Between them there was great competition and rivalry and [posterity] may well debate whether father or son should take the palm. Both were victorious. The father triumphed over his foes, quenched the fires of civil war and brought his people lasting peace. The son was born to a greater destiny. He it was who banished from the altars undeserving men and replaced them with men of worth. Presumptuous popes were forced to yield before him and when Henry VIII bore the sceptre true religion was established and, in his reign, God's teachings received their rightful reverence.

There could be no clearer evidence of the oppressive weight of his father's legacy which Henry felt or of his determination to escape from it. He would have loved to be able to set in the balance against Henry VII's achievements the winning of a crown in France or the brokering of international peace. Since he could not make such claims, he chose to be remembered as the king who reformed the English church. So, was this the objective he had set himself at the beginning of the 1530s? Did this pleasure-and-glory-seeking king, halfway through his reign, metamorphose himself into a serious religious hero? Let us return to 1530 and review the evidence.

Up until the Hampton Court conference the only task occupying the king and his emissaries was that of persuading Rome to grant him release from his marriage. The realization that the pope had no say in the matter changed everything. It was not only old authorities which declared that kings were supreme within their own realms. Cranmer and the Boleyns returned from the continent having learned much about the current state of thinking in radical circles. Therefore, as the debate intensified, it changed not only in tone, but also in content. The seedling arguments about royal power, the nature of a commonwealth, religious freedom and the status of clergy which were to dominate much of English life over the next century-and-a-half were sown in these increasingly tense months. The basic issue of the Reformation was the nature of authority in church and state. It was not a new problem but it came to a head at this time because of Luther's challenge and the spread of vernacular Bibles. Any reading of the New Testament revealed that the granting of primacy to the bishops of Rome could only be supported by extremely strained interpretation of a couple of proof texts. Humanists and heretics throughout Europe were united in believing that the deplorable state of the church was, in large measure, due to Rome's involvement in secular politics.

Jean Mair (1469–1550), a Scottish theologian teaching in Paris, expressed in his writings a widely held opinion that kings exercised their power by consent of their subjects and not by permission of the pope and had no right to bow to papal authority without their consent. This chimed perfectly with the old English chronicles, which were accepted as factual and which demonstrated that the intrusion of papal authority into the kingdom dated only from 1213, when King John had – scandalously – placed his realm under the suzerainty of the pope. Influential schools of history, theology and political philosophy, therefore, combined to challenge papal claims and Henry began to see his conflict with Clement as a celebrated test case in a wider debate. Cranmer and other Boleyn scholars represented Henry's marital problem to him not as the cause of strained relations with Clement, but as the result of the pope's clinging to an authority to which he had no right. Henry was immensely excited and energized by the evidence his team of researchers had turned up because it presented him as a pious ruler campaigning for the reform of the church rather than as a selfish monarch who simply wanted to ditch his wife – which is exactly what he still was.

The *Collectanea* gave Henry a new self image. It did not define supreme headship with any precision; rather, it left it open for the king and his advisers to interpret it as they wished. Naturally, the king chose to rely on those who held the most exalted view of his sovereignty. This view has been described as 'caesaro-papalism', the uniting in the royal person of all temporal and spiritual authority. If the pope was no longer recognized as the Vicar of Christ in the English church – so ran the argument – then that role must belong to the king who, at his anointing, was gifted with the responsibility to exercise control of doctrine, discipline and liturgy. His *imperium* resembled that of the Byzantine rulers of old. Cranmer went so far as to assert that the royal conscience was directed by the Holy Spirit. Small wonder that the diffident Cambridge don now became Henry's favourite theologian. Simon Grynaeus, a Swiss reformer visiting England in 1531, reported that the king spent much time in discussion with Cranmer and never declared his mind on any theological issue without first checking it with his new expert.

Cranmer's rise marked More's fall. For more than a decade Sir Thomas had enjoyed a measure of intimacy with the king, according to his biographer, William Roper, who has left us the familiar picture of Henry and his minister strolling arm-in-arm through the corridors of Greenwich and Richmond deep in conversation or standing on the palace roof to gaze at the stars and discourse on 'astronomy, geometry, divinity and. . .worldly affairs'.[113] Henry knew that More did not support his intention to end his marriage. They had reached a tacit agreement that the king would not press the issue and More would not air his opinion in public but, inevitably, this fundamental disagreement put a strain on their relationship and Anne's intense dislike of the lord chancellor did not help matters. More, who boasted to Erasmus that he regarded evangelicals as 'absolutely loathsome' and was determined to be 'as hateful to them as anyone can possibly be',[114] inevitably found himself doing his level best to counteract Anne's influence. Thus, for example, when Simon Fish returned to England, More was aching to arrest him. He was balked in this because, thanks to Anne's support, the radical author enjoyed the king's protection. That did not stop the lord chancellor writing a refutation of Fish's *Supplication for the Beggars*. He even went so far as to order the arrest of Fish's wife on the specious grounds that she did not share the immunity extended to her husband. It seems that Mistress Fish was only saved by the fact that she was nursing a daughter sick with the plague. Such were the vicious eddies swirling around the court in the early days of the Reformation.

More was one of the few people who could see what was at stake as the religious conflict gathered momentum. How much Henry understood of the consequences of the royal supremacy is very much open to question. He certainly did not share Anne's evangelical zeal to change doctrine, purge ceremonies and improve clerical standards but, at this stage of their relationship, love would have covered any divergence of opinion.

In all probability he was not aware of any divergence. There
was much common ground between Lutherans and humanists
and the king regarded himself as being sympathetic to the
moderate demands of the latter. In September 1527, he had
written to Erasmus:

> In my tender years when I first knew you, I entertained for you
> no slight regard; and this has been daily augmented by the
> honourable mentions you have made of me in your writings.
> Now, seeing the unwearied labours you have suffered in the
> cause of Christianity, I am desirous of succouring your pious
> efforts, for I have myself felt for some years the same desire of
> restoring the faith and religion of Christ to its pristine dignity
> and repelling the impious attacks of the heretics, that the Word
> of God may run on purely and freely but such is the infelicity of
> the times and the prostration of good manners that all things
> degenerate.[115]

Henry shared two basic tenets with the Erasmians and the
wider body of evangelical opinion: popes are subject to holy
scripture and Christians (including clergy) are subject to kings.
He approved the stance of Tyndale (and Luther) that rulers
have the responsibility of reforming the churches in their lands
to bring teaching and conduct into harmony with the Bible. If
the pope opposed the will of the godly prince he was setting
himself up against the word of God and must be resisted.
Whether Henry would have reached such strongly held convictions if the necessity of wriggling out of his marriage had not
arisen may well be doubted. For him theology was the servant
of the royal will and not vice-versa. He certainly did not think
through the implications of his stance on the Bible. When he
referred to 'restoring the faith and religion of Christ to its
pristine dignity' as indicated in the Bible he was using evangelical language. This was precisely what Luther and even more
radical reformers were doing. However, if he really believed
that allowing the word of God to operate 'purely and freely'
would eradicate heresy then he understood neither the word of

God nor contemporary heresy. It was the very freedom being given to Scripture that was producing the unorthodox doctrines he personally deplored. His real concern was not to replace the authority of the pope with the authority of the Bible but to replace the authority of the pope with the authority of Henry, and what he meant by the pure and free word of God was the word of God as interpreted by himself.

The distinction between Henry's treatment of Scripture and the evangelical treatment of Scripture is clearly illustrated by the rival interpretations of Leviticus 20.21. Henry convinced himself that the Mosaic law forbade marriage to the widow of a deceased brother. That was what he wanted the Bible to say: it was the bedrock of his case for the annulment. Both Tyndale and Luther contradicted this interpretation. Had they been motivated by a desire to win the king's support for reform, it might have been supposed that they would have agreed with him but faithfulness to the 'plain word of God' came before the desire to seek the approval of princes. Although their take on the king's dilemma differed slightly in detail, both reformers were clear that Leviticus referred to bigamy and not marriage to a dead brother's wife. Tyndale affirmed that, in marrying Catherine, Henry had performed a holy act, in accordance with Deuteronomy 25.5. Luther thundered that for Henry to divorce Catherine and bastardize their daughter would be an offence against both God and man.

There was no consistency in Henry's attitude towards the German reformer and his followers. When it suited him he was quite prepared to enlist their aid. The king who had actually ventured into print to condemn Luther as a 'detestable trumpeter of pride, calumnies and schism' now told Chapuys that, though there was a certain amount of heresy in Luther's writings, 'that was not sufficient reason for reproving and rejecting the many truths he had brought to light'.[116] He even had the gall to blame Wolsey for urging him to write the *Assertio*. Henry's one-track mind saw no contradiction in attempting to enlist the support of the arch heretic for his own anti-papal campaign. He despatched agents to Wittenberg and tried to lure Luther's assistant, Philipp Melanchthon, to England.

The extent of his indifference to the church's war against heresy is indicated by the career of Robert Barnes. Barnes had been a marked man ever since 1526 when, as a member of the Austin friary at Cambridge, he had preached a suspect sermon, been examined by Wolsey, forced to recant and placed under virtual house arrest in the London headquarters of his order. Not chastened by the experience, Barnes had made contact with radical groups in the capital and actually used his place of confinement as a distribution centre for Tyndale's New Testament. When this came to the attention of Bishop Tunstall the troublesome friar was moved out of London and placed under stricter surveillance. Fearing worse treatment as a relapsed heretic, Barnes now faked his own suicide by leaving a pile of clothes together with a note on a river bank and returning to London disguised as a pauper. From there he took ship for the continent and made his way to Wittenberg. Here English agents tracked him down but, instead of trying to lure him back to face a fresh trial and an inevitable burning, they offered him royal employment. Henry commissioned him to obtain Luther's support for the annulment proceedings. As we have seen, Luther was not prepared to dance to Henry's tune but Barnes' failure did not affect his standing with the king. The heretical friar had by now ventured into print and his writings left no doubt whatsoever about his Lutheran credentials. This did not bother Henry who believed that Barnes could still be useful to him in his negotiations with German scholars and Protestant princes. The friar was given safe conduct back to England where, almost certainly, he was received in audience by the king in 1531. For the next nine years he enjoyed royal patronage. He travelled to and fro between England and Germany as an official diplomat, was appointed a royal chaplain, received ecclesiastical preferment and became one of the country's most prominent evangelical preachers. Then he was burned as a heretic. With protégés such as this, it is small wonder that some observers believed the king of England to be, as one French reformer dubbed him a veritable Hezekiah (the great eighth-century BC king of Judah who was famed for purifying the worship of the temple).

Egotist that he was, Henry made the mistake of believing his own publicity. Just as he had once eagerly paraded before his people as the epitome of chivalric knighthood, a reincarnation of Arthur and Henry V, so now he assumed the robes of sacerdotal imperium and actually began to believe that he had a destiny to fulfil as the scourge of the English church. The emphasis in court festivities moved gradually from the antics of the tiltyard to plays and songs lampooning the pope, expounding biblical themes or celebrating the virtues of Henry's royal ancestors. The most popular writer of the new style entertainments was John Bale, a renegade monk and evangelical controversialist dubbed 'Bilious Bale' because of the crude nature of his anti-papal invective. The title of his earliest known stage work provides a good idea of the kind of fare now being offered to courtiers: *A Brief Comedy or Interlude of John Baptist's Preaching in the Wilderness, opening the crafty Assaults of the Hypocrites* [i.e. friars and monks] *with the glorious Baptism of the Lord Jesus Christ*. Henry responded to the new revelation he had received with a new vigour in promoting it. Chapuys reported with some surprise that the king was now devoting himself assiduously to business rather than regarding it as a tiresome interruption to his pleasures. Henry's old dreams of battlefield glory were now transferred to his conflict with Rome.

That prompts the question why a further six years passed before the royal supremacy was fully established. The answer is twofold: it took a long time to work out how to put into effect the constitutional revolution which naturally followed from the crown's new identity and Henry was all too well aware of the forces ranged against him. Even when he was at his most bullish, he experienced moments of doubt about where his campaign was taking him. Chapuys recorded one conversation between Henry and Anne in which the king expressed his anxiety about the emperor's hostility. Anne was dismissive. 'He can do you no harm,' she said. Moreover, she continued, if push came to shove the Boleyns were ready to pledge 10,000 armed men at their own expense.[117] The image of Henry boldly taking on the cohorts of Rome and relentlessly pursuing his cause is an over-simplification. As long as Anne was behind him, screwing his courage to the sticking place, and as long as he entertained no doubts about the importance of marrying her, he was Henry the Lionheart. However, when he contemplated the strength of conservative opinion at home and abroad and mused on the wider conflict between orthodox faith and heresy, he wavered.

He had good reason to be hesitant. The international scene was both confused and confusing. As long as Wolsey had been swaggering his way around Europe England had been able to make its voice heard in the councils where important decisions were made. Henry felt the loss of the cardinal's massive personality. Without it England was forced to the diplomatic sidelines. The fear that haunted Henry and his advisers was that Charles and Francis would mend their differences and that, egged on by the pope, they might direct their combined resources against secessionist England. In fact, there was little chance of this happening. Anne was right in her assessment that the emperor was in no position to make trouble. He had bigger problems to deal with than his aunt's wounded pride and even than his continuing feud with Francis – problems involved in maintaining the unity and integrity of the empire in a changing world. Muslim pressure in the East and the Mediterranean was radically changing the map. Developments in defensive architecture were changing the nature of warfare; military sieges were becoming impossibly lengthy to sustain. And the spread of Luther's pestilential doctrines among the ruling class in Germany was changing the religious cohesion of western Christendom. In his earnest attempts to restore political and religious harmony to the empire, Charles found himself between a rock and a hard place. The Protestant princes, who formed themselves into a political/military alliance, the Schmalkaldic League, in 1531, demanded the reform of abuses in the Catholic church and the popes (Clement VII, 1523–34, and Paul III, 1534–49) set their faces firmly against any demand for a general council to deal with such abuses.

Henry found it difficult to know how to deal with this changed situation. The diplomatic imperative was no longer a matter of maintaining and exploiting the Habsburg-Valois balance; he had to find a way of relating to the German princes. That, in its turn, raised religious issues. In February 1531, the Schmalkaldic League formally approached Henry, seeking diplomatic support in its quarrel with the emperor and the pope. The writers were eager to dispel calumnies put about by their Catholic enemies that they were opportunists, using religion as a cloak for their disloyalty to their temporal and spiritual overlords and they claimed affinity with English scholars such as John Colet, who had called on Rome in vain to root out corruption and vice in the church. In his cautious reply, the king welcomed their concern for reform but counselled them to avoid extremism. There was a commercial aspect to the relations now being established with Protestant northern Germany. With Low Countries trade being inhibited by poor relations with the emperor, England's other partners, the Hanseatic merchants operating from Baltic and North Sea ports, assumed new importance. However, it was the marriage issue which dominated everything else and Wittenberg's failure to endorse Henry's plans prevented the development of close ties with the Schmalkaldic League at this time. His only practicable political ally remained Francis I and friendship with France was never popular at home.

In England, Henry had to face the ecclesiastical establishment and, beyond it, a people who had, for generations, been set in their ways. Towards the clergy he became increasingly bitter. He could not directly harm the pope but he could vent his anger on the pope's minions and over the next couple of years he devised ways of bullying them. Yet, a certain amount of caution was necessary because the pope had within his power the ultimate sanctions of excommunication and interdict. The latter was, in effect, an order to all clergy to go on strike, forbidding them to offer any of the sacraments and ministrations of the church. Henry's subjects might grumble about incompetent, arrogant, venial, money-grubbing clergy but would they accept a reform programme which risked setting them at odds with the priesthood, with all the consequences that might ensue – in this world and the next? Henry was forced to have regard to public opinion – and that only made him more resentful. Furthermore, since winning the people to his side involved employing authors, pamphleteers, playwrights and preachers who could demonstrate how the popes had usurped the power rightly belonging to kings, he could not avoid taking into his service propagandists who were more extreme than the government might have liked. Henry wanted to bring about change that was draconian but, at the same time, restricted and which certainly fell well short of heresy. It was a difficult, if not impossible, tightrope to negotiate. How were people to differentiate between banned books and those which had the king's blessing?

The pamphlets and books that went out from the king's presses played upon incipient nationalism, hoping to stir up indignation against the dastardly influence of a foreign pope in the dynastic affairs of England. However, any xenophobia among the people at large was traditionally directed against France (and was, by extension, in favour of the emperor) and both Catherine and Mary were very popular. In a letter of June 1531 to Thomas Boleyn, the Earl of Wiltshire, Cranmer considered arguments being put forward by the enemy. He feared that some of their opinions had substance and that conservative reaction in the country at large might prove to be the main stumbling block. While acknowledging that the king's matrimonial affairs 'belongeth not to their [the people's] judgement', he thought that the majority were content with the prospect of the crown passing to Mary and resentful of any change to that arrangement. There was, he feared, some truth in the argument that most of the king's subjects were scandalized at the prospect of Henry setting aside his wife and were unlikely to be persuaded by any scholarly rationale:

> For what loving men toward their prince would gladly hear that either their prince should be so infortunate to live so many years in matrimony so abominable or that they should be taken and counted so bestial [as] to approve and to take for lawful, and that [for] so many years, a matrimony so unlawful and so much against nature. . .when they hear this matrimony dispraised and spoken against, neither by their own minds nor by reasons that be made against this matrimony, can they be persuaded to grudge against the matrimony, [rather] they do grudge against the divorce.[118]

Such considerations carried little weight with Wiltshire and his daughter. The people might grumble but Anne knew herself to be heading a holy crusade and one which relied only on the continued support of the king. It was with good reason that Chapuys identified her as 'the principal cause of the spread of Lutheranism in this country'.[119] Henry was caught in a trap which he, himself, had set. To change the metaphor, he was driving a machine of which he was not in full control. In order to achieve his limited objective he had authorized lively criticism of the traditional church and he could not stop that criticism going too far.

Only in parliament could the new relationship between crown and church be precisely defined and when that much-deferred assembly met in January 1532, Henry's managers set about drafting the required legislation. This is the point at which one of the most controversial figures of the age, Thomas Cromwell, enters the story. He was the archetypal self-made man, a thrusting go-getter who, inevitably, attracted admirers and detractors. As a teenager he had left his home in Putney which was dominated by a father whose business success derived in part from his sailing close to the legal wind. After an adventurous life as a mercenary soldier, merchant and lawyer, Cromwell was head-hunted by Wolsey as an ideal agent for handling his legal affairs and property transactions. John Foxe later described him as 'pregnant in wit. . .in judgement discreet, in tongue eloquent, in service faithful, in stomach courageous, in his pen active'[120] but his principal asset was his mastery of cool logic. If Robert Graves was right in identifying a genius as someone who 'not only diagnoses the problem, but supplies the answers', then Thomas Cromwell was a genius. He had the ability to work at stubborn, brain-teasing questions from first principles, without being deflected by irrelevant facts, distracting emotions or opposition. He was a member of the parliament that was summoned in 1523 and, on Wolsey's fall, he looked to the House of Commons as the best arena in which to continue his upward career. He offered his services to the Duke of Norfolk as someone who could advance the government's policies in the lower house and, with the duke's patronage, he obtained a seat. As an MP and someone on the fringe of court life, he was well aware of the stalemate over the king's great matter and he knew how desperate Henry was to find men with fresh ideas. Convinced that he came into that category, all Cromwell had to do was engineer an audience with the king.

Cromwell's leap from relative obscurity into the position of Henry's principal adviser took observers by surprise. Chapuys reported that this upstart had got to speak with the king on the pretence of seeking royal mediation in a private dispute, whereupon he addressed Henry, 'in such flattering terms and eloquent language – promising to make him the richest king in the world – that the king at once took him into his service and made him councillor, though his appointment was kept secret for four months'.[121] The ambassador was sourly reminiscing some five years after the event and what he wrote was coloured by subsequent happenings. It is unlikely that Cromwell made a bald offer to enrich the king or that the king would have believed him if he had. Nor need we assume that Cromwell's rise was quite so abrupt. He would have been adroit enough to commend himself to the dominant court group and he had something important in common with them. During his travels and his studies (he was a voracious reader) he had become an adherent of the evangelical cause. He was well versed on the controversy surrounding the issue of papal supremacy and intellectually he put most other members of the council in the shade. It would have taken the Boleyns very little time to welcome Cromwell as a useful addition to their team and to recommend him to Henry. As for Henry, he never warmed to Cromwell and certainly never regarded him as another Wolsey but he did recognize a man whose talents he could use. With Cranmer as their chief spokesman in ecclesi-astical councils and Cromwell taking on preparation of the royal case in parliament, Anne and her supporters were well placed to see the success of their campaign. But it would still be a long haul.

The next couple of years witnessed what was arguably the most profound upheaval in English life and there is a temp-tation to regard the break with Rome as the result of clear-cut policy. It was not. Henry and those carrying out his will were trying various tactics simultaneously. This makes it difficult to determine who was doing what at any one time. Did the king keep a tight rein on the minutiae of policy implementation or did he allow Cromwell a free hand? England was excised from Latin Christendom but who wielded the scalpel? The answer is that, while Henry was the chief surgeon, he depended on other members of the theatre staff. When necessary, Henry inter-vened personally but most of the time Cromwell and the court party in parliament were responsible for steering policy.

Ever since Wolsey's fall the threat of Praemunire proceedings had been used to put the frighteners on the whole body of the English clergy. The cardinal had been obliged to acknowledge as unlawful his exercise of legatine jurisdiction. It followed – or at least it was arguable – that any church officers who had acted with him in his capacity as legate were also guilty of Praemunire. Several of the more obdurate higher clergy (particularly Fisher, whom Henry had always loathed) had been singled out for prosecution in King's Bench and the potential for further legal action was limitless. This demonstrated that Henry could match any sanctions the pope could levy. In January 1531 the church leaders tried to buy themselves out of trouble. The southern convocation offered Henry £100,000 in return for a blanket pardon, a clear and limited definition of Praemunire and confirmation of the rights of the clergy as laid down in Magna Carta. It was a smart move by a clerical assembly who knew how cash-strapped the government was. Henry was tempted and he spent some days discussing the offer with his councillors. The radicals insisted what Henry must have understood anyway, that to give in at this point would be to limit royal authority over the English church. Farewell supremacy! So, the king now added his own condition to the granting of a pardon: the convocations were to acknowledge that he had been charged with the cure of his subjects' souls and that, accordingly, they were to accept him as 'sole protector and supreme head of the Church of England'. After a lot more haggling, during which Henry and Archbishop William Warham had, in private, a 'full and frank exchange of views', a compromise formula was found. The ecclesiastical establishment agreed to accept Henry's titles 'as far as the law of Christ allows'. Since what that law did allow would always be open to debate, round one had clearly gone to the king.

However, the contest was far from being a simple one between a godly sovereign and a church in need of discipline. The matrimonial issue remained at the centre of Henry's thinking. He still had his agents in Rome trying to stall the judicial process there and he maintained continuous pressure on Francis I. He persisted in the hope that diplomatic influence would wear down Clement's resistance. This suggests one of the fascinating 'ifs' of history. If some compromise could have been found which allowed the Curia to remit Henry's case to

England without obvious loss of papal face, how would that have changed the king's attitude? Once he had got his own way over the annulment would he have quietly abandoned his dreams of being a reformer of the church? Might he have reverted to his role as a defender of the Catholic faith, turning his face decisively and firmly against the heretics and operating in harmony with Rome? In his bargaining with the pope he certainly made offers, admittedly vague, of fighting his holiness's enemies in return for help with his own problem. From what we know of Henry so far, how do we think he would have reacted? These questions are not as pointless as they might seem, at first sight, because they enable us to focus on the king's character, his motives and the extent to which he directed policy.

It is my opinion that this unprincipled monarch was so concerned about his reputation that he would have had no hesitation about changing tack as soon as it suited him. He was a man with no ideological anchor. We have seen how he disassociated himself from unpopular policies such as the Amicable Grant and how his attitude towards prominent Lutherans veered to and fro. He instructed his representatives in Rome to make it clear that he cared not a fig for papal anathema but this was blatantly not true. A couple of incidents indicate just how concerned he was about popular opinion. In February 1531 members of William Warham's household were stricken with food poisoning. Two people died and it was probably the aged archbishop's abstemiousness which saved him from at least serious illness. A certain Richard Roose was arrested and confessed to having deliberately contaminated the ingredients of the household porridge. Since this occurred at a time when Warham was figure-heading the church's resistance to royal demands, the rumour inevitably spread that the king was behind a plot to assassinate him. Henry's reaction was an example of extraordinary overreaction. He had a parliamentary bill introduced which identified poisoning as the most heinous of crimes and established a new (and mercifully short-lived) mode of execution: those found guilty were henceforth to be boiled to death. More significantly, he went personally to parliament and delivered himself of a ninety-minute speech condemning poisoning in general and specifically the incident at Lambeth. There can be no suggestion that the king was complicit in an attempt on Warham's life but he was obviously enormously sensitive to any suggestion that he might have been.

The other affair revealed a king under-reacting to criticism. The most effective spokesperson against his attempt to put away Queen Catherine was Elizabeth Barton, known as the Holy Maid of Kent. This young, self-styled prophetess had enjoyed great celebrity for her trances, miracles and supposedly inspired utterances since 1525 and was accepted by thousands of devotees as a true messenger from God. Nor was it just the common people who were impressed by her. Among those who implicitly believed in the Maid's 'revelations' were Warham, Fisher, members of several religious houses and various ladies of the royal court. Even Thomas More had an audience with her, though he was careful not to listen to any of her pronouncements on matters of state. From the beginning of the king's great matter Elizabeth inveighed against it and her denunciations became increasingly hysterical as time passed. By 1531 she was forecasting horrific divine judgement against the king if he did not put away his whore and return to his wife. The Holy Maid spoke for the majority of the king's subjects and, if Henry retained any doubt that this was the case, a petition from the Commons asking him (in much more polite language) to return to Catherine dispelled it. Any strong king, determined to pursue his own policies and crush all opposition – and particularly a king who believed himself to be God's representative – would, at the very least, have told his critics to mind their own business and would probably have subjected Elizabeth and her accomplices to investigation, under torture if necessary. Henry did not dare to confront popular opinion so boldly. He sent the Commons a 'slight' answer via the speaker.

As for Elizabeth Barton, even when she forced her way into his presence at Canterbury the following year and made a scene, he did nothing.

Wary and changeable though the king was, the one issue on which he would not yield was his intention to make a fully legal marriage with Anne. By the time parliament reassembled in January 1532 he was desperate and so was his intended bride. So, too, was the new royal 'fixer', Thomas Cromwell, for as yet he had no ready-made programme for achieving whatever it was that he had promised the king. The crucial events of the next three months have all the signs of trial and error. The two houses were in no mood to submit to court guidance. The Commons refused a request to grant the king taxation, ostensibly to face an expected clash with Scotland. Cromwell drafted a bill to authorize the English bishops to adjudicate on the king's marriage but realized that the atmosphere in both houses was too hostile. It was mid-March before Henry was in possession of a parliamentary stick with which to belabour the pope and he only got it with the greatest difficulty.

Weeks before, the royal 'party' in the Commons had initiated a debate on annates, sums paid to Rome on the inauguration of every bishop and archbishop. Parliamentarians 'discovered' that huge sums were being leached from the country to swell papal coffers and petitioned the king to put a stop to it. This manoeuvre was designed to enable Henry to point out that his subjects were angry with the papacy and that he would be unable to curb their hostility – unless, of course, Clement was prepared to accommodate him over that 'other business'. Unfortunately, this fiction was exposed when the petition was turned into a bill, for it aroused enormous opposition in both houses. The spiritual peers, of course, spoke against it and it only squeezed through the Lords after Henry had thrice attended debates there and agreed to insert a delaying clause decreeing that the act, once passed, would only be made operative by letters patent. But why did the Commons resist? The motion had, after all, originated in their

own ranks. The reason was that that the gentlemen and
burgesses had seen through the royal stratagem and knew that
they were being used to attack the ancient rights of the church.
In order to get his own way Henry had to resort to unprecedented tactics. He went to the Commons house in person and
demanded that the members vote in his presence – ayes to one
side, noes to the other. Papal response was anticipated in a
clause which stated:

> Should the pope react by sentence of excommunication or
> interdict, it is further enacted that the King and his lay subjects
> may 'without any scruple of conscience. . .lawfully to the
> honour of Almighty God, the increase and continuance of
> virtue and good example within this realm', continue to enjoy
> the sacraments, ceremonies and services of Holy Church, any
> papal censures notwithstanding.[122]

We may well wonder how many of the king's subjects actually
believed that.

By the time of the Easter recess Westminster had become a
battleground where crown, parliament and church were
fighting for their varied interests. This was something new.
Although parliament had almost always convened there and
though the council usually met in Star Chamber, the southern
convocation had only just moved its locus from St Paul's in
order to be closer to the action and king and court were back
'on site' in the refurbished York House. This proximity of the
contending parties made conflicts more intense. (We have
already seen that Henry was ready to intervene in parliamentary debates.) It was this clash of interests which generated
the heat which finally melted the judicial powers of the church.
The crucial sequence of events began with the 'Supplication
against the Ordinaries'. This was a list of complaints against
the clergy presented to the king by the Commons. It reiterated
most of the grievances which had been expressed in 1529 but
since then resentment, especially in the capital, had grown. The
rapid spread of Lutheran books had resulted in an increase of

heresy prosecutions and that always provoked anticlerical sentiment. When Henry received the deputation he took the opportunity to chastise the Commons for rejecting measures that he had set before it. 'If you will not take some reasonable end,' he warned, 'I will stretch out the extremity of the law.'[123] The king said that he would pass on the complaints to convocation and let them know what he had decided when he received the clergy's reply. It was, on the face of it, at least, a straight 'you scratch my back and I'll scratch yours' message.

But was there more to it than that? Had Cromwell and the court party deliberately provoked the Supplication as a further weapon to be wielded against the papal hierarchy? Henry's reaction after Easter suggests that either he was complicit in stirring up discord or that he quickly realized how the Commons grievances could be exploited. Having received convocation's reply, he handed it to a Commons' delegation with the far from subtle hint, 'we think their answer will smally please you, for it seemeth to us very slender. You be a great sort of wise men; I doubt not but you will look circumspectly on the matter and we will be indifferent between you.'[124]

These seemingly calm and civilized exchanges took place against an emotional and psychological background which was anything but calm and civilized. Church leaders were fighting for the survival of their centuries-old liberties. Upholders of traditional doctrine were trying to contain the rising tide of heresy. Unorthodox believers were incensed at what seemed to them to be the arrival of a version of the Spanish Inquisition. These issues played out on the streets in personal dramas that sometimes involved life and death. When the parliamentarians had their meeting with Henry on 30 April 1532 they were well aware that a respected London lawyer known to several of them was, that very day, being burned at Newgate. The case of James Bainham had been 'headline news' throughout the winter and spring. This son of a prominent Gloucestershire family and member of the Middle Temple was apprehended in December 1531 at the instigation of Thomas More. Bainham had drawn himself to More's attention by marrying the widow of Simon Fish and the lord chancellor took a personal interest in him. It was soon widely known, or rumoured, that the lawyer had been whipped in More's house at Chelsea, then sent to the Tower to be racked. After lengthy interrogations over the next couple of months, Bainham recanted, carried his faggot and was set at liberty. Subsequently, broken by remorse, he rejected his confession and was rearrested as a relapsed heretic. Foxe, the martyrologist, gave an abbreviated account of Bainham's various sufferings:

> For almost the space of a fortnight, he lay in the bishop's coal-house in the stocks, with irons upon his legs. Then he was carried to the lord chancellor's and there chained to a post two nights. Then he was carried to Fulham [the Bishop of London's palace], where he was cruelly handled by the space of a week; then to the Tower, where he lay a fortnight, scourged with whips, to make him revoke his opinions. From thence he was carried to Barking, then to Chelsea and there condemned; and so to Newgate to be burned.[125]

It is difficult to imagine the mood of parliament's deliberations over the next few days. Strong feelings were expressed on both sides. It seems that Henry became impatient at waiting for the response he wanted for, eleven days later (on 11 May), he called representatives before him again. This time he was much more explicit:

> Well beloved subjects, we thought that the clergy of our realm had been our subjects wholly but now we have well perceived that they be but half our subjects, yea, but scarce our subjects; for all the prelates at their consecration make an oath to the pope clean contrary to the oath that they make to us, so that they seem to be his subjects and not ours.[126]

He handed over two documents for parliament's scrutiny. Hall correctly estimated the importance of this meeting: 'The opening of these oaths was one of the occasions why the pope within two years following lost all his jurisdiction in England.'[127] This proved to be the explosion which shifted the log jam. While parliament contemplated drafting new laws to break the power of church courts, the king went straight for the jugular. He demanded that convocation submit all canon law to examination by royal lawyers and enact no further laws without the assent of the crown. This threw the clergy into a panic. They protested. They tried to bargain. Henry simply ordered them to prorogue their assembly and make their submission before doing so. On 16 May 1532, a cowed convocation, from which several members had absented themselves, ratified the Submission of the Clergy. The following day Thomas More resigned as lord chancellor. The urbane scholar who had hailed young Harry as the hero of a bright new age in which tyranny would be unable to raise its head had himself become a petty tyrant and news of his fall was received with joy on the streets of London. Some radicals allowed themselves to believe that their king had, at last, joined the ranks of evangelical reform.

Henry, too, was in celebratory mood. Events were, at last, moving in the right direction. He began to make plans for another meeting with Francis I which would be an echo of the Field of Cloth of Gold but hopefully with a more positive outcome. He now lived openly with Anne and intended to take her with him on the trip to Calais. To enhance her position as royal consort he bestowed on her the marquisate of Pembroke. Suddenly everything was running the Boleyns' way. Old enemies now resigned themselves to the inevitable and fell over backwards to commend themselves to the rulers of the court. Those who failed to accommodate themselves, notably More and Fisher, were out of favour. The Duke of Norfolk had to swallow his pride as he watched his former protégé, Thomas Cromwell, become the most powerful member of the council. In August Archbishop Warham obligingly died and it took Henry very little time to select his successor. His favourite theologian, Thomas Cranmer, became primate of all England. Nothing could now stop the marriage issue being decided in the king's favour.

The visit to France lasted from 11 October to 14 November 1532, the return journey being delayed several days due to bad weather. The festivities were not on the scale of those which had marked the last meeting between the two kings. Henry and Francis were both strapped for cash and had agreed to limit their expenditure on the meeting. Nevertheless, the entertainment managers put on a brave show. Even if there were no elaborate tiltyard contests, there was feasting, dancing, hawking and a wrestling match between French and English teams. The glittering display was such as Henry's courtiers had not seen for some years. It all bespoke a new age or, rather, the return to the 'good old days' when an exuberant Henry and his young queen had presided over an unending round of lavish pleasure-taking. There was much embracing and pledging of eternal friendship between the two monarchs but very little by way of positive diplomatic commitment. Henry and Francis promised to defend Christendom with an army of 80,000 men in the event of a Turkish invasion. Henry agreed to come to the French king's aid if he was attacked by Charles and Francis vowed to do all in his power to forward Henry's case in Rome.

What was ultimately more important was that, in the relaxed and positive atmosphere of their stay in Calais, Henry and Anne finally allowed their desires free rein. They knew that as soon as Cranmer was consecrated, Henry's marriage to Catherine would be dissolved. There was no need to endure further frustration. There was, however, one little technicality to be taken into consideration. Any child of their union would have to be born and, preferably, conceived in wedlock if its claim to the throne was to be uncontested. So, when in mid-January 1533 Anne began to suspect that she was pregnant, something had to be done quickly. On or about 25 January, the couple were privately and very secretly married. At last, Henry could allow himself to believe that the years of conflict and frustration were past. He could compliment himself on having followed, through thick and thin, the dictates of his conscience. He could look forward to God's reward for his faithfulness. Never for a moment did he doubt that the child growing in Anne's belly was a boy.

# Chapter 7

## 'THESE BLOODY DAYS...'

The event of 7 September 1533 was an anticlimax. Anne Tudor, as we must now call her, was safely delivered of a healthy, red-headed baby, the image of its father – except for one crucial fact: the child was a girl (Elizabeth). For the last twelve months everything had been moving towards the final justification of Henry's stubborn defiance of the pope, the English church establishment and the bulk of his own subjects. Many were the advisers who had warned him against casting off Catherine in favour of Anne: Wolsey, More, Suffolk (and his wife, the king's sister), Francis I, Elizabeth Barton and even Martin Luther, but Henry had gone his own way. Had the baby been a boy, as all the augurs had dutifully predicted, Henry would have been vindicated, opponents of the Boleyn marriage would have been forced to accept the new dispensation, diplomats could have begun work on the restoration of relations with the pope and the emperor and the people at large would have welcomed the securing of the succession. The clouds would have drifted away to leave a landscape bathed in sunlight. As it was, little had changed. Anne's friends could take comfort from a successful pregnancy and safe birth. Her enemies were quick to insist that God would never bless a bigamous marriage.

Henry and Anne had kept their wedding secret throughout the preceding winter. This was vital because they needed Cranmer to declare the king's first marriage void. He could not do that until he had become archbishop and he could not become archbishop until the necessary papal bulls had been received. They arrived in mid-March 1533. Then regime change shifted into top gear, led by the two 'TCs'. On 14 March Cromwell introduced into parliament the measure which would be the legislative lynchpin of the English Reformation – the Act in Restraint of Appeals. Its celebrated preamble was a forthright statement of the royal supremacy:

> Where by sundry old authentic histories and chronicles it is manifestly declared and expressed that this realm of England is an empire. . .governed by one supreme head and king and having the dignity and royal estate of the imperial crown of the same, unto whom a body politic, compact of all sorts and degrees of people divided in terms and by names of spiritualty and temporalty, be bounden and owe next to God a natural and humble obedience; he being also institute and furnished by the goodness and sufferance of Almighty God with plenary, whole and entire power, pre-eminence, authority, prerogative and jurisdiction to render and yield justice and final determination to all manner of folk resiants or subjects within this realm, in all causes, matters, debates and contentions happening to occur, insurge or begin within the limits thereof, without restraint or provocation to any foreign princes or potentates of the world.[128]

The immediate object of the Act was to scotch, once and for all, the attempt of Catherine and her supporters to have her case heard in Rome but its impact was very much wider. The court party used every stratagem to ensure that this vital piece of legislation got through the parliamentary machine unscathed. Cromwell had worked industriously over several months to evolve the draft now presented to parliament and the king had then vetted it personally. Vacancies that had occurred in the lower house were filled by 'reliable' new members. Henry had appointed as the new lord chancellor Sir Thomas Audley, groom of the chamber, ex-speaker of the Commons, a friend of Cromwell and a king's man through and through. Audley's place in the Commons was taken by Humphrey Wingfield, another 'safe' candidate. The bill met with determined opposition, particularly from burgesses who feared imperial retaliation which would impact on trade, and it was only on the eve of the Easter recess that the measure cleared both houses.

In the meantime Cranmer had taken up his new post. He was consecrated on 30 March 1533. He immediately set about convening an archiepiscopal court to decide on the issue which had been at the centre of English political life for six years. He chose Dunstable as the meeting place – well away from London and close to Ampthill whither Catherine had been, to all intents and purposes, banished. In the event, the queen made it easier for her opponents by refusing to recognize the proceedings. Thus, after only four sessions, Cranmer was able to give judgement in Henry's favour on 23 May. Of course, Henry and Anne had not waited for this ecclesiastical blessing on their union. They allowed the news of their wedding to leak out and behaved in public as husband and wife. At Easter Anne attended mass in all the panoply of queen and her coronation was confidently fixed for Whit Sunday, 1 June.

This was to be the ultimate propaganda exercise. By having his wife crowned in a full traditional ceremony Henry was proclaiming his triumph to the skies. He was trumpeting his defiance to the pope, the emperor and anyone else who saw fit to criticize the fundamentals of Tudor policy. The emblem that appeared over and again in all the London pageants on the eve of the coronation was the crown imperial. What had been expressed in the Act in Restraint of Appeals was now symbolically displayed for all to see: 'this realm of England is an empire'. Weeks were spent preparing the ceremonial route the queen would travel from the Tower to Westminster on 31 May. The road was gravelled to prevent horses slipping. Gates, conduits and frontages were regilded and painted. Barriers were put up to hold the crowds back. Platforms were erected for the performance of music and the delivery of orations. Barrels of wine were brought in so that the fountains could run with claret on the great day. Streets were made gay with bunting. Henry was determined to make his 'true' queen's great day one to be remembered.

Remembered it most certainly was but by various people in different ways. Some of the thousands who turned out to watch the spectacle or perform in the various pageants recalled Anne's progress through the city as one of exciting spectacle on a fine summer's afternoon. Hall described the various stages of the procession with his usual enthusiasm for gorgeous costume and high ceremony. At the corner of Gracechurch Street, he recorded, the Steelyard merchants put on a fine display:

> for there was the mount Parnassus with the fountain of Helicon, which was of white marble and four streams without pipe did rise an ell [approximately 115cm] high and met together in a little cup above the fountain, which fountain ran abundantly racked Rhennish [i.e. cheap wine made from the leas of the grapes after the first pressing] till night. On the mountain sat Apollo and at his feet Calliope and on every side of the mountain sat four muses, playing on several sweet instruments.[129]

As the procession stopped to receive the homage of the German merchants Apollo serenaded the queen and prophesied the advent of happy days ushered in by the king's marriage. He praised Anne's beauty and assured her of producing fine sons to grace the royal line. The muses, in turn, made more reference to Anne's fecundity and to Henry's patience in remaining in bachelor state(!) until he had found his perfect mate. Similar adulation was offered at further halts along the pageant route.

Other observers told a different story. Unfortunately, most of the descriptions that have survived are the bitchy reports of diplomats whose principals opposed Henry's wife-change. Some made observations such as that the queen was ugly, that her crown was ill-fitting and that she wore a high-necked gown to cover a goitre. They delighted to point out a faux pas on the part of the organizers. They had had banners erected along the route bearing the interlinked initials 'H' and 'A'. Spectators gleefully drew one another's attention to this by pointing and calling out 'Ha! Ha!'. Chapuys, inevitably, wrote sourly of the event. According to him, the crowds looked on grim-faced and funereal. His more objective Venetian counterpart highlighted the enormous crowd which, he said, behaved with 'the utmost order and tranquillity'. More than one witness claimed that very little cheering was to be heard and that few citizens did their queen the courtesy of doffing their hats as she passed. Insofar as we can glean anything of the mood of the day, we would probably be right in concluding that Anne's triumphant procession was not received with wild rejoicing. For the vast majority of onlookers this was their first opportunity to catch a glimpse of Anne. Curiosity must account for the large turnout – that and a day off work with free booze supplied. Mayor, aldermen, livery companies and merchant bodies took part in the ceremonial because they knew what was expected of them and because they could not afford to give offence. Whether people greeted Anne with dumb insolence or not, we cannot now say. Feelings were undoubtedly mixed. While there was widespread sympathy for Catherine, there was also a sense of hopeful expectation, for one thing that was obvious to all those who craned their necks to see Queen Anne as she passed by was that she was noticeably pregnant. If she gave the people their longed-for prince they would forgive her much.

Members of court and council who were – and who were known to be – opposed to the new marriage had no option but to be present for the religious ceremony in Westminster Abbey, the coronation feast which followed and the joust held on the Monday. One man was prominent by his absence. Thomas More chose to spend the time quietly in his house at Chelsea, well away from all the brouhaha. Some of his friends urged him not to make an issue of the queen's coronation. They even clubbed together to give him £20 to buy a suitably expensive gown for the occasion. More took the money – and stayed away. When his benefactors called on him to remonstrate, he riposted by accusing them of condoning, by their silence, the king's attack on the holy church. He offered them a parable which was a very thinly veiled attack on Henry as a tyrant. The Emperor Tiberius, he said, had once issued a law making a certain offence punishable by death but exempting virgins from the extreme penalty. When a virgin whom he particularly wanted out of the way was found guilty of the crime he was in a dilemma until a cunning courtier suggested a simple solution: first deflower the girl, then kill her. It was not difficult to identify the main characters represented in the story – Henry, Cromwell and the church.

For More the political wheel had come full circle. He had once identified Henry VII as a latterday Tiberius and looked to his son to deliver the land from tyranny. Now England, he believed, was in a worse state than it had ever been under the first Tudor. It was not the firm, even cruel, exercise of power that he objected to, but the fact that power was being used against the church rather than being turned on heretics. The growing rejection of traditional customs and doctrines was something about which he could not be neutral. More's psychology was complex. The man who was torn between the desire to live in monastic seclusion and the ambition to be an influential *homme d'affaires*, the man who wore a hair shirt next to his skin spent part of his retirement from public office in a long literary battle with one of Cromwell's major propagandists. Christopher St German was a venerable lawyer of prodigious intellect whose magnum opus, *Doctor and Student*, which expounded the theoretical basis of law, remained a primary text until well into the nineteenth century. In 1533 he turned his attention – at Cromwell's behest – to the relationship between canon and common law (*A Treatise Concerning the Division Between the Spiritualty and the Temporalty*). The author went to the heart of the matter by refuting the idea that church law was based on the ineluctable law of God and was, therefore, superior to man-made law codes. Specifically, he objected to the inequitable treatment meted out to suspected heretics. More was stung into a defence of church courts and the printed dialogue went on for a couple of years. The issues raised were not dissimilar to those aired in our own day relating to the treatment of suspected terrorists. More insisted that those who deviated from religious orthodoxy were such a threat to society that they excluded themselves from the normal rights of citizens accused of common law offences. The church was fully justified in its use of detention without trial, interrogation and denial of trial by jury.

Although undeniably important, More's defence was but one contribution to a range of ideological arguments which now raged with increasing ferocity throughout the country. Henry had assumed that his triumph had ended the religious conflict, an assumption which, more than any of his many miscalculations, reveals the paucity of his political understanding. His clash with the papacy had not settled anything beyond his own marital status. Rather, it had encouraged disharmony between the 'spiritualty' and the 'temporalty' at all levels. This revealed itself in numerous ways. Reports came to the government's attention of evangelical activists protesting against local clergy or attacking objects of 'superstition' in their parish churches. Rival preachers assailed each other from their pulpits. The tide of books and pamphlets rose higher. More and more people were coming into direct contact with the Bible. The stench of burning flesh became increasingly common in the land. However, before we try to gain some flavour of the troubled 1530s we must return to Sunday 7 September 1533, the day when someone told Henry that he was the father of a healthy baby daughter.

It is a temptation of biographers to look for defining moments, turning points which have a profound effect on a subject's

psychology. Was this just such a key point? Knowing as we do
the atrocities for which an increasingly irascible king was responsible over the next dozen years we might easily imagine that this
crushing disappointment had a profound effect. Of course,
Henry rationalized, and allowed others to comfort him, with the
thought that his wife was young and had proved that she could
bring a baby to term. Next time, they assured him, it would be a
son. By the year's end, Anne was pregnant again, but in the
privacy of his own chamber Henry must have indulged blacker,
self-pitying thoughts. He had followed the dictates of his
conscience. He had obeyed God – at enormous cost. He had not
allowed himself to be deflected from his holy purpose. He
deserved some sign of divine approval. Instead, he had been
humiliated. His enemies and critics would be secretly exulting at
his discomfiture. For all the anxieties and pains he had been
through he still had not secured the dynasty. As he cancelled the
celebratory jousts which had been planned to welcome the
prince, he must have recalled the fabulous feats of arms held in
1511 which had marked the birth of his first son – the boy who
had died ten days later. The staple of Greek tragedy was the story
of the hero cursed by the gods, who moved inexorably to
destruction along a painful path of growing self-knowledge.
Henry had not yet travelled far enough along that path to
question his own conduct. Whatever had gone wrong was not his
fault: childbearing was women's business. Therefore, Anne was
responsible for the sex of their child. But, just as Henry was incapable of acknowledging personal error, so he would not allow the
world to witness any rift between himself and his wife. The end
result was that he channelled his anger into his dealings with
others. The time had come to take revenge on those who had
dared to oppose him.

The first to feel the full extent of the king's wrath were the
Maid of Kent, Elizabeth Barton, and her accomplices.
Hitherto, Henry had not been inclined to proceed against this
popular prophetess but now he was determined to turn her
ravings against herself and all who had been gullible enough to

believe them. In order to keep her in the public eye, her mentors had pushed her to make ever more outrageous prognostications until, inevitably, she had overreached herself. She had confidently asserted that, within a month of his marriage to Anne, Henry would no longer be king. As the summer days passed and he remained in good health, the hysterical seer adapted her revelation: Henry was no longer king – in the eyes of God. This tied in with a provisional excommunication issued by Clement VII which gave Henry until September 1533 to renounce Anne. In the event, the pope lacked the resolution to impose the ultimate sanction but many of Henry's subjects took the threat seriously and were very worried by it. Only those who were fully convinced that the pope did not possess the spiritual power that generations of Englishmen had believed that he did possess could shrug off Clement's posturing. They were a minority. The rest faced with deep misgivings the loss of the church's blessings. There was a measure of truth in the exaggerated report Chapuys made to the Emperor in December:

> You cannot imagine the grief of all the people at this abominable government. They are so transported with indignation at what passes that. . .I am told by many respectable people that they would be glad to see a fleet come hither in your name to raise the people; and if they had any chief among themselves who dared raise his head they would require no more.[130]

That there did exist at all levels of society such a deep-rooted papalism was, of course, proof of Henry's assertion that he could not be king in his own country until such divided loyalty was completely eradicated – a process he now set about with fierce energy.

In September 1533 Henry had Elizabeth Barton and her coterie arrested and lodged in the Tower, where the ministrations of the lieutenant, Leonard Skeffington, and his staff soon extracted detailed, grovelling confessions. Skeffington was an apt tool for the purpose. He did not flinch from the application of torture to extract information from prisoners. He even added his own instrument to the Tower's collection of instruments of terror: Skeffington's Gyves was a contraption for doubling up a victim's body so that his head touched his feet and had an advantage over the rack in that it could be carried from cell to cell as required. What inducements were applied to the Holy Maid and her accomplices we cannot know but they were sufficient to make them confess that Elizabeth's visions and miracles were fraudulent. They were now sufficiently broken in spirit to be used by Henry's propaganda machine and he was determined to extract maximum capital from them:

> On St. Clement's Day, the 23rd of November, being Sunday, the Holy Maid of Kent and two monks, two Friars Observants, a priest and two laymen were brought from the Tower of London to Paul's Cross and there stood on a scaffold all the sermon time, where was declared by him that preached [John Capon, Benedictine monk, Bishop-elect of Bangor and strong supporter of the royal supremacy] the abuse of a miracle done on the said Holy Maid at Our Lady of Court-at-Street, in Kent, by the craft of the said monks friars and a priest.[131]

That was only the beginning. The conspirators were returned to the Tower to await the reconvening of parliament, when they were proceeded against by Act of attainder. One of them died in custody. The remainder were condemned for treason. This meant that now others who had dabbled in the Holy Maid affair were vulnerable. Among those who had supported Elizabeth or simply visited her were some marked out for Henry's vengeance. The king personally insisted that the names of Fisher and More should appear on the indictment. The bishop was found guilty and had his capital sentence commuted to a fine. More's knowledge of the law enabled him to extricate himself and his name was removed from the list. Henry would have to wait for his revenge against the ex-chancellor – but not for long. The king was determined to break the man who had once been his friend but had abandoned his loyalty. Loyalty was, for Henry, a one-way street.

These were confusing times for religious enthusiasts of all hues. There was scarcely a pulpit in the land from which preachers were not assailing their hearers with their opinions about the burning issues of the day. Some were independent radicals proclaiming heresy and running the risk of arrest by both ecclesiastical and civil authorities. Others were hired by Cromwell to hammer home official anti-papal policy. In many instances the two groups overlapped, undoubted heretics being employed by the government. Yet, at the same time persecution of Lutherans and Sacramentarians (followers of Ulrich Zwingli and other continental reformers who denied the real presence of Christ in the bread and wine of holy communion) continued with Henry's blessing. Thus, those who enjoyed public executions could watch ardent papists (such as Elizabeth Barton and her group) being hanged, drawn and quartered for treason as well as convicted heretics being burned alive for their unorthodox convictions.

The treatment meted out to two prominent evangelicals in the summer and autumn of 1533 highlights the problems faced by those heading the new regime in church and state as they tried to steer a popeless English church across the minefield of irreconcilable beliefs. John Frith was a bright Cambridge graduate who, some years before, had been head-hunted by Wolsey to grace his new college at Oxford. Subsequently, he had come under Tyndale's influence and found himself in trouble with the university authorities. Wolsey had personally intervened on his protégé's behalf but Frith, considering it wise to emigrate, joined Tyndale on the continent and helped him in his literary labours. He was soon venturing into print on his own account with works attacking the doctrine of purgatory. In 1532 he returned to England, probably to seek financial assistance for himself and his young family. Thomas More ordered his arrest and Frith soon found himself in the Tower. Strangely, the lord chancellor did not pour the vials of his wrath upon this earnest young academic. Frith was actually allowed pens and paper and spent all the daylight hours in a frenzy of writing.

His new books were devotional treatises and closely reasoned rejections of the church's sacramental theology. Not only did More not have the prisoner subjected to torture, he actually replied in print to some of Frith's propositions. How can we account for More's uncharacteristic leniency? Partly, it was a response to Frith's character. There was nothing of the abrasive polemicist about him. On the contrary, he struck even his captors as being remarkably gentle and devout. However, this alone would not have saved him from More's determination to eradicate all traces of heresy from the land. What stayed his hand was the fact that Frith had the backing of Cromwell and, probably, Henry. The minister visited Frith in the Tower in an attempt to enlist him in the royal propaganda service and held out the offer of the king's protection. All that was necessary was for the prisoner to modify some of his extreme views, or at least to keep them hidden, but the ardent evangelical refused to compromise what he believed was the truth. Cranmer devoted several hours to trying to reason Frith out of his opinions. He examined the young man at Lambeth Palace and at his country residence at Croydon but all to no avail. So, with real reluctance, the archbishop referred him back to Bishop John Stokesley of London and Frith was burned at Smithfield on 4 July 1533.

The most electrifying preacher of the day was Hugh Latimer, a university lecturer at Cambridge whose sermons in St Edward's church held students and townsfolk spellbound, but both his style and his content were non-PC:

> Setting up candles, gilding and painting, building of churches, giving of ornaments, going on pilgrimages, making of highways and such other be called voluntary works. . .necessary works and works of mercy are called the commandments. . .and works of mercy consist in visiting and relieving thy poor neighbours.

Now then, if men be so foolish of themselves that they will bestow the most part of their goods in voluntary works. . .and leave the necessary works undone. . .they and all their voluntary works are like to go unto everlasting damnation. And I promise you, if you build a hundred churches, give as much as you can make to gilding of saints and honouring of the church; and if thou go as many pilgrimages as thy body can well suffer and offer as great candles as oaks; if thou leave the works of mercy and the commandments undone, these works shall nothing avail thee.[132]

Latimer fell foul of his bishop for his attacks on formal religion and his advocacy of vernacular Scripture. Like Frith, he was examined by Wolsey and, like Frith, he was leniently handled. And again like Frith, attempts to discipline him were hampered by his popularity at court. He was an early supporter of the annulment of Henry's marriage and had helped to gain his university's endorsement of it. In 1530, the king invited Latimer to preach at Windsor and soon afterwards Anne's patronage gained him a rich living in Wiltshire. He took this support as licence to campaign vigorously for evangelical reform and, much to the chagrin of the ecclesiastical top brass, he proved to be untouchable. When he was detained at Lambeth in 1532 to be examined for suspected heresy, intervention by friends at court secured his speedy release. A year later, though, he was in trouble again. This time he had stirred up a hornets' nest in Bristol. Lenten sermons provoked an angry response from the local clergy. Soon there was a fierce and unseemly pulpit war in progress. Citizens travelled from church to church to listen to Latimer and his enemies lambasting one another. Particularly diverting were the performances of one William Hubberdine, who was so incensed by Latimer that the pulpit shook with the ferocity of his tirades. Eventually, it gave way altogether and Hubberdine was killed in the crash, an incident which drew from one of the churchwardens the nonchalant comment, 'We made our pulpit for preaching, not dancing.' Once again, Latimer escaped the backlash. In fact, it was his opponents who took the blame. Latimer was invited to deliver the Lenten sermons at court in 1534. Though Henry certainly did not approve of everything Latimer said, his popularity as a preacher and his defence of the king's dealings with Rome made him invaluable to the regime. It was because Henry used religious radicals for his own purposes that they were able to use him for theirs.

The 'Henrician Reformation' of the 1530s is a misnomer. It suggests that there was a clearly defined programme of doctrinal and liturgical change but this was not the case. Whatever objectives the king had were distorted in the process of execution by interested parties at court and in the country at large. Moreover, several of the prime movers were not established in fixed positions. In the fierce debates that were raging about Christian truth, thinking men changed their minds. Cranmer's theology underwent a slow metamorphosis during these years as a result of his discussions with German and Swiss reformers. He ended up holding the same opinion of the Lord's Supper for which Frith had been sent to the stake. Henry, as we shall see, gave his support first to one group, then another and historians have always found it difficult to decide what exactly he did believe. He, of course, had the advantage that whatever doctrine he espoused could not possibly be heresy. Lesser men had to walk more circumspectly. Cromwell was once asked to declare his faith unequivocally. He replied, 'I believe even as my master, the king, believes.' It was not true but it was the only safe answer he could give. Those who framed policy were liable to change their minds out of conviction, out of political caution, out of ambition or out of fear. As a result the religious life of the people was pushed and pulled in different directions, pummelled and stretched and twisted. By the end of the decade it had acquired a very irregular shape – and it was still evolving.

In parliament Cromwell set about pushing through those changes implied in the legislation of 1529–32. A number of statutes were required to make the royal supremacy absolutely watertight and Cromwell's fine bureaucratic mind was well equal to the task of drafting them. Henry realized this. Egotists have an unerring knack of recognizing those who can be useful to them and Henry was incredibly lucky to have found a succession of men who had the will and the ability to do his bidding. This explains the confidence he reposed in Wolsey and the speedy promotion of Cranmer, Latimer (who became Bishop of Worcester in 1535) and Cromwell. The latter was appointed chancellor of the exchequer in 1533, secretary and also master of the rolls in 1534. However, at the end of that same year, he received a newly created title as important as it was fine sounding: 'vicar general and special commissary' to exercise all jurisdictions inherent in the supreme head of the church in England. This was an extraordinary creation and one whose significance cannot be overemphasized. The king who had fought so hard to make himself England's pope now handed over the exercise of his new powers to a latterday Wolsey, a kind of lay cardinal-legate.

Cromwell had gained what he had long aspired to gain, absolute authority for the root-and-branch reform of the English church. He lost no time in instigating a general visitation of all churches, monasteries and religious personnel. Having gathered via his army of agents all the information he required, Cromwell turned to parliament for the tools he needed to attack the edifice of medieval Catholicism. Between 1534 and 1536, the anti-papal revolution was completed by a series of Acts which not only replaced papal power with royal power but actually extended it. Thus, the legislation diverting all ecclesiastical payments from Rome to the king increased the income derived from such sources from less than £5,000 in 1534 to over £50,000 by 1536. If Cromwell ever did promise to make Henry the richest king in Christendom, he was certainly beginning to deliver. A new Supremacy Act defined Henry's absolutism with great precision and a Treasons Act made it a capital offence 'to wish, will or desire by words or writing or by craft imagine, invent practise or attempt' any harm to the king or his family but equally condemned anyone who proclaimed the king to be 'heretic, schismatic, tyrant, infidel or usurper of the crown'.[133] But the lynchpin of the new legislation was the Act of Succession of March 1534.

Drafted in the form of a petition to the king, the Act claimed to be grounded in the people's desire to be permanently delivered from 'the great divisions which in times past hath been in this realm by reason of several titles pretended to the imperial crown of the same'. We should not dismiss this as merely the colourful wrapping used to make a sinister law appear more attractive. By 1534 few were alive who had any personal memories of pre-Tudor England but the dislocations of fifteenth-century conflict had not faded from the national consciousness any more than the miseries of two world wars have disappeared from the communal psyche of twenty-first-century Britain. What the Act claimed was that a benevolent king had taken the action he deemed appropriate for the security of the realm. It now only remained for all his subjects to accept what had been done on their behalf and swear allegiance to Henry, his new wife and their heirs forever.

The crunch point for many came in the uncompromising renunciation of interference by popes, who had 'presumed in times past to invest whom should please them to inherit in other men's kingdoms and dominions, which thing we your most humble subjects both spiritual and temporal do most abhor and detest'.[134] Commissioners were sent out with a whole sheaf of oaths which Henry's people were to swear. All adult males had to subscribe to the Act of Succession and the clergy were ordered to acknowledge the royal supremacy and the rejection of papal jurisdiction. It was not sufficient for all Englishmen to accept the dictates of a distant king; they were bound to give their personal approval to the decisions made in their name by their parliamentary representatives. Cromwell had been excruciatingly thorough. Nothing was left to chance. Every man's conscience was bound.

There were those who could not submit. Two religious groups – the Carthusians and the Observant Friars – had proved most troublesome over the renunciation of Rome and were targeted as soon as the weapons to attack them came to hand. They were handled with the utmost severity. All the friars' houses were closed down. Those who refused the oath were sent to prison, where many of them died. The rest were relocated to the houses of their rivals, the Conventual Franciscans, where, it is claimed, they were treated worse than if they had been locked up in the Tower. Seven leading Carthusians were hanged, drawn and quartered and, although many members of the London house had submitted, their monastery was confiscated and they were sent to Newgate, where they were left to starve to death.

The most prominent martyrs were John Fisher and Thomas More, both of whom were sent to the Tower in April 1534 for refusing the oath. More had talked himself out of implication in the treasons of Elizabeth Barton and Henry was determined that there would be no escape this time; he would have the ex-chancellor's public submission or his head. Back in 1529, when he wanted to win More to his team (and, therefore, away from Catherine's), the king had promised him free exercise of conscience over the annulment issue. 'First look unto God and, after God, unto me,' he had said. It was an empty offer. In England only one man was allowed to follow his conscience. Henry had taken the place not only of the pope, but of God. For more than a year the two state prisoners were subjected to repeated sessions of interrogation and cajoling, masterminded by Cromwell. Both remained adamant. While they were ready to swear allegiance to the king and his heirs by Anne, they could not accept the rejection of papal authority. For this Fisher and More went to the block on 22 June and 6 July 1535 respectively.

This orgy of blood-letting needs to be explained. There is no doubt that the responsibility lies squarely with Henry. Common feeling throughout the country was that the 'king's whore' was to blame. The Abbot of Whitby asserted that the king was ruled by a common prostitute 'who made all the spiritualty to be beggared and the temporalty also'.[135] By 1535 Anne was a universal hate figure. Moreover, subjects hesitant about criticizing the king inevitably blamed either his consort or his ministers for the evils of the time. Prejudice later entered the literary record: 'How many famous and notable clerks have suffered death, what charitable foundations were perverted from the relief of the poor unto profane uses. . .if eyes be not blind men may see, if ears be not stopped they may hear, and if pity be not exiled they may lament the sequel of this pernicious and inordinate carnal love'.[136] There is no doubt that Anne loathed More. As well as opposing the king's remarriage, he stood for that stubborn papalism which opposed everything she held dear. One story which has a ring of truth is that when she heard the news of More's death she gleefully threw a portrait of him out of the window. However, Henry did not need his wife's advocacy to pursue his old friend to death. Cranmer tried hard to persuade him to allow More and Fisher to subscribe to a modified form of the oath but Henry would not budge. Cromwell also interceded for some of the monks and friars on the grounds that in their secluded lives they represented no threat to the government. The pragmatic politician was also well aware that public execution of popular figures could be counter-productive. Again the king was adamant.

Were there sound political reasons for the uncompromising treatment of religious dissidents? The king's policy created outrage at home and abroad. Sackloads of reports reached Cromwell from his agents throughout the country of 'murmurings' against government policy. A woman in Oxfordshire grumbled that 'it was never merry in England since there were three queens' (i.e. the Virgin Mary, Catherine and Anne). A priest in Yorkshire told his flock, 'They say there is no pope but I know well there is a pope.' A Cheshire husbandman aired the opinion that if the clergy had stood up to the king he could not have made himself head of the church. A Cambridge ostler got into a fight with a customer who declared that the king was a heretic and that all the nation's ills could be put down to his marriage to Anne.[137]

Chapuys, as we have seen, assessed the mood of the country as one of incipient rebellion but his analysis was not sound. Once the independent power of church leaders had been destroyed by their taking of the supremacy oath there was no group in society able to turn discontent into revolt. This poisonous intriguer had allowed his indignation at the plight of Catherine and Mary to obscure his understanding of the realities of national or international politics. His master, the emperor, was fully absorbed in halting the Muslim advance in the Mediterranean and the distress of his aunt and cousin were distinctly peripheral to his concerns. There was no question of his sending troops or even money to support a popular rising in England, especially when Catherine refused to encourage her supporters to take up arms. Chapuys was frustrated to have to report that she was 'so overscrupulous that she would consider herself damned eternally were she to consent to anything that might provoke a war'.[138] The imperial ambassador acknowledged that noble opposition to Henry lacked potential leadership but thought that some promise of aid form Charles might toughen their resolve. He was wrong. Even if a sizeable cabal of the English aristocracy had been prepared to unite in a religious cause, which is extremely doubtful, they were in no position to do so. By the 1530s the cohesion of the nobility had been irreparably weakened. Henry VII had created centralized government which no longer relied exclusively on the great magnates and their retinues. Men like Buckingham had resented this but Buckingham's fate was a potent warning to any who might plot a return to the 'good old days' before their master had paid more attention to a Wolsey or a Cromwell than he did to them. New patterns of relationship were emerging. The focus of attention was much more on court and capital than it had been in earlier centuries. One reason for the frequent feats of arms, whether in war or tiltyard combat, was to keep the attention of the warrior caste focused on royal service and the unusually long sessions of parliament brought distant lords much more often to London than hitherto.

However, Henry lacked the advantage of detached historical analysis. He was wary of his more powerful subjects. John Russell, Earl of Bedford, who served the regime in several capacities and knew the king well, described him as 'very suspicious and much given to suspicion'.[139] His anxiety, bordering on paranoia, is illustrated by the case of Lord Dacre of the North. In the spring of 1534, when the government was fully absorbed in getting its crucial Reformation legislation through parliament, someone laid information against the warden of the West March suggesting that he was in collusion with the Scots. Henry sent commissioners to seize and ransack Dacre's houses in search of evidence. They found nothing. The charges against Dacre had to do with local rivalries, not disloyalty to the crown. When he was brought to trial in July, he was acquitted by a jury of his peers. This unexpected and unprecedented result was greeted with general rejoicing and that, in itself, was troubling to the king. He had not finished with the fortunate nobleman. Dacre was sent back to the Tower and there subjected to further interrogation. After two weeks he was induced to confess to a technical crime of concealing documents from the court. Henry put a high price on the pardon he now issued. He imposed a crippling £10,000 fine, stripped Dacre of his offices and ordered him to remain in London. This man who had never been a threat was disgraced and ruined. Henry VII could not have managed it better.

A fanatic has been described as someone who redoubles his efforts when he has lost sight of his objectives. Henry may not have taken his eyes off his ultimate goal of securing the Tudor dynasty but this had become tied up with other more fundamental issues of religious belief and individual freedom that were no part of his real concern. It was Henry's massive ego that would not permit him to stand back and allow reason – or even humanity – to dictate his course. Like a gambler convinced that the next throw of the dice will wipe out all his previous losses, he plunged deeper and deeper into decisions that were increasingly irresponsible and often mutually contradictory. Some allowance needs to be made for Henry's age and health. In 1535 he was forty-four. His once athletic frame had filled out and was tending towards obesity. When he was measured for a new suit of armour in 1535, his girth was recorded as 71.5 inches (182 cm) and he had begun to suffer from a complaint which was exacerbated by his increased weight. In modern times the affliction in the king's legs has been variously diagnosed as osteomyelitis, a bone infection, possibly resulting from a fall in the hunting field or tiltyard, or deep vein thrombosis. The latter, which I believe to be the more likely, would have led to attacks of inflammation (cellulitis) so painful that it would have been difficult for him to be distracted. Walking would have been uncomfortable during these bouts and would have obliged him to limp or lean on the shoulder of an attendant.

This affliction did not improve Henry's temper or assist in the making of rational decisions, but it had deeper, psychological implications. Poor health is an attack on the ego. It forces us to acknowledge that we are vulnerable, dependent on others and no longer in full control of our faculties. Henry's response was denial. No one apart from his physicians was allowed to draw attention to his condition. He only changed his routine when pain prevented him following his accustomed pursuits but, inevitably, his ability to enjoy hunting, tennis, jousting and sex was affected. To a vigorous man like Henry this could only be humiliating. However, there was a yet deeper response to his suffering. For sixteenth-century churchmen life, death and health were in the hands of God and were inextricably bound up with morality. The Almighty meted out rewards and punishments according to a man's desserts. Just as Henry believed that he had been denied an heir because of his sin in marrying his brother's widow, so he now struggled to understand what he had done to deserve the fresh trials imposed on him by providence. As he wrestled with his conscience his behaviour became increasingly incomprehensible to contemporaries and has presented historians with real problems.

The first person to suffer as a result of Henry's growing desperation was Anne. Ten months after the two most celebrated opponents of the royal supremacy had gone to the block, the female heretic they had blamed for all their woes joined them in death. The reason for Anne Boleyn's judicial murder has puzzled commentators for centuries. Several theories have been advanced to explain why Henry turned against the woman he had passionately loved, the woman for whom he had defied pope, emperor and the bulk of his own people, the woman who had fundamentally and permanently changed the life of England. Most explanations have proved unsatisfactory because they seek a rational answer where there is none.

The king's summer progress in 1535 was a triumph for the evangelical cause. Henry ventured much farther than usual, taking in Gloucestershire, Somerset, Wiltshire and Hampshire. This was a personal exercise intended to impress the royal supremacy upon his subjects but, since religious radicals were its principal exponents, the court's itinerary gave publicity to the advocates of doctrinal change. Well-vetted preachers were sent on ahead to prepare the ground and to warn opponents of the new dispensation to keep their views to themselves. Prominent West Country evangelicals were singled out to receive visits and special favours from the royal party. Cromwell took the opportunity to make personal visitations of monasteries in the area. The tour ended up in September with a visit to Winchester during which Cranmer consecrated three new bishops, all evangelicals. John Hilsey followed Fisher at Rochester; Edward Foxe was appointed to Hereford; and the forthright Hugh Latimer became Bishop of Worcester. As if all this was not a clear enough indication of which way the wind was blowing, Cromwell later issued a special commission to Hilsey to license preachers in the diocese of London, thus going over the head of the conservative Bishop Stokesley.

During the progress Henry received a copy of a new edition of Philipp Melanchthon's doctrinal compendium, *Loci Communes* (*General Arguments*), which the author had fulsomely dedicated to him. The gift symbolized hopes for a closer relationship between Henry and the Lutheran princes of Germany. A fresh round of diplomatic activity led by Robert Barnes and Bishop Foxe occupied much of the rest of the year. The delegates at Wittenberg discussed the possibility of Henry joining the Schmalkaldic League and the drafting of a common confession of faith. The Lutherans moved significantly towards the official English view on the Levitical prohibition of marriage to a brother's widow. Although agreement on all points had not been reached by the following Easter, the prospects for a political and religious alliance of reformed states seemed good.

Fanned by political interest, the flames of evangelical revival spread in many places and at all social levels. Throughout the country men and women were responding to sermons and books they found liberating and thrilling. Robert Plumpton, a law student, sent his mother a copy of Tyndale's New Testament and excitedly urged her to read it. 'Mother,' he wrote, 'you have much to thank God that it would please him to give you licence to live until this time, for the gospel of Christ was never so truly preached as it is now.'[140] An illiterate London bricklayer learned by heart gobbets of holy writ read to him by others and became a self-appointed preacher. 'He declared Scripture as well as [if] he had studied at the universities,' in the estimation of the chronicler, Charles Wriothesley.[141] In 1537, Bishop Foxe warned his colleagues in a sermon, 'Make not yourselves the laughing-stock of the world; light is sprung up and is scattering all the clouds. The lay people know the Scriptures better than many of us.'[142]

Queen Anne was at the heart of this revolution. Her influence was enormous even by the standards of power exercised by royal consorts. Between 1532 and 1536 ten appointments were made to the episcopal bench. Seven of them – all reformers – owed their promotion to Anne's patronage. This was her single most important contribution to the Reformation. Throughout the troubled times ahead it was the authority wielded by the 'Boleyn bishops' that appointed clergy, licensed preachers, adjudicated in disputes and thus prevented the impetus of change being wholly lost. She also found jobs lower down the ecclesiastical scale for men who showed promise as effective evangelists. Her relationship with Dr Edward Crome suggests that Anne worked to a definite strategy. Crome, another product of Cambridge radicalism, was an effective preacher in one of the City churches. Although popular with the king because of his advocacy of the annulment, he got up the noses of the church establishment and had been obliged, in 1531, to recant his 'erroneous' rejection of purgatory. In 1534, Anne obtained for him the wealthy and fashionable living of St Mary Aldermary[143] so that he might further 'virtue, truth and godly doctrine' among the burgesses and rich merchants of the congregation. Crome apparently needed some queenly arm-twisting before accepting this post. So did another popular preacher, Matthew Parker (later Archbishop of Canterbury), when Anne wanted him as one of her chaplains.

The queen did not content herself with quiet and cautious support of the reformed cause. Like Esther of old, she was outspoken in her defence of 'God's people'. Thomas Patmore, a Hertfordshire parson, had been locked up by the Bishop of London on suspicion of heresy but she secured his release: 'Howbeit one of his brethren afterwards made such suit unto the king (by means of the queen) that, after three years' imprisonment, he was both released out of prison and also obtained of the king a commission. . .to inquire of the injurious and unjust dealings of the bishop and his chancellor'.[144] Richard Herman, a merchant, was arrested by imperial authorities for dealing in banned books and subsequently dismissed from the English House at Antwerp. When this news came to Anne's attention she wrote to Cromwell with instructions to have the man reinstated because he did 'both with his goods and policy, to his great hurt and hindrance in this world, help to the setting forth of the new testament in English'.[145]

Determined that her own household should set a devout and morally impeccable example, the queen surrounded herself with, 'men of great learning and no less honest conversing, whom she with hers, heard much, and privately she heard them willingly and gladly to admonish her, and them herself exhorted and encouraged so to do'. The royal court, where fortune-hunting and lust were common pastimes, was not the easiest place for the queen's attendants to maintain unsullied reputations, as Sir Thomas Wyatt's cynical advice to a courtier attests:

In this also see you be not idle:
Thy niece, thy cousin, thy sister, or thy daughter,
If she be fair, if handsome by her middle,
If thy better hath her love besought her,
Advance his cause and he shall help thy need.[146]

Anne watched diligently over her female court, just as the Archduchess Margaret had strictly overseen her household when Anne herself had been one of its adolescent members. She impressed upon her chaplains, 'I have carefully chosen you to be the lanterns and light of my court', to watch over its morals and, above all things, to teach its young ladies and gentlemen 'to embrace the wholesome doctrine and infallible knowledge of Christ's gospel'.[147] Such a 'holiness regime' could only impose a strain on the fun-loving young people of the court and certainly provoked resentment among those who did not share the queen's commitment to evangelical religion. A prayer in one of the little devotional books Anne gave to her ladies beseeches God to grant understanding of 'the glad tidings of our salvation, this great while oppressed with the tyranny of thy adversary of Rome'.[148] Such heresy ensconced at the very heart of the royal household infuriated religious conservatives such as Anne's own uncle, the Duke of Norfolk, whose proud boast was that he had never read the Bible and never would.

It was Anne's assertiveness that was a contributory factor to her downfall. She was a stronger character than her husband and, when the mortar of sexual passion that bound them began to wear thin, Henry became a prey to jealous whispers that he was being manipulated by his wife. By 1535 the relationship between them was seven years old. The first fine, careless rapture had inevitably faded. More importantly, the marriage had failed to yield its expected fruit. Anne miscarried in July 1534 and again in January 1536. Henry was devastated by the crushing of his hopes. Why, he must have asked himself over and again, was God still withholding his favour? Why had he been cursed with a second wife who was not only unable to bear a healthy prince, but was also insufferably pious and insufficiently submissive? If he found no answers to these self-pitying questions it was because he refused to believe that he was at fault. It was his father and father-in-law who had, he was convinced, suckered him into his first marriage but had not the second been entirely of his own making? Well, perhaps not. Might it not possibly be true that he had been bewitched? At some stage that idea occurred to him and remained lodged in his mind. Meanwhile, court watchers observed occasional rows between king and queen. One reason was Anne's response to her husband's wandering affections. For most of her brief married life she was pregnant. Henry neglected her and began flirting with one or other of the bright young things about the court. In all probability, his attentions never went beyond chivalrous courtship until the early spring of 1536 but that was no solace to Anne. She resented his behaviour because of the slight offered to herself and the bad example it set to members of her entourage. She did not hesitate to say so. Henry responded that she would have to put up with it, as her predecessor had done. There was one flaw in that argument. Kings married for political and dynastic reasons. They looked for love elsewhere. It was a widely accepted convention, but Henry had married Anne for love and she felt that she had the right to receive his undivided attention. Thus, a thin crack was appearing in the royal marriage and the Boleyns' enemies were ready with wedges to insinuate into it.

However, it was Death who held the strongest hand as the days shortened towards the year's end and, over the winter, he played his cards in such a way as to cause maximum confusion among mere mortals. The execution of More and Fisher had profoundly shocked foreign courts. It moved the new pope, Paul III, to call for Charles V and Francis I to compose their differences and direct their united efforts against England. From her confinement at Kimbolton on the edge of the fens Catherine sent messages to Rome urging his holiness to issue the excommunication his predecessor had hesitated to declare. Had he done so with the combined backing of the Catholic powers his action would have sparked off at least a diplomatic offensive against Henry's kingdom. It is just possible that this might have been sufficient to provoke the internal rebellion for which Chapuys had longed and intrigued. However, just as the ex-queen's letters arrived, the Duke of Milan died, without heir. This sparked off once more the old Habsburg-Valois rivalry for control of this strategically placed dukedom. Neither the French king nor the emperor had much thought to spare for heretic England. Henry's excommunication was again put on hold. By this time Catherine knew that she, too, was dying as cancer advanced inexorably through her body. The end of her sad life came on 7 January 1536. This transformed the diplomatic situation, literally overnight. The very next day instructions were on their way to Henry's ambassador at the French court:

> The emperor, having none other cause or quarrel to the king's highness will of great likelihood by all ways and means seek for the king's highness's amity. The only matter of the unkindness betwixt them now abolished by death of the said lady. Ye, therefore, in your conferences and proceedings with the French king and his council shall not only keep yourself the more aloof. . .but also. . .shall seem most expedient to set forth this matter [i.e. Anglo-Imperial rapprochement].[149]

There was, at least in Henry's mind, a return to the old pattern of European diplomacy in which England could play off her continental rivals against each other.

The king felt rejuvenated. Clad all in yellow, he celebrated his ex-wife's death with feasting, music and dancing, and he summoned the flower of English manhood to take part in a tourney. It was in the tiltyard that the king himself was brushed by death's shadow. On 24 January he had a bad fall from his horse in full armour. For two hours he was unconscious. Physicians fussed. Chamber staff anxiously watched over the massive, recumbent figure. Councillors busied themselves with calculations of what to do if their master should not recover. He did recover, although it seems to me that his accident had a profound effect on his personality. Whether the fall made a physiological impact or whether Henry was simply brought face to face with the dynastic implications of his sudden death, his behaviour took a definite lurch towards irrational, impulsive cruelty. Five days later Anne miscarried what was, according to some accounts, a male foetus.

Over the next three months all occupants of the political centre were busy working out the implications of these dramatic events. The diplomatic turnaround was bad news for Anne and good news for the pro-imperialists at court. It meant that Henry was no longer reliant on the French king's good offices and had no need of an alliance with the German Protestant princes. Norfolk and his conservative friends even allowed themselves to hope that normal relations with Rome might be re-established. Catherine's death had reinforced the public sympathy for Mary and made Anne even more unpopular. Cromwell was widely hated and might now prove vulnerable, as his predecessor had been. The king was seen to be grappling once more with his conscience. If he could be skilfully manipulated the disastrous policies of the last few years might be put into reverse. Unfortunately for Norfolk and his allies, they were as devoid of positive ideas now as they had been after the fall of Wolsey. Left to their own devices they would never have been able to take advantage of the changed situation. There were, however, two men sufficiently bold and unscrupulous to grasp Fortune by the hem of her gown and hazard all.

The first was Thomas Cromwell. He possessed several of the qualities of his former master. Like Wolsey, he was affable, witty and a generous host (though not on the same lavish scale as the cardinal). He was a workaholic. He maintained an efficient intelligence network. He was highly adept at anticipating the king's desires. He had a mind which was as sharp as Toledo steel. However, in one attribute he far outpaced his old employer; he was completely ruthless. He may be seen as one of the originators of the concept of *raison d'état*, the acknowledgement that there are issues on which the good of the whole people is of such paramount importance that all other considerations, including moral ones, no longer apply

Niccolò Machiavelli wrote in his treatise, *The Prince*, first published in 1532, 'a prince, so long as he keeps his subjects united and loyal, ought not to mind the reproach of cruelty; because with a few examples he will be more merciful than those who, through too much mercy, allow disorders to arise, from which follow murders and robberies'.[150] Cromwell probably read *The Prince* but he certainly understood at first hand the intellectual dialogue to which it belonged. He had travelled in the rival states of Renaissance Italy; he had fought in their wars. When he entered royal service he was a committed evangelical and social reformer with a clear idea of what needed to be done to make England a truly Christian commonwealth. By 1535, a good start had been made. Henry VIII was master of his realm in a way that he had not been six years earlier. Now was not the time to draw back, to rest on laurels. Cromwell's legislative programme embraced more than religious change and he was not afraid to take on vested interests. For example, he pushed for agricultural reform but the bills he introduced into parliament were severely mauled by the great landowners. However, the major war he waged was against the power and wealth still wielded by the religious establishment and he was confident of having royal support. He knew Henry had a weakness. Money. That meant he could be manipulated.

The second man who now emerged into prominence was Sir Edward Seymour. This son of an upwardly-mobile Wiltshire gentry family was a member of the new generation of courtiers, young men Henry liked to have around him to maintain the impression of a lively court, well up with the latest fashions. They had reached years of maturity in an age when new ideas were in vogue and old allegiances *passé*. Ambition drove them to seek places close to the fount of all patronage, but no one was more ambitious than Edward. Sir John Seymour of Wolf Hall had succeeded in placing his eldest son at court in about 1531. His eldest daughter, Jane, was by then already a member of the queen's entourage. The family achieved a particular mark of favour when the royal party stayed under Sir John's roof during the summer progress of 1535. Quite when Henry began to take an interest in Jane is not clear but he was certainly aware of her by the time that Anne was recovering from her second miscarriage. Edward Seymour recognized his opportunity. He knew that the king had a weakness: sex. That meant he could be manipulated.

Cromwell's legislative onslaught on the medieval church was now directed at the monasteries. There were two reasons for this. The greater and lesser houses of religion dotted over the land constituted the most formidable bastion of traditional Catholicism remaining to be overrun. Because the monastic orders were under the control of foreign superiors and not Henry's bishops, they were, in effect, still subject to indirect papal authority. The cloisters were potential and, in some cases, actual, centres of disaffection. They had to be neutralized. Of course, there was another motive for getting rid of at least some of them. They were rich. Endowments heaped upon them over the centuries had made them, collec-tively, far wealthier than the king or any of his subjects. The idea of dissolving houses which, through dwindling vocations, found it difficult to maintain their function or administer their estates was not new. As we have seen, the king's grandmother, Bishop Fisher and Cardinal Wolsey had all closed monasteries in order to fund colleges at the universities. The government was under pressure from reformers to continue and extend this process. They could point to the continent where, in states which had embraced the Reformation, monasticism was withering on the vine, often without need for government legislation. Luther, the ex-monk, had always claimed that, as the Bible became widely available, the cloistered life would fall without being pushed.

The argument of English evangelicals was simple and, perhaps, unanswerable: while there was a great need to improve educational standards generally, and especially among the clergy, vast potential funds were locked up in the maintenance of minor religious houses which were long past their sell-by date. Others were in favour of monastic closures for less exalted motives. The potential release on to the market of large tracts of land provided opportunities for landowners to consolidate and extend their holdings. Small wonder that when Cromwell introduced his dissolution bill into parliament in February 1536 it sailed through the House of Lords; even before it had received the royal assent, king and minister were receiving bids for specific properties from interested parties.

It was the future use of confiscated monastic property which caused the fatal rift which now opened between Cromwell and the queen. Anne, an enthusiastic and large-scale patroness of scholars, had assumed that the income from the dissolved houses would be used for charitable purposes, which in turn would further the advance of the gospel. When she discovered that the money was destined for the royal coffers she confronted Cromwell and, doubtless, also the king. She occupied the moral high ground and did so very effectively. We know both how strongly she felt and what her concerns were from a sermon she had her chaplain, John Skip, preach at court on 2 April 1536. He denounced the greed of those who were casting covetous eyes on church property and hypocritically covering their real motives with a cloak of evangelical fervour. He went further. The king, he said, should be careful which counsellors he listened to, since there were those who would, by telling lurid stories about the behaviour of individual clergy, stir him to acts against the clerical body in general. The climax of his sermon came when he alluded to the story of Esther. It was a remarkably apt illustration. In the Bible narrative, Haman, the evil adviser of the Persian king, persuaded his master to massacre his Jewish subjects but Queen Esther turned the tables on him and it was Haman who was sentenced to death.

It takes little reading between the lines to understand why this sermon set the court by the ears and why its consequences were so dramatic. It was delivered after the Act dissolving all religious houses with less than twelve inmates and less landed wealth than £200 p.a. had been passed by parliament but before it had received the royal assent. It was an attempt to stir resistance in court and council and was, therefore, a deliberate interference in the workings of government. It directly accused the vicegerent of deception and hypocrisy. The Act Cromwell had drafted made a blanket condemnation of all small religious houses:

> Manifest sin, vicious, carnal and abominable living is daily used and committed amongst the little and small abbeys, priories and other religious houses of monks, canons and nuns. . .the governors of such religious houses and their convent spoil, destroy, consume and utterly waste as well their churches, monasteries, priories, principal houses, farms, granges, lands, tenements and hereditaments, as the ornaments of their churches and their goods and chattels to the high displeasure of Almighty God.[151]

Cromwell had put a great deal of effort into this measure and backed it up with a massive publicity campaign. Now Anne was publicly dissociating herself from it. She was no friend of the abbeys but she was quite prepared to denounce grasping individuals who, in her opinion, brought the evangelical cause into disrepute, even if this might appear to offer some comfort to conservatives. She was challenging her husband to choose between herself and his minister.

Henry could only find this irritating, for a number of reasons. One was that his relationship with Cromwell was not one of unrelieved cordiality. The vicegerent's confidence in his own judgement and abilities sometimes made him overstep the mark in his dealings with the king. About this time the two men were observed to have a serious row. Courtiers heard them shouting at each other and saw Cromwell withdraw with the briefest of obeisances to his master. However, if Henry did not see entirely eye to eye with his servant, he was also not prepared to countenance his wife's interference in politics. Yet, I believe that fundamentally his annoyance was a defence mechanism. He doubtless believed the sweeping libels against monks and nuns because he wanted to believe them and he wanted to believe them because he needed the wealth the new Act was about to deliver to him. He became angry when his pious motives were challenged. If anyone other than Anne had dared to cast doubt on his good faith he would soon have found himself in prison – or worse.

Signs of disharmony between king and queen were as manna to the Seymours. Edward was among those who hoped to gain substantially from the redistribution of monastic land. Now there appeared the possibility of even greater rewards by dangling Jane before the sex-starved king. Towards the end of March 1536 Edward was appointed a gentleman of the privy chamber, presumably in order to act as liaison between his sister and Henry. Edward was, of course, allocated rooms at the royal residences and Cromwell 'graciously' vacated his chamber at Greenwich to accommodate him. This arrangement had another advantage for all concerned; a private corridor connected this room with the royal apartments. Therefore, discreet meetings could be arranged between Henry and Jane. Mutual ambition was now drawing Seymour and Cromwell together and there was only one group who stood in the way of them achieving their desires. They now worked in tandem to consolidate a court faction aimed at dislodging the insufferable Boleyns. The key figure in their intrigues was Jane Seymour who, in the words of David Starkey, was 'a woman of no family, no beauty, no talent and perhaps not much reputation'.[152] This vapid creature was simply a tool of her family's ambition. She was drilled by Edward to encourage the king and, once he was hooked, to refuse her royal victim sex without marriage. She was also to take every opportunity to disparage the queen, an exercise in which she was backed up by Edward, Cromwell and their allies. In the claustrophobic atmosphere of the court it was not difficult to breathe life into long-standing jealousies and resentments. The Boleyns had been cocks of the walk for a long time and had acquired many enemies. So, throughout April, a poisonous atmosphere was built up by whispers, innuendos and gossip against the oh-so-holy queen and her overbearing clique.

Yet, we must be careful to avoid the temptation to argue backwards from Anne's tragic fate and regard it as the inevitable end result of a carefully planned plot. There is all the difference in the world between a smear campaign and judicial murder. When Cromwell made his do-or-die move against Anne in May 1536 it took many people completely by surprise, not least among them Archbishop Cranmer. He, like most observers not privy to the internal politics of the royal household, had become accustomed to regarding queen and minister as the joint heads of the religious reform programme. That programme was, at this very time, achieving its most notable triumph to date. Henry had been induced to sanction the distribution of an English Bible. It was the work of Miles Coverdale, another evangelical exile who cobbled together his translation from the work of Tyndale as well as Latin and German versions. It was completed in October 1535, and furnished with a dedication to the king and an impressive title page by Hans Holbein, a member of Cromwell's propaganda team and shortly to be elevated to the position of king's painter. By the new year, it was selling well in England with royal sanction (though not under royal licence). Anne persuaded Henry to instruct all parish priests to acquire a copy and there is evidence that, by the spring, several bishops were relaying this order to their clergy. Conservative leaders could only regard this as a major threat and it reinforced their resolve to make maximum capital out of the rift now opening in the evangelical leadership.

However, even they were stunned by the news which broke at the beginning of May. This was how Cromwell reported it in a letter to Bishop Stephen Gardiner, in France:

> The queen's abomination both in incontinent living and other offences towards the king's highness was so rank and [close to being implemented] that her ladies of her privy chamber and her chamberers could not contain it within their breasts, but detesting the same had so often communications and conferences of it that at the last it came so plainly to the ears of some of his grace's council that with their duty to his majesty they could not conceal it from him, but with great fear, as the case [inspired], declared what they heard unto his highness. Whereupon in most secret sort certain persons of the privy chamber and others of her side were examined.

Interrogation, Cromwell explained, had revealed 'a certain conspiracy of the king's death, which extended so far that all we that had the examination of it quaked at the danger his grace was in'.[153]

Anne was arrested and taken to the Tower on 2 May. Among the malicious fictions alleged against her were that she had committed adultery with several men of the court, including her own brother, she had wished for the king's death (the charge of planning to kill him was dropped as being too far-fetched), she had promised to marry Henry Norris, groom of the stool, she had poisoned Catherine of Aragon and had planned to poison Princess Mary. The Queen of England was beheaded on 19 May 1536 and five of her 'accomplices' were also executed.

The details of this notorious travesty of justice – the interrogations, the suborning of witnesses, the dubious interpretation of the statute under which Anne was condemned – have frequently been explored and space does not permit a re-examination here.[154] The question we must ask is 'Where was the king in all this?'

There are two possibilities. Either Cromwell conceived and executed the entire plot or he was working to the king's orders. Let us consider these alternatives in turn. Cromwell certainly had the Machiavellian clarity of mind, mental stamina and lack of moral scruple necessary for such a major exploit. He knew full well that the Seymours and their allies would never be able, unaided, to triumph over the Boleyns. Just as Norfolk and the council had been unable to think their way through the problem of how to end Henry's first marriage, so now they needed the guidance and leadership of someone who could unite them and nerve them in the task of terminating his second. Of course, in the previous case, it was Henry who was determined to get rid of Catherine and we are assuming, for the moment, that he had not voiced any desire to disembarrass himself of Anne. Professor Ives argues that Cromwell was fighting for his political life (and, indeed, perhaps for his mortal life). Skip's sermon had thrown down the gauntlet and the minister had no alternative but to take it up.

Replenishing the treasury from the proceeds of confiscated church lands was a cornerstone of Cromwell's political strategy. If Henry was persuaded to fritter away substantial sums on charitable works, that would unravel all Cromwell's careful bookkeeping. Anne's francophilia was also an obstacle to the realignment of foreign policy to which the minister was committed. Rapprochement with Charles was necessary to restore good commercial relations with the Netherlands, another plank of Cromwell's financial policy. The fact that Catherine was out of the way should have made it easier to normalize relations with the empire but Henry was making that process difficult. He was stubbornly insisting that the emperor should recognize the validity of his second marriage and the bastardizing of Mary. On 18 April Chapuys was tricked into a symbolic acknowledgement of Anne. He had always steadfastly refused to honour the queen in any way but on that day Henry and the Boleyns outwitted him. They were all attending mass in the chapel at Greenwich. Chapuys skulked behind a door in order not to make obeisance as Anne passed. However, she stopped and bowed in his direction, signifying her respect for the emperor. The ambassador had no alternative but to return the compliment. In a world where etiquette was all, this was a minor triumph and Chapuys, knowing that, stalked off in a huff. Right up until the end of April Henry gave no indication either to his council or to the diplomatic community that there was a serious rift between him and his wife or that he was contemplating a third marriage. This might be considered to support the thesis that the news of Anne's infidelities came as a bolt from the blue; that Cromwell's letter to Gardiner was a true account of the course of events; that the minister was the sole author of the plot against Anne.

However, if Henry was still basically content in his marriage and insisting that the diplomatic and political communities accommodate themselves to it, it is surely inconceivable that Cromwell would have dared to call for the death of the queen and also of the king's close friend, Henry Norris. Henry would not have been prepared to countenance such a draconian undertaking unless, beneath the public persona, there lurked a private Henry committed to a very different agenda. Consider the enormity of what Cromwell had in mind. He was not just offering Henry a way out of his marriage; he was proposing nothing less than the public humiliation and execution of the king's wife. This would involve some implicit acknowledgement that the popular criticisms of Anne had been right all along, that she was an evil whore and Henry had been foolish to get involved with her. It would follow from her condemnation that most people would expect the government's anti-papal policies to be reversed and that would concentrate hostile attention on Cromwell. He would need to be very sure of his ability to survive the inevitable attacks of his conservative enemies. So, if we take Cromwell's report to Gardiner at face value and if we believe that the revelation of Anne's alleged misdeeds came as a genuine surprise to the king, we must concede that Cromwell was taking an enormous risk. As for Henry, if he was ready to believe the fantasy plot that Cromwell revealed to him, then he must have been insecure and suspicious to the point of paranoia.

Let us look at the other alternative. It is what we may call the traditional explanation of the fall of Anne Boleyn. It goes like this: the king had grown tired of his second wife and fallen in love with another woman. He realized his mistake in marrying Anne because, like Catherine, she was unable to fulfil her primary function of bringing into the world a Tudor prince. Only a new wife could make good this omission. Always sensitive to public opinion, Henry knew that throwing over Anne would be popular. So, just as he had instructed Wolsey to get him out of his first marriage, he now told Cromwell to unravel his second. It is a neat and tidy explanation but, unfortunately, it does not square with the evidence. Right up until the beginning of May 1536, Henry, for personal and diplomatic reasons, showed no signs of wishing to get rid of Anne. Also, if he simply wanted to change wives, it was not necessary for him to kill Anne. He now had the church in his pocket and could have instituted annulment proceedings. In fact, after the queen's condemnation, Cranmer did pronounce the marriage void on the basis of Henry's previous relationship with Mary Boleyn (thus, in effect, making a nonsense of the treason verdict, since, if Anne and Henry had never been legally married, her supposed affairs were neither adulterous nor treasonous).

The trouble with the traditional explanation is that it is too pat, too logical. The judicial murder of Anne Boleyn and her accomplices was a *crime passionnel*. Henry, becoming steadily more unstable, ordered their destruction in a fit of fury. Some historians have recognized this and looked for incidents that might have triggered the king's wrath. It has been suggested that Henry's pathological fear of witchcraft lay at the root of his anger. Fifty years after the event a story went the rounds of Catholic recusant communities that, in January 1536, Anne had miscarried of a deformed foetus, proof positive of a pact with the devil, and that Henry had recoiled from her in horror. However, Henry did not shun his wife after her unsuccessful pregnancy and Catholic propagandists made no capital out of this story for half a century. The instinct to look for some non-rational explanation for Henry's conduct is, I am sure, correct but we are unlikely to discover some specific event which tipped him over the edge into uxoricide.

If we look for a pointer to the truth, we should consider the means – the extremely cumbersome and illegal means – used to bring Anne down. This was a quite unwarranted extension of the existing treason law. Cromwell and his legal experts asserted that adultery by or with a queen was high treason. It was not. Once Anne's enemies decided to go down this route, they had to find men they could fit up as the queen's lecherous partners. So, the net had to be spread wider and confessions forced out of Anne's supposed paramours. All this was complicated and messy. Simple annulment would have been enough to end the marriage. If it was necessary to blacken Anne's name it would have been possible to fabricate an attempt by her on the king's life (something which was initially considered, but then dropped). The only reason Cromwell would devise an unnecessarily complex scheme was that it was what Henry wanted. At the heart of the murder of Anne Boleyn lies sex – sex and the jealousy and fear that only sex can provoke.

As we have seen, Henry was desperate to have male children. It was important to him for both personal and dynastic reasons. When it did not happen he invariably blamed his current wife, but he was plagued by doubts. We have discussed his quest for spiritual answers as to why God was punishing him by withholding an heir to the throne, but beneath that there lurked a fear of personal sexual inadequacy. An outburst to Chapuys in 1533 is significant. When the ambassador suggested that his new wife was no more likely to give birth to a prince than his old one, Henry bellowed, 'Am I not a man like other men? Am I not? Am I not?'[155] Edward Seymour knew, and took advantage of, the king's need to demonstrate that his virility was not flagging. When Jane, a woman eighteen years Henry's junior, responded to his advances, it flattered his ego as well as holding out the possibility of a third and more successful marriage. Anne's angry reaction to the growing affair only strengthened Henry's resolve, but that, in itself, was not sufficient to make him want his wife killed.

There was another person at court who wanted to be released from an unsatisfactory marriage and who bristled with hatred for Anne. This was her sister-in-law, Lady Rochford. George Boleyn's wife resented the closeness of the two siblings and her own exclusion from the charmed circle of the queen's intimates. She could not resist spreading gossip about Anne and became one of Cromwell's most important sources of information. A foreign observer described Jane Rochford as a woman, 'who, more out of envy and jealousy than out of love towards the king, did betray this accursed secret and together with it the names of those who had joined in the evil doings of the unchaste queen'.[156] Among the tales this virago repeated was an assertion that Anne had confided in her brother that Henry was not much good in bed. It is not difficult to imagine the effect such an alleged revelation must have had on the king. It was, in itself, quite sufficient to determine him to hit back and hit back hard, and not only against Anne. To whom else had she blabbed the secrets of the royal bedroom? And if there was one person who would also know the more intimate details of Henry's life, that person was his closest attendant, Henry Norris. Such people had to be silenced.

Resentments, fears, jealousies and suspicions now multiplied in Henry's fevered brain. He saw Anne at the centre of a group of admiring males, singing, laughing dancing, sharing jokes – perhaps at his expense. And this was the woman who had the gall to lecture him about the attentions he was paying to Mistress Seymour. He saw also the pious queen who set her preachers up to humiliate him, who thought she knew more about Christ's religion than God's appointed head of the English church. Now, as love turned to hatred, Henry was determined to expose what he convinced himself was the hypocrisy of his loathsome consort. As he had done with Catherine, he simply withdrew from Anne. After 1 May 1536 he never saw her again and he ignored messages she tried to send by other hands. For him she had ceased to exist. It remained only for his trusted lieutenant to make her non-being permanent.

Thomas Wyatt was among those who found themselves in the Tower under suspicion for his close relationship with the queen. From his cell he watched her execution. It inspired his poetic reflections on life at Henry's court:

Who list his wealth and ease retain,
Himself let him unknown contain.
Press not too fast in at that gate
Where the return stands by disdain,
For sure, *circa Regna tonat*. ['thunder rolls around the throne']
The high mountains are blasted oft
When the low valley is mild and soft.
Fortune with Health stands at debate.
And sure, *circa Regna tonat*.
These bloody days have broke my heart.
My lust, my youth did them depart,
And blind desire of estate.
Who hastes to climb seeks to revert.

Of truth, *circa Regna tonat*.
The Bell Tower showed me such a sight
That in my head sticks day and night:
There did I learn out of a grate,
For all favour, glory or might,
That yet *circa Regna tonat*.[157]

# Chapter 8

## MOLOCH*

1536 had started badly. It would get worse. In the last days of July a wagonload of hay made its way from St James's Palace to the Carthusian priory of Thetford in Norfolk. It was attended by a small troop of soldiers, which was, in itself, curious. What was more odd was that the man in charge of the party was the Duke of Norfolk. At journey's end Thomas Howard's men brought out from its concealment a lead coffin. With the minimum of ceremony it was interred in Norfolk's family chapel. The king's only son, the seventeen-year-old Henry Fitzroy, Duke of Richmond, had come to his last resting place (although the remains were, in fact, removed three years later to Framlingham when the monastery was dissolved). The duke was, of course, carrying out his master's order in supervising this secret burial. Yet, days later, he received an angry message from the king demanding to know why Richmond had not been more honourably interred.

*Moloch *n.* a pagan god of the Old Testament to whom human sacrifices were believed to be made – see Jeremiah 32:35.

Henry's behaviour had now become so changeable that it is difficult for us to know exactly what was going on in his mind. As long as his son lived the king had a dynastic fall-back. He had bastardized both his daughters. A new Succession Act had just been passed which ensured the crown to the children of Henry's third marriage but an entirely novel clause provided that, if Jane Seymour did not provide the required heir, Henry might will the crown to any individual of his choice. Presumably, he had Henry Fitzroy in mind. The young man's death was a serious blow and the king's first reaction, it seems, was to throw over it the cloak of forgetfulness: let his body be buried quickly and quietly so that as few people as possible would be aware of this latest royal embarrassment. Then, on further reflection, he seems to have decided that no Tudor should receive such a hole-in-the-corner interment. And, of course, having so decided, he laid the blame on someone else – in this case Norfolk.

No sooner had Anne Boleyn been out of sight than she was out of mind. Henry never spoke of her so, of course, no one else at court spoke of her. All images of the late queen were removed from royal and noble residences, which explains why no unchallenged portrait of Anne has survived. The day after the execution Henry and Jane Seymour were betrothed. Ten days later they were married quietly at Whitehall. Contemporaries and historians have struggled to discern any engaging features about the pinch-cheeked, tight-lipped woman depicted by Holbein. David Starkey may be right in concluding that it was Jane's very ordinariness that attracted Henry. Yet, it may be the fact that we know so little about her that inclines us to regard her as a nonentity. Anne had been vivacious and exciting, a talented, strong-willed woman with a mind of her own, but she had grown into a dominatrix and that was something Henry could not handle. His own burgeoning ego needed a consort who was quiet and submissive. But was Jane such a wife? On at least two occasions that we know of she argued with Henry – once about the treatment of Princess Mary and once about the plight of the dispossessed religious. Henry had no hesitation in warning her not to meddle in politics, like her predecessor. Above everything else, what he wanted was a wife who would lie back and think of the Tudor dynasty. There can be no doubt that Henry immediately set about the business of baby-making, but month succeeded month and there was no sign of Jane becoming pregnant. With his son dead, his daughters disowned and his latest marriage as yet proving unfruitful, Henry's basic problem was no nearer solution. Jane must have been well aware of his impatience and cannot have been ignorant of the fact that her husband's eye was soon roving again. When he noticed a couple of court beauties and commented that he wished he had seen them before he was married, the queen may well have experienced a chill of apprehension. Fortunately for her, Henry soon had other things to worry about.

Cromwell emerged stronger from the putsch of April-May and he was able to pursue his own policies with unremitting vigour. Henry stepped back and allowed his new major domo the kind of latitude he had allowed Wolsey. Cromwell now discovered, as the cardinal had found, that being allowed political freedom involved both power and peril. Cromwell was running ahead of the pack, exposed, the recipient of syco-phantic adulation and mounting contempt. If the court conser-vatives expected Anne's downfall to be followed by a purge of evangelicals and a reversal of religious policy, they were swiftly undeceived. Cromwell had given the king what he wanted and in doing so had not flinched from barbarity. Henry was not slow to reward him by elevating him above all his other coun-cillors and courtiers. He raised his minister to the peerage as Baron Cromwell of Wimbledon and gave him the office of lord privy seal, which was stripped from Thomas Boleyn. What was more immediately important was that Cromwell was able to build up his following at court. He filled the vacancies which had appeared in the privy chamber by the death or disgrace of previous holders with his own supporters. Not content with that, he broke the conservative faction headed by Norfolk and Gardiner. He exposed their attempt, in alliance with Chapuys, to have Princess Mary reinstated, something to which Henry was irrevocably opposed. When they were threatened with the loss of royal favour, they urged the princess to save their skins by giving in to the king. It was only with tearful reluctance that she finally acknowledged that her father was head of the church and that she had been born in sin.

Such closet triumphs were won against a national background of mounting discontent. The religious/social/political/ economic revolution organized from the centre was now reaching into every locality and was profoundly disturbing. In towns and villages throughout England the rhythm of life was being upset by both official and unofficial change and the king's subjects might be excused if they found it difficult to tell one kind of innovation from another. Vandalism of churches was becoming, if not common, certainly more frequent. Zealots opposed to 'superstition' and 'idolatry', like today's animal rights activists, made their protests with axes and fire-bombs. At Rickmansworth, Hertfordshire, a gang wrapped tarred rags around the figures on the rood loft of a church and set them ablaze. Another posse pulled down the image of Thomas Becket on London Bridge. These and others were the uncoordinated acts of idealists who, when caught, were appropriately punished by the authorities. However, how were ordinary parishioners to distinguish between such crimes and the activities of government agents such as the commissioner despatched to take possession of an abbey in Kent? He reported:

> I found the image of the rood called the Rood of Grace, the which heretofore hath been had in great veneration, certain engines and old wire, with old rotten sticks in the back of the same, that did cause the eyes of the same to move and stare in the head thereof like unto a lively thing and also the nether lip in likewise to move as though it should speak. . .I did convey the said image to Maidstone. . .[on] market day and in the chief part of the market time did show it openly unto all the people there

being present to see the false, crafty and subtle handling thereof, to the dishonour of God and [delusion] of the said people.[158]

For the last few years, Cromwell's agents and pamphleteers had been attacking the misuse of religious images and, in August 1536, he issued injunctions to the parish clergy which, among other matters, instructed them not to, 'set forth or extol any images, relics or miracles for any superstition or lucre, nor allure the people by any enticements to the pilgrimage of any saint'.[159] His intention was actually to put an end to unauthorized iconoclasm by removing the cause of it but people who were told to abandon age-hallowed rituals or who saw the income they derived from selling pilgrim trinkets dwindle were unlikely to take a detached view of the changes being forced on them.

The king was enthusiastically behind his vicegerent's reforming measures. He was intent on making it clear that he would be no mere figurehead in spiritual matters. He could only justify his assumption of caesaro-papistical power to his critics and to his people at large by actually stamping his authority on the church. That meant making changes. He was determined to purify and unify doctrine and liturgy. In other words he wanted to make everyone believe what he believed. In the summer of 1536 he had his bishops in convocation draw up the 'Ten Articles' of official English religion, so that, 'all occasion of dissent and discord. . .be repressed and utterly extinguished'. The publication of the articles was accompanied by a ban on sermons until the end of September. After this cooling-off period preachers were warned not to interpret the articles 'after their fantastical appetites'. The approved formularies were mildly reformist in tone. For example they reduced the number of sacraments from the seven that Henry had defended in his controversy with Luther to three. Because the articles were neither fish nor flesh, nor good red herring, they satisfied neither conservatives nor evangelicals. The weakness of the royal position was that the definition of 'abuses' rested with the king. If he could detect errors that needed correcting what was to stop eager preachers and zealous laymen, with the Bible open before them, doing the same?

Everything was done in the king's name and the principles were ostensibly his, but it would be wrong to think of Henry and his minister as working in complete harmony. Cromwell used his relative freedom to steer the nation in the direction he thought it should go. He employed preachers and writers who were well to the 'left' of official policy. He tried to lure Tyndale back to England, both for the reformer's safety and also in the hope of enlisting him for his propaganda team. He maintained his Lutheran contacts even after Henry had gone cold on the idea of alliance with the Schmalkaldic princes. He encouraged and sustained the group of evangelical merchants known as the Christian Brethren who imported and distributed Lutheran books. Some of them were impulsive firebrands and Cromwell was certainly taking risks in aiding them. Sometimes, he had members of the group locked up for their own safety but he could not always save them from Catholic vigilantes who were as committed as themselves. In the small hours of a misty November morning, one of their number, Robert Packington, a member of parliament well known as someone who 'talked somewhat against the covetousness and cruelty of the clergy',[160] was shot dead in front of his house in Cheapside. He was probably the first victim in London to be murdered with a firearm.

These were violent times but worse trouble was brewing in the Midlands and the North. It began in the fenland of Lincolnshire as a series of protests against Cromwell's 'Big Brother' tactics. The people of this semi-isolated region were not used to the close scrutiny of their affairs by central government but, in October 1536, they were subjected to no less than three groups of royal commissioners. First came those sent to collect the latest round of taxes approved by parliament. Then others appeared to gather the clergy together to explain the Ten Articles and ensure that they were enforced. As well as these unwelcome intruders from the metropolis men arrived to strip smaller monasteries of any items of value and ensure that the inmates departed peacefully. The convergence of these bands of government snoopers was seen by many as a monstrous infringement of their civil liberties. Not only were the clergy being told how to do their job (they were to preach regularly against popular superstitions, remove offending images from their churches, teach the Lord's Prayer and the Creed in English and to set a high moral standard), but certain holy days were abolished, as were age-hallowed customs. The disappearance of religious houses threatened the livelihoods of those who were monastic tenants and also men who worked for the cloistered communities in various capacities. The sight of carts trundling southwards carrying furniture, books, hangings, roofing lead, as well as the precious votive offerings which had decked ancient shrines, was particularly offensive. Anxious and angry crowds gathered. In Louth the cry went up that the king was bent on despoiling the church of all its treasures. At Caistor two of the local gentry were taken prisoner. The government had a rebellion on its hands.

As with most popular risings, the demands of the Lincolnshire rebels were, initially at least, incoherent. They aired several grievances before their leaders managed to draft a petition which reduced their protests to three:

No more taxes
No more suppression of religious houses
Surrender to the people of Cromwell and all the king's heretical advisers.

When Henry VII had been faced with rebellions he had ridden out at the head of his troops to confront his enemies and cower any who might contemplate joining them. His son's reaction was to shut himself up in his strongest fortress at Windsor and panic. He fired off instructions to various nobles to muster their men, then created confusion by countermanding or changing his orders. His responses indicate the conflicting messages which were coming in from all over the country. For days it was impossible to assess the true extent of the problem, though most of the news reaching Windsor was not good. The Lincolnshire malcontents, it seemed, could not be dismissed as a peasant rabble brandishing pitchforks and scythes; several of the leading gentry, to whom the government looked to keep order, had made common cause with the lower orders. Henry assumed that the rebels would march southwards and there was every indication that their numbers would grow as they went. There was news of discontent among the cloth workers of East Anglia and loyal men hastening to join the king spoke of householders in the Home Counties standing ready with food and drink to succour the Lincolnshire 'heroes'. Only 5 miles (8 km) from Windsor a priest was arrested for preaching that the insurrectionists were 'God's people, who did fight and defend God's quarrel.' A butcher taken with him had promised to have his best meat ready for 'the good fellows of the North'.[161]

After a week, the government got its act together. Henry sent a very stern message to the insurgents. Charles Brandon, the Duke of Suffolk, entered the area at the head of a royal army. The rebel host, which had always lacked cohesion and leadership, dissolved. By mid-October there was nothing to be done but round up the ringleaders and carry out an appropriate number of executions – at least, Suffolk thought that the retribution he meted out was appropriate, but now that the crisis was past Henry was baying for more blood. However, there was good reason for Brandon's leniency. He knew that the trouble was far from over.

Beyond the Humber more determined resistance was stirring. The Pilgrimage of Grace had the backing of some of the marcher lords and was effectively led by the charismatic lawyer, Robert Aske. At its height, it had 40,000 men in the field. The Pilgrims, marching under banners portraying the five wounds of Christ, took control of York, Hull and Pontefract. Henry despatched the Duke of Norfolk to face them. Reluctantly. He was none too sure of Howard's loyalty. The duke hated Cromwell and was all for turning back the religious clock. He was marching north with only 4,000 men. Even when he linked up with the Earl of Shrewsbury he still had an inadequate force of 8,000. There was a risk that, when he was confronted by the overwhelming size of the enemy army, he might throw in his lot with them, overthrow the cursed Cromwellian regime and force the king to reverse his policies. Fortunately for Henry, Norfolk was not made of such stern stuff. Chapuys was right when he concluded that Howard was of too 'versatile and inconstant a humour' to be of any value to the Catholic cause.[162] Then again, the duke's reticence may have had something to do with the fact that Henry had ordered him to leave his two sons behind. He did not call them hostages but that is what they were.

The perception of the crisis as it appeared to the government was frightening. By the end of the year, a third of England, from the undrained marshland along the Don to the Scottish border, was either in arms against the crown or awaiting the call to arms. The rebellion embraced all strata of society, and there were many reasons for it. Religious change was only a symbol of widespread discontent. It underlined a feeling of resentment among northerners that they were being marginalized. Just as London merchants dominated the nation's commercial life and creamed off most of the profits, so government in the distant capital was imposing changes on the people against their will. Even when parliament was summoned, nobles and members of the Commons were expected to go to the expense of travelling to London and finding accommodation. Full-scale civil war seemed to be only a hairbreadth away. Henry's generals were in an impossible position. Vastly outnumbered, in hostile territory and leading troops who had little stomach for fighting against fellow Englishmen, it was obvious to them that military victory was out of the question. It was not obvious to Henry. From the distant safety of Windsor he ordered Norfolk to crush the rebels mercilessly. If that was not immediately possible, he was

to fall back and wait for the arrival of reinforcements. The latter
was not a realistic option. Norfolk knew well that a retreat
would only encourage the opposition and probably inspire
them to launch an immediate offensive.

There is a telling difference between the truculent bluster of
messages Henry sent northwards and the way he handled
dissent nearer home. Peace and stability in London were brittle
after Packington's murder. Robert Barnes further heightened
the tension by preaching an inflammatory sermon at the
merchant's funeral. News from abroad was even more
alarming. Reginald Pole, ardent Catholic and one of the few
surviving limbs of the Yorkist tree, had long been living in exile.
When news of the rebellion reached Rome, the pope decided
that this was the moment to come to the aid of loyal opponents
of the Reformation. He made Pole a cardinal legate with
instructions to mobilize support in France and the Low
Countries. Henry reacted by sending agents across the Channel
to track Pole down and bring him to England for trial. If forced
extradition did not succeed, they were to assassinate him. Both
royal and papal parties failed in their objectives but Henry
vented his spleen against members of Pole's family who were
within his reach (see below). Meanwhile, Henry handled the
situation in the capital with mingled firmness and conciliation.
Hugh Latimer condemned the northern rebels at St Paul's
Cross but he was instructed to be discreet and cautious, an inhi-
bition which certainly went against the grain with him. Over
the ensuing days, Barnes and other prominent evangelicals were
taken out of circulation and locked up. Henry now sent a
panicky round robin to all the bishops. The Ten Articles, he
assured them, was an orthodox statement of belief and he disso-
ciated himself from radical interpretations of the document –
including Latimer's recent sermon. To reinforce this, the bishop
made a repeat appearance at St Paul's Cross in December 1536,
under strict orders from Cromwell to preach 'unity without
any special note of any man's folly'.[163] News of the
government's apparent U-turn reached the rebel leaders and

encouraged them to believe that England's brief flirtation with heresy was over.

It was what they were intended to think. Norfolk, meanwhile, on his own initiative had held talks with Aske. What he offered amounted to a complete capitulation. If the rebels disbanded they would receive a free pardon, a parliament would be summoned to meet in York to discuss their grievances and the closed religious houses would be reopened. Henry was not pleased. He was quite ready for Cromwell to make conciliatory gestures in the capital but would not back his generals when they did the same in that 'other country' which was the north of England: how dare they negotiate with traitors? 'We marvel much,' he grumbled, 'that you do all write unto us in such extreme and desperate sort, as the world should be, in a manner, turned upside-down, unless we would, in certain points, condescend to the petitions of the rebels.'[164] Henry instructed Norfolk to play for time. He convinced himself that the rebels, who, after all, had families to look after and jobs to do, would have no more stomach for a long confrontation than the troublemakers of Lincolnshire. The onset of winter would cool their ardour. Then would be the time for savage reprisals. So, Norfolk met with a handful of the Pilgrims' leaders and solemnly discussed their complaints. He gave the impression that the king would give his gracious ear to what they had to say and that he would pardon their recent presumption. (He was careful not to actually issue a pardon himself.) On the strength of these assurances Aske ordered his followers to disperse and he set off for London at the king's invitation. So much for not negotiating with traitors. When the two men met, Henry 'received him into his favour and gave unto him apparel and great rewards'.[165] He did not hesitate to make some of the promises he had recently castigated Norfolk for making. There would be a parliament at York and the Pilgrims' grievances would be impartially considered. Henry even hinted that he might bring Queen Jane to York for her coronation.

When Aske reported back to his colleagues he discovered that some of them were, quite rightly, not convinced by the king's gentle words and empty promises. One of them was Sir Francis Bigod, a twenty-eight-year-old evangelical and one of Cromwell's henchmen in the north. Headstrong, but highly intelligent, this young man tried to revive the Pilgrimage. His change of heart reveals something of the complexity of the northern risings. He had enthusiastically embraced the 'new' faith and supported Cromwell's programme of reform. Then, like Anne Boleyn, he discovered that royal supremacy did not mean a realignment of religious and social life in accordance with the gospel, but an unscrupulous appropriation of church property by the crown. He knew, now, that the king was not to be trusted and he warned the people of the East Riding. A crowd flocked to this eccentric man's banner but failed to capture Hull or Scarborough. Quite what Bigod expected to achieve is not clear. His movement was imbued with a sense of northern independence. He was striking a blow against tyranny and, presumably, hoped to bring the king to genuine negotiation.[166] All he achieved was to provide Henry with an excuse to abandon his 'Mr Nice Guy' disguise. Now there would be no pretence at pardon or discussion of grievances; just suppression and punishment. The Pilgrimage had lost its momentum and cohesion. Over the winter months the last pockets of resistance were cleaned out and the rebel leaders sent southwards for their state trials. Lesser fry were rounded up and dealt with more summarily. One hundred and seventy-eight traitors were hanged and their bodies displayed on gallows or hung from church steeples. And still Henry wanted more blood.

It remained only to deal with the Yorkist menace. The surviving leaders of the clan were known to be opposed to the breach with Rome and Henry's treatment of Catherine and Mary but they remained loyal and had sided with the government against the northern rebels. It was Reginald Pole's activities that sealed their fate. In the summer of 1538 Geoffrey Pole, the cardinal's brother was arrested. Subjected to some of the Tower's more refined methods of persuasion, he was driven to attempt suicide but not before he had informed against Henry Courtenay, the Marquess of Exeter, his elder brother Henry Pole, Baron Montague, Sir Edward Neville and others. Montague and a score of associates were rounded up, including his mother, the sixty-eight-year-old Countess of Salisbury. Over the next few months a bloody purge eliminated once and for all the threat – real or imaginary – posed by the White Rose of York.

Henry, of course, claimed the collapse of the rebellion as a personal triumph. It was no such thing. The power of the regional magnates to assert themselves against central government had been broken by the first Tudor. Therefore, what started as a rising of peasants and clergy, with the reluctant support of some of the gentry, was not taken over by the leaders of northern society and turned into a movement capable of shaking the throne. The descendants of the warring barons of the fifteenth century were far less sure of themselves than their grandfathers had been:

'The Pilgrimage presents then the picture of a constructive search for non-violent political forms through which an opposition could express itself. But the movement also signalises the crumbling away of the traditional oppositionist role of the great lords. In 1536 the northern magnates. . .confronted authority in a mood of uncertainty and moral ambivalence'.[167]

By the spring of 1537 Henry was exultant. He had overcome all obstacles to his forthright 'imperial' policies and, to cap it all, his new queen was pregnant. This was the background to the creation of the painted image of Henry which has done more than anything else to mould all subsequent thinking about him. We have already referred to this fresco which the king ordered Holbein to create for his privy chamber, but now we can explore it more fully in its historical context. First and most obviously it is a group portrait. Jane Seymour is included because she is Henry's only wife, his two previous marriages having been declared void. Secondly, it is a dynastic portrait. It exalts the family which has successfully held the throne for half a century against several attempts (like the most recent one) to dislodge it. Thirdly, it presents Henry as the 'star'. The other three figures are very much there as a supporting cast. Fourthly, Henry is shown as the embodiment of sheer, naked power. This representation is unique among Renaissance royal portraits. Holbein took as his pattern Jakob Seisenegger's 1532 painting of Charles V and transformed an elegant official portrait into a massively awe-inspiring piece of propaganda. The emperor's refined gaze is slightly to his right. Henry glares full-face from the canvas (or, rather, from the plastered wall). Charles' pose is relaxed, one hand resting on his hunting dog. Henry shares his space with no other creature and he looks anything but relaxed. In showing the king with splayed legs Holbein departed radically from painterly etiquette as set by the Burgundian court, where it was thought that 'an excessive separation of the feet is blameworthy'.[168] The fact that this image colours our perception of Henry five-hundred years later indicates what a powerful piece of propaganda it was. This is Henry as he wanted to be seen and he was obviously pleased with his painter's handiwork because he commissioned copies to be made of that part of the fresco which showed himself and presented them as gifts to favoured courtiers.

It would be a mistake to believe that this was what Henry really looked like or that this image, exuding total self-confidence, was how he saw himself. He was podgy and the redness of his cheeks indicated high blood pressure. He was in intermittent pain from his legs, which were probably already bandaged and this will have shown itself in the lines of his features. Even in victory, he was not prepared to venture into the north, as he had promised. A personal tour of the troubled regions would have done much to stamp his authority on the distant counties but he declined the risk, blaming his wife's condition. The Latin inscription on the plinth exalted Henry as the reformer of the church, as we have seen. Again, this is the impression he wanted to convey and it was far from the truth. The toing and froing of religious policy over the next three years dispel any idea that the king was working to a plan of his own devising.

Jane did not have an easy pregnancy and when she went into labour on 10 October 1537 it was a long-drawn-out affair. It is not difficult to imagine Henry's mingled anxiety and impatience. Would it be a boy this time? After all his previous disappointments he may scarcely have allowed himself to hope. Day after day he waited at Esher for news from Hampton Court where the queen was in confinement. At last, a messenger clattered into the courtyard in the small hours of Friday 12 October. Henry was woken and told the news. And it was good. Hours later London reverberated with the sound of church bells and cannon fire. Te Deums were sung throughout the city in thanksgiving for the birth of a prince, who was christened Edward. Celebrations continued over the weekend and Henry went to Hampton Court to meet his son. The Seymour clan were triumphant. Edward was created Earl of Hertford and confidently expected even more favours.

However, all was not well with the queen. She appeared to make a good recovery but, after a week, her condition began to deteriorate. As she grew steadily weaker, her physicians and her ladies hovered round her bed, doing all they could to make her comfortable until her death on 24 October. One person who was absent was Henry. He returned to Esher. He was good at meting out death to others but he could not face it himself. If he grieved he did so in private and not for long. Doubtless, he consoled himself with the thought that the dynastic problem had, at long last, been solved. He had found a wife who had fulfilled her primary function. Beyond that? Well, life goes on.

For him it certainly did. Once more he was footloose and fancy free. By the end of the year he was contemplating another marriage, even though the court remained in mourning until 2 February 1538. This time, and for the first time in all his forty-six years, Henry would actually be choosing a wife from a wide field, rather than from his own court. All the royal beauties of Europe were at his disposal, or so he fondly believed. He now had a legitimate heir, so, although the siring of more children was important, it was no longer critical. He could take his time and weigh up the diplomatic pros and cons of a marriage alliance. Accordingly, his ambassadors were instructed to keep an eye out for likely princesses. However, he was not prepared to allow politics to dominate his choice. Unlike most of his royal contemporaries, he refused to be yoked to a wife he did not find sexually attractive. Was this mere self-indulgence or is it a further indication of a sexual problem? Taken together with other evidence, there is a distinct possibility that he needed strong stimulus in order to be able to perform in bed.

Cromwell never understood his master's feelings on this matter. He shared the common perception that for kings love and marriage were quite distinct. Naturally, it was on his shoulders that the task of finding a bride was laid and he had his own set of priorities. Henry had to be steered firmly away from the beauties of the court. The low-born minister could not risk another of the great families gaining power by placing one of their own women in the royal bed. The king would have to find his new wife abroad and that presented Cromwell with a real opportunity. If he could engineer a 'suitable' marriage alliance he could stabilize English diplomacy and stop it seesawing between support for either the Valois or Habsburg camps. Nor was it only the king's hand that Cromwell had to offer in marriage. Henry had three unwed children. All four Tudors were valuable counters on the board of Christendom politics and he was intent on playing them as advantageously as possible. This became for him a fatal *idée fixe*. Cromwell was a brilliant executive – the best Henry ever had, as he later ruefully acknowledged – but in foreign affairs he was not in the same league as Wolsey. The cardinal's antennae had been constantly sensitive to subtle changes of diplomatic vibes. He never lost sight of the fact that foreign policy was the preserve of princes and was careful to make sure that Henry owned all the decisions made in his name. He would certainly have been extremely cautious about choosing a wife for him. Cromwell, *per contra,* was writing within days of Jane's death to the English ambassador in France:

> Sundry of his grace's council here have thought it meet to be most humble suitors to his majesty to consider the state of the realm and to enter eftsoons into another matrimony. . .his tender zeal to us his subjects hath already so much overcome his grace's disposition and framed his mind both to be indifferent to the thing and to the election of any person from any part that with deliberation shall be thought meet for him.[169]

If Cromwell really thought that Henry was 'indifferent' to the question of his remarriage, his evaluation of the king and his own relationship with him was gravely at fault. That relationship was certainly unusual. The two men socialized and Henry sometimes went to Cromwell's house to dine but, as we have already seen, they had their arguments, some of which, apparently, were violent. It seems that Cromwell was sufficiently confident of his standing with the king to speak straight to him and that he got away with behaviour that, in others, would have been presumptuous. With someone as unstable as Henry that was risky, especially in view of the numerous enemies Cromwell had at court.

Be that as it may, Cromwell continued with his work of reforming the church and enriching the king. Now that opposition to the suppression of the smaller monasteries had been neutralized, he continued with what he had intended all along: the complete abolition of the institution. His task was made easier by the involvement of some monks in the recent insurrection. The sight of habited figures swinging in the breeze from wayside gibbets served well *'pour encourager les autres'*. The vicegerent's visitors resumed their tours of religious houses, urging inmates to gossip about their superiors and inevitably finding fault everywhere. Several heads of houses, seeing the writing on the wall, voluntarily gave up their convents to the king. They had every material incentive to do so. Not only were compliant ex-religious well compensated for abandoning their vows, they were often encouraged by local families who had for generations supported them but now coveted their property. Cromwell knew that he could count on the support of most of the nobility and landed gentry, irrespective of their religious convictions. Even Norfolk wrote complaining to Cromwell that, while others had been able to buy monastic land from the crown, his petitions had been overlooked. In April 1539 the last legal block was put in place with an Act enabling the king to receive all property that had been or would be handed over. A year later the last English monastery closed its doors.

Whatever one may think about the secularization of monastic land and buildings, what cannot be denied is that the most momentous transfer of property since the Norman Conquest was carried out with incredible efficiency. Cromwell was well aware of the potential for disruption in the Dissolution and he put in place the machinery to handle it as smoothly as possible. Hundreds of thousands of pounds worth of property passed through the Court of Augmentations, the royal estate agency set up to handle the reception and disposal of this great bonanza. Thousands of monks were relocated and paid off. Employees of the monasteries were, as far as possible, taken care of. Then, there was the security problem to be dealt with:

> The poor people. . .in every place be so greedy upon these houses when they be suppressed that by night and day, not only of the towns, but also of the country, they do continually resort as long as any door, window, iron or glass or loose lead remaineth in any of them. . .I keep watch as long as I tarry and prison those that do thus abuse themselves, and yet others will not refrain.[170]

So reported one of Cromwell's agents from Warwick and it is unlikely that his experience was unique.

Cromwell turned Henry into a modern Croesus. Crown revenues increased by over £100,000 p.a., which was more than the total income the government had received in 1530. Within the space of a very few years, England's landscape – both physical and social – changed drastically. New patterns of ownership gave a boost to domestic architecture throughout the land. Local gentry bought up monastic buildings, either to demolish them and re-use the materials or to convert them to secular use. Merchants and lawyers grabbed the opportunity to improve their status by acquiring country estates. Many of the great entrepreneurial and political families of future centuries were established on the spoils of the monasteries.

But what of those lower down the social scale? The old canard that the Dissolution escalated the poverty problem has proved tenacious but the emotive anecdotal evidence of hardship does not amount to solid proof that the disappearance of relief provided by the religious created massive hardship to the rural poor. Secular and conventual clergy were supposed to devote a third of their tithes to poor relief but this rule was honoured more in the breach than the observance. Poverty and vagrancy were mounting problems for various reasons, little concerned with the collapse of monasticism. When abbeys and nunneries changed hands their lands still had to be farmed and maintained and most tenants and labourers stayed on to serve new masters. Cromwell certainly cannot be blamed for increasing unemployment and beggary. The 1536 Act stipulated that future owners of monastic estates should 'maintain an honest continual house and household'. In the same session Cromwell introduced a revolutionary poor law bill. It proposed setting the able-bodied poor to work on public projects, to be paid for by a graduated income tax. He even persuaded Henry to come into the Commons house to promote the proposed legislation (an event which offers us another glimpse of the relationship between king and minister.). To no avail. However great the problem, lords and gentlemen were not prepared to dip into their purses to solve it. The Act which they eventually approved was a much watered-down version of Cromwell's original.

In 1538 Cromwell resumed his work of religious reform – or, rather, he tried to. The extraordinary stop-go process of change over the next couple of years reveals just how divided England was and how difficult Henry found it to cope with the discord he had done so much to foment. The nation was like a ship being blown along by the winds of evangelical enthusiasm and dragged backwards by conservative currents. Henry opposed the excesses of both parties and tried to curb them in the interests of unity but that is not to say that he had a positive doctrinal/liturgical package to offer his people. One current theory advanced in academic circles represents Henry as a steadfast captain at the helm, skilfully negotiating wind and wave to bring his realm into the safe haven of the *media via* (middle way).[171] This view is untenable on any careful analysis of the king's character and any impartial study of the turbulent events of 1538–40.

On 8 September 1538, king and minister were together at Canterbury to witness the destruction of the richest and most important shrine in the land. The vicegerent's workmen had spent three days hacking away at the masonry of Thomas Becket's tomb, removing the saint's bones and carefully cataloguing the gold, silver and jewels with which the shrine was bedecked. We can imagine Henry rubbing his hands with glee at the sight of two enormous chests of jewels and twenty-four wagon loads of plate setting off under guard for the Tower. That same night John 'Bilious' Bale presented a play to the king and court – almost certainly his *On the Treasons of Becket.* For Henry it was a symbolic moment; the reversing of the humiliation imposed by the pope's church on a king of England.

At the same time copies of another set of injunctions were on their way to clergy throughout the land. They imposed on the church the most extreme evangelical principles that had yet been put forward. Parish priests were given three months to place in their churches, 'one book of the whole Bible of the largest volume in English'. (The following spring the Great

Bible, Coverdale's revision of his earlier work, was published under royal warrant.) Parishioners were to be encouraged to come and read it. They were to be taught to recite the Lord's Prayer and the creed in their native tongue. Four times a year the clergy were to preach against idolatry and pilgrimages and remove from their churches all images tending to idolatry. They were to report to the king's council any members of their flock who resisted these changes. And they were to keep registers of births, marriages and deaths (an innovation of enormous benefit to later historians, though at the time resented by many as an invasion of privacy). Cromwell, in the king's name, was bent on imposing a culture shift of the first magnitude. He and his fellow reformers were trying to wean the people away from the remote, latinized, priestly magic, focused on holy 'things', to a personal, direct faith which called on them to understand for themselves the all-sufficient truth contained in Holy Scripture. The Reformation drum was beating and Harry of England was leading the march. Or so it seemed.

Only a few weeks later, Henry went over his vicegerent's head and issued a proclamation which was intended as something of a corrective. Just as during the northern troubles the king had been bounced into actions which declared his orthodoxy, so now he was at pains to let his subjects know that the recent injunctions did not imply any departure from the ancient Catholic faith. The proclamation was basically an attack on Sacramentarians, the religious extremists who denied the real presence of Christ in the consecrated elements at the mass, and Anabaptists, the more extreme radicals who separated themselves entirely from all existing churches. With such an attack Cromwell, Cranmer and their allies had no argument, but Henry took the opportunity to issue tight restrictions on the publication and dissemination of the Bible and all other religious books. He ordained that certain devotional practices, such as creeping to the cross on Good Friday, were not superstitious, that clergy were not to marry and that any who had taken wives were to be defrocked.

These semi-contradictory instructions could do nothing but sow confusion. An incident in Salisbury Cathedral the following Easter illustrates the point. Worshippers in one of the side-chapels were queuing to kiss a statue of Christ. In strode John Goodall, under-bailiff of the city, and promptly removed the image. He claimed to be acting in obedience to the 1538 injunctions. The cathedral clergy accused him of being a Sacramentarian demonstrating in defiance of the royal proclamation. Their action against Goodall went all the way to the Star Chamber before collapsing, doubtless on the initiative of Bishop Nicholas Shaxton of Salisbury, supported by Cromwell. With no clear direction being provided as to what the doctrine of the independent Church of England was, such unpleasant confrontations became commonplace. What most of Henry's subjects could not know was that he shared their confusion. For all his seeking advice from his bishops, his perusing of the documents drawn up by Cromwell and his cursory reading of theological treatises, he could never get his head round the fact that Catholic and evangelical doctrines were incompatible: salvation was either by faith or by ritual observance; Scripture was either available for all believers to read and interpret according to conscience or it was only safe in the hands of the clergy; man-made images either moved worshipers to contemplate the invisible God or they were idolatrous distractions; the priesthood was either a sacerdotal caste with quasi-magical powers or it was a professional body whose primary responsibility was preaching and teaching the pure word of God. There were no compromises. There was no such thing as a *media via*. The concept was one which no one at the time would have recognized. Nor was Henry looking for some mythical middle ground. His actions were governed by two priorities. One was a genuine search for religious truth and the other was the maintenance of his standing in foreign courts. Since these two did not necessarily pull in the same direction, they only added to the confusion of the times. Henry's religious pilgrimage was not and could not be purely personal. When he found what, to his mind, passed for truth, he imposed it on his people. When his own quest led him to change his mind it did not strike him as at all nonsensical that the entire population of England should move with him to the newly discovered understanding.

In these months the king was going through one of his bouts of renewed interest in theology. The reason for this was twofold. Religious conflict had flared up in various places and it touched him closely because it was tied up with his search for a wife. Throughout 1538–9 a number of high-profile cases kept religious discord in the public eye. These ranged from the examination of Robert Croukar, a conservative rabble-rouser who preached fire and brimstone against the government for its attacks on traditional devotion, to the trial of the Sacramentarian, John Lambert, over which Henry presided in person. Unorthodox belief did not fall into tidy categories. Take, for example, the case of one Collins, a London lawyer, who was driven from his wits by the desertion of his wife. Going into church one day at the elevation of the host, he mimicked the priest by grabbing a little dog and holding it above his head. As Foxe recorded, he was 'condemned to the fire and was burned, and the dog with him'.[172] These events coincided with the return, in September 1538, of Stephen Gardiner, Bishop of Winchester, at the end of a three-year embassy in France. He was a prickly customer. Henry disliked him. Cromwell loathed him and the feeling was mutual. However, he had a fine brain, was politically astute and he was the best intellectual weapon the court Catholics had. The bishop had personal and theological reasons for wanting to spike Cromwell's guns and his very presence was the kind of encouragement the lesser intellects, such as Thomas Howard, urgently needed if they were to throw sand in the well-oiled evangelical machine. Gardiner was not welcomed back at court for six months but he made his presence felt in convocation and parliament as well as through informal contacts.

News of religious turmoil in England reached the continent where matters seemed much more clear cut. Pope Paul III had

just succeeded in persuading Charles and Francis to compose
their differences and join with Venice in a holy league against the
Turk. Nothing came of this crusade but it did mean two things
for England: Henry's fellow monarchs appeared as good sons of
the church and English diplomacy could no longer rest on the
foundation of playing them off against each other. In January
1539, two alarming things happened. Charles and Francis
cemented their new friendship in the Peace of Toledo and Paul
III issued the long-pending excommunication of the man he
characterized in a letter to the emperor as 'that most cruel and
abominable tyrant'. Henry was shaken by his sudden diplomatic
isolation. Invasion fever gripped the country. The king ordered a
survey of coastal defences and devoted a large chunk of the
income from the Dissolution to the biggest programme of castle
building in two-and-a-half centuries. From Berwick round to
Carlisle, but especially along the Channel coast, fortifications
were either modernized or created from scratch.

The pope's bull threw a spanner in the works of Henry's
marriage negotiations. It made it difficult for Catholic
monarchs to unite their families with the 'great heretic'.
Henry's convoluted negotiations with various royal houses
had narrowed the field to two candidates. Top of the list was
the lovely young Christina of Denmark, who was the widow
of the late Duke of Milan and a niece of Charles V. Holbein had
been commissioned to make her portrait and, when Henry saw
it, he reputedly drooled over the prospect of marriage with this
sixteen-year-old beauty. Unfortunately, because Christina was
the grand-niece of Catherine of Aragon, her marriage to Henry
required a papal dispensation and there was no way that Paul
was going to oblige. Henry's marital 'fallback' was Anne, sister
of William, Duke of Jülich-Cleves-Berg. To Henry this alliance
was potentially attractive because the duke's territory was
strategically situated on the middle Rhine, where it could be of
considerable annoyance to both Charles and Francis.
Cromwell favoured the match because William was a member
of the reformed camp. He was more Erasmian than Lutheran

but was closely involved with the Schmalkaldic League, since its leader, John Frederick of Saxony, was his brother-in-law.

Henry was in a cleft stick. He wanted to pursue the German alliance but was anxious not to appear out of step with the orthodox rulers of Christendom. The result was several months of wildly fluctuating policies. At the beginning of 1539, his diplomats were in serious discussions with Duke William, the Schmalkaldic princes and the Protestant King Christian III of Denmark. If he expected these northern rulers to be elated at the prospect of closer diplomatic ties with England, he was disappointed. The general response was cool. In particular, the German princes insisted that Henry should commit himself to the religious basis of their league. Henry's reaction was violent. As soon as the next parliamentary session began in April 1539 he forced through – again by personal intervention – the Act Abolishing Diversity of Opinions, better known as the Act of Six Articles or, by its opponents, as the 'bloody whip with six strings'.

The statute was precisely what its title proclaimed. Henry had grown impatient with debate and dissension and was making an ill-tempered attempt to impose traditional Catholic tenets with the threat of death to the disobedient. The Act reasserted transubstantiation, clerical celibacy, the validity of private masses, auricular confession and vows of chastity, and upheld the withholding of the communion cup from the laity. The penalties for disobedience were draconian. The stake, the prison cell or loss of all property awaited any who fell foul of the statute. Cranmer and the evangelical bishops did all they could to oppose the new measure in parliament and convocation but in vain. Latimer and Shaxton resigned their sees. Within a few weeks, 500 heretics had been indicted under the Act. From the Protestant courts Henry's envoys sent back reports expressing shock and outrage. To many of Henry's subjects it seemed that the clock had been put back.

Then, suddenly, everything changed. The Six Articles Act came into force at the end of June. Within two months it was

virtually a dead letter. Gardiner was dismissed from the
council. Cromwell did not get round to issuing commissions to
the inquisitors who were to seek out offenders against the Act.
Franz Burchard, the Saxon emissary, reported home:

> The king seems already displeased at the promulgation of the
> decree and little favourable to those who have so astutely done
> this in order to supplant Cromwell and the Archbishop of
> Canterbury and the Chancellor [Audley], excellent men and
> most friendly to the purer doctrine of the Gospel. But God in
> his mercy seems to have turned the wicked counsel upon the
> heads of its authors, for those excellent men are now in greater
> favour than ever and the papistical faction has in no wise
> obtained its hoped-for tyranny, nor, God willing, ever will in
> England. These hypocrites, indeed, endeavoured, when
> occasion offered, to suppress the truth and confuse the king
> with their sophistries but they have only succeeded, so far as to
> obtain the statute, not its execution.[173]

There can be little doubt that Henry had meant the Act to
shock. He was alarmed by the spread of religious extremism
and intended to scare free-thinkers into conformity. He may
have decided that the mere promulgation of the Act had
achieved this purpose. Yet, his dismissal of Gardiner and his
distancing of himself from other conservative bishops suggests
that Burchard was basically right. The strong medicine had
produced undesirable side effects and, typically, Henry put the
blame for its inefficacy on someone else. Gardiner's fall from
grace see-sawed Cromwell back into favour. On 24 September
1539 the marriage contract between Henry of England and
Anne of Cleves, which the minister had enthusiastically backed,
was signed. It seemed that king and country were emerging
from a region of storms into clearer waters. However, Henry
had already noticed a new arrival at court, the nineteen-year-
old niece of the Duke of Norfolk – Catherine Howard.

The king had now been without a wife for two years. If he
was to take a foreign bride – and months of diplomatic activity

had created an irresistible momentum – he was running out of options. The diplomatic situation favoured the German alliance, for the moment, at least. Thus, on 27 December, the 'Flander's Mare' arrived on English soil. This ungallant comment that Henry is wrongly supposed to have made about his bride has become firmly entrenched in mythology and is repeated over and again about the second Tudor.[174] Another untruth is that Holbein painted a flattering portrait of the German lady and that Henry was appalled when the reality did not live up to the image. It is important to correct these common misconceptions if we are to understand what Henry's relationship with his fourth wife tells us about him. The prospective queen of England whom the king's painter met at Düren, near Cologne in August 1539 was a comely, homely twenty-three-year-old of pleasant, quiet demeanour. Brought up in a small ducal court, Anne lacked many of the accomplishments which were thought desirable in European royal circles. In terms of sophistication she was light years away from someone like Anne Boleyn. Holbein's painting of her did not lie. It would have been more than his job was worth to distort the reality. He did, of course, place his subject in the most advantageous pose. The only other portrait of Anne shows a woman of rather sharp features. By painting her full-face the artist was able to hide her pointed nose. By accentuating her rich costume he also distracted the viewer's gaze from Anne's features, but he captured her meekness and represented her as a not unattractive young woman. There is no indication that the king believed that Holbein had deceived him.

Why, then, was Henry so distressed when he met his fiancée the following January? The first point to bear in mind is that he had formed his opinion from second-hand information. Anne was the only one of Henry's wives that he had not met and become attracted to before the approach of their wedding. He could, therefore, as was his wont, blame others for his disappointment. Written reports he had received from his diplomats had certainly talked up Anne's character and appearance but Sir

Nicholas Wotton, head of the English delegation to Cleves, had been quite clear about the lady's limited accomplishments. She had no French or Latin, he reported, 'nor yet she cannot sing, nor play any instrument, for they take it here in Germany for a rebuke and an occasion of lightness that great ladies should be learned or have any knowledge of music'.[175] So Henry's expectations should not have been impossibly unrealistic.

What seems to have put him off just as much as his first impression of her was her reaction to him. A crucial part of Henry's self-image was that of the gallant ladies' man. Thirty years of courtly dalliance and cringing flattery had firmly convinced him that he was a past master at charming the opposite sex. He had had no opportunity to woo Anne so, at their first meeting, he felt he had to make up for lost time. The encounter took place at Rochester where the bride's suite was spending New Year before moving on to Blackheath and her ceremonial reception by her husband-to-be. Henry decided on a romantic surprise. With a small entourage he rode to her lodging and, in elaborate disguise, entered her room, where he offered her intimate greetings 'in the name of the king'. According to chivalric convention, true love should have penetrated the disguise so that Anne would immediately recognize her visitor. She, of course, knew nothing of this and was merely flummoxed by the unseemly advances of a total stranger. Thanking him curtly, she turned to gaze out of the window at a bear-baiting in progress in the courtyard below. For Henry, who was not used to playing to unappreciative audiences, this was not a good beginning. He had been made to feel like a clumsy adolescent. When he returned, unmasked, it was Anne's turn to be embarrassed. Because she had had no time to prepare, to dress and bejewel and perfume herself appropriately, she felt even more awkward than she would have done with a more conventional wooing. Thus, Henry was confronted by a bashful, gauche, plain woman. He decided – apparently on the spot – that he did not want to go through with the wedding. He only had himself to blame. He had made no allowance for the fact that Anne was at a huge disadvantage, among strange people whose language and customs she did not understand. It was not her fault that she did not know the rules of Henry's love games.

The die was cast. Henry had decided that this German woman was not for him and, as the moment of their wedding drew closer, he became more and more petulant. He had been tricked into this union. Others had deceived him. 'She is nothing as fair as she hath been reported,' he complained to Cromwell. He decided that the marriage must be aborted but when he instructed his council to find a way of extricating him, they informed him that he was legally obliged to go through with it. Moreover, offering an affront to the Duke of Cleves would be diplomatically disastrous. At this very time Charles V was being sumptuously entertained by Francis I in Paris and swearing eternal friendship with his old rival. To alienate himself from the German princes would leave Henry completely isolated. When he grumbled in the privacy of the privy chamber to his groom of the stool, that attendant pointed out, quite correctly, that in matters of marriage subjects were better off than rulers, 'for princes take as is brought them by others and poor men be commonly at their own choice and liberty'.[176] This was something Henry was never able to accept. Although he did enjoy the occasional extramarital fling, the idea of marrying for duty and keeping mistresses for pleasure was alien to him. The reason for that has already been hinted at but it becomes clear when we consider the intimate details of Henry's relationship (or non-relationship) with his fourth wife.

The wedding took place on 6 January 1540 at Greenwich. After the usual feasting and entertainments, the royal couple retired to bed for the final act which would cement the marriage. Nothing happened. Next morning, when Cromwell cautiously enquired about the events of the night, Henry blamed Anne for his own failure to consummate their union. In a somewhat confused narrative he replied that he had examined the bride's body and concluded that she was not a virgin. But, he went on, if she had brought her maidenhead to England, he had not deprived her of it. On subsequent nights, Henry did try to do his matrimonial duty but without success. He assured his doctors that there was nothing wrong with him. He was perfectly capable of sexual relations (he had 'wet dreams' to prove it!). It was just that his wife did not arouse his passions.

If he was frustrated and distressed, so was Anne. Very early on she brought herself to confide in Cromwell, doubtless in very fumbling English. Knowing how sensitive the king was on such matters, he did not dare to broach them with his master but he did speak to the queen's lord chamberlain. All the advice that official could give was to urge Anne to take the initiative and make herself more alluring, something this very modest young lady may have found difficult. This evidence disposes of the account of a conversation Anne is supposed to have had with some of her ladies the following June. When they suggested to her that she was still a virgin, she retorted that this was impossible because every night when the king comes to bed, 'he kisses me and takes me by the hand and bids me goodnight, sweetheart, and in the morning kisses me and bids me farewell, darling. Is not this enough?'[177] Now, Anne may have had a sheltered upbringing but she was not stupid. She knew how babies were made and how important it was for royal consorts to perform their basic function. The attendants who made this deposition did so when Henry was seeking a divorce on the basis of non-consummation. They knew what was expected of them: they had to provide evidence that Henry and Anne had not had sexual relations and that Anne's naivety was responsible for that state of affairs. Moreover, one of the ladies who set her name to the statement was the poisonous Lady Rochford, who, as we shall see, had her own reasons for wanting to put an end to the royal marriage.

Henry's increased bulk and his painful legs will have made intercourse difficult for him and added to the problem he had long experienced – a weak sex drive. He was in his forty-ninth year when he married Anne and it is significant that he sired no more children. In order to complete the sex act he required considerable stimulus. He persisted in believing that there was no defect in himself and to prove his potency he started pursuing Catherine Howard within three months of his latest marriage. He was to be seen quite openly being rowed across the Thames to Lambeth where Catherine lodged with her step-grandmother, Agnes, Dowager Duchess of Norfolk. Unlike Anne, Catherine was an experienced young woman, well versed in the ways of love. She knew how to excite a man and it is difficult to believe that Henry could have imagined that he was the only one to have been given proofs of her affection. Perhaps he did know and preferred to pretend that he did not. It may well be that he did not, at first, contemplate matrimony. Four failed marriages might have been enough even for Henry.

However, other forces were very soon at work. Seeing his king on the rebound from Queen Anne, Norfolk fell to scheming. Might it be that the old trick would work yet again with this emotionally unstable man? Could Henry, who had defied the world in his love for Anne Boleyn and committed murder in order to swap her for Jane Seymour, be manoeuvred into marriage with his niece, Catherine? If so, the benefits would be immense in terms of family advancement for the Howards and the reversal of recent disastrous policies. The prize must have seemed well worth the risk. Howard forwarded the liaison and was aided by Gardiner who made his own riverside palace available for parties where the couple could enjoy themselves discreetly. But, in truth, there was little need for intrigue. Catherine used her many talents to achieve the prize of becoming queen of England and Henry was totally besotted.

Cromwell was not going to sit still and let the conservatives insinuate their way back into power, so the spring and summer of 1540 became a time of ferocious infighting at court. The shape of the executive had changed. Wolsey had achieved his position by keeping king and council apart and by maintaining an ecclesiastical power base partially free of royal control. Despite his semi-independence, he had always had to watch his back and prevent his influence being negated by potential rivals with access to the king. Unlike Wolsey, Cromwell's political career did not grow out of court office. He did not belong to the inner circle of privy chamber staff, trained as personal attendants on the king. He was always an outsider; a sparrow in an aviary of exotic birds. Whatever ranks and offices he achieved, he could never feel completely at home in the extravagant, fun-loving court. And, unlike Wolsey, he had no outside power base. Despite his vicegerency, his freedom of manoeuvre in religious affairs was limited. His power lay in his control of parliament and the council.

However, the 'council' was not what it had been, a body existing largely separate from the peripatetic court. From 1536–7 it had become an executive 'privy council'. Henry's oft-expressed desire to be served by his own group of intimate advisers achieved reality because of the crises of the 'great matter' and the northern rebellion. These events called for secret executive decisions to be made by a small committee Henry could trust. By 1540 this body consisted of nineteen councillors including nobles, household officers and bureaucrats chosen for their talents. Conservatives were in the majority and policy, theoretically, was arrived at by vote. In reality, Cromwell dominated the body by adroit handling, force of personality and access to the king. He shored up his position by packing the privy chamber with his supporters. The purge of Yorkists had left a number of gaps in the inner circle and Cromwell was careful to fill them with his own protégés, men like Anthony Denny, committed to religious reform. However, by the spring, his position needed further strengthening.

On the continent Charles V was stamping his authority on his dominions. He had just suppressed a revolt in the Netherlands and was turning his attention towards the neighbouring state of Cleves, where Duke William was opposing the consolidation of Habsburg power. There seemed a distinct possibility that England might be drawn into a war to aid Anne's brother. Diplomatic feelers put out in Paris disclosed that there was no immediate prospect of Francis and Charles directing their combined strength across the Channel. Indeed, the smart money was on the imminent disintegration of the brittle Valois-Habsburg friendship. Henry concluded that he had no need of foreign alliances and that he was refreshingly free to follow his own fancy in matters of the heart. He made it clear to Cromwell that he held him responsible for getting him into his current marriage and ordered him to get him out of it. This was tricky for the minister. If he failed to secure a divorce for the king he was sure to go the way of Wolsey. If he succeeded, he would be playing into the hands of the Howards and their supporters. His enemies were already girding themselves for an offensive, particularly by gathering or manufacturing evidence that Cromwell was flooding the kingdom with heretics.

Cromwell responded by advancing his own precedence among the nobility and the holders of household offices. Henry Bourchier, the elderly Earl of Essex, had recently been killed in a riding accident. Bourchier was also lord great chamberlain of the household. Cromwell persuaded the king to bestow both titles on him. He also put through parliament an Act of Precedence which cut the hereditary nobility down to size by giving all the household officers privileged positions in parliament and council irrespective of their positions in the peerage. As both vicegerent and chamberlain the 'Putney cur' now outranked the Duke of Norfolk. Henry also appointed Cromwell head of the privy chamber. It seemed that, by June 1540, he had covered all his bases.

That was not how court watchers saw the situation: 'Things are at such a pass that either the party of. . . Cromwell must succumb or that of the Bishop of Winchester with his adherents.'[178]

Such was the opinion of the French ambassador. The atmosphere of fear, hatred and intrigue was so thick that it might have been cut with a knife. Accusations and counter-accusations flew back and forth. Spies and informers were hard at work. Men and women were arrested and interrogated as the rivals desperately tried to find evidence of heresy or treason

that could be used against their adversaries. And over it all
brooded a king now in an advanced state of paranoia who,
when he could drag his thoughts away from Catherine, was
ready to believe anything of anyone. Henry's only concern was
to push the divorce through as quickly as possible. Had
Cromwell regarded it with the same urgency he might have
saved himself but he was busy seeing through parliament
another raft of important measures, including securing for the
king a miraculously large grant of taxation. Although they
knew that his coffers were bursting with the proceeds of the
Dissolution, members voted him a massive £220,000 for the
period 1541–4, more than any parliament had promised for
many years. But Henry was impatient with the slow progress
Cromwell was making in gathering all the necessary documents and conducting the sensitive diplomatic negotiations for
the divorce. It was this that gave the Norfolk clique their
opportunity. On 10 June 1540, when he entered the council
chamber, Cromwell was confronted by the captain of the
guard with a warrant for his arrest on charges of treason and
heresy. Cromwell blurted out in shock and anger. 'Is this my
reward for years of faithful service?' It was a fair question.

# Chapter 9

## 'GOD WILL NOT, I HOPE, ALLOW THIS TYRANNY MUCH LONGER'

Some eight months after Cromwell's death on 28 July 1540 Henry lambasted members of the council for bringing about the minister's downfall. 'On pretext of some trivial faults,' he complained, 'they had made several false accusations to him, as a result of which he had put to death the most faithful servant he had ever had.'[179] The king was not speaking out of remorse, nor indulging his usual petulance in blaming others for his own mistakes. His complaint was an expression of self-pity. He had discovered that he was alone. Throughout his entire reign to this point he had been served by faithful and brilliant ministers who had run the country for him. After the death of Wolsey, ten years earlier, he had found another talented politician eager and able to step into the cardinal's shoes. These two men had carried out his policies (or tactfully persuaded him to change them) and lifted from his shoulders the burden of day-to-day administration. They had made him master of his own domain and given him financial security (in stark contrast to Charles V and Francis I, who were heavily in debt). Henry had taken them for granted, and used and monstrously abused them.

Now he discovered that there was not another trustworthy political genius waiting in the wings. The most able of the royal advisers was Stephen Gardiner but he was arrogant, argumentative and had his own agenda. Henry – rightly – did not trust him. Cranmer was a dutiful yes-man who could be relied upon to do as he was told in terms of religious policy. Henry felt some affection for the archbishop and relied on his advice in matters theological but Cranmer was essentially an academic and not equipped for the cut and thrust of national and international statecraft. The other members of the executive team were lightweights, second-rate men who lacked Wolsey and Cromwell's talent for sheer hard work and were fearful of taking initiatives without the king's detailed approval (scarcely surprising in view of what had happened in 1530 and 1540). Moreover, they were given to squabbling among themselves. Willy-nilly, Henry had to become more involved in the minutiae of government. And he made a mess of it.

It is difficult to know whether to react to the record of Henry's last six-and-a-half years with pity or indignation. He was fat, ill and, after the failure of his fifth marriage (see below), seriously depressed. He could no longer take his pleasures in the tennis court or tiltyard and hunting was progressively difficult. What was harder to bear was the realization which eventually dawned on him that he would have no more legitimate children. He hobbled around his palaces, increasingly dependent on his intimate attendants. Had he emulated the behaviour of his father he would have left his country strong and secure. When Henry VII's last years had been dogged by declining health, he had concentrated on leaving his son a full treasury and a nation at peace. He had been notoriously miserly in accumulating wealth and had buttressed the kingdom with foreign alliances. There is no reason why Henry VIII should not have done the same. He could have avoided European conflict, arranged useful marriages for his children and brought into being a council of sage advisers to assist young Edward in the likely event of his son inheriting the crown at an early age. What he did bequeath to Edward VI was a nation that was bankrupt, reeling from disastrous and unnecessary wars with France and Scotland and increasingly divided along religious lines.

Historians have, until recent years, portrayed Tudor government in this last phase of Henry's reign as a kind of tug-o-war between rival factions. Latterly, revisionist thinkers have presented a picture of the king taking a firm hold on the reins and steering England towards a destiny of his own devising. I believe we must be content to accept a much more messy understanding of what was going on between 1540 and January 1547. Let us first consider the consistency of Henry's policy-making:

> The king is a dilettante and has no serious intentions. This we have certainly found out from the English who have been here, although at times out of Christian love we had to believe that he was serious. But finally, when we had debated *ad nauseam.* . .everything was sealed with a sausage [i.e. worthless] and left to the king's pleasure. The English themselves said, 'Our king vacillates. . .Our king in no way respects religion and the gospel'.[180]

Thus Martin Luther, in October 1539, reporting to the Elector of Saxony on the interminable negotiations of the English delegates with the Protestant states. His frustration is understandable but was his estimate of Henry's character distorted by his distaste for the tortoise-like reality of international diplomacy? Is his opinion supported by that of other contemporaries free enough or bold enough to express themselves fearlessly? In the reign of Mary, Gardiner delivered a sermon at St Paul's Cross in which he assured his hearers that, in 1540, 'Master Knyvet and I were sent ambassadors unto the emperor, to desire him that he would be a mean between the pope's holiness and the king, to bring the king to the obedience of the see of Rome'.[181] Did Henry really contemplate abandoning the royal supremacy or was Gardiner presenting a deliberately distorted version of the truth to please the Catholic queen?

In 1546, Henry authorized Cranmer to have letters drawn up ordering the clergy to 'pull down the roods in every church and to suppress the accustomed ringing on All hallow-night'. The archbishop bent to his task and delivered the necessary documents for the king's signature, only to meet with the following response:

> I am now otherwise resolved. . .I have received letters from my lord of Winchester. . .and he writeth plainly unto us that the league [proposed between France, England and the Empire] will not prosper nor go forward if we make any other innovation, change or alteration, either in religion or ceremonies, than heretofore hath already been commenced and done.[182]

Such U-turns do not convey the impression of a king clearly focused on his vision for the country. And such changeableness was not, apparently, uncommon. The French ambassador, Charles de Marillac, reported that the king's mood swings were now so violent and impacted so unpredictably on policy that he often changed his opinion drastically between morning and evening. The picture of the ageing Henry that emerges from contemporary records is of a man distracted by pain, influenced by his advisers and companions and responsive to national and international events. As far as religion was concerned, Henry's beliefs were not set in aspic. He devoted a considerable amount of time to theological debate with his bishops and preachers. He was concerned enough about continual disputes and rival demonstrations to draw up new statements of official doctrine but his own thinking continued to develop. It dawned even upon this pious autocrat that it was not possible to outlaw ancient ceremonies and practices such as pilgrimage and the decking of shrines without negating or, at least, casting doubt upon the dogmas underlying them. His beliefs, insofar as we can determine them, were certainly not theologically consistent. While accepting transubstantiation, he downplayed sacerdotalism. The primary function of priests was not, in his view, mediating between God and human souls, living and dead, but preaching and teaching (a distinctly evangelical emphasis). As for purgatory, scripture, he thought, had as much to say about that as did 'the tale of Robin Hood'.

Nor, I think, can we put the toing and froing of policy down to the ebb and flow of the influence of court factions, if by 'faction' we mean a group of activists bound together by some ideological or political *raison d'être*. The privy council after Cromwell's fall was new and, yet, it was not new. It had shaken off control by a powerful minister and now emerged as a body with its own secretariat and regular working procedures, but the old problem remained of how to maintain effective government when the head of state was peripatetic and the executive body was static. Inevitably, the privy chamber maintained its political importance. Thanks to the fact that Cromwell had packed the royal inner sanctum with his own supporters, most of Henry's day-to-day companions – his gentlemen, his doctors and his body servants – were men of a reformist stamp. The more dependent an ailing king became on his close attendants the more this dependence reflected itself in the influence on policy. Since these men exercised patronage, they could bring in their own clients to the royal household. Thus, the outer circles of the court also took on a predominantly reformist hue.

By contrast, the privy council was now a bastion of the conservative aristocracy. As a result of the Act of Precedence this body was now dominated by the holders of the great offices of state, most of which were held by hereditary peers. Policy decisions came to be made by about a dozen lay and ecclesiastical lords. This gave government the superficial appearance of a reversion to the medieval model: the king advised by his barons. However, after all that had happened since 1509, things could never be that simple. It may help us to grasp something of the complexity of relationships among the political elite if we think of each member of that elite as having numerous strings attached. They connected him to colleagues in chamber or council, to family members, to co-religionists, to protégés close to the court and out in the shires. The strings were constantly being tugged and relaxed and, sometimes, severed (usually because an individual had fallen from royal favour). There was nothing novel about this but the situation after 1540 was more than usually fraught. The king was tetchy, unpredictable, ready to listen to slanderous innuendos, prepared to strike out viciously at anyone he could be persuaded to suspect. For those prepared to risk riding his moods the results could be gratifying. Also, Henry could not be expected to live many more years. Soon there would be a new young king – and new opportunities. Lacking control by the king, or an all-powerful minister, the privy council degenerated into a body of men who, according to the cynical Marillac, 'Seek only to undo each other to gain credit and, under the colour of their master's good, each attends to his own. For all the fine words of which they are full, they will act only as necessity and self-interest compel them.'[183]

Cromwell was not destroyed because the international situation had changed and Henry wanted to distance himself from the architect of current policy. He was not destroyed because he had pushed religious change beyond the limits set by the king. He was not even destroyed because he had manoeuvred his master into a distasteful marriage. His fate was sealed because Henry was impatient to make Catherine his wife and his minister seemed to be dragging his heels over the matter. Apart from his infatuation with his new mistress, Henry was, as ever, sensitive about his sexual inadequacy. His lack of arousal with Anne brought him face to face with this again. Cromwell was one of the few who knew about the king's sexual embarrassment and Henry may not have been sorry to be sure of his silence. Certain it is that he could not wait to get Catherine with child and thus prove to the world his undiminished virility. If we assume that he and his nymphet were already sleeping together, Catherine might have fallen pregnant at any time and it was vital that any baby should be born, and preferably conceived, in wedlock. Like a spoilt child throwing a tantrum over his parents' reluctance to indulge his latest whim, Henry was vulnerable to the approaches of those who expressed sympathy for his plight. These were, of course, Cromwell's enemies. They saw the chink in their adversary's armour and grabbed their opportunity to exploit it. The garish mosaic of fictitious offences they devised would not have stood up even in a Tudor court of law so it was necessary to proceed against the accused by Act of Attainder, a parliamentary procedure which required only the approval of both houses and the royal assent. Cromwell never knew the detailed accusations of treason, heresy and even witchcraft assembled by his enemies. All he could do from his quarters in the Tower was write to the king with grovelling appeals for mercy. There were aspects of Cromwell's disgrace which mirrored those attendant upon Wolsey's fall. Henry sent his own messengers to the Tower to cheer the prisoner and invite him to respond privately to his accusers. This kept Norfolk, Gardiner and company on tenterhooks and, perhaps, explains the hodge-podge of crimes they desperately cobbled together.

They need not have worried. Henry was too preoccupied with the mechanics of dissolving his marriage to care greatly about the plight of his minister. Understandably, Anne was confused and frightened when her husband's envoys came to tell her that the king had determined on a divorce and to demand her cooperation. Even with the aid of an interpreter she could not grasp what Henry expected of her. On the other hand, she knew well enough what happened to wives who failed to please this irascible man. Small wonder that she fainted on receiving the news or that she listened with tears to the explanation of why Henry was resolved to repudiate her. Anne was not a passive nonentity. She had already stood up to the king by questioning his behaviour towards Princess Mary. Now she insisted that she had vowed before God to take

Henry for her husband till death should them part and that she had comported herself at all times as a dutiful wife.

Tremblingly she demanded to know what she had done to displease the king. It was only with difficulty that she was persuaded that Henry had no animosity towards her and would behave honourably, giving her the title of 'sister' and allowing her precedence beneath members of the king's immediate family. The face-saving formula that Henry had accepted as the basis for his case for annulment was that he had only with reluctance agreed to the marriage and had deliberately refrained from consummating it because there was some question of Anne's having been pre-contracted to Francis of Lorraine. It was at this time that Anne's ladies were quizzed as to what they knew of their mistress's intimate relations with the king and provided the evidence of non-consummation and Anne's supposed naivety. A previous union had, indeed, been agreed when Anne and Francis were both children. No formal written evidence of the repudiation of this contract had reached England and it was on this technicality that Henry now pressed for an annulment. Anne was not allowed to consult her brother or to receive independent advice. She was required to consent speedily to an investigation into her marriage. By this time she knew Henry well enough to realize the futility of resistance. On 9 July 1540 convocation dutifully declared Henry's fourth marriage null and void. Anne was allocated an estate of £3,000 per annum.

There was a price – a cruel price – to be paid for her privileged position. She was forbidden ever to leave England. She was allowed no communication with her family in Cleves except under supervision of the king's officers. She was, however, ordered to write to Duke William, with a copy and translation to the council, expressing that she agreed to the annulment of her own free will, without any pressure from her spouse. This was, according to Henry, an insurance policy in case, because of her 'womanish nature', she changed her mind. In fact, what Henry was buying was not only her agreement to divorce, but also her silence. The secrets of the royal bedroom would not be noised abroad. On 28 July two ceremonies took place. Henry and Catherine were married quietly at the royal manor of Oatlands and, on Tower Hill, Thomas Cromwell was beheaded by a clumsy executioner who badly bungled the job.

Henry was nothing if not a crowd pleaser. Throughout his reign he sought the adulation of London's citizens with public displays, jousts and river pageants. In this long, hot summer of 1540 – the driest and most uncomfortable anyone could remember – the people did not want for gruesome entertainments. Cromwell's death was hugely popular – another good reason for Henry's abandoning him. Two days later he gave them another rare treat:

> The thirty day of July, were drawn on hurdles out of the Tower to Smithfield, Robert Barnes, Doctor in Divinity, Thomas Garrett and William Jerome, Bachelors in Divinity, Powell, Fethersone and Abel. The first three were drawn to the stake, there before set up, and were burned and the latter three drawn to the gallows, likewise there set up, and were hanged, beheaded and quartered.[184]

Barnes we have already met as the confidant of Cromwell and Henry's ambassador to Lutheran princes. He had recently fallen foul of Bishop Gardiner by engaging in pulpit controversy with him. Garrett and Jerome had also been despatched to the Tower for their suspect sermons. The other three had been convicted for treason under the Act of Supremacy. A stranger witnessing the executions was puzzled to understand what religion the king actually espoused, 'his sword cutting on both sides',[185] and he cannot have been alone in his bewilderment. Historians have debated whether this was a deliberate show of Henrician impartiality; a demonstration that he would kill any religious deviant of whatever hue – papist, evangelical, Sacramentarian or Anabaptist – who failed to toe the party line. In fact the king's actions at this time did not smack of vicious even-handedness. On 4 August a dozen men earlier apprehended by Cromwell on suspicion of a Catholic conspiracy in

Calais suffered as traitors at Tyburn. At the same time, the king issued a general pardon to most of the 500 Londoners who had been arrested for suspected infractions of the Six Articles Act.

Henry was encountering the problems which face all persecutors. On the one hand, it was necessary to enforce the laws pertaining to religion. On the other hand, too great zeal would create martyrs and thus be counter-productive. It was easier to deal with Catholic extremists because, by rejecting the royal supremacy, they had committed a political act. In the same way, Anabaptists, who were wedded to beliefs (such as the rejection of oath-taking) which were destructive of civil order, could be classed as political offenders, but evangelicals were in another category. They were loyal subjects who happened to believe in doctrines not approved by the government. Wholesale punishment of such heretics might all too easily play into the hands of the clergy and risk stirring up that anti-clericalism which was never far below the surface.

Suppression certainly had an effect. For the first time ever there was the beginning of a religious exodus. Several people who could afford to do so travelled abroad to centres of reform such as Strasbourg, Basel and Zurich. One pessimist, the London merchant Richard Hilles, reported to friends in Switzerland:

> A man may travel from the east of England to the west and from the north to the south, without being able to discover a single preacher who, out of a pure heart and with faith unfeigned, is seeking the glory of God. . .The king has now prohibited [Latimer and Shaxton] from preaching or coming within two or three German miles of our two universities, the city of London, or their own dioceses! God will not, I hope, allow this tyranny much longer.[186]

However, ardent Catholics were equally despondent. With the advantage of hindsight, a devotee of the old faith reflected a decade later that the Reformation had gathered momentum towards the end of the old king's reign:

A great many I am sure, that would have said once within these twenty years, that no man living, no, nor an angel of heaven or all the devils in hell, should never have perverted you from the sure affiance and fast faith that you had toward the blessed sacraments of the church. But after that there came among you a great multitude of pleasant preachers, preaching liberty, and so pleasures following of such lewd liberty: how soon you have been overthrown and turned another way.[187]

Liberty was, indeed, the heady intoxicant of the Reformation. Too many of Henry's subjects had now tasted the freedom from priestly domination and the fear of eternal punishment on which it rested to be persuaded back into Catholic abstinence. Henry only realized slowly that he had no way of imposing religious unity. All he could do was try to check the new faith with sporadic persecution, while at the same time also restraining the Catholic backlash.

For him, the months following his fifth marriage were the happiest or, at least, the most stress free that he had enjoyed for a long time. He had the company of a lively wife to foster in him the illusion of youth and vitality. He lavished attention and gifts on her – the estates confiscated from Cromwell, chests of jewels, all the clothes she was ever likely to wear – and loved to show her off. He threw parties for her, lavish banquets and dances where the queen and the nimbler guests could enjoy themselves even if he had to sit out some of the newfangled galliards. Catherine's response to being appallingly spoiled by her obsessed sugar-daddy is not difficult to understand. She took him and his generosity for granted. Perhaps, secretly she despised this fat old man whose feeble, lumbering attempts at love-making were not only uncomfortable but ridiculous. Putting up with them was a small price to pay for being the grandest lady in the realm with the members of a large court scurrying around her, eager to pander to her every whim.

It is customary to dismiss Catherine Howard as a flibberti-gibbet, characterized in the words of one biographer by 'juvenile delinquency, wanton selfishness, and ephemeral hedonism'.[188] I believe we may allow ourselves to be a little more sympathetic. Catherine was a young woman scarcely out of her teenage years who learned slowly and with difficulty the dignity and restraint expected of a queen. The few glimpses of her provided by extant records suggest that she had a natural warmth that made her dismissive of protocol. When Anne of Cleves (now always referred to as the Lady Anne) visited the royal court for the New Year celebrations in 1541, which cannot have been an easy experience for her, Catherine was at pains to put her guest at her ease. She refused to allow her predecessor to kneel in her presence. The atmosphere became markedly less relaxed when the king entered his wife's chambers: Anne was required to occupy a seat 'near the bottom of the table at supper'. However, 'after the king had retired, the queen and Lady Anne danced together and the next day all three dined together'. When Henry sent Catherine yet another present of a ring and two small dogs, she 'passed them over to Lady Anne'.[189] About the same time, she made efforts to repair a breach which had opened with Princess Mary. The king's daughter had been very distant towards her and she had responded by having two of Mary's attendants dismissed. However, Catherine was unable to harbour a grudge for long and, by January 1541, the two women were exchanging costly gifts. Catherine clearly had a warm heart – too warm for her own good.

If her sympathetic nature extended to encouraging Henry in the intimacy of their bedroom, her feminine wiles were unproductive. When Chapuys reported to his master the emperor on 4 January 1541, his first snippet of news was 'the queen is not yet enceinte'. People, he wrote, were even talking of a rapprochement between Henry and the Lady Anne. Personally, he could see no sign of it but, he assured Charles, he would 'indirectly thwart' any such reunion.[190] Everyone with access to the court was watching for some change in Catherine's 'condition'. In April, Marillac believed he had a scoop: 'the queen is thought to be with child which would be a very great joy to this king who, it seems, believes it and intends, if it be found true, to have her crowned at Whitsuntide'.[191] But Whitsun came and went and their was still no prospect of a happy event.

By this time Henry had decided on a mammoth excursion to the north. In the aftermath of the Pilgrimage of Grace he had promised to visit the remote shires but always put off venturing his person in a society where religious conservatism and old feudal loyalties remained strong. He might have hoped that the sacrifice of Cromwell would satisfy the northerners and he had also thrown them another sop by exempting them from the taxation voted in 1540 but, in April 1541, trouble had flared up again in the shape of a mini-rebellion around Pontefract. Therefore, Henry steeled himself for the arduous and painful trek. He had another reason for making the journey; he planned a face-to-face meeting with his nephew, James V. He had always regarded Scotland as an English vassal state and was concerned at the close ties between James and the family of his wife, Marie of Guise. Henry frequently patronized the Scottish king with advice and particularly urged him to bring the church to heel as he had done but James, under the influence of Cardinal David Beaton, remained firmly loyal to Rome and resented his uncle's interference. It was arranged that the two monarchs would meet at York. Henry had good political reasons for this initiative. As the accord between Charles and Francis began to fall apart, he returned to the old policy of trying to make gains from their rivalry. If this was to result in open hostility with France, he wanted to secure his 'backdoor'.

The expedition which set out on the last day of June 1541 seems to have been doomed from the start. For most of the following month the weather was foul. Henry had assembled a vast entourage to impress his northern subjects. As well as a large court contingent and the wagons needed to carry every-thing needed to overawe his subjects – sumptuous clothes, food, kitchen equipment, chamber hangings, furniture and chests of silver plate – the king was attended by a guard of 1,000 soldiers and even some pieces of artillery. These churned rain-soaked roads into muddy morasses and made a nonsense of the planned itinerary. The journey was sheer misery for everyone involved. Queen Catherine found ways to relieve her dreary days – and nights. At several stopping places along the route she had assignations with her cousin, Thomas Culpeper, a gentleman of the privy chamber. The couple were aided by Jane Rochford who entered fully into the conspiracy by vetting the apartments designated for the queen and calculating how best Culpeper's nocturnal visits might be accomplished. Quite what can have possessed Catherine and her co-conspirators it is difficult to comprehend. They can have entertained no doubts about the king's massive insecurity, jealousy and suspiciousness. Jane Rochford, in particular, had been close to the traumatic events surrounding the downfall of Anne Boleyn and should have been acutely aware of the risks involved in deceiving Henry. Undoubtedly, sexual desire was the motor driving Catherine's foolhardy adventure. This was a young woman with a history of dangerous liaisons and the prospect of tying herself exclusively to her corpulent, sexually incompetent husband must have been unbearable to her. Was it just the overconfidence of youth that convinced the queen and her lover that they could get away with it?

It may be that this is not the most important question to ask. Perhaps we should be probing more persistently the relationship between the king and queen. The fact that Catherine could devote several nights to her lusty visitor indicates that Henry was not with her. There are other indications that his ardour may have been cooling. In the previous spring he had banned his wife from his privy chamber for ten or twelve days. This may have been because his ulcerated legs were particularly bad but observers gossiped about a marital row and they may have been right. The rumours about Henry possibly returning to Anne of Cleves were persistent and the fact that Chapuys was prone to dismissing them does not prove that the king was not weighing his options. Henry was confronted by the unpalatable fact that his new wife was no more able to give him a son than three of her predecessors. It must have been torment for him to watch Catherine preening herself with flirtatious gallants of her own age and to know that, though she belonged to him, he could not give them the irrefutable proof of his own virility.

However, for the moment, the king was ignorant of his wife's adultery as the royal cavalcade lumbered its way to York. All along the route civic dignitaries and local gentry turned out to display their allegiance. This took very tangible forms. The burgesses of Stamford presented him with £20, Boston managed £50 and Lincoln £40. The royal cash register jangled agreeably at every stop, but it was as the party entered the region which had been most disaffected four years earlier that the leaders of society were particularly anxious to prove their loyalty: 'When he entered into Yorkshire, he was met with two hundred gentlemen of the same shire in coats of velvet and four thousand tall yeomen and serving men well hosed, which on their knees made a submission. . .and gave to the king nine hundred pounds.[192]

Unfortunately, James of Scotland was not among the number of those who rushed to acknowledge Henry's sovereignty. He failed to turn up for the appointed rendezvous at York. He later claimed that he had been advised that it was too dangerous for him to venture south of the border but the reality was that the pro-French king fully intended to snub his overweening uncle. Henry waited eight days in mounting impatience. Then, still fuming and vowing revenge, he set out to make for home as fast as he could. It was the end of October 1541 before he arrived back at Hampton Court. He was greeted with the news that Prince Edward was seriously ill with a fever. It was a worrying postlude to what had been a dismal summer but worse was to come.

The rump of the privy council that had been left in the capital during the progress was headed by Cranmer, Edward Seymour and Thomas Audley, all religious progressives. Gardiner was, once more, absent on a foreign embassy and

Norfolk was travelling with the king. In several small ways, such as making clerical appointments, appointing preachers and suppressing heresy prosecutions, the councillors swung the pendulum back towards ongoing reformation. It was the absence of the conservative leaders that emboldened some junior members of the king's household to play for high stakes. John Lascelles was one of Henry's table waiters and the first sign of his disaffection was recorded a year earlier. In a conversation with three of his colleagues he lamented the downfall of Cromwell and the fact that Gardiner and Norfolk appeared to be cocks of the walk. They discussed ways that the conservative group might be attacked. One of them had overheard Norfolk angrily opposing the distribution of the vernacular Bible and the abolition of monasticism. 'By God's body sacred,' the duke had thundered, 'it will never be out of my heart as long as I live!' Surely, the reporter suggested, this opposition to royal policy was enough to bring Norfolk to account. Lascelles had counselled caution. 'If we wait quietly and do not oppose Norfolk and Winchester, but rather suffer a while in silence, they will overthrow themselves. For they stand so obviously against God and their prince that they cannot long survive.'[193] The prudent zealot waited a year before grasping his opportunity. In October 1541, he came to Cranmer with information about Queen Catherine. It related to her pre-marital sexual adventures in the household of the dowager Duchess of Norfolk. Lascelles sister, Mary Hall, had been a servant at Lambeth and had first-hand evidence to give, particularly of Catherine's relationship with Francis Dereham, one of Norfolk's gentlemen, who had wanted to marry his mistress and had certainly slept with her.

Cranmer was in a spot. He did not want to cause the king distress. He probably was not motivated by evangelical triumphalism, but, of course, there was no question of concealing the information that had come his way. That would have made him an accessory to Catherine's misdemeanours. He discussed the problem with his conciliar colleagues and they decided that the archbishop was the best person to convey the unpalatable truth to Henry. However, Cranmer was not prepared to confront his master face-to-face. He wrote the allegations in a letter and slipped it to Henry as they were leaving mass on 2 November. It only revealed Catherine's pre-marital activities and Henry was initially disposed to disregard it as malicious gossip. He ordered Lascelles and his sister to be examined in order to break their story. Three days later, Marillac reported that the king spent time with the queen and her ladies and was 'as gay as ever he had seen him' but that was the day that reports were brought back that the informers were sticking to their story. There was no confrontation. Henry did what he usually did with wives, ministers and servants he intended to destroy; he simply walked away from them. Or, rather, on this occasion he had himself rowed away from Hampton Court. He now authorized a full investigation and the secret arrests began. The net spread gradually wider. Confessions were obtained, some or all by the usual methods. Within days the full extent of Catherine's sexual liaisons before and after her marriage was known.

When the government officially released the news, exaggerated stories began to circulate about Henry's response. One portrayed him roaring around the palace, brandishing a sword and vowing vengeance. The privy council's version of events, as set down in a letter to William Paget, ambassador in France, was more restrained: 'the king's heart was pierced with pensiveness, so that it was long before he could utter his sorrow, and finally, with plenty of tears, which was strange in his courage, [he] opened the same.'[194] There has been a tendency to melodrama in the recording of this sad collapse of Henry's fifth marriage: 'the end of life, if not of the reign had arrived. He stepped forth. . .a grey and crippled old man.'[195] Well, I wonder. This supposedly shattered king was sufficiently detached to order all his wife's jewels to be impounded and to begin taking thought for his next marriage. Within days, Chapuys reported, 'The king pretends that Dereham had actually been betrothed to the queen before her marriage, which is, therefore, invalid. . .In two days time the king will have that published and three months hence [parliament] will be assembled. . .to cancel their former declaration of the nullity of the Cleves marriage.'[196]

The ambassador assumed that this was in response to information brought back by Gardiner, recently returned from Germany. The changed complexion of international affairs, he guessed, was now making an alliance with the Protestant princes once more appear attractive. This degree of calculation on Henry's part does not square with the image of a man utterly broken by having his love rejected. Certainly, he was humiliated by his wife's misdemeanours. She had come to him as, supposedly, a spotless virgin and she had, again supposedly, been a faithful wife. On both counts she had deceived him. No doubt he did weep. No doubt he was rendered momentarily speechless. However, he was not mourning lost love or the departure of youth. His were tears of petulance and self-pity. Why, he must have asked himself, had he been so cursed in marriage? All his wives, with the possible exception of Jane Seymour, had failed him. The latest one had promised so much but he had, I believe, already begun to be disillusioned with her. Catherine had not produced another Tudor baby. The recent illness of little Edward underlined just how important this was and it was not the only warning sign. In Scotland, James V's second wife had given him two sons but, in the spring of 1541, the infant princes had died within a few days of each other. It is, I believe, more than possible that, despite Catherine's physical attraction, Henry had failed to have satisfactory sexual intercourse with her. The truth was – and perhaps it was beginning to dawn even on him – that no woman could satisfy him because he could satisfy no woman. He was psychologically and probably physically incapable of love. His obsessive generosity towards Catherine is a typical sign of emotional deficiency. He lavished on her things in abundance because he could not give her himself.

If the revelations about his wife's amours had forced him, as it forces every cuckolded husband, to contemplate his own inadequacy, he soon brushed aside any such misgivings. As usual, he blamed everyone except himself. Just as others had 'tricked' him into marriage with Anne Boleyn and Anne of Cleves, so the Howard clan had conspired to foist Catherine on him. Henry made sure that the guilty parties were punished. The only surprising fact about the fallout from failed marriage number five is that the king's vengeance did not extend more widely than it did. Culpeper and Dereham both had to die as, in February 1542, did Catherine and Lady Rochford. Several members of the Howard clan, excluding Norfolk, who went to desperate lengths to distance himself from his niece, were incarcerated in the Tower and had their property confiscated but, within months, they were pardoned and allowed to resume their lives.

It is tempting to see Henry's plunge into war as, in part at least, a reaction to the disaster of his private life, a defiant assertion of his power and importance. It is certainly difficult to find any rational reason for the disastrous international policies which dominated the last years of the reign. On 29 December 1541, the king held meetings with Chapuys which lasted most of the day. Their discussions ranged over all the major aspects of the contemporary European scene and the adroit, seasoned diplomat later boasted that he 'got the king into very high spirits by such flattering words which. . .are never thrown away upon him'.[197] Chapuys congratulated himself on inducing Henry to speak openly about his relations with Francis and Charles and reported that the English king would sell his support to the highest bidder: 'he was quite independent, he said [and] if people wanted him they might come forward with offers.' Meanwhile, he would 'temporise with both sides in order to avoid spending money in preparing for war'.[198] Perhaps the underlying reason for Henry reverting to the military adventurousness of his youth is simply that he could. For the first time in years he had money to lavish on men and armaments and now there was no minister at his elbow urging thrift. Moreover, Henry had at his court a new generation of potential military commanders – men like Edward Seymour and John Dudley – ambitious for the fame and fortune of war. Henry had spent the 1530s making himself fully master at home and he was proud of his achievement. Now he wanted to reassert his position on the international stage and time was running out.

Before he could venture across the Channel Henry had unfinished business to settle with Scotland. At the end of October 1541, while he was still returning from his progress, news had reached him that Margaret, the Scottish queen mother, had died. Henry's only remaining sibling had striven over the years to maintain cordial relations between her brother and her son. Now her restraining hand was removed and Henry was still smarting from the insult he had received at York. Over the next months, he tried by unyielding diplomacy and the threat of force to neutralize Scotland in preparation for his own preoccupation with European war. His efforts, culminating in an ineffective but irritating cross border incursion led by the Duke of Norfolk, only provoked James V into retaliation. In November 1542, he despatched an army of 20,000 men to invade England. They were met at Solway Moss, near Gretna Green, by a hastily gathered force of 3,000. Surprisingly, the Scots fled the field and sustained heavy losses. To add to Henry's good fortune, James V died a few days later, shortly after responding angrily to the news that his queen had given birth to a daughter. 'Devil take it!' he is reputed to have grumbled. 'It will end as it began. It came with a lass and will go with a lass!'[199] Henry VIII was not the only monarch to suffer dynastic misfortune.

The infant Mary, Queen of Scots now became, as she was destined to remain, the victim of national and religious rivalries. In distant London, Henry believed that he could now take the northern kingdom under his wing. He sent his secretary and close companion, Sir Ralph Sadler, to Edinburgh with what amounted to instructions for the governor, the Earl of Arran. He was to reform the Scottish church along English lines, agree to the marriage of Mary to Prince Edward and send her to be educated in England. The Scottish government was to have no dealings with France. As a reward for his compliance Henry offered his daughter, Elizabeth, as a bride to Arran's eldest son. So much for the carrot. The stick came in the form of a threat. If the Scots should look to an alliance with Marie of Guise's country, Henry would, after settling with France, 'so look upon them that they should see their unkind and deceitful behaviour requited to their extreme damages'.[200]

Poor Sadler thus became the latest of those royal servants whom Henry regarded as agents of his will. Having told the ambassador what he wanted, and without any understanding of the actual situation in Scotland, he expected the envoy to carry out his instructions to the letter. Sadler discovered that Arran was a weak man, ready to say anything to keep Henry happy, that the governor was involved in a struggle with Cardinal Beaton, the queen and the pro-French party and that the people in general were bitterly resentful of interference by the 'auld enemy'. On one occasion the house where he was staying was surrounded by an angry mob. On another, someone took a shot at him while he was walking in the garden. Small wonder that the envoy was really alarmed when Henry proposed to appoint him as a permanent representative in Scotland. Only with difficulty did Sadler manage to wriggle out of this 'honour'. On 1 July 1543 a treaty of sorts was agreed between the two nations at Greenwich. Its terms represented a much modified version of what Henry had demanded but even this the Scots had no intention of keeping. On 8 September, Arran came to terms with his opponents, renounced the Reformation and agreed to power-sharing with the queen mother. Henry ranted that he had been deceived and that he would never trust the Scots again. In fact, he only had himself to blame. It would have taken another Edward I, ready to commit himself to the use of force and, preferably, to lead his army in person, to make the Scottish nobles yield their infant queen into his hands. Henry VIII was not in the same league as the 'Hammer of the Scots'.

He was not even in the same league as his contemporaries, Charles V and Francis I. They were monarchs who led their own armies. They discussed tactics with their captains in the field. They rode into battle. They enthused their soldiers. They took risks and, as we have seen, the French king was actually captured. Henry was an armchair general. He sent his commanders into the fray with detailed written instructions which usually proved impossible to accomplish on the ground. He angrily berated their failures – from the comfort of his privy chamber. He talked of marching with his troops, but talk was all he ever did. There was talk of his leading the invasion of 1523. There was talk of his personal suppression of the northern rebels in 1537. Nothing came of either. Just as he fell in love with love rather than with women, so he was enamoured of the idea of war rather than its reality. The king, who was now about to bankrupt his country by fresh military adventures in France, was not using war as a last resort to obtain some necessary political objective. He was pitting himself against a rival because that was what kings did; war was part of the essence of kingship.

His fascination with military conflict centred on two of its aspects – technology and pageantry. Henry was genuinely interested in the latest developments in the art of warfare. In land fighting it was fortifications and artillery that principally fascinated him. The invasion scare of 1539 had energized him into ordering the biggest overhaul of coastal defences before the nineteenth century. He took the opportunity to have his engineers apply the latest innovations. The Renaissance re-volution in the building of castles and town fortifications was a response to the development of artillery and it was inevitable that interest in the two aspects of warfare should go hand-in-hand. Henry ordered the construction of new cannon foundries. By 1544 he was able to ship 250 pieces of ordnance across the Channel for deployment in the campaign of that year. All the major military engagements of his reign after

Flodden Field in 1513 were sieges. Henry's armies were never called upon to fight pitched battles in open field.

About the same time, the king commissioned one Thomas Audley, a gentleman usher of the privy chamber (not to be confused with the lord chancellor), to write a manual of warfare for Prince Edward. The *Booke of Orders for the Warre both by Sea and Land* was a compendium of information of all aspects of military activity from tactical formations to discipline. It drew on existing English and foreign works and on the writer's own experience in France (he had been captain of Guisnes castle in 1544). The *Booke of Orders* urged the young prince to keep himself up to date with current developments on the continent. This was something that the younger generation of Henry's captains took very seriously. Norfolk and Suffolk were military leaders of the old school, whose effectiveness was marred by an unimaginative traditionalism. The new men, like Seymour and Dudley, were prepared to learn not just from the ancient masters, but from Italian, Swiss and German experts who were turning warfare into a science. Dr John Dee later reminisced about Dudley that he:

> . . .did disclose his hearty love to virtuous sciences and his noble intent to excel in martial prowess when he with humble request and instant soliciting got the best rules (either in time past by Greek or Roman or in our own time used, and new stratagems therein devised) for ordering of all companies, sums and numbers of men. . . with one kind of weapon or more appointed; with artillery or without; on horseback or on foot; to give or to take onset [i.e. assault]; to seem many, being few; to seem few, being many; to march in battle or journey – with many such feats to fight in [open] field, skirmish or ambush. . . [arithmetical formulae relevant to military formations were] enclosed in a rich case of gold he used to wear about his neck, as his jewel most precious and counsellor most trusty.[201]

It was Dudley who now supervised what may reasonably be called the foundation of the Royal Navy. Henry was always fascinated by ships but since the early years of the reign, which had seen the building of the impressive *Henri Grâce á Dieu*, the laying down of warships had almost ceased. Henry had relied largely on commandeering merchant vessels when he needed to carry out cross-Channel raids or convey troops abroad but, between 1540 and 1546, he doubled the size of his navy by new construction, purchase and capture. Of the new vessels laid down, fifteen were in excess of 300 tons. Several of them were built to a new design with greatly increased fire-power. For the first time cannon were installed amidships. The age of naval artillery had arrived. This involved building or extending royal dockyards at Deptford and Woolwich and creating a huge naval base at Portsmouth. If the navy was now to be a permanent feature of England's offensive and defensive capabilities its organization would need to be put on a more effective footing. In January 1543, John Dudley, now Viscount Lisle, was appointed lord admiral. Over the next couple of years he developed an administrative machine, the Council for Marine Causes, the direct forerunner of the Admiralty, a professional bureaucratic institution with its own specialist officials for administering every aspect of naval development and maintenance.

Thus, for the remainder of the reign, England was on a war footing. By 1543 Henry had committed himself to campaigning in France. The treaty he signed with the emperor in February proposed what was, in essence, a repetition of the military strategy that had so signally failed before: a coordinated advance into French territory by imperial forces through Champagne and English troops from Calais to converge on Paris. This was all scheduled for the coming summer but, by the spring of 1544, Henry's army had not departed. The reason was Scotland. Or, rather, the reason was Henry's belligerence. His high-handed bullying had achieved what the local politicians could not achieve: it had united the people and their leaders against England. The king was furious. Charles was waiting with mounting impatience for the English contingent to cross the Channel and the Scots were making him lose face by demonstrating that he could not even secure his own border. Henry despatched Edward Seymour, Earl of Hertford, north-wards with an army to deal with the 'traitors'. The general advised a moderate approach – to secure and garrison a chain of strategically placed strongholds to prevent any Franco-Hibernian distraction. Henry rejected this counsel emphatically. He was intent on a bloody demonstration of his wrath. Hertford was instructed to:

> . . .burn Edinburgh town and so deface it as to leave a memory for ever of the vengeance of God upon their falsehood and disloyalty. . .sack Holyrood House and sack, burn and subvert Leith and all the towns and villages round, putting man, woman and child to fire and sword where resistance is made, then pass over to Fifeland and extend like destruction there, not forgetting to turn upside down the cardinal's town of St. Andrews, so as the upper stone may be the nether and not one stick stand by another, sparing no creature alive, especially such as be allied to the cardinal. . .take order with the wardens of the Marches to burn and destroy to the uttermost, not leaving Jedworth behind if it may be conveniently destroyed.[202]

These instructions, faithfully, if reluctantly, carried out by Hertford were vindictive and politically inept. The harrowing of Edinburgh and the Lowlands generated a decade and more of ill will.

Meanwhile, life at court had been very eventful. In July 1543, the king got married again. His sixth and last wife was the only one he chose for himself without any kind of outside influence or manoeuvring. For that reason it is difficult to discern Henry's motives for plunging once more into the troubled waters of matrimony. Perhaps, like his renewed warmongering, it was an attempt to convince himself and others that he still possessed the mental and physical vigour of a man half his age. Or, it may be that we need look no further than his desire to be loved. Like all weak characters, Henry needed to have people around him who offered support, praise and flattery. If a Tudor wife's first responsibility was child-bearing, her second was ego-massaging. Catherine Parr was a caring, sympathetic woman who, at the age of thirty-one, had already devoted herself to nursing two aged husbands. She came from a border family and her second spouse, John Neville, Lord Latimer, had only narrowly involved impli-cation in the Pilgrimage of Grace. However, he had subse-quently sufficiently proved his loyalty to be appointed to the Council of the North. Catherine's brother, William, Lord Parr, quitted himself well during the troubles with Scotland and was marked out as a young man with a promising future. At the end of 1542, he was designated to take over from John Dudley as warden of the Scottish Marches on the latter's appointment as lord admiral. Catherine had not spent all her life in the distant shires. On the contrary, she was no stranger to the royal court. Her mother had been a lady-in-waiting to Catherine of Aragon and she herself had been a schoolroom companion of Princess Mary. Her sister, Anne, was married to William Herbert, an esquire of the body. When Lord Latimer went to London for parliamentary or royal business his wife accom-panied him. Catherine, then, was well known at court where she had a wide circle of relatives, friends and acquaintances. It can have been no surprise, therefore, that when Latimer was ordered to court at the end of 1542, he was instructed to bring his wife with him.

What dramatically changed her fortune was that, sometime in the next few weeks, Lord Latimer died. This did not leave his widow prostrate with grief. She was soon contemplating her third marriage. This time, she resolved, it would be for love and not for duty or family ambition. The man she had fallen for was the charming, plausible, womanizing, rakehell brother of Lord Hertford, Thomas Seymour. Catherine is usually thought of as something of a high-minded bluestocking but her attachment to Seymour indicates that there was a definite passionate side to her nature. She was no witty sophisticate like

Anne Boleyn but neither was she flighty and empty-headed like Catherine Howard or pleasantly dull like Anne of Cleves. Catherine was a mature, well-educated, devout and capable woman in her prime and it must have been these qualities which attracted the king – these and the prospect of putting Seymour's nose out of joint and proving that he was still more than a match for any slick, smooth-tongued courtier. In May 1543, Seymour was despatched on an embassy to the Netherlands. On 12 July 1543, at Hampton Court, Harry of England took Catherine Parr to be his wife.

The arrival of the new queen and her kith and kin changed the composition of the court. It reinforced the progressive elite which now had the upper hand in the royal apartments. Catherine was an intelligent and pious woman with an independent mind which led her in an evangelical direction. Labels are suspect but her spiritual pilgrimage brought her to what we might reasonably call 'humanistic Lutheranism'. She described that journey in a devotional book she wrote herself, *The Lamentation or Complaint of a Sinner, Bewailing the Ignorance of her blind Life led in Superstition*. Interestingly, she seems not to have arrived with hard and fast evangelical convictions already formed but rather to have developed them as a result of the new influences prevailing in the royal court.

Just how strong those influences were is indicated by the conversion of another even more unlikely candidate, Norfolk's son, the turbulent Henry Howard, Earl of Surrey. On a January night in 1543, he and some rowdy companions rampaged through the City of London attacking prostitutes and smashing the windows of churches and prominent citizens, actions which he defended in truculent verse:

In secret silence of the night
This made me with a reckless breast,
To wake thy sluggards with my bow:
A figure of the Lord's behest,
Whose scourge for sin the Scriptures show.

Surrey presented himself as God's agent of vengeance against London, the new 'shameless whore of Babylon':

> Thy martyr's blood by sword and fire
> In Heaven and earth for justice call. . .
> The flame of wrath shall on thee fall. . .
> Thy proud towers and turrets high,
> Enemies of God beat stone from stone;
> Thine idols burnt, that wrought iniquity.[203]

This incident conventionally merits little more than a footnote in standard histories but it is evidence of the boldness and confidence with which many members of the upper classes were now adhering to the new faith and which was changing the tone of court life. In the queen's chambers Catherine was discussing doctrinal intricacies with her ladies, among whom the most formidable was Catherine Brandon, Duchess of Suffolk, who kept a pet dog name 'Gardiner'. In the privy chamber most of those closest to the king – Anthony Denny, Lord Parr (now created Earl of Essex) and the royal doctors, William Butts and Robert Huick – were dedicated evangelicals. Young Prince Edward's education was, from 1544, entrusted almost entirely to scholars of the New Learning such as John Cheke, Anthony Cooke and Roger Ascham. Even the privy council experienced an influx of reformist members – Hertford, Lisle, Parr and William Paget, the new secretary.

The changed situation would not have been so alarming to the conservative faction had the king been his old self, more addicted to pleasure than policy and accessible to a wide circle of courtiers, councillors and clergy. Now, he spent more time in his chambers, gave more attention to state affairs, was prone to discussing theology with his familiars and had a smaller circle of close attendants. Two old attributes were still constant in his personality: his dependence on sage political advice and his refusal to acknowledge that dependence. No one was appointed officially to step into Cromwell's shoes but that did not mean that Henry made all his decisions all alone. The man he relied on increasingly was Anthony Denny, whose behind-the-scenes influence increased to the point that, by the last months of the reign, he was authenticating royal documents (see below). The queen and other close attendants also wielded increasing influence with the king, as did Archbishop Cranmer. All this gave the expression 'chamber government' a new meaning. It was frustrating for Norfolk, Gardiner and their ally, Thomas Wriothesley (lord chancellor from 1544), when decisions reached in council could be reversed as the result of a few whispered words at the king's bedside or a discussion across the card table during one of Henry's sleepless nights. They were also fully aware that time was not on their side. Henry was so incapacitated that Chapuys declared himself surprised that he had not taken permanently to his bed.

This explains why the conservatives resorted to a series of desperate measures in an effort to regain the ascendancy. The Bishop of Winchester's machinations have been likened to a sinister tale from the *Arabian Nights*. In 1543 Gardiner's agents proceeded against a nest of alleged heretics in Windsor whose circle overlapped with members of the castle establishment. As a result three men were burned, though a fourth, John Marbeck, a lay clerk of St George's Chapel and an early English disciple of John Calvin, was released. Despite lengthy interrogation, Gardiner had failed to persuade the prisoner to implicate court personnel and he drew back from prosecuting someone whose friends in high places might have created difficulties. However, he felt himself on safer ground with Cranmer. The archbishop's enemies in Canterbury complained that he was encouraging the spread of unorthodox teachings. Gardiner's agents collected evidence and he ensured that it came to the king's attention, but Henry was not about to throw his primate to the wolves and he devised a little melodrama to drive the point home. The archbishop's enemies had planned a re-enactment of the coup against Cromwell; they would have him arrested in the council chamber. However, the previous night Henry summoned Cranmer from Lambeth under cover

of darkness and warned him what was afoot. In the subsequently reported version of their conversation, the king
supposedly chided the primate for his political naivety. 'Do
you not know that once they have you in prison three or four
false knaves will soon be procured to witness against you?' He
gave Cranmer a ring with instructions to produce it when his
accusers confronted him. The effect, the next day, was electrifying. The plotters had to hurry, shamefaced, to the privy
chamber and listen to an admonitory homily from the king.

If we read between the lines, what this reveals is Henry's
tendency to theatricality and his enjoyment of power over the
lives of others. He had no illusions about the dirty tricks his
councillors performed against each other. It amused him to let
them play their games, even when life and death issues were at
stake, and it was one way of keeping his control over them. In
this instance, the Catholics' machinations rebounded against
them. Cranmer's allies struck back against his accusers.
Germaine Gardiner, the bishop's nephew and secretary, was
subsequently found guilty of denying the royal supremacy. He
and three of his associates suffered the death of traitors. Henry,
genuinely bemused by the escalating religious conflict, could
do nothing but exhort his people to unity and continue the
policy (if such it can be called) of making occasional examples
of unrepentant enthusiasts from both sides.

Henry's preoccupation was the war. Chapuys reported that
he was obsessed with his invasion of France. Since Charles,
fresh from a convincing victory over the Duke of Cleves, was
heading up the imperial forces, the king was determined to lead
the English contingent himself. This would not have involved
him actually facing any danger; the vanguard would have been
commanded by his generals. Nevertheless, the lack of wisdom
of having the gross, crippled monarch anywhere near the battle
zone was obvious to everyone from the emperor downwards.
There was also disagreement between the allies over strategy.
Henry had abandoned the plan for a march on Paris: war was
about forcing an advantageous peace and that meant capturing

strategic towns and holding them to ransom. Another problem was that Henry had fallen out with his German mercenary leaders over payment. While these matters were being argued at the top level the momentum of war had carried the English army across the Channel. By 22 June 1544 it was quartered in and around Calais awaiting instructions. Norfolk wrote testily that he had expected by now to have been told what he was supposed to be doing. Eventually, Henry decided to conquer two ports. Howard was ordered to proceed to lay siege to Montreuil, while Suffolk was to bombard Boulogne into submission. Howard failed. Suffolk succeeded. Henry arrived in mid-July to watch the fun. The experience of being on campaign rejuvenated him, even though he had to wait until 18 September for his moment of triumph:

> The king's highness, having the sword borne naked before him by the Lord Marquis Dorset, like a noble and valiant conqueror, rode into Boulogne, and the trumpeters standing on the walls of the town sounded their trumpets at the time of his entering, to the great comfort of all the king's subjects, there beholding. . .there met him the Duke of Suffolk and delivered unto him the keys of the town.[204]

Henry had his moment of glory – but that was all he did have. After weeks of battering by the English artillery the town was a wreck, many buildings having been reduced to rubble and the defences severely breached. If Henry was to hold on to his prize he would have to spend considerable amounts on repairs. That was the least of his worries, however. On the very day that Henry entered the shattered port, Charles, impatient with his ally's refusal to adhere to the original plan and eager to set about a final reckoning with the German Protestants, signed a peace treaty with Francis. Henry now faced the full might of the French army.

It had all been an immensely costly fiasco. The campaign and the re-fortification of Boulogne cost a staggering £1.2 million. Defending England from the French backlash would take that figure to well over £2 million by the end of 1545. This was appreciably more than the total cash that had come into the royal coffers as a result of the Dissolution, the plundering of shrines and other confiscations from the church. When Cromwell made Henry master of the monastic estates it had been his intention to provide the crown with an annual income that would make it independent of parliament by minimizing the need for taxation revenue. Military expenditure made it necessary for Henry to alienate two-thirds of the ex-ecclesiastical lands and thus severely cut his income. So far from being less dependent on tax, he had to impose swingeing new levies. When that did not produce enough, he resorted to debasement of the coinage and when that failed to meet his needs, he borrowed heavily on the international money market. However, the cost of war is never adequately measured in money terms. The suffering of English troops as a result of foul weather, inadequate victuals, disease and poor leadership was appalling. One eye-witness has left a moving description of Henry's homeward straggling troops:

> The soldiers coming from Calais and Boulogne were dying along the road from Dover to London and along the roads from London to every quarter of the kingdom while trying to go to their homes. After they had come home, those who were well fell sick and those who were sick got worse and from this sickness and feebleness and pest they died in every part of England.[205]

This was the direct result of the king exercising unbridled control of the nation's affairs. It shows up the importance of Wolsey and Cromwell. As long as Henry had at his right hand a minister who combined vision and competence two things happened: his more irresponsible whims were, to some extent, restrained and, when they could not be restrained, they were realized with thrift and efficiency.

By the end of the year no one at the centre of the nation's life was in any doubt that the king was ruining the country. The acerbic Gardiner summarized the nation's plight with surgically accurate precision:

We are at war with France and Scotland, we have enmity with
the Bishop of Rome, we have no assured friendship. . .with the
Emperor and we have received from the landgrave [of Hesse],
chief captain of the Protestants, such displeasure that he has
cause to think us angry with him. . .Our war is noisome to our
realm and to all our merchants that traffic through the Narrow
Seas. . .We are in a world where reason and learning prevail not
and covenants are little regarded.[206]

It would be difficult to overemphasise the distressed state of the
English people. As well as death and injury in the war, unemployment and trade dislocation, Henry's subjects were
suffering as a result of poor harvests in 1543 and 1544 which
pushed the price of grain to double its level at the beginning of
the decade. Chapuys, for once, may not have been exaggerating
when he reported in June 1545: 'every man of wit in England
blasphemes at the war and most of them call Boulogne the "new
Milan" which will work their destruction.'[207] Henry's recent
conquest had, indeed, become a bitter bone of contention
between the two sides. All attempts at mediation foundered on
the stubborn determination of Francis and Henry, the one to
regain the port and the other to retain it.

Refusing peace, Henry's only option was to escalate the
conflict, regardless of cost. He demanded a 'benevolence' of
two shillings in the pound from his subjects and this time there
was to be no backing down as there had been over the Amicable
Grant. Refusal to pay was met with swift punishment. One
venerable London alderman who complained about the ille-
gality of the impost was despatched to serve in the army on the
Scottish border. The official line put out to justify Henry's
financial demand was that he was defending the nation against
French aggression. Once again, as in 1539, fear of invasion
gripped the popular imagination. Fighting was confined to skir-
mishing around Boulogne and minor naval engagements in the
Channel, in which the 'new men', Hertford and Lisle quitted
themselves well, but everyone was waiting for a determined
assault either on the south coast or close to the Scottish border.

Fortunately, when the 'invasion' of July 1545 came, it turned out to be something of a damp squib. The French admiral, Claude d'Annebault, had amassed a large fleet in the Channel ports for a seaborne attack on Boulogne but Lisle provoked him into a raid on the English navy anchored in Portsmouth roads. Like so many naval engagements of this period the resultant clash was brief and inconclusive, its outcome determined more by weather than seamanship. Only two factors made it remarkable. One was the presence of the king, who was actually dining aboard the *Great Harry* when the French approach was announced. The other was the loss of the *Mary Rose*, one of the English capital ships, which, attempting to get to grips with the French galleys, keeled over during a too-hasty manoeuvre and lay at the bottom of the harbour until its dramatic salvaging in 1982. D'Annebault's attempt to land further along the coast was thwarted by the local levies. It was, in fact, the two admirals who became the agents for concluding a peace in the following spring. Meeting at Calais, Lisle and d'Annebault haggled over terms for the cessation of hostilities. Their task was made more difficult by the need to refer back to their respective masters every detail of the treaty but, thanks to their patience, persistence and occasional fierce arguments, peace was finally concluded on 7 June 1546.

The absence of Lisle and Hertford from the council gave the conservatives an opportunity to strike at them. It was becoming obvious that these two successful generals were so high in the king's favour that, unless checked they would hold the future in their hands. That future was now clamouring for attention. No one could ignore the fact that England would, almost certainly, soon have a minor for a king and the jockeying for powerful positions close to the throne became intense. Perpetual pain now dominated Henry's life. He relied heavily on those around him who could ease his physical discomfort and distract his mind from it. The death of William Butts, his physician, in November 1545 was a serious blow. Following closely on the demise of his brother-in-law and old friend, Charles Brandon,

Duke of Suffolk, in August, it came as an unwelcome reminder of his own mortality. Henry still had those around him on whose commitment he could rely, though. Will Sommers, his diminutive fool, could still coax a laugh from the invalid with his lampoons of self-important councillors, courtiers and diplomats. Queen Catherine endured the smell of his suppurating sores as she changed his bandages and proved a knowledgeable and stimulating conversationalist when the king's mind turned, as it now frequently did, to religious matters. And ever, at his side was the faithful Anthony Denny. Not only did the groom of the stool discuss policy with his master, he also increasingly lifted from his shoulders the burden of daily administration. He kept the privy purse and was responsible for royal expenditure, which averaged more than £50,000 per annum. He sifted the documents that came to the king for signature and, significantly, in 1545 he actually assumed a measure of control over that signature. To save himself the bother of taking up a pen to scrawl his name on important papers, Henry resorted to using a dry stamp. This made a light impression which a clerk then carefully went over in ink. By the autumn of 1545 he had given custody of the dry stamp to Denny and promoted him to chief gentleman of the privy chamber. The office of groom of the stool went to Catherine Parr's brother-in-law, William Herbert.

Influential conservatives were now outnumbered and outmanoeuvred in the inner circles of power. However, they felt that they could always rely on the king's sensitivity to heresy. On Christmas Eve, 1545, he had made a moving speech to parliament on the subject of religious unity. 'What love and charity is among you,' he had chided, 'when the one calleth the other heretic and anabaptist, and he calleth him again papist, hypocrite and pharisee?' He upbraided the clergy for their controversial preaching. As for the laity, they were:

> . . .not clean and unspotted of malice and envy, for you rail on
> bishops, speak slanderously of priests, and rebuke and taunt

preachers, both contrary to good order and Christian fraternity. . .although you be permitted to read Holy Scripture and to have the word of God in your mother tongue, you must understand that you have this licence only to inform your own conscience and to instruct your children and family and not to dispute and make Scripture a railing and taunting stock against priests and preachers. . .I am very sorry to know and hear how unreverently that most precious jewel, the word of God, is disputed, rhymed and jangled in every alehouse and tavern, contrary to the true meaning and doctrine of the same.

Unless disputes ceased, Henry warned, 'I, whom God hath appointed his vicar and high minister here, will see those divisions removed and those enormities corrected, according to my very duty.'[208] It was a remarkable acknowledgement of failure, perhaps of genuine confusion. Henry was confronted by a foe more powerful than himself: the hydra-headed beast of religious conviction. The truth dawned on him that he would die without having tamed it.

This truth was also obvious to all members of the political establishment and it dominated life in court and council from this point on. Throughout 1546, Henry's health oscillated between lumbering semi-mobility and bedridden incapacity. It was obvious that he was approaching his end. The prospect of the massive void soon to be left at the political centre produced reactions as highly charged as they were confusing. Because radicalism was so well ensconced in the circles closest to the king, it was vital for the conservatives to clean out the Augean stables of the royal court if they were to prepare the ground for a rigorous reactionary campaign in the next reign. Somehow, they had to induce that purge which they had so far failed to bring about. Had the Catholic leaders formed a real faction capable of following a consistent, united strategy they just might have succeeded. In the event, individuals pursued their own agendas, launched uncoordinated attacks, fell out among themselves and were more concerned with preserving themselves than any religious ideology. They managed to turn the king against them, with surprisingly little help from their enemies.

What must have seemed the most promising approach was to try to entangle court evangelicals in the continuing prosecution of heretics. With complete disregard for Henry's plea for peaceful coexistence, the conservative bishops made fresh attempts to weed out offenders against the Six Articles Act. They might have been warned when Henry ordered the commissioners in Essex to wind up their activities until 'a more commodious time' but the stakes were too high and the time too short for counsels of caution to prevail. It was Thomas Wriothesley who took the initiative. As lord chancellor, he had a close knowledge of what was going on in the law courts and, specifically, of those who were being apprehended on offences against the Six Articles.

His first victim was Dr Edward Crome, one of the queen's favourite preachers who had more than once been in trouble before. When threatened by the fire, Crome not only agreed to recant but also provided his accusers with names. Among them were John Lascelles, who had been instrumental in the destruction of Catherine Howard, the royal physician, Robert Huick, and some other lesser fry about the court. So far, so good, but Wriothesley's reach was more extensive. He sent agents into the shires to bring in any suspects who might serve his purpose. Among them was a Lincolnshire gentlewoman destined to become one of the more celebrated of Protestant martyrs. Anne Askew (or, more accurately, Ayscough), the 'Fair Gospeller', was a member of Crome's congregation at St Mary Aldermary and had been examined by Bishop Edmund Bonner earlier in the year. On her release she had returned to her father's home near Caistor but she was not destined to be left in peace. Anne was something of an evangelical celebrity with admirers in the City and, more importantly, in the court. One of her brothers was a member of the Gentlemen Pensioners and she had been introduced to some of the ladies of the queen's circle. Wriothesley had her brought back to the capital at the end of May 1546. This time it was members of the privy council who interrogated her – several times. It was, to say the least, unusual for the king's leading advisers to devote so much time to bandying theology with a woman from 'out in the sticks'. Clearly, their main concern was to convict her, imprison her and force her to reveal the names of members of her 'sect' in the king's court.

Simultaneously (although we have no way of calculating the precise chronology of events), Gardiner attempted a direct assault on the queen. He happened to be present at a slight altercation between the royal couple over some point of religion and took the opportunity to hint to the king, when they were alone, that Catherine's religious opinions were not above suspicion. He obtained permission to have the queen detained and questioned. Fortunately, Catherine got wind of her danger. She went straight to Henry and protested her innocence. If she had appeared over-assertive in her arguments, she claimed, it was in order to provoke discussion so that she might learn from her husband and distract him from his pain. The king was mollified and, when the lord chancellor turned up at the appointed time to effect Catherine's arrest, he felt the full blast of the royal wrath. 'Knave! Arrant knave, beast and fool!' Henry shouted as he sent Wriothesley packing.

A lesser man would have known when to quit but Wriothesley had learned much from his erstwhile master, Thomas Cromwell. Ruthlessness and single-mindedness could be more effective than caving in before Henry's bullying. He vented his anger and desperation on Anne Askew. When he had her safely locked up in the Tower, he used all available interrogation techniques to try to extract information against the Ladies Suffolk, Hertford, Denny, Sussex and Fitzwilliam. The news was soon out that the inquisitors had gone so far as to stretch Anne on the rack and that Wriothesley himself had turned the screw. All he succeeded in doing was making another evangelical martyr. Having failed to extract either information or a recantation, he was forced to authorize Anne's burning, She perished, along with John Lascelles and

two other convicted heretics, in the flames of Smithfield on 16
July 1546.

Court evangelicals had been protected by the fortitude and
faith of an incredibly brave woman. Rather than endanger the
cause by telling her persecutors all that, undoubtedly, she
could have told them about her highly placed co-religionists,
Anne had kept her silence. The tension at court was almost
tangible. On the day after her execution, two members of the
king's household who were in the Tower and expecting to
share her fate were released. Other events, comparatively
trivial in themselves, show how on-edge everyone around the
throne was. The Duke of Norfolk had given up his struggle
with the new men. He swallowed his pride and proposed a
marriage alliance with the upstart Seymours. His plan was
scuppered by his daughter, Mary, the lamb designated for
sacrifice on the altar of matrimony. She refused to be a party to
it. When her brother Henry, the Earl of Surrey, learned of the
dynastic proposal, he was furious. He might share his religious
outlook with the Seymours but he had not the slightest
intention of sharing power. He looked to a future in which his
father would head a regency government during the minority
of King Edward. He actually proposed to Mary that, in order
to gain Howard supremacy, she should become the king's
mistress. Her response was that she would rather cut her own
throat. Surrey continued his hubristic, irresponsible and, ultimately, fatal way. He talked unguardedly of his vision for the
political future and vaunted his family's close connection to the
throne. He even displayed a new coat of arms which quartered
Edward the Confessor's device with those of the Howards and
the baronial house of Mowbray. If Henry, now preoccupied
with the trouble-free succession of his son, ever got to hear of
this he might consider the Howards a serious threat. Surrey
recklessly made enemies at court. They ensured that the king
would get to hear of the earl's indiscretions. By August 1546,
Hertford and Lisle were back at court and confronting their
opponents across the council table. In one argument, a few

weeks later, Lisle slapped Gardiner's face. Henry banished the offender for a month but the report of the incident may very well have lightened his dark days.

Inevitably, we have a mixed picture of the fifty-five-year-old king as he appeared in the autumn of 1546. The latest pictorial images show a man markedly different from the one represented in the official iconography of Holbein. An illustration from the king's Psalter (now in the British Library) depicts Henry as a greatly aged man strumming a harp. It is not a portrait but it does evoke a feeling of a life which has become closed in on itself. Cornelis Massys (or Metsys) has left a more telling image. His engraving after a lost original depicts the same fleshy contours as the face in the Whitehall cartoon but the eyes have become slits squinting out, as it were, from a mask and the impression given is almost that of a sneering caricature. Rumours about the king's health and life expectancy ran through Europe. Henry assiduously did everything he could to dispel them. In August 1546, he set off on progress, as usual, but this was not like the pleasure pilgrimages of earlier years. He travelled first to Hampton Court, then, by easy stages, to Windsor, before returning to Whitehall in November. Still he mounted (or was hoisted on to) his horse for hunting expeditions, but now it was to watch his servants flush out the deer for courtiers to fell with their arrows. He frequently took to his bed for days at a time but his chamber staff were instructed to announce only that he had a cold. When he was up and about the impression carefully given was one of 'business as usual'.

The major diplomatic event was the arrival of d'Annebault for the official signing of the Anglo-French peace treaty. In a specially-erected banqueting house at Hampton Court, Henry showed the jovial face of friendship to the visitor. His chosen companion during the informalities of the occasion was Cranmer. According to the archbishop, the king proposed an extended agreement between the two monarchies, one feature of which would be the replacement of the mass with a simpler communion service. Henry had already sanctioned Cranmer to experiment with vernacular liturgy. This was the first step towards worship for the English church in English, the change which, more than any other, would bring the Reformation home to every man, woman and child in the country. In these weeks Henry also made fresh overtures to the German Protestant princes. Whether he was seriously signalling a further advance towards the reformed communities of the continent or, as so often in the past, responding to transitory shifts in international diplomacy we shall never know. However, Charles' decisive victory over the Schmalkaldic League early in 1547 would certainly have discouraged his continued support for the Lutherans.

The changes and chances of political life continued to the end of the year. Georges de Selve, the French ambassador, reported, on 10 November 1546, 'Here is a great bruit of dissension. . . among the principal men of this realm'. Rivalries and concerns about the future were not confined to the inner circles of power, as he went on to explain: 'the day before yesterday, command was given to the mayor of this town and to the justices of the peace in the provinces to enquire secretly for such as talk treason against this king or knew of any talk or conspiracy against him'.[209] Everyone realised that a change of reign was imminent and it was vital to ensure that it went smoothly. Gardiner chose this moment to upset the king. Henry's accumulation of ex-church property had not abated in the years since the Dissolution. By a constant stream of transactions, royal estates were augmented and consolidated. In November, the Bishop of Winchester was 'requested' by the lord chancellor to agree an exchange of lands with the crown. He demurred. He said that he could not consent without discussing the matter personally with the king. The only reason Gardiner can have had for this affront was to use the property issue as a means of access to the king in the hope of exerting influence. Henry was furious, not only, with Gardiner's hubris, but also with his request for an audience at a time when, in order to conceal as much as possible his physical deterioration, he was seeing very few people. It did not take very much for Gardiner to fall from favour and this was very far from being the first time he had alienated the king, but it was the last and the timing could not have been worse. A few weeks later when plans were drawn up for a council of regency, Henry deliberately excluded the bishop. It must be said that there is no guarantee that the king would have endorsed Gardiner's membership of the new governing body. He knew the bishop's hankering after a rapprochement with Rome and he was determined that nothing should interfere with his son's enjoyment of the royal supremacy.

Much the same concern turned Henry against the Howards in the closing days of the year. On 2 December, the Earl of Surrey was, without warning, seized at Whitehall Palace and hustled away to Wriothesley's house in Holborn. After ten days he was transferred to the Tower and was joined there by his father. Exactly who instigated this fall from grace is not clear but there is no doubt that its real cause was Henry's suspicion. Wriothesley was only his master's mouthpiece when he claimed that a Howard plot hade been unmasked to kill members of the council and gain control of the prince. Henry's reign was ending as it had begun with the incarceration of politically inconvenient men on trumped up charges. By this time the king was seeing very few people. He stayed at Whitehall for Christmas but sent the queen and most of the court to Greenwich. The official explanation of his retreat into purdah was that he was giving detailed, confidential attention to the case against the Howards but imperial ambassador Van der Delft suspected, probably correctly, that the king's rapid deterioration was being kept from prying eyes. The ambassador had to resort to stratagems to discover was going on behind locked doors. He sent a servant to Whitehall, ostensibly to deliver a message to Lisle. By discreet questioning below stairs, this man discovered that 'the king was not at all well although he had been seen dressed the previous day'.[210]

The ambassador's assessment of political realities was dire. 'Affairs here change almost daily,' he lamented. The position of

Hertford and Lisle appeared unassailable. Ever since their return to court all prosecutions of heretics had ceased. The privy council now met regularly in Hertford's town house. They would probably be granted custody of the young king after Henry's death and that would mean a further lurch away from continental Catholicism, for the two powerful councillors were supporters of the 'sects'. And they were far from being alone: 'The majority of the people are of these perverse sects and in favour of getting rid of the bishops and they do not conceal their wish to see Winchester and other adherents of the ancient faith in the Tower with the duke. Probably parliament, which meets next month, will pass some strange Acts.'[211] It was remarkably accurate prophecy. Surrey was tried in the Guildhall on 13 January 1547. The outcome was never in doubt. He was beheaded on Tower Hill on the 19 January. By then parliament had already condemned Norfolk by Act of Attainder. It remained only for it to receive the royal assent and Henry appointed a small commission to give this on 27 January. The king was by now beyond enjoying one of his favourite pastimes – exercising the power of life and death over his subjects. A few hours more and he was beyond everything.

It was towards the end of that same day that Sir Anthony Denny performed the last office of a loyal servant. He told his master that he was dying. Henry instructed him to send for Cranmer – but not until he had slept a little. The messenger was not despatched until the night was well advanced. By the time he reached the archbishop's manor at Croydon and returned with him, the king was unconscious. The final scene is familiar. Cranmer kneels by the bedside and holds the king's hand. England's first evangelical primate has no truck with the oils and paraphernalia of unction. He simply urges the dying man to give some sign that he trusts only in the merits of Christ for his salvation. And to his own dying day, Cranmer will remain convinced that the king squeezed his hand. About two o'clock on the morning of 28 January 1547 Henry Tudor died, but it was hours before that he had uttered his 'last words'. He confided to Denny his assurance that Christ would forgive all his sins, 'though they were greater than they be'. Henry had always expected everyone to give him whatever he wanted. Why make an exception for God?

# Epilogue

## SO, WHO WAS THE REAL HENRY?

Written controversy about Henry VIII began soon after his death. Before 1547 was out the Welsh-born scholar, William Thomas, living in Bologna, had set down a lively defence of the late monarch, entitled *The Pilgrim: A Dialogue on the Life and Actions of King Henry the Eighth*. It purported to report a discussion Thomas had had with a group of Italian friends and consisted of a detailed refutation of fourteen accusations made against Henry. He was, Thomas concluded:

> . . .undoubtedly the rarest man that lived in his time. . .I will confess that he did many evil things as the publican sinner, but not as a cruel tyrant, or as a pharisaical hypocrite; for all his doings were open to the whole world, wherein he governed himself with so much reason, prudence, courage and circum-spection, that I wot not where, in all the histories I have read, to find one private king equal to him.[212]

Two facts should be noted about the author of this piece: Thomas was a zealous Protestant, whose only personal complaint against

Henry was that he had not pushed the Reformation far enough, and he was also angling for a job in the new regime of Edward VI.

John Leslie was another early commentator. Safe in Scotland from any Tudor backlash, he described Henry as cruel, dishonest and not very bright. All the king's dealings with the Scottish court, he claimed, were characterized by dissimulation and deceit. Even the ironic Philipp Melancthon described Henry as another Nero.

The best known verdict on Henry was penned by Sir Walter Ralegh, who wrote his *History of the World* more than sixty years later. 'If all the pictures and patterns of a merciless prince were lost in the world,' Ralegh suggested, 'they might all again be painted to the life out of the story of this king.' The author decried Henry's executions of faithful wives and servants. Then, broadening his attack, he continued:

> But besides the sorrows which he heaped upon the fatherless and widows at home and besides the vain enterprises abroad, wherein it is thought that he consumed more treasure than all our victorious kings did in their several conquests, what causeless and cruel wars did he make upon his own nephew, King James the Fifth? What laws and wills did he devise to establish the kingdom in his own issues, using his sharpest weapons to cut off and cut down those branches which sprang from the same root that himself did.[213]

Ralegh's assessment was no more disinterested than that of Thomas. At the time of writing, the son of James V of Scotland now ruled as James I of England and the prisoner in the Tower was eager to ingratiate himself at court. What unites both these evaluations – and, indeed, every critique of Henry VIII ever made by biographers and historians – is an acknowledgement of the king's offences. Whether they are to be condemned or excused, they cannot be ignored. Because the events of his reign have been so formative of England's character and destiny it has always been difficult for chroniclers to stand back and view them objectively. The Reformation inevitably touched deep beliefs and has been applauded or deplored, according to the varied convictions of the recorders. The Dissolution of the Monasteries trampled the aesthetic sensibilities of later historians outraged at the loss of beautiful medieval treasures. Henry's treatment of the women in his life gives offence not only to feminists. No less than Thomas or Ralegh, we each bring our own beliefs and prejudices to our evaluation of the life of this extraordinary man. However, detachment is something the modern historian must, at least, attempt and in these concluding paragraphs I will try to draw together the threads of my account as even-handedly as I can.

Politics is all about style and substance. Whether we are assessing the career of a Margaret Thatcher, a Tony Blair or a Henry VIII, we do well to keep these two elements separate. The politicians and their image-makers will always try to bamboozle us by wrapping up policy in the tinselled paper of presentation. It is up to the intelligent voter not to allow himself to be fooled by rhetoric, photo opportunities or soundbites. At the beginning of our canter through the life of this remarkable king I suggested that we ought to put from our minds the official image generated by Holbein on the instructions of his royal patron. We must not allow ourselves to be mesmerized by the 'Henry the Magnificent' icon as we go to work creating our own portrait with the pigments of established facts and contemporary comments. This requires considerable mental discipline because Henry was larger than life. He was the consummate showman who spared no expense to impress his audience, whether at court, on progress or in the arena of international diplomacy. For example, this explains what many observers found difficult to comprehend – his support for Wolsey, who, apparently, presided over a rival court. So far from being jealous or mistrustful of the cardinal, Henry applauded his magnificent alter ego because he extended the splendours of the Tudor regime into areas, at home and abroad, where Henry could not or did not choose to go. For the same reason we need to be careful what use we make of contemporary chronicles. Edward Hall's pages glow with enthusiastic accounts of tourneys, pageants and diplomatic spectaculars. His breathless prose brings to life for us the vivid costumes, the theatrical conceits and the cheering crowds attending the numerous royal displays of the reign. This, no less than Holbein's painting, is fact doctored and garnished by Tudor political correctness.

Any assessment of Henry's role in the history of England must start with the recognition that he battled against enormous obstacles to achieve his primary objective, the preservation of the dynasty. The peaceful succession of his only son was unchallenged and his training was in the hands of wise and gifted tutors. It must have given the old king considerable satisfaction to know that the prince was being better prepared for his future responsibilities than he had been by his own father. Thanks to his ruthless elimination of all possible rivals and over-mighty subjects, including his last minute destruction of the Howards, Edward's throne was secure. Thanks to the establishment of the royal supremacy, he would enjoy a degree of power over the spiritual and temporal nation much greater than that which Henry had inherited. The departing king had also enhanced Tudor prestige in Europe. He had two footholds on the mainland – Calais and Boulogne – footholds which could be used as bases for further conquest. He had built up a standing navy of over fifty ships, some equipped with up-to-date gunnery and backed by newly built dockyards. The Council for Marine Causes was the most sophisticated regulatory body of its kind in Europe. England's own coasts were now protected by a defensive chain of fortresses and Henry's chastening of the Scots would, hopefully, deter them from succouring French ambitions. It all looked very impressive.

Unfortunately, most of these achievements proved to be hollow or to be overtaken by events. Henry's aggressive foreign policy had simply come at too high a price and could not possibly be sustained. In 1509 he had inherited a modest reputation in Europe and a full treasury. The situation he handed on to his son was quite the reverse – a bankrupt nation unable to support an over-ambitious stance among the leading nations. The people had been taxed to the hilt. Royal revenue had been boosted by devaluation of the coinage but this, though bringing in more than the entire proceeds of Henry's ecclesiastical takeover, still left the treasury dependent on raising government loans. The new regime hastened to make peace with France and was only too glad, in 1550, to return Boulogne, which was an expensive white elephant. Eight years later, Calais also was lost. The damage done north of the border was not so easily reversed. Henry's bullying of the Scots simply drove them into the arms of the French. The triumph of style over substance had proved disastrous. What added to these misfortunes was that Henry's marital misadventures sealed the fate of his dynasty. Edward VI died of consumption in 1553 and Queen Mary's marriage to Philip II of Spain the following year made England a Habsburg dependency. After her sister's mercifully brief reign, Elizabeth was determined not to make the same mistake and remained unwed. Thus, the bloodline of Henry VII died out – or was considerably diluted in the person of James VI and I.

Alone among Henry's military innovations the Royal Navy remained and was destined to play a vital role in the worldwide expansion of English influence. Yet, even this significant contribution to the life of the nation cannot be attributed solely to the king. Henry was certainly the inspiration for the building of a fleet of capital ships but, as Professor David Loades observed in his survey of England's maritime history, 'outside the arts of war and courtly love the king had no imagination'.[214] He took no initiatives to encourage overseas exploration or challenge the supremacy of the Iberian nations. It was John Dudley, Lord Lisle (later Duke of Northumberland), who, as Lord Admiral (1543–7, 1549–50), presided over and organized the work of the Council for Marine Causes, set up a school for mariners under the leadership of veteran navigator,

Sebastian Cabot, oversaw the incorporation of the Merchant Adventurers of England for the Discovery of Lands, Territories, Isles, Dominions and Seignories Unknown (1553) and provided the initial impetus for the historic voyages of Elizabeth's reign.

Of course, the English Reformation, with all its political and social ramifications, remains the most momentous transformation of the nation between the Norman Conquest and the Industrial Revolution. It resulted from the activities of the king, his ministers, religious activists and massive changes in the ideological and cultural framework of Europe. Exactly to what extent responsibility should be apportioned to each of these participants has been debated by historians for centuries. By the terms of his coronation oath Henry was bound to preserve the church in his territory and there is no reason to suppose that he did not take this commitment seriously. In 1537, when Henry projected in the Whitehall cartoon the image that he wanted everyone to have of him, he elected to go down to posterity as the king who purified the national religion. But, again, we have to be wary of taking him at face value. Since before the beginning of the reign humanist scholars had been calling for the redress of ecclesiastical abuses and a new, vital approach to Scripture. Luther had launched his protest a full twenty years before. These were the real reformers. They spoke for the frustrated minority of devout men and women throughout Europe who resented the power of a priestly caste for which they had scant respect and who yearned for a deep, personal faith and a church life which nourished it. If that is how we understand the word 'reformer', then Henry was not a reformer. Whatever his theological convictions, they became entwined, masked and confused by his dynastic concerns and personal ambition.

There is no evidence that the king saw himself as a dedicated agent for religious change before the development of his quarrel with the pope. The man who wrote a defence of the church's sacramental system, campaigned long and hard for the title *Defensor fidei* and banned the import of heretical books was a Catholic king in the traditional mould. 'Nothing,' he assured Pope Leo in 1521, 'is more the duty of a Christian prince than [to study] how to preserve the Christian religion against its enemies'.[215] It was as he pursued his determined quest for a sexually compatible wife who could provide a Tudor heir that Henry embraced any man and any theological conviction that would support his cause. He was never at home in the world of ideas and so could not grasp the issue of faith versus works. He was obliged to borrow from other men those principles which happened to suit him at the time. This explains his see-saw relationships with radical thinkers and his own genuine distress at the deepening religious divisions which rent the country during his latter years. His last speech to parliament revealed his bewilderment at the conflicts between 'papists' and 'heretics'. He had been forced to recognize that substantial minorities of his subjects were not prepared to believe what they were told to believe. It was his own concept of orthodoxy and not any appeal to a higher truth which lay behind Henry's plea to his people to exercise 'charity and concord'. His was the anguished incomprehension of a pragmatist confronted by stubborn idealism. For the idealist, it is conviction which informs will and leads to action. For Henry it was the royal will which provided the motive for political initiatives; religious convictions were simply brought in to justify them. Henry simply did not live on the same exalted plane as people who were prepared to go to the fire or the scaffold for what they believed.

Nothing illustrates more clearly his Machiavellian attitude to religious change than his instructions of 1543 to Ralph Sadler, his envoy in Scotland. In preparation for an alliance of the two nations, he urged that the Scottish regent should follow the pattern of change which had been so successful in England:

The extirpation of monks and friars requires politic handling. First, the governor should send commissioners as it were to take order for their living more honestly. . .with a secret commission to groundly examine all the religious of their conversation and living. . .then, he and the chief noblemen agreeing together for the distribution of some of the abbey lands among them, he should devise to allot a good portion of the abbey lands to the king and the young queen, their heirs and successors whereby they may maintain their estate and not be enforced to seek such ways as their late king did whereby to grieve and annoy his people.[216]

This would be the most naked, shameless cynicism were it not for the fact that Henry had convinced himself that monarchs were divinely appointed to regulate all ecclesiastical affairs. For the supreme head of the church political acts, even underhand political acts, were infused with spiritual grace. In describing the way the dissolution had been achieved in England Henry was actually appropriating to himself the methods devised and employed by Cromwell. It was the minister who had master-minded the political Reformation. Just as the king took the credit for the military achievements of his generals, so he used for his own glory the accomplishments of his ministers. Few rulers have ever been served by a more talented succession of executive officers. Just as Wolsey established his master as a lead player in continental affairs, so Cromwell and Cranmer severed the English church from Roman obedience and set about giving it its distinct doctrinal and liturgical identity. Henry backed their initiatives simply because they were to his advantage. Cromwell and Cranmer, by contrast, were religious thinkers committed to the new beliefs. Their actions had theological foundations. Henry believed he could change the government of the English church without disturbing the doctrinal framework which supported it. He could not get his head round the theological ramifications which lay behind the changes imposed on the people. But, then, he did not have to.

The question is often asked whether the English Reformation would have happened if Henry had not wanted to wriggle out of his first marriage. The answer is undoubtedly, 'yes', and that for two reasons. First, Henry's realm could not have escaped the impact of new, exciting ideas originating on the continent and among the English intelligentsia which were merging with old native heresies. Secondly, the government would have found it impossible to suppress these ideas. England was not Spain, where the state-backed Inquisition held sway. Nor was it France, where, by tradition, crown and church were mystically linked and heresy smacked of rebellion. Prosecution for heresy in English church courts was sporadic and sometimes provoked local resentment. In London, particularly, it tended to bring civic and episcopal authorities into conflict. Parliament and convocation fell out over it from time to time. Henry, always sensitive to public opinion, was very careful not to allow religious persecutors their head. From 1539, the Six Articles Act was on the statute book and could always be wielded when the king wanted to make a point but in practice he inhibited its use. In the same year that the 'bloody whip with six strings' appeared the Great Bible was issued. It was destined to have infinitely greater impact than the repressive Act. It would have been impossible for any government, however orthodox, to prevent the intoxicant of vernacular scripture from entering the English bloodstream. Once that had happened it was all up for domineering Catholic sacerdotalism.

Any attempt to portray Henry VIII as a wise and devout monarch carefully charting for his church and people a 'middle way' between Rome and Wittenberg is anachronistic nonsense. The religious situation was much more complex than a straight choice between Catholicism and Protestantism. The theological waters of the 1530s and 1540s were turbulent with doctrinal cross-currents and the submerged rocks of political implication. By 1537, Henry had achieved his main religious objective of the supremacy, disposed of those individuals who rejected it and put down the rebels who had presumed to criticize his ecclesiastical innovations. He spent the last decade of his life trying to impose a degree of order on 'his' church. He failed. The man who lit the blue touch paper of the English

Reformation was not the man who was responsible for the pyrotechnic display.

How justified are we in applying the word 'tyrant' to Henry VIII? A sixteenth-century writer defined a tyrant as a prince who 'accounteth all his will as a just law and hath no care either of piety, justice or faith'.[217] Reginald Pole, from the safe haven of Rome, castigated the English king as one who had 'robbed every kind of man, made sport of the nobility, never loved the people, troubled the clergy and torn like a wild beast the men who were the greatest honour to his kingdom'. Henry instigated several state trials, the outcome of which was seldom in doubt. The prison quarters of the Tower were never as full as they were during his reign. He consigned to death hundreds of subjects who were real or perceived threats to his regime or who rejected the imperium he sought to establish in church and state. The evidence against the defendant would seem to be overwhelming; the prosecution's case scarcely worth arguing.

However, historical judgement has to take a wider perspective, setting this king's record beside that of other rulers and, particularly, contemporary rulers. Henry has by some commentators been placed in the same category as Nero or Stalin. One referred, almost in passing, to 'Henry's sadistic brutalities',[218] but that precisely underscores the danger of overemphasis. We can be just as misled by the outrage of later chroniclers as by Henry's official iconography. Henry was not a sadist comparable to the monsters who ruled in first-century Rome or twentieth-century Moscow. He took no pleasure in watching his victims being executed. As far as I can determine, he never actually witnessed death at close quarters. On the contrary, he was careful to distance himself from suffering. The merest suggestion of contagion in London was sufficient for him to order the royal bags to be packed for a swift journey into the countryside and that was not entirely motivated by fear of contagion. When he had marked some unfortunate wife, minister, courtier or friend for destruction, he simply withdrew his support and left others to do the dirty work. He never told a victim face-to-face that he had issued a death warrant, partly because he knew that, confronted with a grov-elling penitent, he would almost certainly relent. This was why it was so important for leaders of the court factions to prevent those whose downfall they had engineered from gaining access to the king. In terms of personal relationships, Henry was more a 'soft touch' than an 'implacable avenger'. If he savoured the power of consigning people to death, he also enjoyed the role of magnanimous monarch, graciously extending pardon to those who had offended him.

Henry VIII was an autocrat living in an age of autocrats. Charles V and Francis I, no less than the English king, regarded themselves as holding office by divine appointment and felt justified in enforcing the obedience of their subjects. Charles was determined to extirpate religious radicalism from his own vast territories. In Germany he was obliged to play cat-and-mouse with the Protestant princes but elsewhere he had no hesitation about using the full power of the state to enforce Catholic orthodoxy. The Moriscos of Valencia felt the unre-strained force of the Inquisition. In 1540 the city of Ghent was punished for rebellion in a manner designed to live long in the communal memory. As well as making maximum use of torture and execution, Charles had the senior citizenry parade before him barefoot and draped in penitential black. Then he had a large part of the town demolished in order to make way for a fortress. Such personal interventions were a long way from the suffering Henry imposed indirectly on the Pilgrimage of Grace rebels.

Francis ruled with the support of a small council of royal appointees. He never summoned a meeting of the Estates General, the nearest body France had to a parliament. He levied taxes at will without any pretence at popular consent and, in 1542, he had to face a 10,000-strong revolt against the salt tax. France could not escape the Reformation and Francis took firm action to suppress Lutheranism. He proscribed 'heretical' books and authorized purges which resulted in the massacre of over 3,000 people. Yet, at the same time, he extended state control over the French church. All senior ecclesiastical appointments were made by the king. In the 1530s and 1540s all European governments were facing similar problems. Henry VIII was no more extreme than his brother monarchs in dealing with them.

There were two sources of restriction on royal power in England – or, at least, on power as Henry wielded it: parliament and public opinion. Theoretically, he had no need to concern himself with either. Parliament was a body summoned entirely at the royal behest, as and when the king required a forum for the discussion of matters of moment, but its function and importance changed during the reign. It met more frequently because Henry needed its support in two areas – money and religion. The enormous increase in royal expenditure necessitated the voting of taxes and the intrusion of secular government into spiritual affairs meant that the crown had to take parliament more fully into partnership. Cromwell based the Reformation takeover on statute law. Therefore, the arguments of lords, burgesses and gentlemen in parliament assembled had to be listened to. The royal case had to be argued. Members had to be bullied, cajoled or manipulated. Elections, where possible, had to be rigged. Parliament could not be ignored and the more often it met the more jealous its members became of their privileges. As to public opinion, while Henry affected to be entirely his own man, he was always sensitive to the will of the people. The war of new and old ideas raging throughout Europe was entangled with ancient social and economic grievances and could at any time explode into violence. It happened in Germany in 1524–5. It happened in England in 1536–7 and threatened to happen at other times. This was why government policy had to be backed by a vigorous campaign of sermons, pamphlets and pictorial propaganda. Henry could not neglect the necessity of persuasion and when persuasion failed, as over the Amicable Grant, he had to back down. All in all, as tyrants go, Henry VIII was very far from being in the premier league.

How shall we rate him as a king? Medieval monarchs were judged by their achievements in war, in diplomacy, in the maintenance of law and order, in their keeping of a cultured court and in their provision for the welfare of their subjects. Henry never exposed his person in battle. Save for the long-term pacification of the northern border, the military exploits of his generals produced negligible results. In the French campaigns his armies never came face to face with the full battle strength of the enemy. Apart from the needless suffering of English troops, war took its toll of the civilian population, particularly those members of it who relied on overseas trade. Henry failed to achieve by negotiation what he had not achieved by force of arms and so left his son an unsustainable role in international affairs. By his own admission, the nation was also cruelly divided along religious lines.

Can we set down to Henry's credit that he was a brilliant, cultured Renaissance prince? Not really. Without doubt, he presided over a glittering court, especially throughout the first half of the reign. Henry VII had begun the process of employing leading foreign artists, such as Pietro Torrigiano, but his son was half-hearted about building on this cultural foundation. A few masters were enticed to England from Italy and the Netherlands but, towards the end of the reign, Henry decided that he wanted 'no more strangers sent from Rome'.[219] In terms of avant-garde culture the English court lagged far behind those of Burgundy, France, Rome and the Italian principalities. Hans Holbein was Henry's biggest 'catch' but the Basel artist only arrived in London as a result of patronage by Erasmus and More and after having failed to gain admission to the court of Francis I. Nor, if we are to believe Sir Thomas Elyot's *Boke Named the Governour* (1531), was the employment of foreign masters discouraged by the wealth of native talent. On the contrary, English craftsmen were not being sufficiently encouraged by wealthy patrons from the king downwards. In the higher arts, he complained, 'Englishmen be inferior to all other people'.[220] Henry was obsessively acquisitive of all manner of beautiful and costly artefacts but this did not imply a cultivated aesthetic appreciation. He spent hugely on houses, for example, and owned about thirty-five at his death. However, at Hampton Court and York Place he can scarcely be credited with having improved upon Wolsey's Renaissance palaces and the incredible Nonsuch, designed to rival Francis's Fontainbleau and Chambord, was, as far as we can tell from early drawings, considerably over-the-top.

What we rightly look for in any charismatic national leader is vision. We need to know what he stands for, what he desires for his people. In an age when scholars were eagerly debating the characteristics of a 'Christian commonwealth' we seek in vain any concept of national identity from Henry. He had very firm and clear ideas about kingship, about his own place in the divine order of things but 'England', insofar as it existed at all in his thinking, was little more than an extension of his own personality. Reduced to those few sentences, the appraisal of Henry as king is not impressive. However, on the other side of the scales we have to place the fact that England was, in his reign, a nation secure and strongly governed. That, given the turbulence of the century preceding Henry's accession and the convulsive changes foisted upon the realm, was remarkable in itself. This was not only accomplished by negative actions such as the ruthless removal of all possible contenders for the throne and the suppression of rebellion. Nor was it achieved by the spectacular talents of royal ministers. Peace and stability relied on a network of conscientious and loyal local officials. Justices of the peace, the gentry of the shires and the aristocratic landowners who controlled large tracts of the country worked, for the most part, with central government to prevent unrest getting out of hand and to provide rough-and-ready justice for the bulk of the population. One aspect of the continuously changing pattern of land ownership was the need to place and maintain men Henry could trust in positions of responsibility. In keeping men loyal to himself the king's main asset was the force of his personality.

I referred above to the need to differentiate between style and substance in judging the careers of national leaders. However, there is an important difference between today's politicians and the sixteenth-century wielders of autocratic power. Display was an important part of the job for a man who, in a very real sense, embodied the national spirit. Appearances mattered if subjects were to be kept in awe of their monarch and to discern in him a focus of national pride. Henry understood this from the very beginning and was determined to be demonstrably 'kingly', in contrast to his father who, in his latter years, had almost retreated from the world. It was the outward show that the new king was so good at and which chroniclers, in search of sensational copy, picked up on. Raphael Holinshed, in 1577, emphasized Henry's physical attributes as well as his intellectual abilities and moral virtues:

> Of personage he was tall and mighty, in his latter days somewhat gross, or, as we term it, burly ['gross' and 'burly', in the sixteenth century, had the sense of 'massive' and 'impressive']; in wit and memory very perfect; of such majesty tempered with humanity as best became so high and noble an estate; a great favourer of learning. . .[His] fame and renown. . .made itself known by restless forces, and others submitting themselves for fear of utter desolation. . .Sufficient cannot be said in his high and merited commendation.[221]

However, Holinshed's book was separated by almost a generation from the events it recorded. Elizabeth's reign was, by then, well advanced and England had taken on a new identity as Protestant champion against the threat of Catholic Spain and France. In the light of this changed situation the realm needed the myth of a heroic king who had been the agent of divine providence, freeing his people from papal error and taking the fight into enemy territory. As literate Englishmen looked back across the unhappy interlude of the reigns of Edward VI and Mary they were ready for an interpretation of the past which demonstrated that the English were God's chosen people, an interpretation erected on the unstable foundation of Henrician propaganda. That propaganda had been vital to Henry's success. The royal showman had to impress all spectators. Foreign diplomats had to be kept from discerning the king's weaknesses. Councillors, bishops and members of parliament had to be made aware at all times that they were in the presence of greatness.

Elizabethan and Stuart Puritans devised a picture of England as an elect nation, comparable to Old Testament Israel, and they looked to their sovereigns to emulate the virtues of Moses, David and Hezekiah. We can see this process beginning in Henry's reign. Around 1535, Holbein created, perhaps for some sycophantic courtier to give the king as a New Year's gift, a miniature depicting Henry as Solomon receiving the homage of the queen of Sheba. It bore the inscription in letters of gold, 'How fortunate are the men who serve you, who are always in your presence and are privileged to hear your wise sayings.' This, doubtless, reflected Henry's self-image but as a photo-fit of the godly ruler of a godly people it was a poor match.

So, at last, we come to the central issue. What lay behind the courtly charade? What can we know about the inner man? What reality is concealed as much by later accusations of monstrous cruelty as by the official Tudor images? A list of some of the royal attributes pointed out by contemporaries is revealing. Henry, they said, was vain, affable, competitive, suspicious, acquisitive, given to violent outbursts of temper, hypochondriac and, by turns, stubborn and accommodating. These are all marks of the egotist and they relate to all of us in varying degrees. It is only when massive egotism is coupled with virtually unlimited power that you get a Henry VIII. The egotist has an exalted idea of his own importance. When, in defiance of logic and the evidence of experience, other people are fed to the Moloch of this delusion it verges on paranoia. In Henry's case, intense self-regard was encouraged, during childhood, by being the leading male in a predominantly female household and, throughout his life, by the daily attentions of flatterers. This explains how he could come to believe in the royal supremacy. As an anointed king Henry was convinced that he stood in a special relationship with God. One would love to have been privy to his prayers. Did repentance, one wonders, feature much in them? His moral sense was centred in his own will, as Thomas More recognized when he urged Cromwell to tell the king not what he could do, but what he should do. Henry wrestled with the evidence of divine disapproval but did not accept personal responsibility for having incurred it. It was the pope's fault that he had married his brother's widow. It was Wolsey's fault that the people were subjected to unjust taxes. It was the fault of successive wives that, for twenty-eight years, he had no legitimate male heir. The egotist can never admit to being wrong. Convinced of his own righteousness he tends to pursue his objectives even when this means stumbling from failure to failure – hence Henry's determination to achieve the annulment of his first marriage despite being balked over and again.

The essential point about egotism is that it is a defence mechanism. It is one way that the mind deals with failure, inadequacy and self-doubt. Beneath the bluster, the bonhomie and the belligerence Henry VIII was intensely insecure. He had to prove himself to himself, to his country and to the world. This explains the apparent contradictions in his personality; how he could be both domineering and also manipulated by court factions and ministers; how he could be nagged and reduced to tears by wives and mistresses and yet coldly, cruelly dispose of them when they displeased him; how he could be aggressively independent while relying heavily on the emotional support of wives and close companions; how he could rule despotically but always be conscious of public opinion. It tells us why he craved applause at court entertainments and why he relished the competition of the tiltyard (as long as he won). And it provides us with the basic reason for his fruitless foreign wars. Henry had to demonstrate that he was more than a match for his royal contemporaries. Charles and Francis had real border disputes to sort out. Their rivalry was inevitable. Henry, by contrast, had to revive the ambitions of the Hundred Years' War and manufacture *casus belli* in order to be taken seriously in international affairs.

However, the real competition was internal. The vital contest was with the demons in his mind. One was his sexual inadequacy. He found it difficult to be aroused, a problem which worsened with the passing of the years, doubtless partly as a result of anxiety. He was desperately sensitive about this, because it cast doubt upon his manhood but also because it suggested that he was the real cause of the dynastic problem which dogged him and the nation for the greater part of his life. He compensated for this by macho boasting about his sexual exploits – and most people, it seems, believed him. The merchant, Richard Hilles, while reporting London gossip to friends on the continent in 1541, poured scorn on the idea that Anne of Cleves could have preserved her virginity after a night with her husband. 'That is a likely thing, indeed,' he scoffed. 'Who, judging of the king by his fruits, would believe him to be so chaste?'[222] No one was allowed to draw attention to Henry's 'problem' and the elaborate fiction of Anne Boleyn's faithlessness had to be invented to prevent the truth coming out.

However, the demon with which he contended most fiercely was his father. He was always in competition with the founder of the dynasty. The first Tudor had won his crown in the hazard of battle. His son had done nothing to earn his; it had come to him by default on the death of his brother. Henry VII had never believed that his younger son would amount to much. He had ignored him while lavishing attention on his beloved Arthur. He had restricted his freedom in the years after Arthur's death while neglecting to train the new Prince of Wales for his future duties. He made no secret of his disapproval of young Henry's attitude and it is not surprising that, consciously and unconsciously, the son should have striven passionately to prove the father wrong. History suggests that Henry VII's judgement was sound.

# NOTES

1. Gairdner, J. ed., *Letters and Papers Illustrative of the Reigns of Richard III and Henry VII*, 1861–3, vol. I, 231–40
2. Thomas à Kempis, *The Imitation of Christ*, G.F. Maine, ed., 1957, p. 322
3. T. Malory, *Works of Sir Thomas Malory*, E. Vinaver, ed., 1967
4. S. Anglo, *Spectacle, Pageantry and Early Tudor Policy*, Oxford, 1969, p. 97
5. Ibid., p. 87
6. Ibid., p. 100
7. J. Leland, *De Rebus Brittanicis Collectanea*, vol. V, pp. 373–4
8. E. Hall, *The Union of the Two Noble and Illustre Families of Lancastre and Yorke*, H. Ellis, ed., 1809, pp. 499–500
9. Duque de Berwick y de Alba, ed., *Correspondencia de Gutierre Gómez de Fuensalida,* Madrid, 1907, p. 449
10. Author's translation
11. T. Malory, *Le Morte Darthur*, H. Cooper, ed., Oxford, 1998, pp. 50–51
12. E. Hall, *The Triumphant Reign of King Henry VIII*, 1904, vol. I, p. 1

13. G.A. Bergenroth and P. de Gayangos, eds, *Calendar of State Papers, Spanish,* 1862–6, I & II Supplement, 21–2

14. E. Hall, 1809, op.cit., p. 507

15. Ibid.

16. E. Hall, 1809, op.cit., pp. 96–8

17. E. Dudley, *The Tree of Commonwealth*, D.M. Brodie, ed., Cambridge, 1948, pp. 25–6

18. T. Malory, op.cit., p. 93

19. D. Hoak, 'The iconography of the crown imperial', in D. Hoak, ed., *Tudor Political Culture*, Cambridge, 1995, p. 71

20. G.A. Bergenroth and P. de Gayangos, eds, op. cit. vol. II, p. 71

21. E. Hall, 1809, op.cit., p. 515

22. S. Anglo, op.cit., pp. 111–12

23. T. Malory, op.cit., pp. 481–2

24. E. Hall, 1809, op. cit., p. 8

25. J. Stevens, ed., *Music at the Court of Henry VIII*, 1969, p. 66

26. P.S. and H.M. Allen, eds, *Letters of Richard Fox*, Oxford, 1929, p. 44

27. H. Miller, *Henry VIII and the English Nobility*, Oxford, 1986, p. 12

28. E. Herbert, Lord Cherbury, *History of Henry VIII*, 1719, p. 6

29. P.S. and H.M. Allen, op.cit., pp. 53–4

30. J. Skelton, *Magnifycence: A Moral Play by John Skelton*, R.L. Ramsay, ed., 1908, 1958, lines 77–80, pp 121–5

31. M. Johnson, *The Borgias*, 1981, p. 179

32. J. Gairdner, ed., *Letters and Papers, Foreign and domestic of the Reign of Henry VIII*, 1861–3, vol. I, 354, 1740

33. Ibid.

34. G. Cavendish, *Thomas Wolsey Late Cardinal, His Liyffe and Deathe*, R.S. Sylvester, ed., Oxford, 1959, p. 12

35. E. Hall, 1904, op. cit., vol. I, p. 43

36. Ibid., p. 44

37. P.S. and H.M. Allen, op. cit., pp. 57–8

38. Ibid., p. 96

39. J. Gairdner, ed., *Letters...Henry VIII*, op. cit., vol. III, 217

40. P. Henderson, ed., *The Complete Poems of John Skelton*, 1948, p. 47

41. G.A. Bergenroth and P. de Gayangos, eds, Further Supplement, 164

42. J.A. Guy, *The Cardinal's Court: The Impact of Thomas Wolsey in Star Chamber*, 1977, p. 26
43. H. Ellis, *Original Letters illustrative of English History*, 1824–46, 2nd series, vol. I, p. 237
44. Ibid., 1st series, vol. I, pp. 116–7
45. J. Gairdner, ed., *Letters. . .Henry VIII*, op. cit., vol. II, 80
46. J. Barlowe and W. Roye, *Rede Me and Be Nott Wrothe*, D.H. Parker, ed., Toronto, 1992, p. 64
47. Author's translation
48. E. Surtz and S.J. and J.H. Hexter, eds., *The Complete Works of St. Thomas More*, New Haven, 1963, vol. IV, p. lxxiv
49. E. Hall, 1809, op. cit., p. 594
50. R. Brown, *Four Years at the Court of Henry the Eighth*, 1854, vol. II, p. 177
51. J. Gairdner, ed., *Letters. . .Henry VIII*, op. cit., vol. III, 1233
52. Ibid., 1297
53. Quoted in C. Creighton, *A History of Epidemics in Britain*, 1891–4, vol. I, p. 234
54. E. Hall, 1809, op. cit., p. 597
55. J. Skelton, *Why Come ye Not, Poetical Works* (ed. A. Dyce), 1843 vol. II, pp. 657–76
56. J. Gairdner, ed., *Letters. . .Henry VIII*, op. cit., vol. III, p. 1
57. J. Skelton, op. cit., vol. II, p. 29
58. William Tyndale, *Doctrinal Treatises*, ed. H. Walter, 1848, pp. 8–9
59. Archbishop Fitzralph of Armagh (*d.*1360). See W.A. Pantin, *The English Church in the Fourteenth Century*, 1962, pp. 132–3
60. Thomas à Kempis, op. cit., Bk 1, Ch. 5
61. W. Tyndale, op. cit., p. 394
62. P. Marshall, ' Evangelical conversion in the reign of Henry VIII', in P. Marshall and A. Ryrie, *The Beginnings of English Protestantism*, Cambridge, 2002, p. 36
63. T. More, *A Merry Jest How a Sergeant Would Learn to Play the Friar*; c.f R. W. Chambers, *Thomas More*, 1976, p. 90
64. J. Foxe, *Acts and Monuments*, J. Townsend, ed., 1837, vol. IV, p. 582
65. Ibid., p. 582
66. E. Hall, The Union of the Two Noble Families. . .fascimile ed. Menston, 1970, fol. lxxxxviii
67. Ibid., fol. c

68. J. Gairdner, ed., *Letters. . .Henry VIII*, op. cit., vol. IV(i), p. 510
69. E. Hall, 1970, op. cit. fol. cxxxi
70. Ibid., fol. cxxxix
71. Ibid., fol. cxli
72. Ibid., fol. cxlii
73. Ibid., fol. cxiiii
74. J. Gairdner, ed., *Letters. . .Henry VIII*, op. cit., vol. IV (i), p. 1318
75. J. Barlowe and W., op. cit., p.57
76. E. Hall, 1809, op. cit., fol. cxliii
77. Ibid.
78. Ibid., fol. cxl
79. G.W. Bernard, *The King's Reformation*, New Haven, 2005, pp. 5–9
80. J. Gairdner, ed., *Letters. . .Henry VIII*, op. cit., vol. IV (ii), p. 2556
81. Ibid., p. 3200
82. Ibid., p. 3137
83. Ibid., p. 3253
84. Ibid., p. 3400
85. Ibid., p. 3644
86. G.R. Elton, ed., *The Tudor Constitution. . .*, Cambridge, 1960, p. 323
87. N. Tjernagel, *Henry VIII and the Lutherans*, St Louis, 1965, p. 33
88. E. Hall, 1970, op. cit, fol. clxxxi–clxxxii
89. J. Strype, *Ecclesiastical Memorials*, Oxford, 1822, vol. I, p. 173
90. W. Tyndale, op. cit., pp. 206–7
91. E. Hall, 1970, op. cit., fol. clxxxiii
92. E. Herbert, Lord Cherbury, *The Life and Raigne of King Henry the Eighth*, 1649, p. 174
93. J. Gairdner, ed., *Letters. . .Henry VIII*, op. cit., vol. IV (ii), p. 4649
94. R.S. Sylvester and J. Harding, eds, *Two Early Tudor Lives*, New Haven, 1962, pp. 103–04
95. Ibid., p. 105
96. G. Cavendish, op. cit., pp. 76–7
97. E. Hall, 1970, op. cit., fol. clxxxviii
98. E. Ives, *The Life and Death of Anne Boleyn*, Oxford, 2004, p. 128
99. J. Gairdner, ed., *Letters. . .Henry VIII*, op. cit., vol. IV, p. 6295
100. G.A. Bergenroth and P. de Gayangos, eds, op. cit. vol. IV, i, p. 819

101. R. Rex, 'The Friars in the English Reformation', in P. Marshall and A. Ryrie, eds, *The Beginnings of English Protestantism*, Cambridge, 2002, p. 41

102. E. Ives, op. cit., p. 260

103. J. Foxe, op. cit, vol. V, p. 135

104. E. Ives, op.cit., p. 275

105. Ibid., p. 33

106. T. Amyot, ed., 'A memorial from George Constantine', in *Archaeologia*, 1831, pp. 272, 419

107. E. Ives, op. cit., pp. 122ff

108. E. Hall, 1970, op.cit.. fol. clxxxix

109. D. MacCulloch, *Thomas Cranmer*, New Haven, 1996, p. 41

110. J. Gairdner, ed., *Letters...Henry VIII*, op. cit., vol. IV, p. 6667

111. G.W. Bernard, op.cit.

112. S. Foreman, *From Palace to Power*, 1995, p. 7

113. W. Roper, *The Life of Sir Thomas More*, 1935, p. 11

114. P.S. and H.M. Allen, eds, *Opus Epistolarum Desiderii Erasmi Roterodami*, vol. X, p. 2831

115. J. Gairdner, ed., *Letters...Henry VIII*, op. cit., vol. IV (ii), p. 3438

116. G.A. Bergenroth and P. de Gayangos, eds, op. cit., vol. IV, p. 224

117. Ibid., p. 634

118. J. Strype, *Memorials of the Most Reverend Father in God, Thomas Cranmer*, 1853, Appendix 1

119. G.A. Bergenroth and P. de Gayangos, eds, op. cit., vol. V, p. 85

120. J. Foxe, op. cit., vol. V, p. 363

121. G.A. Bergenroth and P. de Gayangos, eds, op. cit., vol. V, p. 359

122. G.R. Elton, op. cit., pp. 343–4

123. E. Hall, 1970, op. cit., fol. cciii

124. Ibid., fol. ccv

125. J. Foxe, op. cit., vol. IV, p. 704

126. Ibid.

127. E. Hall, 1970, op. cit., fol. ccvi

128. G.R. Elton, op. cit., p. 344

129. E. Hall, 1970, op. cit., fol. ccxv

130. J. Gairdner, ed., *Letters...Henry VIII*, op. cit., vol. VI, p. 1528

131. C. Wriothesley, *A Chronicle of England During the Reigns of the Tudors*, ed. W.D. Hamilton, 1875, vol. I, p. 23

132. G.E. Corrie, ed., *Sermons of Hugh Latimer*, Cambridge, 1844, p. 23

133. G.R. Elton, op. cit., p. 62

134. Ibid., p. 7
135. J. Gairdner, ed., *Letters. . .Henry VIII*, op. cit., vol. V., p. 907
136. G. Cavendish, op. cit., pp. 105–6
137. H. Ellis, ed., *Original Letters Illustrative of English History, 1824–46*, 3rd series, vol. II, pp. 333, 343, 351; J. Gairdner, ed., *Letters. . .Henry VIII*, op. cit., vol. VII, p. 754
138. G.A. Bergenroth and P. de Gayangos, eds, op. cit., vol. IV, ii, p. 649
139. D. Willen, *John Russell, First Earl of Bedford,* RHS Studies in History, vol. 23, 1981, p. 32
140. A.G. Dickens, *Lollards and Protestants in the Diocese of York,* Oxford, 1959, pp. 131–2
141. C. Wriothesley, op cit., pp. 82–3
142. R.W. Dixon, *History of the Church of England,* 1878–1902, vol. I, pp. 413–4
143. Not Aldermanbury – see E. Ives, op. cit., p. 261
144. J. Foxe, op. cit., vol. V, p. 37
145. H. Ellis, op. cit., 1st series, vol. II, p.45
146. Sir T. Wyatt, *Collected Poems,* J. Daalder, ed., Oxford, 1975, p. 112
147. M. Dowling, 'Anne Boleyn and Reform' in *Journal of Ecclesiastical History,* no. 35, i, 1984, pp. 39f
148. Ibid., p. 33
149. R.B. Merriman, ed., *Life and Letters of Thomas Cromwell,* Oxford, 1968, vol. II, p. 2
150. N. Machiavelli, *The Prince,* trs. W.K. Marriott, 1992, p. 75
151. G.R. Elton, op. cit., p. 374
152. D. Starkey, *Six Wives: The Queens of Henry VIII,* 2003, p. 585
153. R.B. Merriman, op. cit., vol. II. p. 12
154. For the best modern narrative see E. Ives, op. cit., pp. 319–56
155. J. Gairdner, ed., *Letters. . .Henry VIII*, op. cit., vol. VI, p. 351
156. E. Ives, op. cit., p. 331
157. Sir T. Wyatt, op.cit., p. cxliii
158. H. Ellis. op. cit., 3rd series, vol. III, pp. 138–9
159. M. Aston, *England's Iconoclasts,* 1988, vol. I, p. 224
160. E. Hall, 1970, op. cit., fol. ccxxxii
161. Ibid., fol. ccxxxi
162. G.A. Bergenroth and P. de Gayangos, eds, op. cit., vol. V, ii, p. 269
163. D. MacCulloch, op. cit., p. 172
164. *State Papers of Henry VIII,* 1830–52, vol. I, pp. 518–9
165. E. Hall, 1970, op. cit., fol. ccxxxi

166. For a discussion of the strange history of Francis Bigod, see A.G. Dickens, *Lollards and Protestants in the Diocese of York*, Oxford, 1959, ch. 3.

167. M. James, *Society, Politics and Culture: Studies in Early Modern England*, Cambridge, 1986, p. 353

168. L. Campbell, *Renaissance Portraits*, New Haven, 1990, p. 95

169. R.B. Merriman, op. cit., vol. II, p. 97

170. H. Ellis, op. cit., 3rd series, vol. III. p. 139

171. G.W. Bernard, op. cit., New Haven, 2005

172. J. Foxe, op. cit., vol. V, p. 251

173. J. Gairdner, ed., *Letters. . .Henry VIII*, op. cit., vol. XIV, ii, p. 423

174. The canard appears to have originated with Bishop Gilbert Burnet in the late seventeenth century and to have become anchored in the historical account by Tobias Smollett in his popular *History of England*, 1748.

175. J. Gairdner, ed., *Letters. . .Henry VIII*, op. cit., vol. XIV, ii, p. 33

176. J. Strype, 1822, op. cit., vol. VI, p. 218

177. Ibid., pp. 221–2

178. J. Gairdner, ed., *Letters. . .Henry VIII*, op. cit., vol. XVI, p. 1638

179. J. Gairdner, ed., *Letters. . .Henry VIII*, op. cit., p. 590

180. *Luther's Works,* H.T. Lehmann and J. Pelikan, eds, St Louis, Missouri and Philadelphia, Pennsylvania, 1955–86, vol. 50, pp. 205–6

181. J. Foxe, op. cit., vol. VI, p. 578

182. Ibid., vol. V, p. 562

183. J. Gairdner, ed., *Letters. . .Henry VIII*, op. cit., vol. XV, p. 954

184. E. Hall, 1970, op. cit., fol. ccxliii

185. C. Wriothesley, op. cit., p. 121n

186. J. Gairdner, ed., *Letters. . .Henry VIII*, op. cit., vol. XVI, p. 578

187. R. Edgeworth, *Sermons Very Fruitful, Godly and Learned: Preaching in the Reformation c.1535–c.1553*, J. Wilson, ed., Cambridge, 1993, p. 364

188. L.B. Smith, *A Tudor Tragedy: The Life and Times of Catherine Howard*, 1961, p. 205

189. J. Gairdner, ed., *Letters. . .Henry VIII*, op. cit., vol. XVI, p. 436

190. Ibid., vol. XVI, p. 421

191. Ibid., vol. XVI, p. 712

192. E. Hall, 1970, op. cit., fol. ccxlv

193. J. Gairdner, ed., *Letters. . .Henry VIII*, op. cit., vol. XVI, p. 101

194. Ibid., p. 1334
195. L.B. Smith, op. cit., p. 182
196. J. Gairdner, ed., *Letters. . .Henry VIII*, op. cit., vol. XVI, p. 1328
197. Ibid., p. 1482
198. Ibid.
199. His reference was to Queen Margaret, whose death in 1289 had led indirectly to the invasion of Edward I.
200. J. Gairdner, ed., *Letters. . .Henry VIII*, op. cit., vol. XVIII, i, p. 364
201. Preface to *Euclid's Elements of Geometry,* trs. Henry Billingsley, 1570
202. J. Gairdner, ed., *Letters. . .Henry VIII*, op. cit., vol. XIX, i, p. 314
203. *Henry Howard Earl of Surrey: Poems,* E. Jones, ed., Oxford, 1973, no. 33
204. E. Hall, 1970, op. cit., fol. cclix
205. J. Childs, *Henry's Last Victim – The Life and Times of Henry Howard, Earl of Surrey,* 2007, p. 218
206. J.A. Muller, ed., *Letters of Stephen Gardiner,* Cambridge, 1933, pp. 185ff
207. J. Gairdner, ed., *Letters. . .Henry VIII*, op. cit., vol. XXI, i, p. 984
208. J. Stow, *Annals of the Reformation,* 1601, p. 590
209. J. Gairdner, ed., *Letters. . .Henry VIII*, op. cit., vol. XXI, ii, p. 381
210. Ibid., vol. XXI, ii, p. 605
211. Ibid.
212. W. Thomas, *The Pilgrim: a Dialogue on the Life and Actions of King Henry the Eighth,* ed. E.J. Froude, 1861, pp. 79–80
213. Sir W. Ralegh, *The History of the World,* ed. C.A. Patrides, 1971, pp. 56–7
214. D. Loades, *England's Maritime Empire: Seapower, Commerce and Policy, 1490–1690,* 2000, p. 43
215. J. Gairdner, ed., *Letters. . .Henry VIII*, op. cit., vol. III, p. 1297
216. Ibid., vol. XVIII, i, p. 364
217. P. de la Primaudaye, *French Academy,* trs. Thomas Bowes, 1586–94, vol. I, p. 601
218. W.G. Hoskins, *The Age of Plunder: the England of Henry VIII,* 1976, p. 233
219. C. Reynolds, 'England and the Continent: artistic Relations', in R. Marks and P. Williamson, eds, *Gothic: Art for England, 1400–1547,* 2003, p. 84
220. Ibid.

221. R. Holinshed, *Chronicles of England, Scotland and Ireland,* 1808, vol. III, p. 864
222. J. Gairdner, ed., *Letters. . .Henry VIII*, op. cit., vol. XVI, p. 578

# BIBLIOGRAPHY

The place of publication is London unless otherwise indicated.

## Printed and Early Sources
Allen, P.S., et al, eds, *Opus Epistolarum Des. Erasmi Roterodami*, Oxford, 1906–58

Allen, P.S and H.M., eds, *Letters of Richard Fox*, Oxford, 1929

Bacon, Sir Francis, *History of the Reign of Henry VIII*, J. Weinberger, ed., Ilhaca, 1996

Bain, J., ed., *Hamilton Papers: Letters and Papers Illustrating the Political Relations of England and Scotland in the Sixteenth Century*, Edinburgh, 1890

Bergenroth, G.A. and de Gayangos, P., eds, *Calendar of State Papers, Spanish*, 1862–6

Brown, R., *Four years at the Court of Henry VIII*, 1854

Brown, R., Bentinck, C. and Brown, H., eds, *Calendar of State Papers, Venetian*, 1864–98

Byrne, M. St C., ed., *The Lisle Letters*, Chicago, 1980

Cavendish, G., 'The Life and Death of Cardinal Wolsey' in R.S. Sylvester and D.P. Harding, eds, *Two Early Tudor Lives*, New Haven, 1962

Corrie, G.E., ed., *Sermons and Remains of Hugh Latimer. . .*, Cambridge, 1844, 1845

Cox, J.E., ed., *The Works of Archbishop Cranmer*, Cambridge, 1844–6

Dasent, J.R., ed., *Acts of the Privy Council of England*, 1890–1907

De La Primaudaye, P., *French Academy*, trs. T. Bowles, 1586–94

Dowling, M., ed., 'William Latymer's chronickille of Anne Bulleyne', *Camden Miscellany 30*, 4th series, no. XXXIX, 1990, pp. 23–66

Dudley, Edmund, *The Tree of Commonwealth*, D.M. Brodie, ed., Cambridge, 1948

Duque de Berwick y de Alba, ed., *Correspondencia de Gutierre Gómez de Fuensalida*, Madrid, 1907, p. 449

Edgeworth, R., ed., *Sermons Very Fruitful, Godly and Learned: Preaching in the Reformation, c.1535–c.1553*, J. Wilson, ed., Cambridge, 1993

Ellis, H., ed., *Original Letters, Illustrative of English History*, 1824–46

Elton, G.R., ed., *The Tudor Constitution, Documents and Commentary*, Cambridge, 1960

Erasmus, D., *The Praise of Folly*, trs. C.H. Miller, New Haven, 1979

Fish, S., *A Supplication for the Beggars*, F.J. Furnivall and J.M. Cowper, eds, 1871

Fortescue, J., *The Governance of England*, C. Plummer, ed., Oxford, 1885

Foxe, J., *Acts and Monuments*, G. Townsend and S.R. Cattley, eds, 1838

Frere, W.H. and Kennedy W.M., *Visitation Articles and Injunction*, 1910

Gairdner, J., ed., *Letters and Papers, Foreign and domestic of the Reign of Henry VIII*, 1861–3

Gairdner, J., ed., *Letters and Papers Illustrative of the Reigns of Richard III and Henry VII*, 1861–3

Gairdner, J., ed., *Paston Letters, AD 1422–1509*, 1904

Giustinian, S., *Four Years at the Court of Henry VIII. . .January 12th 1515 to July 26th 1519*, R. Brown, ed., 1854

Gough Nichols, J., ed., *Documents of the English Reformation*, Cambridge, 1994

Hall, E., *The Union of the Two Noble and Illustre Families of Lancastre and Yorke*, H. Ellis, ed., 1809

Hall, E., *The Union of the Two Noble and Illustre Families of Lancaster and Yorke*, facsimile edition, Menston, 1970

Hardyng, J. and Grafton, R., *Chronicle of John Hardyng...*, H. Ellis, ed., 1812

Hay, D., ed., *The Anglica Historia of Polydore Vergil, 1485–1537*, Camden Society, 3rd series, no. LXXIV, 1950

Herbert, E., Lord Cherbury, *The Life and Rayne of Henry VIII*, 1872

Hillerbrand, H.J., ed., *Erasmus and His Age, Selected Letters of Desiderius Erasmus*, New York, 1970

Holinshed, R., *Chronicles of England, Scotland and Ireland*, H. Ellis, ed., 1807–8

Howard, H., Earl of Surrey, *Poems*, E. Jones, ed., Oxford, 1973

Hughes, P.L. and Larkin, J.F., eds, *Tudor Royal Proclamations*, New Haven, 1964, 1969

Kaulek, J., *Correspondence Politique de M.M. de Castillon et de Marillac...*, Paris, 1885

Kingsford, C.L., ed., *A Survey of London*, Oxford, 1908

Latimer, H., *Sermons*, G.E. Corrie, ed., Cambridge, 1844

Leland, J., *De Rebus Brittanicis Collectanea*, T. Hearne, ed., Oxford, 1715

Leland, J., *Itinerary in England and Wales*, L. Toulmin Smith, ed., 1964

Loades, D.M., ed., *Papers of George Wyatt Esquire...*, Camden Society, 4th series, no. V, 1968

Luther, Martin, *Works*, H.T. Lehmann and J. Pelikan, eds, St Louis and Philadelphia, 1955–86

Machiavelli, N., *The Prince*, trs. W.K. Marriott, 1992

Malory, Sir T., *Le Morte Darthur*, H. Cooper, ed., Oxford, 1998

Mancini, D., *The Usurpation of Richard III*, C.A.J. Armstrong, ed., 1969

Merriman, R.B., *The Life and Letters of Thomas Cromwell*, Oxford, 1902

More, T., *Selected Letters*, F.F. Rogers, ed., New Haven, 1961

More, T., *The Complete Works of St Thomas More*, New Haven, 1963

Muller, J.A., ed., *Letters of Stephen Gardiner*, Cambridge, 1933

Mynors, R.A.B. et al, eds, 'Correspondence of Erasmus' in *The Collected Works of Erasmus*, Toronto, 1975

Nichols, J.G., ed., *Chronicle of the Grey Friars of London*, Camden Society, 1st series, no. LIII, 1852

Nichols, J.G., ed., *Narratives of the Reformation*, Camden Society, old series, no. LXXVII, 1859

Nott, G.F., ed., *Works of Henry Howard*, New York, 1965

Ralegh, Sir W., *The History of the World*, C.A. Patrides, ed., 1971

Reynolds, E.E., ed., *The Life and Illustrious Martyrdom of Sir Thomas More by Thomas Stapleton*, trs. P.E. Hallett, New York, 1966

Rogers, E.F., ed., *Correspondence of Sir Thomas More*, Princeton, 1947

Roper, W., 'The Life of Sir Thomas More' in R.S. Sylvester and D.P. Harding, eds, *Two Early Tudor Lives*, New Haven, 1962

Roye, W., *Rede Me and Be Nott Wrothe*, D.H. Parker, ed., Toronto, 1992

Skelton, J., *Magnifycene: A Moral Play*, R.L. Ramsay, ed., 1908, 1958

Skelton, J., *The Poetical Works*, A. Dyce, ed., 1843

Starkey, T., *A Dialogue Between Pole and Lupset*, T.F. Mayer, ed., Camden Society, 4th series, no. XXXVII, 1989

Starkey, T., *The Complete English Poems*, J. Scattergood, ed., 1983

*State Papers Published under the Authority of His Majesty's Commission, King Henry VIII*, 1830–52

Stow, J., *Annales*, 1615

Strype, J., *Ecclesiastical Memorials*, Oxford, 1822

Strype, J., *Memorials. . .of Thomas Cranmer*, P.E. Barnes, ed., 1853

Tawney, R.H. and Power, E., *Tudor Economic Documents*, 1924

*The Complete Works of St Thomas More*, New Haven, 1963

Thomas, W., *The Pilgrim: A Dialogue on the Life and Actions of King Henry the Eighth*, E.J. Froude, ed., 1861

Thomas à Kempis, *The Imitation of Christ*, G.F. Maine, ed., date unknown

Tyndale, W., *Answer to Sir Thomas More's Dialogue, the Supper of the Lord. . .and William Tracy's Testament Expounded. . .*, H. Walter, ed., Cambridge, 1850

Tyndale, W., *Doctrinal Treatises. . .*, H. Walter, ed., Cambridge, 1848

Tyndale, W., *Expositions and Notes on Sundry Portions of the Holy Scriptures together with the Practices of Prelates. . .*, H. Walter, ed., Cambridge, 1849

Vergil, P., *Anglica Historia*, D. Hay, ed., Camden Society, new series, no. LXXIV, 1950

White, B., ed., *Eclogues of Alexander Barclay*, Oxford, 1928

Wright, T., ed., *Three Chapters of Letters Relating to the Suppression of the Monasteries*, Camden Society, no. XXVI, 1843

Wriothesley, C., *A Chronicle of England During the Reigns of the Tudors*, W.D. Hamilton, ed., Camden Society, new series, nos XI, XX, 1875–7

Wyatt, Sir T., *Collected Poems*, J. Daalder, ed., Oxford, 1975

## Secondary Works – Books and Articles

Ackroyd, P., *The Life of Thomas More*, 1998

Allen, J.W., *A History of Political Thought in the Sixteenth Century*, 1960 edition

Alvarez, M.F., *Charles V – Elected Emperor and Hereditary Ruler*, trs. J.A. Lalaguna, 1975

Anglo, S., *The Great Tournament Roll of Westminster*, 1968

Anglo, S., *Spectacle, Pageantry and Early Tudor Policy*, Oxford, 1969

Aston, M., *England's Iconoclasts, I, Laws Against Images*, Oxford, 1988

Aston, M., *The King's Bedpost, Reformation and Iconography. . .*, Cambridge, 1993

Bagchi, D., '"Eyn Mercklich Underscheyd": Catholic reactions to Luther's doctrine of the priesthood of all believers' in W.J. Sheils and D. Wood, eds, *The Ministry: Clerical and Lay Studies in Church History*, no. XXVI, Oxford, 1989

Bates, C.J., *Flodden Field, A Collection of Some of the Earliest Evidence*, Newcastle, 1894

Baumann, U., ed., *Henry VIII in History, Historiography and Literature*, Frankfurt, 1993

Beckingsale, B.W., *Thomas Cromwell: Tudor Minister*, 1978

Beer, B.L., *Northumberland: The Political Career of John Dudley, Earl of Warwick and Duke of Northumberland*, Kent, Ohio, 1973

Bennett, H.S., *The Pastons and Their England*, Cambridge, 1922

Bernard, G.W., 'Anne Boleyn's religion', *Historical Journal,* no. XXXVI, 1993

Bernard, G.W., 'The fall of Anne Boleyn', *English Historical Review*, no. CVI, 1990

Bernard, G.W., *The King's Reformation: Henry VIII and the Remaking of the English Church*, New Haven, 2005

Block, J., *Factional Politics in the English Reformation, RHS Studies in History*, no. LXVI, 1993

Bowker, M., *The Henrician Reformation: The Diocese of Lincoln under John Longland 1521–1547*, Cambridge, 1981

Bradshaw, B. and Duffy, E., eds, *Humanism, Reform and the Reformation: The Career of Bishop John Fisher*, Cambridge, 1989

Brenan, G. and Statham, E.P., *The House of Howard*, 1907

Brigden, S., *London and the Reformation*, Oxford, 1989

Bromiley, G.W., *Thomas Cranmer, Theologian*, 1956

Burnet, G., *History of the Reformation of the Church of England*, Oxford, 1865

Cameron, E., *The European Reformation*, Oxford, 1991

Campbell, L., *Renaissance Portraits*, New Haven, 1990

Chamberlain, A.B., *Hans Holbein the Younger*, 1913

Chambers, R.W., *Thomas More*, 1976 edition

Chapman, H.W., *The Sisters of Henry VIII*, 1969

Chibi, A.A., *Henry VIII's Bishops*, Cambridge, 2003

Childs, J., *Henry VIII's Last Victim: The Life and Times of Henry Howard Earl of Surrey*, 2006

Chrimes, S.B., *Henry VII*, 1972

Coleman, C., and Starkey, D., *Revolution Reassessed*, 1986

Condon, M., 'Ruling elites in the reign of Henry VII' in C. Ross, ed., *Patronage, Pedigree and Power in Late Medieval England*, Gloucester, 1979

Connell-Smith, G., *Forerunners of Drake*, 1954

Cross, C., *Church and People, 1450–1600: The Triumph of the Laity...*, Henocks, 1976

Cross, C., Loades, D. and Scarisbrick, J.J., 'Law and government under the Tudors', essays presented to Sir Geoffrey Elton, Cambridge, 1988

De Molen, R.L., ed., *Leaders of the Reformation*, Selinsgrove, 1984

Demaus, R., *Hugh Latimer, A Biography*, 1869

Demaus, R., *William Tyndale: A Biography*, 1904

Dickens, A.G., *The English* Reformation, 1989

Dickens, A.G., *Later Monasticism and the Reformation*, 1994

Dickens, A.G., *Lollards and Protestants in the Diocese of York 1509–1558*, 1982, revised edition

Dickens, A.G., *Thomas Cromwell and the English Reformation*, 1959

Dickens, A.G. and Jones, W.R.D, *Erasmus the Reformer*, 1994

Dickens, A.G. and Tonkin, J.M., with Powell, K., *The Reformation in Historical Thought*, Oxford, 1985

Dodds, M.H. and R., *The Pilgrimage of Grace and the Exeter Conspiracy*, Cambridge, 1971 edition

Dowling, M., 'Anne Boleyn and reform', *The Journal of Ecclesiastical History*, vol. XXV, no. I, January 1984, pp. 30–46

Duffy, E., *The Stripping of the Altars: Traditional Religion in England 1400–1580*, New Haven, 1992

Elton, G.R., *England Under the Tudors*, 1955

Elton, G.R., 'King or minister? The man behind the English reformation', *History,* no. XXXIX, 1954, pp 216–32

Elton, G.R., *Policy and Police: The Enforcement of the Reformation in the Age of Thomas Cromwell*, Cambridge, 1972

Elton, G.R., *Reform and Reformation*, 1977

Elton, G.R., *Reform and Renewal: Thomas Cromwell and the Common Weal*, Cambridge, 1973

Elton, G.R., 'Sir Thomas More and the opposition to Henry VIII', *Studies in Tudor Politics and Government*, 1974, pp. 129–56

Elton, G.R., *Studies in Tudor and Stuart Politics*, 1974–84

Elton, G.R., *Thomas Cromwell*, ed. J. Loades, *Headstart History Papers*, 1991

Elton, G.R., 'Thomas More, councillor', *Studies in Tudor and Stuart Politics and Government*, 1974

Elton, G.R. *The Tudor Constitution*, Cambridge, 1960, 2nd edition, 1982

Elton, G.R., 'Tudor government: the points of contact', *Royal Historical Society*, 1976, p. 21

Elton, G.R., *The Tudor Revolution in Government: Administration Changes in the Reign of Henry VIII*, Cambridge, 1953

*English Reformation: Religion, Politics and Society Under the Tudors,* Oxford, 1993

Fleisher, M., *Radical Reform and Political Persuasion in the Life and Writings of Thomas More*, 1973

Fox, A., *Thomas More: History and Providence*, Oxford, 1982

Fox, A, and Guy, J., eds., *Reassessing the Henrician Age: Humanism, Politics and Reform, 1500–1550*, Oxford, 1986

French, K.L., et al, *The Parish in English Life, 1400–1600*, Manchester, 1997

Gikes, R.K., *The Tudor Parliament*, 1969

Gunn, S.J., *Charles Brandon, Duke of Suffolk c.1484–1545*, Oxford, 1988

Gunn, S.J., *Early Tudor Government, 1485–1556*, 1995

Gunn, S.J. and Lindley, P.G., eds, *Cardinal Wolsey: Church, State and Art*, Cambridge, 1991

Guy, J.A., *The Cardinal's Court: The Impact of Thomas Wolsey in Star Chamber*, 1977

Guy, J.A., *The Public Career of Sir Thomas More*, Brighton, 1980

Guy, J.A., *Tudor England*, Oxford, 1988

Haigh, C., ed., *The English Reformation Revisited*, Cambridge, 1987

Hammond, E.A., 'Doctor Augustine, physician to Cardinal Wolsey and King Henry VIII', *Medical History*, no. XIX, 1975, pp. 215–49

Harris, B.J., *Edward Stafford, Third Duke of Buckingham, 1478–1521*, Stanford, 1986

Harrison, C.J., 'The petition of Edmund Dudley', *English Historical Review*, 1971, pp. 82–99

Harrison, S.M., *The Pilgrimage of Grace in the Lake Counties*, 1981

Haugaard, W.J., 'Katherine Parr: the religious convictions of a Renaissance queen', *Renaissance Quarterly*, no. XXII, 1969, pp. 346–59

Head, D.M., *The Ebbs and Flows of Fortune: The Life of Thomas Howard, Third Duke of Norfolk*, Athens, Georgia, 1995

Heal, F. and O'Day, R., *Church and Society in England, Henry VIII to James I*, 1977

Higgs, L.M., *Godliness and Governance in Tudor Colchester*, Michigan, 1998

Hoak, D., 'The iconography of the crown imperial' in D. Hoak, ed., *Tudor Political Culture*, Cambridge, 1995

Hoskins, W.G., *The Age of Plunder: King Henry's England, 1500–1547*, 1976

Howarth, D., *Images of Rule, Art and Politics in the English Renaissance 1485–1649*, 1997

Hoyle, R.W., *The Pilgrimage of Grace and the Politics of the 1530s*, Oxford, 2001

Huizinga, J., *Erasmus of Rotterdam*, 1952

Hunt, E.W., *Dean Colet and His Theology*, 1956

Hutton, R., *The Rise and Fall of Merry England*, Oxford, 1994

Ives, E.W., *Anne Boleyn*, Oxford, 1986

Ives, E.W., 'Anne Boleyn and the early Reformation in England: the contemporary evidence', *Historical Journal,* no. XXXVII, 1994, pp. 389–400

Ives, E.W., *The Common Lawyers of Pre–Reformation England; Thomas Kebell: A Case Study*, Cambridge, 1983

Ives, E.W., 'Faction at the court of Henry VIII', *History*, no. LVII, 1972, p. 69f

Ives, E.W., *Faction in Tudor England, Historical Association Appreciations, VI*, 1979

Ives, E.W., *The Life and Death of Anne Boleyn*, Oxford, 2004

Ives, E.W., 'The queen and the painters: Anne Boleyn, Holbein and Tudor royal portraits', *Apollo*, July 1994, pp. 36–45

James, M., ed., 'Obedience and dissent in Henrician England: the Lincolnshire rebellion, 1536[prime], in *Past and Present*, no. XLVIII, 1970, pp. 1–72

James, M., ed., *Society, Politics and Culture, Studies in Early Modern England*, Cambridge, 1986

Knowles, D.E., *The Religious Orders in England*, Cambridge, 1948–59

Lake, P. and Dowling, M., eds, *Protestantism and the National Church in Sixteenth-Century England*, 1987

Lehmberg, S.E., *The Later Parliaments of Henry VIII 1536–1547*, Cambridge, 1977

Lehmberg, S.E., *The Reformation Parliament 1529–1536*, Cambridge, 1970

Loach, J. and Tittler, R., *The Mid-Tudor Polity, c.1540–1560*, 1980

Loades, D., *John Dudley, Duke of Northumberland, 1504–1553*, Oxford, 1996

Loades, D., *The Papers of George Wyatt Esquire,* Camden Society, 4th series, no. V, 1968

Loades, D.M., *Politics and the Nation, England 1450–1660*, Oxford, 1974

Loades, D., *The Tudor Court*, 1987

Lodge, E., *Illustrations of British History*, 1791

MacCulloch, D., *Reformation; Europe's House Divided 1490–1700*, 2003

MacCulloch, D., *Thomas Cranmer, A Life*, New Haven, 1996

MacCulloch, D., 'Two dons in politics: Thomas Cranmer and Stephen Gardiner, 1503–1533[prime], *Historical Journal*, no. XXXVII, 1994, pp. 1–22

MacCulloch, D., ed., *The Reign of Henry VIII, Politics, Policy and Piety*, 1995

Marius, R., *Thomas More*, 1984

Marks, R., and Williamson, P., eds, *Gothic Art for England, 1400–1547*, 2003

Marshall, P., and Ryrie, A., *The Beginnings of English Protestantism*, Cambridge, 2002

Martienssen, A., *Queen Katherine Parr*, 1973

Martin, J.W., *Religious Radicals in Tudor England*, 1989

Mattingley, G., *Catherine of Aragon*, 1942

Mattingley, G., *Renaissance Diplomacy*, 1955

Mayer, T.F., 'On the road to 1534: the occupation of Tournai and Henry VIII's theory of sovereignty' in D. Hoak. ed., *Tudor Political Culture*, Cambridge, 1995

McConica, J.K., *English Humanists and Reformation Politics Under Henry VIII and Edward VI*, Oxford, 1965

Miller, H., *Henry VIII and the English Nobility*, Oxford, 1986

Moat, D., ed., *Tudor Political Culture*, Cambridge, 1995

Mozley, J.F., *Coverdale and His Bibles*, 1953

Mozley, J.F., *William Tyndale*, 1937

Neame, A., *The Holy Maid of Kent: The Life of Elizabeth Barton 1506–1534*, 1971

Oberman, H.A., *Masters of the Reformation: The Emergence of a New Intellectual Climate in Europe*, Cambridge, 1981

Ogle, A., *The Tragedy of the Lollard's Tower*, 1949

Olin, J.C., *The Catholic Reformation: Savonarola to Ignatius Loyola: Reform in the Church 1459–1540*, New York, 1971

Pollard, A.F., *Thomas Cranmer and the English Reformation, 1489–1556*, 1905

Porter, H.C., *Reformation and Reaction in Tudor Cambridge*, Cambridge, 1958

Porter, H.C. and Thomson, D.F.S., *Erasmus and Cambridge*, Toronto, 1963

Raymond, J., *Henry VIII's Military Revolution*, 2007

Redworth, G., *In Defence of the Church Catholic: The Life of Stephen Gardiner*, Oxford, 1990

Reynolds, E.E., *The Life and Death of St Thomas More*, 1978

Richardson, W.C., *Stephen Vaughan, Financial Agent of Henry VIII*, Baton Rouge, Louisiana, 1953

Ridley, J.G., *Henry VIII*, 1984

Ridley, J.G., *The Statesman and the Fanatic: Thomas Wolsey and Thomas More*, 1982

Ridley, J.G., *Thomas Cranmer*, Oxford, 1962

Rowlands, J. and Starkey, D., 'An old tradition reasserted: Holbein's portrait of Queen Anne Boleyn', *Burlington Magazine*, no. CXXV, February 1983, pp. 88–92

Rupp, E.G., *Studies in the Making of the English Protestant Tradition*, Cambridge, 1947

Russell, J.G., *The Field of Cloth of Gold: Men and Manners in 1520*, 1969

Scarisbrick, J.J., *Henry VIII*, New Haven, 2nd edition, 1997

Scarisbrick, J.J., *The Reformation and the English People*, Oxford, 1984

Simon, J., *Education and Society in Tudor England*, Cambridge, 1966

Slavin, A.J., *Politics and Profit: A Study of Sir Ralph Sadler, 1507–1547*, Cambridge, 1966

Smith, L.B., *Tudor Prelates and Politic*, 1953

Smith, L.B., *A Tudor Tragedy: The Life and Times of Catherine Howard*, 1961

Starkey, D., 'Court, council and the nobility in Tudor England' in R.G. Asch and A.M. Birkie, eds, *Princes Patronage and the Nobility. The Court at the Beginning of the Modern Age c.1450–1650*, Oxford 1991

Starkey, D., *Six Wives; The Queens of Henry VIII*, 2003

Starkey, D., ed., *Henry VIII; a European Court in England,* 1991

Stevens, J., ed., *Music at the Court of Henry VIII*, 1969

Strong, R., *Holbein and Henry VIII*, 1967

Tawney, R.H. and Power, E., *Tudor Economic Documents*, 1924

*The Collected Works of Erasmus*, Toronto, 1986

Thomas, K., *Religion and the Decline of Magic*, 1971

Tjernagle, N.S., *Henry VIII and the Lutherans: A Study in Anglo–Lutheran Relations from 1521 to 1547*, St Louis, 1965

Tracy, J.C., 'Ad Fontes: the humanist understanding of Scripture as nourishment for the soul' in J. Raitt, ed., *Christian Spirituality – High Middle Ages and Reformation*, New York, 1988

Tucker, M.J., *The Life of Thomas Howard, Earl of Surrey and Second Duke of Norfolk, 1443–1524*, The Hague, 1964

Tyacke, N., *Aspects of English Protestantism, c.1530–1700*, Manchester, 2001

Walker, G., *John Skelton and the Politics of the 1520s*, Cambridge, 1988

Walker, G., *Writing Under Tyranny: English Literature and the English Reformation*, Oxford, 2005

Warnicke, R.M., *The Marrying of Anne of Cleves: Royal Protocol in Tudor England*, Cambridge, 2000

Warnicke, R.M., *The Rise and Fall of Anne Boleyn*, Cambridge, 1989

Wegg, J., *Richard Pace, Tudor Diplomat*, 1937

Wernham, R.B., *Before the Armada: The Emergence of the English Nation, 1485–1558*, 1966

Williams, N., *Henry VII and His Court*, 1971

Williams, N., *Thomas Howard, Fourth Duke of Norfolk*, New York, 1964

Wilson, D., *England in the Age of Thomas More*, 1978

Wilson, D., *Hans Holbein: Portrait of an Unknown Man*, 1996, 2003

Wilson, D., *In the Lion's Court: Power, Ambition and Sudden Death in the Reign of Henry VIII*, 2001

Wilson, D., *Out of the Storm: The Life and Legacy of Martin Luther*, 2007

Wilson, D., *A Tudor Tapestry: Men, Women and Society in Reformation England*, 1972

Wilson, D., *Uncrowned Kings of England: The Black Legend of the Dudleys*, 2003

# INDEX